T0355780

 Indigenous
Confluences

Charlotte Cotè, Matthew Sakiestewa Gilbert,
and Coll Thrush, *Series Editors*

Indigenous Confluences publishes cutting-edge works on the larger, universal themes common among indigenous communities of North America, with a special emphasis on Pacific Coast communities. Focusing on transnational approaches and decolonizing perspectives, this interdisciplinary series seeks to bring nuance and depth to the indigenous experience by examining a wide range of topics, including self-determination and resurgence efforts, identity, environmental and food justice, urban histories, language preservation, and art, music, performance and other forms of cultural expression.

A Chemehuevi Song: The Resilience of a Southern Paiute Tribe
by Clifford E. Trafzer

*Education at the Edge of Empire: Negotiating Pueblo Identity
in New Mexico's Indian Boarding Schools*
by John R. Gram

A Chemehuevi Song

The Resilience of a Southern Paiute Tribe

CLIFFORD E. TRAFZER

Foreword by Larry Myers

UNIVERSITY OF WASHINGTON PRESS

Seattle and London

Printed and bound in the United States of America
Design by Dustin Kilgore
Composed in Charter, a typeface designed by Matthew Carter
19 18 17 16 15   5 4 3 2 1

UNIVERSITY OF WASHINGTON PRESS
www.washington.edu/uwpress

Library of Congress Cataloging-in-Publication Data
Trafzer, Clifford E.
A Chemehuevi song : the resilience of a Southern Paiute tribe / Clifford E. Trafzer ;
foreword by Larry Myers. — First edition.
    pages   cm — (Indigenous confluences)
Includes bibliographical references.
ISBN 978-0-295-99458-1 (hard cover : alk. paper) 1. Chemehuevi Indians—History.
2. Chemehuevi Indians—Government relations. 3. Chemehuevi Indians—Ethnic
identity. I. Title. II. Title: Resilience of a Southern Paiute tribe.
 E99.C493T73 2015
 979.1'3004974576—dc23

                                              2014034909

The paper used in this publication is acid-free and meets the minimum requirements
of American National Standard for Information Sciences—Permanence of Paper for
Printed Library Materials, ANSI Z39.48–1984.∞

I dedicate this book to the extended families of Dean Mike, Jennifer Mike, Matthew Hanks Leivas, Joe Mike Benitez, Betty Cornelius, Vivienne Jake, Richard Arnold, and Larry Eddy. These families are among those that keep the Chemehuevi and Southern Paiute songs and stories alive.

Contents

Foreword

PROFESSOR CLIFFORD TRAFZER BEGAN HIS ASSOCIATION WITH THE Twenty-Nine Palms Tribe in 1997, when the tribal council invited him to visit members of the tribe's Business Committee to discuss cultural projects. At that time, Cahuilla tribal scholar Luke Madrigal directed the Twenty-Nine Palms Cultural Committee and offered monthly cultural exchanges with members of the San Manuel, Hualapai, Torres-Martinez, Chemehuevi, and other reservations in Southern California and western Arizona. In the mid-1990s the Twenty-Nine Palms Tribe became interested in preserving its tribal history by collecting oral interviews. Scholars had written very little about Chemehuevi people and essentially nothing on the Twenty-Nine Palms Tribe. As a result, tribal members decided to capture their history through the words of tribal members and other Indians who knew Chemehuevi culture, language, and history. They invited Cliff to work with them to develop a scholarly effort that carefully represented the tribe's history and culture.

Some members of the Twenty-Nine Palms Tribe had attended a workshop on American Indian oral histories taught by Muscogee-Creek scholar Duane Hale at the University of Oklahoma, and they wanted to learn more about oral histories. One Monday evening in September 1997, Luke Madrigal introduced the tribe to his brother, Cahuilla historian Anthony Madrigal, and his friend Cliff Trafzer. At that time, Cliff was director of American Indian studies and professor of ethnic studies at the University of California–Riverside. Cliff and Anthony presented the tribal leadership with a host of ideas about possible historical and cultural projects that the tribe might wish to undertake, including an oral history project. After an enthusiastic discussion about possible projects, tribal members in attendance agreed on an oral history project.

Members of the Business Committee asked Cliff and Anthony to return the next week to interview Dean Mike, who at the time was tribal chair. Shortly after that, Cliff participated in the first of several oral histories with members of the Twenty-Nine Palms Tribe, and Joe Benitez, a Chemehuevi and member of the Cabazon Band of Cahuilla Indians. Cliff also traveled to the Colorado River to interview Gertrude, Matthew, Juliana, Hope, Mary, and June Hanks Leivas—all tribal scholars of Chemehuevi people. From these initial oral history projects, Cliff began an ongoing research project to gather documents and information from the National Archives, the Southwest Museum, the Costo Collection, the Bancroft Library, and other repositories about the history of Chemehuevi people in general and the Twenty-Nine Palms Tribe in particular.

Cliff interviewed numerous subjects about Chemehuevi people and their families. After researching tribal census data and death records of the Mission Indian Agency in the National Archives, Cliff spent hours with Dean Mike, Joe Benitez, and Gertrude Hanks Leivas identifying people listed as Chemehuevi in tribal censuses from the 1890s to the 1940s. This included those living on the Cabazon, Torres-Martinez, Soboba, Agua Caliente, Morongo, and San Manuel Reservations. Cliff also investigated birth and death registers of the Mission Indian Agency in the National Archives. This information has proved invaluable to the present book as well as to the tribe. A great deal of Chemehuevi history is family history, and Cliff has made excellent use of familial aspects of this Native American community.

From 1997 to 2013, he collected boxes of documents, maps, books, articles, and photographs. He made copies of all the sources for the Twenty-Nine Palms Tribe and helped the tribe create an archive. In addition, Cliff worked with the tribe to assist in establishing the Native American Land Conservancy, which formally began in 1998 and continues with an active agenda of preservation today. The Twenty-Nine Palms Tribe and Native American Land Conservancy diligently strives to protect and preserve the cultural, spiritual, and biological heritage of American Indian people. Cliff has been a part of this preservation effort from the outset, and he continues to serve on the Board of Directors of the Native American Land Conservancy.

Unlike many scholars, he has worked with and for the Twenty-Nine Palms Tribe, sharing information and learning from tribal elders. He has used knowledge gained from tribal scholars and elders to enrich his study, and he has carefully documented a portion of the tribe's history by writing in the oral tradition, using oral narratives, contemporary interviews, written historical documents, and a host of other sources. Cliff does not claim that this study, *A Chemehuevi Song: The Resilience of a Southern Paiute Tribe,* is a definitive work. Instead, it is one song that represents a portion of the tribe's history but a story never told before. He presents an original historical work that is groundbreaking in scholarship yet very readable—one that puts Indian people at the center of the story.

In 1997, Cliff worked with Anthony and Luke Madrigal to produce the first book on the tribe, *Chemehuevi People of the Coachella Valley.* To my knowledge, it is the only book to date on the Twenty-Nine Palms Tribe. Isabel Kelly, Catherine Fowler, LaVan Martineau, Martha C. Knack, and others have written major works on Southern Paiute people, and their research has contributed significantly to the foundation of Cliff's study of the Twenty-Nine Palms Tribe. Carabeth Laird expanded the works on the Southern Paiute by recording the oral histories of her husband, George Laird, to write *The Chemehuevis* (1976) and *Mirror and Pattern* (1984). Laird's work is largely anthropological, however, and not focused on the Twenty-Nine Palms Tribe.

The research of Kelly, Fowler, Knack, and Laird is indispensible to this book, offering rich anthropological studies relevant to the cultural past of Southern Paiute people. Yet these past works have only touched on the history of the Twenty-Nine Palms Tribe that once lived along the Colorado River, including in California's Chemehuevi Valley. During the 1860s these people left the Mojave-controlled Colorado River regions for the isolation of the Mojave Desert, moving to the Oasis of Mara. There, one group of Chemehuevi formed a relationship with the Serrano to live in the desert by hunting, gathering, and farming the oasis known for its native palm trees. During the late nineteenth century, other Chemehuevi from the river and villages in the Mojave Desert joined them at the oasis, creating the Twenty-Nine Palms Tribe of Chemehuevi. This is the subject of Cliff's moving study.

Since 1997, his ongoing research project has captured the history and culture of the Twenty-Nine Palms Tribe. This book represents his continued effort to research and write a deeper and fuller study of the people, their families, and their relationships with others. He understands the traditional cultural landscape of Chemehuevi from the Colorado River to the Pacific Ocean, sacred space that includes the Salt Song Trail, Silver Fox, Colorado River, Coco-Maricopa, and other spur trails. After one group of Chemehuevi relocated to the Oasis of Mara, the people of Twenty-Nine Palms formed an intimate relationship with the deserts and mountains of Southern California, while maintaining cultural and familial relationships with Chemehuevi and other Southern Paiute of Arizona, California, and Nevada.

Before completing this fine manuscript, Cliff provided several Chemehuevi people with copies of the work so that tribal members and council members of the Twenty-Nine Palms Tribe could read and comment on the work before submission. He worked especially closely with former tribal chair Dean Mike and current tribal chair Darrell Mike. Cliff has made a tremendous effort to gather written documents and learn from Indian people. I applaud his research model of openness and inclusiveness, respecting tribal elders and including their voices in this work. I duly acknowledge Cliff's academic effort and hope this book encourages other scholars to continue to research tribal histories by conducting oral history projects and using tribal knowledge in a critical fashion in their own works. *A Chemehuevi Song* offers many details about Chemehuevi people in general and specifically about the Chemehuevi of Twenty-Nine Palms. This includes their dramatic relationships with other tribes and non-Indian newcomers. Cliff's thorough historical and community-based research has resulted in an original scholarly work of Chemehuevi people of the Twenty-Nine Palms Tribe that will become the standard work on the tribe.

This book represents a path-breaking study of one group of Chemehuevi people through diverse historical voices and lenses. Cliff presents the first full-length historical work on the Twenty-Nine Palms Tribe, relating their history as part of a much larger historical drama of California, the Southwest, and the United States. He presents a remarkable story—not of vague historical characters but of members of Native American families and people. I think *A Chemehuevi Song: The Resilience of a Southern Paiute Tribe* is a significant book that will be of use and interest to scholars and the general public alike. Anyone the least bit interested in the history of Native Americans will find great value in these colorful and authoritative pages about the Twenty-Nine Palms Tribe of Chemehuevi. I hope this is the first of many songs sung about Chemehuevi Indians and other Native Americans of the Pacific West.

LARRY MYERS (POMO)
Executive Secretary
California Native American Heritage Commission

Preface and Acknowledgments

Eddy and Matthew Hanks Leivas sang Salt Songs long into the night. Salt Songs are typically sung for funerals and memorials, but on this occasion, the elders sang their body of sacred songs in celebration of American Indian Day for one thousand people at California State University–San Bernardino. After singing a few songs, Leivas explained that the male and female dancers performed the Circle Dance, a dance also performed by Chemehuevi Ghost Dancers in the late nineteenth century. He explained that Chemehuevi and other Southern Paiute people believe the spirits hear the singing and gather in the middle of the plaza to be near their loved ones. Dancers surround the spirits, remembering and honoring them as well as their ancestors.

Chemehuevi dancers put songs into motion, re-creating ancient music and movement of the first Chemehuevi who emerged at the beginning of time on their sacred Spring Mountains of southern Nevada. Eddy explained: "It is appropriate to share these songs tonight, because they are the mourning songs of our people, which we sing when someone dies or someone is remembered." In the late nineteenth century, Chemehuevi and other Southern Paiute people had danced the same dances, performing the Ghost Dance—a religion still practiced by some of the people. Leivas pointed out: "We are all mourning, you know, given what happened in New York, Pennsylvania, and Washington." He was referring, of course, to the airplane crashes into the World Trade Center, the Pennsylvania woods, and Pentagon on September 11, 2001. "We all need to listen to these songs and remember the dead and what has happened to all of us." Leivas added: "We need these songs to heal. He and Eddy invited the crowd to join the dancers in the Circle Dance, and soon more than a hundred men, women, and children danced with the Chemehuevi to honor the dead.

Chemehuevi culture is alive today through the dynamic process of ethnogenesis. Their culture has changed in many ways as a result of contact with newcomers, but the essence of cultural identity remains strong among the people. Songs, prayers, and stories call the spirits that have an effect on the lives of all Southern Paiute. Chemehuevi are Southern Paiute, or Nüwü as they call themselves. The people remain connected with each other, the spiritual world, and their grand landscape of mountains, deserts, and river valleys. Their spiritual connection with the world remains the core of their culture, and tribal elders pass along knowledge of spiritual matters through the oral tradition, which includes songs and stories. Singers share elements of this knowledge every time they sing or tell stories, believing that spirits enter their personal and public spaces whenever they gather. Chemehuevi elders, singers, and storytellers believe all human beings have the ability to share a common relationship through the Spirit. Many believe the actions of a single person affects the lives of everyone. Ceremonial spokesmen and -women remind people to teach their children proper behavior and be mindful of their actions. They stress the need to obey traditional tribal laws and continue the Chemehuevi way.

Songs put the Chemehuevi world into motion at the beginning of time, and the people have sung songs since the time when Ocean Woman stretched out her body to create the landform known today as the Western Hemisphere. Songs keep the world in motion, affecting landscapes, animals, plants, and people. Songs tell stories, and many exist. This book is my attempt at a historical song-story presented using written documents, oral histories, and fieldwork among the people. Since 1997, I have worked with several Chemehuevi people to research and write a history—my song—of the Twenty-Nine Palms Tribe of Chemehuevi. This book is but one song about one group of Chemehuevi Southern Paiute people who once lived at the Oasis of Mara in the modern-day town of Twentynine Palms, California. Today, they live primarily in the Coachella Valley near Indio and Palm Springs, California. They have relatives among all other Chemehuevi and Southern Paiute people living in Utah, Nevada, Arizona, and California. All of them are Nüwü. Since 1997, members of the Twenty-Nine Palms Tribe, Chemehuevi Tribe, Chemehuevi people of the Colorado River Reservation, and other Southern Paiute people have worked with me on this book, and many read and commented on the manuscript before and after submission to the University of Washington Press.

A Chemehuevi Song is a collaborative effort that draws on many written and oral sources to frame a book that focuses on spiritual, familial, social, and environmental relationships of the people. It is a story of ethnogenesis, cultural continuance, adaptation, and survival. In the 1970s the people of Twenty-Nine Palms organized a formal government and have functioned successfully since as a federally recognized tribe with trust lands in Coachella and Twentynine Palms. This history represents my song about the Chemehuevi people, built on past and new research, including oral histories and personal participation in song, stories, and ceremonies. It is only one of the many songs historians might create about Chemehuevi in general and the Twenty-Nine Palms Tribe in particular.

In the 1860s, these Chemehuevi moved into the eastern Mojave Desert, about seventy miles west of their relatives along the river. Their story is compelling, a chronicle of ethnogenesis, hardships, and survival that ultimately led them to the Coachella Valley. Dean Mike, Darrell Mike Jr., Jennifer Estama-Mike, Leanna Andrea Mike, Vivienne Jake, Joe Mike Benitez, Gertrude Hanks Leivas, Larry Eddy, Betty Cornelius, Matthew Hanks Leivas, June Hanks Leivas, Mary Hanks Leivas Drum, Julianna Hanks Leivas, Hope Hanks Leivas Hinman, Kenneth Anderson, Alfreda Mitre, Lorene Sisquoc, and other tribal scholars helped me with this research. I also thank Carmen Lucas, Michael Tsosie, Daphne Poolaw, Barbara Levy, Wesley Schofield, Lolita Schofield, Lorey and Linda Cachora, Preston Arrowweed, Barbara Levy, Willa Scott, Anthony Madrigal, Ernest Siva, James Ramos, Pauline Murillo, Sean Milanovich, Ted Vaughn, Linda Ogo, and Manfred Scott, who helped me understand Yavapai, Mojave, Cahuilla, Serrano, Kwaaymii, and Quechan relationships with Chemehuevi.

I thank the officials and institutions that helped me locate documents, including the Twenty-Nine Palms Tribe, Rupert Costo Library, Special Collections and Archives at the University of California–Riverside, Twentynine Palms City Library, Twentynine Palms Historical Society, San Manuel Tribe, National Parks Service, National Forest Service, Malki Museum, National Archives, Huntington Library, Joshua Tree National Park, Smiley Library, San Diego Historical Society, Southwest Museum, Cabazon Cultural Museum, Bancroft Library of the University of California–Berkeley, Colorado Indian River

Tribe's Museum and Library, Quechan Cultural Resources Library, Quechan Tribal Language Program Library, Yuma Proving Ground, Dorothy Ramon Learning Center, and Yuma City-County Library.

I thank the numerous officials at many libraries and special collections, including the Rivera and Orbach Libraries of the University of California–Riverside, Twentynine Palms Library, the Riverside Public Library, the Riverside Metropolitan Museum, Nevada Historical Society, Native American Heritage Commission, California State Parks, the University of Arizona, the Arizona Historical Society, the Twentynine Palms Historical Society, the Smith Collection at the Twentynine Palms Hotel, and personal documents provided by Indians and non-Indians alike.

I wish to thank the Chemehuevi and other Southern Paiute people for sharing their oral histories. I am profoundly grateful to Dean, Theresa, and the entire Mike family as well as the Hanks Leivas family for allowing me to participate and write about wakes and memorial ceremonies. These sacred ceremonies among Paiute people are not public events. I have written about these ceremonies from personal experiences, and I am humbled by the cultural confidence placed in me. The editors and reviewers of the University of Washington Press honored me by allowing this song to be a part of the Indigenous Confluence series. I offer deep appreciation to Ranjit Arab, Mary C. Ribesky, Tim Zimmerman, Dustin Kilgore, and Amy Smith Bell. I thank the anonymous reviewers who reviewed my manuscript and offered constructive criticisms that enhanced the work.

I thank librarians of many institutions, some of which I have just mentioned, for leading me to particular sources and making collections available. I also wish to thank authors mentioned throughout the manuscript and in the bibliography for providing groundbreaking information: Isabel Kelly, Catherine and Donald Fowler, Richard W. Stoffle, Maria Zedeño, Katherine Siva Saubel, Kurt Russo, Dorothy Ramon, Eric Elliott, Carobeth Laird, George Laird, Robert Johnson, Dennis Casebier, Tom King, Paul Smith, Robert Euler, James Sandos, Larry Burgess, Nathan Gonzales, Maria Carrillo, David Halmo, George Phillips, and Martha Knack. Each has greatly contributed to what we know about Southern Paiute people. I owe a debt of gratitude to Bill Houck, Fay McClung, David Saldivar, Emerson Gorman, Nicole Van der Linde-Johnson, and Michael Connoly of the Native American Land Conservancy.

Several scholars read and commented on portions of the work, including Anthony Madrigal, Matthew Sakiestewa Gilbert, Luke Madrigal, Richard Hanks, Kevin Whalen, Robert Przeklasa, Heather Andrews-Horton, Paul and

Jane Smith, Kurt Russo, James Sandos, and Larry Burgess. I also thank members of the Business Council and Cultural Committee of the Twenty-Nine Palms Tribe for critiquing every page of the manuscript. I thank Darrell Mike, Jr., Dean Mike, Jennifer Estama-Mike, Joe Mike Benitez, Matthew Hanks Leivas, Betty Cornelius, Wilene Fisher-Holt, Larry Eddy, Michelle Mike, Melissa Mike Solomon, Dineen Mike, Angelina Mike, Courtney Andrade Gonzales, Lloyd Mike, Darrell Miller, Sabrena Mike, Leanna Mike, Richard Arnold, and Leanna, Earl, and Jordan Thomas for their support and constructive criticism. Without the support of the Twenty-Nine Palms Tribe, this book could not have been researched or written.

Theresa Mike has been a guiding light and supportive mentor. She taught me patience. She traveled with me to historical and cultural sites such as Old Woman Mountain, Twentynine Palms, Joshua Tree National Park, the Colorado River Indian Reservation, and the Chemehuevi Reservation. She traveled to the Colorado River with Anthony Madrigal and me to attended Bear Dances, funerals, and memorials. A Lummi person by birth, Theresa Mike has embraced the Chemehuevi history of her husband's and daughter's tribe.

Lucas Reyes, Maria Carrillo, and Sarah Allison helped format the photographs, and Lee Ann helped format the manuscript, which I greatly appreciate. I thank friends and colleagues: Kim Wilcox, James Sandoval, Steve Cullenberg, Michelle Raheja, Monte Kugel, Jacqueline Shea-Murphy, Joshua Gonzales, James Brennan, Tom Cogswell, Randolph Head, Tom Patterson, Brenda Focht, Wendy Ashmore, Steve Hackel, and Juliet McMullen. The following provided research grants: the Ford Foundation, the Riverside–San Bernardino Community Foundation, the U.S. Corps of Engineers, Faculty Senate Research Grants through the University of California–Riverside, and the Haynes Foundation grant through the Southern California Historical Society; each contributed to the research of the this volume. I thank the Rupert and Jeanette Costo Endowment for creating the chair that provided me time and funds to research and travel. I also wish to thank Melissa Conway, Eric Milenkiewicz, Steve Mitchell, and Sarah M. Allison of the campus libraries, especially Special Collections and the Costo Library, Rivera Library, of the University of California–Riverside. I thank my colleagues of the California Center for Native Nations. I also thank Larry Myers, executive secretary of the Native American Heritage Commission, for taking the time to read the manuscript and write a generous foreword.

Most of all, I thank my family for their support. My mother, Mary Lou, taught me the importance of our Indian heritage and the significance of family, community, survival, and memory—all elements of the Chemehuevi story.

My sisters, Donna and Sally, as well as their husbands, Ron and Alan, helped me complete this work by providing support. Cousins Cathleen and Ron, as well as friends Chris Suter, Jim Fenelon, Kenneth Coosewoon, and the Madrigal family encouraged this book. My sisters took on extra family responsibilities caring for our mother, which meant a great deal to our family. I thank my other mother, Louise Smith, and my children—Tess Nashone, Hayley Kachine, and Tara Tsaile—for listening, editing, formatting, and typing. My best friend and wife, Lee Ann, a historian in her own right, read the manuscript, offered gentle criticism, and improved the presentation. To Lee Ann and all other people mentioned here, I offer my sincere and lasting appreciation, but without the Chemehuevi people, this song could never have been sung.

CLIFFORD E. TRAFZER
Yucaipa, California

A Chemehuevi Song

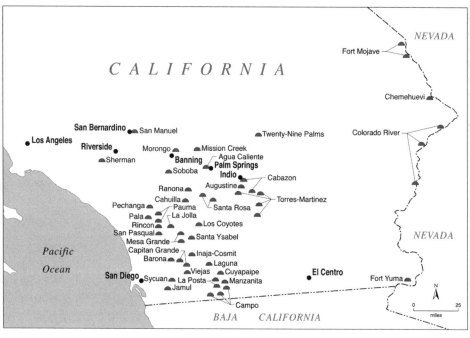

Reservations of Southern California

Introduction

A COLD WIND SWEPT DOWN FROM THE LITTLE SAN BERNARDINO Mountains, racing south through the Coachella Valley to the Torres-Martinez Indian Reservation, where Salt Song singers added their voices to nature's howling chorus. Dust swirled up in the air, sending sand into the eyes and mouths of the singers, but nothing could quiet their songs, neither the dirt nor the cold. Old oil drums sat about the landscape, shooting fire from their open tops. They provided some light and warmth during the dark night in the early winter of 1998. The weather was bitter cold, made worse by the cutting winds. People huddled together around the rusted oilcans, warming their hands over the yellow, red, and blue flames. Some people sipped hot coffee. Others drank hot chocolate. Under a brush arbor not far away, men and women assembled to begin singing. People huddled around the oilcan fires heard the faint sounds of Salt Songs mixed with the howling winds, just as night had fully fallen over the desert valley.[1]

Men, women, and children left the warmth of the fire, walking to the brush arbor to be closer to the singing and warmth of elders. Tribal assistants had set up an altar at one end of the brush arbor, which held a large framed photograph of Theresa Andrea Mike.[2] They had set up folding chairs on either side of the arbor for the male singers on one side and the female singers on the other. They had kept the center open. Speaker and elder Larry Eddy explained that sacred space existed between the chairs in front of the altar. Children could not "fool around" inside the sacred space, but Larry Eddy welcomed people to come forward to speak to the family and "dance" with the picture of the deceased.[3] Only a few people came forward to pray and dance within the sacred space, some taking the photograph from the altar and dancing with it. Over the course of the evening, many people came forward to embrace and kiss members of the Mike family. Many mourned with the Mike family, while the Salt Song singers used their voices and gourd rattles to provide the music, telling a traveling song that delineated a large part of Southern Paiute country, which they shared with other Indians. Salt Songs travel through parts of Arizona, California, Nevada, and Utah. That freezing cold night, Chemehuevi and Southern Paiute singers sang many of the estimated 120 Salt Songs. Contemporary singers shared ancient songs that the Creator had taught the people at the beginning of time and people have passed down through the oral tradition throughout known time to the present. Like many aspects of Chemehuevi culture, the significance of Salt Songs, mourning ceremonies, and their link with the Spirit is alive today and an integral part of Chemehuevi culture.[4]

Salt Songs are a part of a dynamic, adaptive, and pragmatic cultural complex that has bent over time but never broken. Each time singers share Salt Songs, the story explained in song becomes animated. Salt Songs belong to an ancient cultural complex closely tied to the sacred. The songs tell of two women receiving power within a cave on the Bill Williams River of western Arizona; the songs follow a hero's journey down the Bill Williams to the Colorado River before turning north along the river, east into the Hualapai country, and north to the Colorado River west of the Grand Canyon. The song-story describes a vast and rugged landscape of northern Arizona, southern Utah, and Nevada (near modern-day Las Vegas). The song-story travels to the creation site of Southern Paiute people, the Spring Mountains, where the mountainous stone figure of Ocean Woman lies facing heaven and the Milky Way.[5]

The two women part at this point. One woman travels north, the other travels south, taking the songs into and through the Mojave Desert south to the Little San Bernardino Mountains of Joshua Tree National Park. In the Palm Springs area, the woman travels east toward the Colorado River, following a trail near present-day Interstate 10. The woman reaches the Colorado River south of present-day Blythe, California, but does not cross the Colorado River. Instead, she travels north on the California side of the river to the Riverside Mountains and reenters Arizona onto the Colorado River Indian Reservation. The woman who brought the Salt Songs to the people passes through the present homelands of Larry Eddy, Betty Cornelius, and other Chemehuevi who live on the Colorado River Indian Reservation. The woman takes the Salt Songs up

Matthew Hanks Leivas grew up on the Colorado River Indian Reservation and Chemehuevi Indian Reservation, where he resides today. He joined Betty Cornelius, Larry Eddy, and Vivienne Jake to organize and execute the Salt Song Project to preserve the Salt Songs of Southern Paiute people. Leivas is a Native American singer, scholar, and teacher. Photograph by Clifford E. Trafzer.

the eastern bank of the Colorado River to the Buckskin Mountains, then east up the Bill Williams River. The journey ends in the cave on the Bill Williams, thus completing a symbolic circle of Southern Paiute lands that are shared with many other tribes. Salt Song singers are careful not to provide exact information about the trail and its branches in order to preserve and protect the landscape encompassed by the songs. The people say the woman who made this momentous journey, bringing the songs to the people, lives in spirit and listens to the Salt Songs every time the people gather to sing.[6]

On the night of the memorial ceremony in 1998, more than a hundred people met at twilight to honor Theresa Andrea Mike during an all-night ceremony. The gathering represented communal mourning in support of Mike family members, and a ceremony celebrating Theresa's life with song, music, dance, and prayers to help the deceased travel to Naugurivipi, the Land of the Spirits. The ceremony helped the living cope with their loss and deal with their grief. After a year of mourning, the ceremony represented a new beginning for the living to go on in life and continue their journey on earth, never forgetting their identity as Chemehuevi and their obligation to live in the cultural way that binds all Southern Paiute people together.[7]

Theresa's mother and father, Dean and Theresa Mike, arranged the ceremony to honor their daughter in the Chemehuevi way.[8] Many family members living throughout the country came together to participate and support each other. Friends of the family gathered to mourn and share the grief, participating in the singing and dancing in remembrance of the one who had passed. Late that evening, Chemehuevi elder Larry Eddy spoke from his heart, comforting the Mike family and reminding everyone that the Salt Songs tied the past to the present. "A long time ago the Creator gave us these songs," Eddy announced. "But in order to teach you these songs, the Creator said, 'I am going to break your heart.' We sing these songs to help the spirit travel to the next life. We sing these songs to help us with sorrow." Several people cried as he spoke.[9] Eddy asked everyone to think of their own loved ones and remember to live a good life, the right kind of life following the values established by the Creator at the beginning of time. He asked the people to reflect on the great circle that links the living with the dead, the lessons taught by life.[10] Salt Songs provide guidance for the deceased to help the spirit move north to the Land of the Spirits, skyward into the Milky Way that sparkles at night and looks back onto earth, a reminder of another world beyond earth.[11]

At midnight, Salt Song singers shared the Cry Song. The Salt Songs are "traveling" songs and at midnight, singers offer that part of the song-story when two women arrive at the Spring Mountains, the creation site of Southern Paiute. In the mountains located northwest of present-day Las Vegas, the two sisters anticipate their separation. They loved each other but they had to part. Therefore they cried. The Cry Song is a significant element of the Salt Song complex, characterizing the time when the two sisters parted ways, one going north and the other south. They cried, just as mourners cry, knowing they had no choice but to say goodbye. The woman going north symbolically represents the soul of the dead traveling north on her journey to the spirit world, while the other woman traveled south into California's Mojave Desert, thus representing the living.[12]

Only a few Chemehuevi people have served as chair of the Twenty-Nine Palms Tribe, including Dean Mike, the great-grandson of William Mike. He is pictured with his wife, Theresa, who is a member of the Lummi Indian Nation of Washington State but has worked in many capacities for the Twenty-Nine Palms Tribe.

Dean Mike served as chair when the tribe entered high-stakes gaming, and he continues to mentor younger Chemehuevi people, the future leaders of the nation. Notice the flag of the Twenty-Nine Palms Tribe hanging behind Dean Mike. Photograph by Clifford E. Trafzer.

After this song, the singers and those participating in the ceremony take a break. During the intermission, Southern Paiute people often give their condolences to the family or discuss the meaning of the songs or their central position within the modern world of Chemehuevi and Southern Paiute culture. Parents and grandparents educate their children and grandchildren about the tradition, explaining how to act during the ceremony. After refreshments and the warmth of a fire, the ceremony continues. Most often, Salt singers sing through the night until the gray light of morning. But during this particular ceremony, the lead singer, quite elderly, became ill and had to end the singing around 2 A.M. During the last few songs, tribal assistants lit a large bonfire fifty yards from the brush arbor. When the last song ended, participants walked to the fire, where family members had assembled some of the items owned by the deceased. They burned the personal items of Theresa Mike, offering smoke and prayer to the spirit world. Chemehuevi songs, particularly Salt Songs, provide cultural continuity, threads that weave the past with the present, providing hope for the continued renewal of Chemehuevi culture.[13]

Southern Paiute songs helped put the world into motion. Dance, the physical manifestation of song, keeps the world moving. Song, dance, and other elements of Chemehuevi culture remain extant, which form a unique and shared identity of Chemehuevi and other Southern Paiute people. The Salt Songs describe expansive landscapes, water, plants, people, and animals found within four states. The songs flow like a stream, providing a confluence of people, places, plants, animals, and memories in the deserts and mountains of the Great Basin, California, and the Southwest. Like song and dance, landscape and the entire natural environment remain central to contemporary Chemehuevi identity in addition to pragmatism, adaptation, and traveling.[14]

By being adaptive, Chemehuevi people survived many changes throughout their history, from the Pleistocene to the present. Over many years, Southern Paiutes experienced a great diaspora out of southern Nevada into Utah, California, and Arizona. In ancient times, Southern Paiutes radiated out from the Spring Mountains in all directions, including south into the Mojave Desert and Colorado River Valley. Chemehuevi people established their homelands north, south, and west of Mojave people. The Mojave are Yuman-speaking people, closely related to the Quechan, Kumeyaay, and other Yuman peoples. The Mojave enjoyed a large population and could be tremendous warriors that dreamed of fighting prowess and power. The Chemehuevi also had great warriors, but they did not develop a military system similar to the Mojave, Quechan, Cocopah, and other Yuman-speaking Indians. But like the Yuman-speaking tribes, the Chemehuevi had strong familial and kinship relations among themselves and their Southern Paiute neighbors.[15]

Chemehuevi family units and small bands lived in different regions of the desert and mountains of the Mojave Desert and Colorado River Valley. The people survived by depending on each other and working together for the betterment of their communities. Like heroes of ancient oral stories, the Chemehuevi learned to act on behalf of the family and band, acting correctly so that everyone survived the harsh desert conditions. Chemehuevi families adhered to strict marriage laws that the Creator had established to prevent incest and ensure a strong, hardy people. As a result, Chemehuevi people "married out" of their families and bands, carefully selecting husbands and wives. Generally, Chemehuevi people had to be six generations apart if they wished to marry, so parents and grandparents, aunts and uncles were deeply involved in arranging

Salt Song singers visited the cemetery of Sherman Institute, an off-reservation American Indian boarding school located in Riverside, California. The singers knew that school officials had buried students without traditional Native ceremonies, so they sang at the cemetery to send the spirits of the dead on to the next world. While the singers sang, young people danced around the large black headstone depicting the names of several students buried in the cemetery. From left to right: Olivia Tom, Vivienne Jake, Mary Hanks Drum, Larry Eddy, Matthew Hanks Leivas, Roland Meldanado, Junita Tsiniginni, and Hope Hanks Hinman. Photograph by Melissa Nelson, Cultural Conservancy.

and permitting marriage.[16] From an early age, Chemehuevi children learned about marriage laws, and their parents encouraged them to meet other young people when Chemehuevi gathered during the winter to feast, sing, dance, and tell stories at Winter Gatherings. Kinship relations, proper familial behavior, and living for the benefit of the entire group proved highly significant in Chemehuevi history, and these remain important cultural elements to contemporary people. Breaking marriage laws harmed the people involved and all Southern Paiute people who shared a belief system similar to that of covenant theology. Transgressors could expect the wrath of spirits that could harm every Southern Paiute person and sicken or kill offenders.[17]

The Chemehuevi people have always moved about, traveling and trading. The Southern Paiute diaspora began with Creation. A goddess, not a god, put the Southern Paiute world into motion. Ocean Woman, the first creative force, used her skin and body to stretch out over the entire Western Hemisphere. She used her body to push out the hemisphere from the center of the earth, located in the Spring Mountains of southern Nevada. The practice of movement, traveling, and diaspora continues today through the lives, philosophies, and ceremonies of contemporary Chemehuevi. They have always been great travelers, and Chemehuevi continue to move about today, not on foot or horseback but in cars, trucks, busses, trains, and airplanes. In August 2013, Chemehuevi Salt Song singer Matthew Hanks Leivas and his son traveled from their home on the Chemehuevi Reservation in California to Utah, Nevada, Arizona, and New Mexico, traveling by train from Needles, California, to Albuquerque, New Mexico, and then by rented car to Santa Fe. They traveled to share their unique contemporary culture and body of sacred songs with numerous Native communities. They explained how the Salt Songs speak of traveling vast distances and visiting new people. The singers explained that in the songs, the people lived first in the present-day Spring Mountains, but they gradually moved down from the tree-covered peaks of their sacred mountain into the deserts, valleys, mountains, and plateaus of Nevada, California, Arizona, and Utah.

Chemehuevi and Mojave people experienced a special cultural confluence when they met on the Colorado River. Mojave called Southern Paiute people Chemehuevi, meaning mixed with all, and Chemehuevi settled near the Mojave, where they cultivated corn, squash, beans, and melons. Mojave and Chemehuevi shared an amicable relationship for years, sometimes intermarrying and sharing songs and ideas. Chemehuevi honored their great runners, and Mojave marveled at the running ability of their neighbors. Chemehuevi had special runners who could "run in the old way." The Chemehuevi believed their runners could fly.[18] Other Indians respected Chemehuevi for their ability to move and be adaptive in many diverse environments. Chemehuevi learned numerous languages, including Cahuilla, Cocopah, Haldchihoma, Luiseño, Mojave, Quechan, Serrano, Ute, and others. Chemehuevi moved smoothly among other Native nations, sometimes marrying men and women from these tribes and adding to their cultural richness. Recurrent diaspora characterized Chemehuevi throughout their history, and the people continue this tradition to this day.[19]

The arrival of non-Native people significantly influenced the diaspora of Chemehuevi people, just as it did the course of their history. Although representatives of Spain and Mexico visited Chemehuevi and influenced their history with the introduction of domesticated animals, plants, and pathogens, the arrival of white Americans from the United States had a far greater impact on Chemehuevi people. Chemehuevi met American trappers and traders before the war between the United States and Mexico in 1846. But the Treaty of Gua-

Traditional
Southern Paiute Territory:
Band Divisions

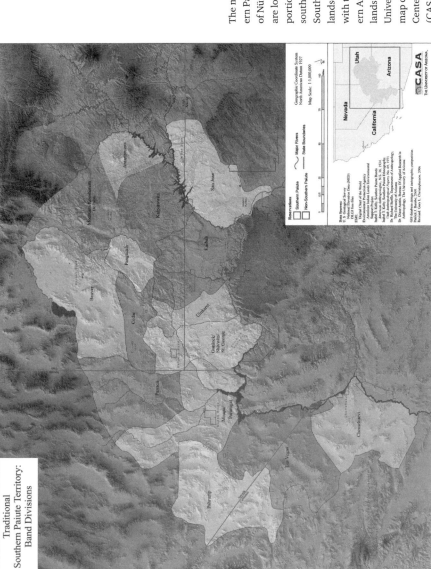

The map depicts Traditional Southern Paiute Territory and the location of Nüwüvi bands. The Chemehuevi are located in the southwestern portion of Paiute territory, the southernmost band of Paiute. All Southern Paiute people shared this landscape and formed an agreement with the Native Americans of Southern Arizona to travel through their lands unmolested. Richard Stoffle, University of Arizona, provided this map created for public use by the Center for Applied Spatial Analysis (CASA).

dalupe Hidalgo of 1848, which brought California and the Southwest into the United States, ushered in a new era of explorers, surveyors, and soldiers who interrupted the traditional lives of Chemehuevi. Americans upset the balance of power between Chemehuevi and Mojave, creating a hostile situation in which the two old friends became enemies. The Chemehuevi-Mojave war of the 1860s destabilized the two peoples and caused some Chemehuevi to remove willingly to the Oasis of Mara, later known as Twenty-Nine Palms.[20] There, under the leadership of Jim Mike and his brother, William Mike, the Chemehuevi lived peacefully with a group of Serrano and established a new life in the heart of the Mojave Desert. At the Oasis of Mara the Chemehuevi continued to hunt, gather, and farm, raising crops of corn, wheat, squash, melons, beans, and varieties of fruit. They worked for miners scouring the desert and mountains in search of gold, and they traveled into the Coachella Valley and Banning Pass to work for cash as laborers. They worked as cowboys, miners, farm hands, house cleaners, babysitters, carpenters, and at other jobs. They survived the destruction of their economic world and kept their families and cultures together.[21]

During the early twentieth century, some Chemehuevi people moved to Banning, Coachella, Indio, Las Vegas, Palm Springs, and Parker, but most of the people remained at Twenty-Nine Palms until 1909 and the tragic murder of William Mike and the untimely death of his daughter, Carlota. Since 1903, William Mike had been the civil and spiritual leader of Chemehuevi at Twenty-Nine Palms. When he died suddenly and violently, the people abandoned the Oasis of Mara, moving temporarily to the Morongo Indian Reservation. Some of the people remained in Banning to live with the Serrano and Pass Cahuilla. Most tribal members moved to the eastern edge of the Coachella Valley near Indio, California, where the Office of Indian Affairs enrolled them on the Cabazon Reservation without the knowledge or consent of the Cahuilla people of the Cabazon Reservation.[22]

Susie Mike, the daughter of William Mike, remained on the Cabazon Reservation, but the other Chemehuevi dispersed, moving in many different directions to find work.[23] The diaspora that so characterized the Chemehuevi of the past continued to mark their history throughout the twentieth century. Still, despite their movement in different directions, some Chemehuevi elders held the people together through informal councils at each other's homes. The people visited each other's residences, worked in the fields and orchards together, and participated in ceremonies together. Chemehuevi also saw each other at funerals, Indian fiestas, weddings, and memorials, where they gathered to dance and sing. In spite of their situation, Chemehuevi always found humor and stories

In 1994 the Twenty-Nine Palms Tribe established Spotlight 29 Casino on its reservation in the town of Coachella, near Indio, California. Originally the casino had no slot machines, but the tribe used its tribal sovereignty to challenge federal and state authorities by buying and operating slot machines.

Today the Twenty-Nine Palms Tribe owns two successful casinos, including Spotlight 29 and Tortoise Rock. Photograph by Clifford E. Trafzer.

in human and animal activities, poking fun at one another as well as outsiders. Chemehuevi experienced an ethnogenesis in the early twentieth century, holding onto key elements of their culture while living in a world greatly influenced by white Americans. Through it all, they kept their human spirit—in part, through their well-known innate humor, which remains intact today.[24]

During the late twentieth century, Chemehuevi of the Twenty-Nine Palms Tribe used informal councils and family meetings to keep the people united. They used these meetings to make decisions as a tribe. In this manner, the families decided not to sell their reservation trust land near the modern town of Twentynine Palms. Through these informal council meetings in the 1970s, they agreed to accept an offer by leaders of the Cabazon Reservation to take a portion of the reservation and create their own formal reservation and tribal government. At the same time, the Twenty-Nine Palms Band of Mission Indians formed their own By-Laws and Constitution, re-creating a sovereign tribal government on their new reservation.[25] In 1994 the Twenty-Nine Palms Tribe took a new direction, establishing a casino on their reservation in Coachella, California, and asserting their tribal sovereignty in defiance of the governments of the United States and California. They pressed their economic and political power, offering high-stakes gambling despite a threat that the entire General Council of the tribe might be arrested and jailed for asserting these rights.[26]

Tribal members moved in concert with some of the other tribes of the Coachella Valley to lead two referendum efforts, Proposition 5 and Proposition 1A, which supported Indian gaming. The tribe became politically active within the nation, state, and city, working closely with political and business leaders as well as civic organizations.[27] For a short time during the early years of the twenty-first century, the Twenty-Nine Palms Tribe partnered with Donald Trump to increase interest in their business and tribe. The partnership with Trump ended in 2005 but not their interest in furthering their tribal community. Tribal members used some of the profits from their casino to support health, religious, and educational charities. The tribe also created a cultural committee and has revitalized their history, culture, religion, and language through various programs.

Now at the beginning of the twenty-first century, members of the Twenty-Nine Palms Tribe are on the move again, this time to advance their economic base and further their cultural programs. In 1998 the tribe formally organized the Native American Land Conservancy, an intertribal nonprofit land conservancy that purchases lands important to Indian people and creates learning and healing landscapes to benefit Indians and non-Indians alike.[28] The tribe sponsored the first organizing meetings for the conservancy in the winter of 1997, when the Native American Land Conservancy identified several sacred areas where members wish to protect plant and animal habitats as well as cultural resources such as village sites and burial grounds. The tribe has supported the Salt Song Project, a grassroots effort of several Southern Paiute tribes to preserve the sacred songs by teaching them to young people. The Salt Song singers visit the places mentioned in the songs, so they may learn more about the places and form a life-long connection to the land and the life in the area.[29] Young people will pass on the songs, keeping them alive for future generations. Members of the Twenty-Nine Palms Tribe believe that by supporting the conservancy, Salt Songs, and other cultural efforts, they are continuing the circle that emerged out of the earth with Ocean Woman and has continued ever since. They recognize their culture has changed, but they treasure their

In 1975 members of the Twenty-Nine Palms Tribe separated from the Cabazon Indian Reservation, establishing their own enrollment, bylaws, and constitution. As a federally recognized tribe, the Twenty-Nine Palms Tribe created its own flag and emblem, depicting the Washington Palm Trees of the Oasis of Mara, mountains, rattlesnake, roadrunner, and sun sign found on petroglyphs of the Mojave and Colorado Deserts. Photograph by Clifford E. Trafzer.

traditional culture and have used modern technology and businesses to retain and perpetuate their cultural ways.

Like Chemehuevi dancers who move in a great circle, the Chemehuevi story has no beginning, no ending. In some respects, the tribe is part cultural change and part continuum of time, place, and people. Tribal members have enlarged their cultural circle, moving to the songs that put them into motion. In its own way, the work is part of the circle—a song of historical stories that originated in part from contemporary people who put this story in motion through the written word. But this song encourages the next song, which will enrich and add to what we know of the Chemehuevi of the Twenty-Nine Palms Tribe and their cultural ways.

CHAPTER 1

The Chemehuevi Way

CONTEMPORARY CHEMEHUEVI ARE SOUTHERN PAIUTE PEOPLE. THEIR culture remains alive among all Nüwü people, including members of the Twenty-Nine Palms Tribe. Their culture has changed over time, but the people maintain their identity as a unique segment of the larger grouping of Nüwüvi people. They are representatives of the southernmost group of Southern Paiute people, and contemporary Chemehuevi hold onto central elements of their ancient culture.[1] Through the process of ethnogenesis, contemporary Chemehuevi maintain their unique place within present-day society, renewing their culture while living in modern society. They hold onto many traditional spiritual beliefs, honor their close relationship to the natural landscape, continue to participate in ceremony, and sing their ancient Salt Songs. Chemehuevi families have survived thousands of years of change through their tenacious and pragmatic character. The people say their culture is alive but transitional, a strong culture able to bend with the time in dynamic ways. Nüwü culture remains at the core of Chemehuevi tribal identity, an ethnic and tribal identity Chemehuevi share with all Southern Paiute.[2]

Chemehuevi people are the Enugwuhype, or ancestral Numic people, who have used the process of ethnogenesis to maintain their tribal sovereignty, connection to the earth, and spiritual beliefs that sustain them today.[3] Contemporary Chemehuevi believe their past history and culture is closely tied to the present. Their culture has always been dynamic. It has never been static as the people learned from other people. Since the Pleistocene era, Chemehuevi have traveled great distances across the Great Basin, the Southwest, and the Pacific states. Because of marriage laws that require people to marry six generations removed, Chemehuevi married widely, taking husbands and wives from many Southern Paiute groups as well as from Cahuilla, Hopi, Luiseño, Mojave, Navajo, Yavapai, and tribes located in present-day northern Mexico. In fact, other Indians claimed Chemehuevi mixed with everyone, and Chemehuevi enriched their culture by adding cultural elements of other Native peoples. Chemehuevi people never lived in a utopia, but they survived in large part by maintaining positive, congenial, and familial relationships with other Indians and later with non-Indians. At the same time, they practiced, remembered, and treasured their ancient way of life: the Chemehuevi way.[4]

Today, Chemehuevi continue their strong spiritual relationship with the natural and spiritual environments of California, the Great Basin, and the desert Southwest. They always have. They are a tribal people strongly tied to the land.[5] In a very real sense, the earth is their religion and their religion is the earth. For some Chemehuevi, this remains the case despite the fact that some contemporary people are also Christians and worship the Creator Spirit in many different ways. During the 1990s, members of the Twenty-Nine Palms Tribe felt so strongly about their ancient relationship with the earth and the need to preserve flora, fauna, and cultural resources that they formed the Native American Land Conservancy. In the past, most Chemehuevi believed in seen and unseen powers, and that spiritual power resided in certain areas of the deserts and mountains. The power radiated out across their traditional homelands like spokes of a wheel. Chemehuevi territory covered a vast landscape, including lands in eastern California, southern Nevada, southern Utah, and western Arizona.[6]

Chemehuevi shared their landscape with other Southern Paiute. Those associated with the Twenty-Nine Palms people had relatives among all the Southern Paiute bands or tribes. At different times they shared the earth with Cahuilla, Halchidhoma, Hopi, Hualapai, Mojave, Quechan, Serrano, Southern Paiute, Yavapai, and others. Chemehuevi men, women, and children had an intimate knowledge of the land, plants, animals, and water resources. Their survival depended on it. Songs tied them to the land and all things encompassed in the natural landscape.[7] Most members of the Twenty-Nine Palms Tribe continue their spiritual relationship with the desert environment and believe that spiritual power rests in the landscapes.

Contemporary Chemehuevi have demonstrated their sustained attachment to the land by supporting the purchase, protection, and preservation of a cul-

In January 2014 members of the Twenty-Nine Palms Tribe held a ceremony to honor and bless a traditional feathered headdress. Chemehuevi elders officiated the headdress blessing ceremony, including Joe Mike Benitez, Dean Mike, and Darrell Mike (from left to right).

These tribal elders are dedicated to the preservation of historical objects and cultural landscapes. They keep songs and traditions through individual acts and tribal programs. Photograph by Clifford E. Trafzer.

tural landscape in the Mojave Desert. For many years, Dean Mike of the Twenty-Nine Palms Tribe served as president of the Native American Land Conservancy and oversaw the purchase of the Old Woman Mountain Preserve in the Mojave Desert. The tribe participated in the purchase with financial and moral support. Mike helped negotiate the purchase of more than twenty-five hundred acres of desert and mountainous land forty miles east of the Colorado River in a remote area. Dean's wife, Theresa, and cousin, Joe Mike Benitez of the Cabazon Tribe, joined in the effort to purchase the Old Woman Mountain Preserve and create a cultural and biological preserve to benefit Indians and non-Indians alike. Matthew Hanks Leivas, a Chemehuevi singer from the Chemehuevi Tribe, also helped with the negotiations that resulted in the Native American Land Conservancy buying the Old Woman Mountain Preserve, including a sacred cave with unique rock sketches that indigenous people had used for thousands of years. These three Chemehuevi men and Theresa led the way to make the purchase and begin a Learning Landscape program to teach young people about their responsibility to the earth and its bounty. Other Indians and non-Indians joined them in an effort to preserve and protect old landscapes of importance to people today.[8]

Chemehuevi do not use the deserts and mountain landscapes like they once did, however. Their economic way of life no longer requires them to enter the desert and mountains to hunt and gather. Non-Indians destroyed the Chemehuevi's old economic way of life in the late nineteenth and early twentieth centuries. Male members of the Twenty-Nine Palms Tribe no longer hunt deer, rabbits, and bighorns, and females no longer gather mesquite, chia, cactus, agave, and yucca. As a result, Chemehuevi no longer sing songs describing the landscape and about places to find food and water. But in the past, Chemehuevi knew the mountains, deserts, valleys, springs, rivers, and roads found within their domain. They had descriptive words to describe the ever-changing colors of the mountains, valleys, clouds, and rocks as the sun cast its rays on the enchanting desert country. Chemehuevi had names for all the plants and animals of the Mojave and Colorado Deserts, and they felt a special kinship with the spirits that inhabited the earth around them. They had songs to commemorate the landscapes owned by certain individuals. They knew all the important landmarks, and they knew shortcuts across the desert and mountains that led to water. They also knew where they could find vegetables, nuts, seeds, and game throughout the year. To many observers today, Chemehuevi territory in the Mojave and Colorado Deserts appears a wasteland. But Chemehuevi viewed the arid region as their home and paradise—a sacred and magical place of spirit that had sustained them since the time of their creation, at least as long ago as the Pleistocene era.[9]

Most contemporary Chemehuevi people know elements of their creation story. They no longer gather in traditional lodges to spend multiple winter nights telling or listening to the creation story, but some members of the tribe know the origin stories of their people. People today continue to find meaning in the stories. For them, the stories are not "fairytales that grow with the telling."[10] They are significant narratives important to Chemehuevi history, and ancient stories and songs still influence the life and well-being of the people today. Western society generally views history in a linear fashion, where point A may influence point B, but points A and B have little relationship to points S or T. This is not so with the Chemehuevi, who believe that point A has a great deal to do with present-day society. The history is thus in a circular fashion, appearing repeatedly as significant to modern society. Some Chemehuevi are profoundly influenced by the past and view history as a great circle in which ancient events are interconnected with today's society, particularly issues involving the sacred, the spiritual, and landscapes. Creation is not something that belongs to the "mythical" past or the "dream time." With each telling of creation stories—with each thought of Ocean Woman, Coyote, Wolf, the Yucca Sisters, the Twins, and their lessons—the events come to life again, influencing both the teller and listener, just as they did generations ago. Far from being fairytales, many Chemehuevi and Southern Paiute view these stories as history—real history that creates events and influences present-day society and the future course of Southern Paiute people.[11]

Children growing up in the Chemehuevi way learned from an early age about a host of characters in their history that put the world into motion. Grandmothers and grandfathers, mothers and fathers, aunts and uncles, relatives and storytellers told the stories. Elders taught children to listen, not with careless attention but with "all their ears" so that they would remember stories and one day tell the narratives in their own words.[12] Chemehuevi still tell stories, but some of the oral narratives have been lost over time. Nevertheless, narratives have been preserved to teach Chemehuevi correct action: honesty, humor, integrity, obedience, sexual conduct, marriage rules, gender roles, proper treatment of plants, animals, and places, and many other ways presented to them in songs and stories. The characters presented in Chemehuevi oral narratives teach lessons through both positive and negative actions of characters or "animal people" such as Coyote, Bear, Wolf, and Cougar. The stories constitute a body of sacred laws, and these rules of life still apply to contemporary Chemehuevi who follow the old teachings. Of course, not all of today's Chemehuevi follow the teachings of ancient stories, but some do and they incorporate traditional beliefs into modern life. In the past, one learned how to act in the Chemehuevi way, and the creation stories offered a central way of knowing and being Chemehuevi. Some tribal elders today still remember the ancient creation stories when the land and people came to be.[13]

In the beginning, Nüwü elders say that water covered the entire Earth and that a small worm fell from the sky onto the surface of the water. The worm transformed into Hutsipamamauu, or Ocean Woman.[14] She took dirt and skin from her own body, especially from her reproductive area, which held special power. She added mud from the bottom of the ocean, and laid it upon the endless sea where it floated. Ocean Woman made the ball of mud, skin, sweat, and oil—composed of elements of the earth and her body. With these natural ele-

In the Southern Paiute Creation story, Ocean Woman used her own fertile skin to spread out on an endless ocean to create solid land. With her arms, legs, and body, Nüwü people say Ocean Woman fashioned mountains, plateaus, and valleys through her movement.

The Spring Mountains of southern Nevada represent the origin site of all Nüwü people, including the Chemehuevi. The outline of Ocean Woman appears at the top of the mountain range. Photograph by Clifford E. Trafzer.

ments, she created land. But the land mass proved too small, so Ocean Woman placed her body onto the land and began stretching it to the north, south, east, and west. She laid down on the earth, and began pushing out the earth with her head, feet, hands, arms, and body, using every extremity and the trunk of her body to spread an extensive land mass. Like a the great ice sheets of old, she worked to make the coastal mountain ranges from Alaska to Chile and from the Pacific Coast to the Atlantic Seaboard. Ocean Woman continued her work while she looked into the blue sky where Sun, Moon, Stars, and Milky Way were. With her hands and feet, she formed mountains, deserts, valleys, plains, plateaus, and coastal regions, making the natural features. She made lakes, rivers, aquifers, seeps, and other water sources. Ocean Woman made the first plants and animals, creating life on what became the Native Universe.[15]

While creating the Earth, Ocean Woman made Sinawavi, or Coyote. She used sweat, skin, dirt, and oil from her pubic area to form Coyote. From the outset, Coyote was a randy character, interested in sex and creating confusion on Earth. He could also be a hero, teaching through his positive and negative acts known through song and story. Coyote, the imperfect one, was at once hero and fool. The female deity continued her creative endeavors by making Tivatsi, or Wolf—first among animal people. Wolf represented the perfect being, a god-like figure. He displayed wisdom, kindness, generosity, bravery, and foresight. Coyote, on the other hand, represented the typical human being with some attributes of Wolf, but a personality flawed with ego, desires, materialism, self-ishness, and lust. Ocean Woman created Tukumumuuntsi, or Mountain Lion, the bold and fearless hunter that provided for others. When Ocean Woman thought she had formed the earth sufficiently, she sent Wolf to the north and south to examine her creation. Wolf returned singing that the earth was not large enough. Ocean Woman sent Coyote to the east and west to inspect her creation, and he too reported that the earth was not large enough. So Ocean Woman continued the earth's creation, stretching it out more and more until Coyote reported that it was large enough.[16]

Wolf and Coyote lived in a cave on Nivaganti, their sacred Snow Mountain (known today as Charleston Peak in the Spring Mountains) of present-day southern Nevada, located northwest of Las Vegas. Wolf and Coyote became great hunters and on one hunting expedition, Coyote discovered the tracks of a woman traveling from the east to the west. Always curious, Coyote followed her tracks, which led him to Poowavi, or Louse. She was a beautiful woman who wore nothing but a jackrabbit apron that flipped up and down in the air with every step, revealing her pubic area. Louse stimulated Coyote's sexual urges, and he longed to have sex with her. He studied her body and became aroused. Coyote wanted to make love to Louse and, intuitively, she knew it. As she continued her journey westward from the Great Basin and the Mojave Desert toward the Pacific Ocean, she sang this song to tease Coyote:

My little jackrabbit apron
flaps up and down
flaps up and down.[17]

Coyote lusted after Louse. Since Louse knew that Coyote wanted to make love to her, she teased him, telling him to race ahead on the trail and build a small lodge where they could have sexual relations. Coyote eagerly built a small brush lodge and waited for Louse. As Louse approached the lodge, she sent sleep medicine that put Coyote to sleep. Louse continued her journey toward the Pacific but eventually used her thoughts to awaken Coyote. When Coyote awoke, he became angry with himself for falling asleep and missing his chance to have sex with Louse. Frustrated, he ran after her. When he caught up to her, she made the same request for a shelter where they could make love. Coyote ran ahead to build the lodge.[18]

Four times the same event took place. After the fourth time of being tricked, Coyote caught up with Louse on the shores of the Pacific Ocean. She explained that she planned to swim the Pacific Ocean to an island where her mother lived. Louse offered to allow Coyote to accompany her, but he explained he could not swim. Louse offered to help Coyote reach the island too by traveling on her back. Coyote liked the idea of being that close to Louse, so he crawled onto her back as they began their journey into the sea. As Louse swam the ocean, Coyote clung to her back until she dived deep into the water, attempting to drown her suitor. Coyote let go, floated to the surface, and changed himself into a water spider. During the transformation, Louse swam away, leaving Coyote far behind. As a spider, however, Coyote moved faster than Louse, skirting across the top of the ocean until he spotted an island and dashed over the water to land. Once Coyote came ashore, he saw an elder woman sitting outside her lodge in the shade weaving a basket. Without saying a word, Coyote went inside the lodge and fell asleep. His journey as spider had tired him greatly.

By and by, Louse arrived and told her mother about horny Coyote and how she had outsmarted him and then drowned him on her journey across the great water. Her mother admonished her daughter, reporting that Coyote was not dead but asleep in the house. Surprised and impressed by Coyote's effort, Louse entered the lodge and made love to Coyote. Sexual relations with Louse proved difficult, owing to the fact that the creative process had armed Louse's vagina with teeth. Despite this obstacle, the couple made love that resulted in Louse becoming filled with fertilized eggs. Within a short time, Louse laid many eggs that her mother placed into a new woven basket, carefully sealing the lid with pine pitch. The elder woman had special plans for the eggs and prepared the container to serve as a womb to carry the eggs back to Wolf.[19]

After making love, Coyote decided to return home to the Spring Mountains of southern Nevada. Before leaving the island, Louse's mother gave Coyote her basket filled with Louse's eggs. She had glued and sewn shut the basket lid and told the trickster not to open it until he arrived home. She gave Coyote strict instructions not to open the basket and to give it to Wolf, who would know what to do with it. Coyote transformed himself into a water spider, skirted across the waves to the mainland, and began his journey east from the Pacific Coast to the Great Basin. Once on the mainland, Coyote changed back to himself, always keeping the special basket close. As he traveled east from the coast to the coastal ranges and inland valleys, Coyote noticed that with each passing day, the basket became heavier. He felt something moving inside the basket. He heard voices. As he traveled toward the deserts and mountains, Coyote became so curious about the contents of the basket that he opened it. Human beings—the first Native Americans—flowed out of the basket. Coyote tried to put the first people back into the basket, but to no avail. They flowed out of the basket like water, traveling in every conceivable direction. The basket had served as a protective womb, and the people now came forth from a basket. Chemehuevi and their Southern Paiute relatives say that the union of Coyote and Louse created the first human beings.[20]

All of the people scurried from the basket except a few remnants of humankind, men and women crushed by the weight of the others. They were too weak and severely injured to climb out. Coyote put the lid on the basket and took these few people to the Spring Mountains of present-day southern Nevada, where Wolf used his breath medicine to bring life to the people. Wolf angrily chastised his brother for not following the old woman's directives and bringing all the people in the basket to him. He had known of the basket of first people and had expected it. Wolf opened the basket and took the weak humans and remolded them. With his breath, a life-giving force and component of indigenous medicine, Wolf blew on the first people. His breath medicine magically revived and reformed the people, making them the heartiest of all human beings. They became the Nüwü, or Southern Paiute people, including Chemehuevi. They became the first Southern Paiute who populated the Spring Mountains, the creation site and mountain of power of Chemehuevi and others. Larry Eddy once explained the power of the Spring Mountains: "When I go up to Mount Charleston, I have to say my prayer. I can't just go walking up there. He'll punish me. I have to pray to Him and ask his forgiveness that I'm coming up into his sacred land."[21]

Chemehuevi and other Southern Paiute people look to the Spring Mountains as a sacred place with many sites of power. The rock sketches found in these mountains and many others have a special place in past and modern culture of Chemehuevi and other Nüwü. "That peckin' in the mountains, you know, where they peck, peck, peck, peck, peck, they're done by the Little People and they live in the mountains." Tribal elders say: "If you're out there on certain days, a real still day, you can hear the pecking." To "a spiritual man," this pecking is evidence the Little People are "still there." The Little People "record the healing, the healing that they did in certain places. This is why it still goes on today."[22] Places of healing are situated throughout the Spring Mountains and many other mountains in the Great Basin, in California, and in the desert Southwest. One highly significant site sits in the Spring Mountains, a mountain cave located on Charleston Peak (11,918 feet) in present-day Toiyabe National Forest.

The people began their existence at Nivaganti (Where Snow Sits or Snow Having), the Chemehuevi name for Charleston Peak. They established themselves first among Coyote, Wolf, Cougar, and others before leaving the mountain and traveling to many other places where they established their homes. The Chemehuevi chose to move in many directions from the Spring Mountains, including south into the Mojave Desert and down the Colorado River where they lived, developing positive relationships with Halchidhoma, Mojave, Quechan, Yavapai, and other Indian people long before the Spanish arrived in Alta California.[23] Chemehuevi and other Southern Paiute people lived in a vast region and had intimate knowledge of the land in present-day Arizona, California, Nevada, and Utah. In addition, Chemehuevi had contact with Indians in what is today Alta California, Baja California, Mexico, and New Mexico. According to Quechan elders Lee Emerson and Henry DeCorse, Chemehuevi people had a positive trading relationship with the Quechan living at the confluence of the Colorado and Gila Rivers.[24]

With their Paiute brothers and sisters, Chemehuevi and other Southern Paiute inhabited and used the region around Las Vegas, Nevada, including the Pahrump Valley, the Ivanpah Mountains, Death Valley, the Clark Range, and the Providence Mountains. They had a close and generally amicable relationship with the Hualapai Indians living in the deserts, plateaus, canyons, and mountains surrounding present-day Kingman and Peach Springs, Arizona. Chemehuevi traded with Hopi, Hualapai, Maricopa, Pima, Tohono O'odham, Ute, and others. They were great travelers and traders, a tradition they continue today. Nüwüvi people had a "passion for investigation and exploration, and a deep-seated love of novelty and change. They delighted to visit strange peoples, speak strange tongues, sing strange songs, and marry strange wives."[25] Chemehuevi became a people that mixed well with all tribes. According to Chemehuevi elder Larry Eddy, Chemehuevi boasted they had some of the most beautiful women among all the tribes, and their families arranged marriages for their daughters so they could establish formal familial relations with many diverse tribes, including Cahuilla, Hualapai, Quechan, and others.[26] Contemporary Chemehuevi continue to exhibit inquisitive, investigative minds and revel in all forms of change and exploration. They today enjoy traveling just as they did in the distant past. As a result, Chemehuevi culture became "a mosaic of elements derived from the various tribes with whom they came in contact during their long wanderings, continuing from the remote past down into recent times."[27] These historical characteristics are evident among modern Chemehuevi people and have their origins in the ancient tribal past.

In keeping with the Chemehuevi propensity to interact and learn from other Native people, some Chemehuevi have pointed out that at one time, their people lived north of the Mojave in villages on Cottonwood Island in the Colorado River Valley. They lived in the western end of the Colorado in Chemehuevi Valley. Other Chemehuevi lived south of the Mojave and in villages near Halchidhoma Indians, a Yuman-speaking people who lived south of the Mojave in the region of present-day Blythe, California. During the 1820s, the Mojave and Quechan became alarmed at the behavior of Halchidhoma, who reportedly attacked small Mojave villages and stole Mojave women and children, selling them to the Spanish for manufactured goods. According to Dan Welch and Pete Sherman, Mojave men and consultants of anthropologist Alfred Kroeber, a small delegation of Quechan and Mojave men had entered a Halchidhoma village near Ehrenberg, Arizona, on a peace mission. Halchidhoma hosts took them to a small lodge to allow them to eat and rest, but Halchidhoma warriors pounced on their guests and took them to a place the Mojave now call Scalps Taken, where they impaled the delegation, allowed them to die slowly, and took their scalps. This incident and the slave trade caused a full-scale war of Mojave and Quechan allies versus Halchidhoma.[28]

Around 1828, a combined force of Quechan and Mojave attacked the Halchidhoma, causing great bloodshed. Quechan and Mojave scouts had urged the Chemehuevi not to take sides, advice the Nüwü chose to follow. Quechan and Mojave warriors drove the Halchidhoma from the field of battle, the defeated people taking refuge briefly at a village at the base of Moon Mountain on the Arizona side of the Colorado River. Halchidhoma remnants fled across the desert southeast, following Tyson's Wash east to Palm Canyon into the Kofa Mountains. They likely took the trail between the Kofa and Castle Dome Mountains, moving east through White Tanks, and on to the Mohawk Mountains, where they took the trail south to live with Cocopah Indians. Later, they moved north near present-day Phoenix to live among the Pima and Maricopa, where many reside today on the Fort McDowell Reservation. Chemehuevi people remained out of the fight, and after the exile of the Halchidhoma and their Yuman-speaking allies, Halyikwamai, and Kohuana, the Chemehuevi provided a buffer zone between the Mojave to the north and the Quechan to the south. Some Quechan and Mojave remained in the lower Parker Valley near the Chemehuevi, but far more Chemehuevi lived in the region. They became early warning allies

The Chemehuevi landscape includes lands in Arizona, California, Nevada, and Utah. Chemehuevi people hunted bighorn sheep in the Kofa and Castle Dome mountains of Western Arizona. This is a photograph of the great Castle Dome, a massive volcanic plug seen from miles away, a landmark located thirty miles east of the Colorado River on the Yuma Proving Ground of the United States Army Command. Mule deer and bighorn sheep as well as rabbits, reptiles, birds, and other animals and plants exist today in the mountain range. Castle Dome in the desert northeast of present-day Yuma, Arizona, and can be seen easily from the desert city. Photograph by Clifford E. Trafzer.

to the Mojave, reporting to their neighbors when enemies approached. The forced exile of Halchidhoma opened the Blythe and Palo Verde Valleys near present-day Blythe, California, for additional Chemehuevi settlement, although Chemehuevi say they had inhabited the area since ancient times. Chemehuevi farmed, hunted, and gathered the region, but they continued to travel great distances to trade and visit Indian tribes in distant lands.[29]

These dramatic events significantly influenced the course of Chemehuevi history, because of their increasing presence north, south, and west of the Mojave. In addition to settling the Colorado River Valley, Chemehuevi moved into the Mojave Desert, slowly moving west into the desert above the San Bernardino Mountains and into the Tejón Pass.[30] In the aftermath of the fighting, Chemehuevi presence expanded into the Parker, Blythe, and Palo Verde Valleys they had once had shared with the Halchidhoma. The Mojave and Quechan considered themselves the "owners" of the Blythe and Parker valleys, but Chemehuevi had lived along the Colorado River farming productively for generations west and north of the major Mojave villages. Although some Mojave remained in the Parker and Blythe Valleys after the war with the Halchidhoma, most Mojave moved north to their homes in the Mohave Valley near present-day Needles, California. The Chemehuevi population in the Blythe and Parker Valleys may well have been greater than estimates provided by contemporary scholars.[31]

Alfred Kroeber estimated the Chemehuevi population at "something between 500 and 800 people."[32] Although the actual number will never be known, the Chemehuevi population may have been a thousand or more people, scattered in many villages found within a huge geographical area. Many Southern Paiute people traveled from one area to another, making it impossible to distinguish which Paiute person was Chemehuevi. In the eighteenth and nineteenth centuries, many settlers and military men used the terms interchangeably, as Chemehuevi and Paiute were synonymous. No one took a census, so numbers are estimates. The people lived in several small groups, known broadly as River Dwellers and Desert People. The people further distinguished themselves by calling each other Southern Desert Dwellers and Northern Desert Dwellers. Chemehuevi generally lived in loose-knit bands of many diverse people, living independently in the greater Mojave and Colorado Deserts. They established villages that became their base but moved into the desert and mountains to hunt and gather. Chemehuevi and Southern Paiute conducted limited farming along the various streams and rivers as well as near springs in the Mojave Desert. "We farmed long before we moved south near the Mojave," Matthew Hanks Leivas explained. "The Mojave did not teach us how to farm, but we learned new forms of irrigation once we lived on the Colorado River."[33] One of the major bands of Chemehuevi included the Shivwits group at Twenty-Nine Palms and their relatives, another group living in the Chemehuevi Valley west of the Colorado River.

In addition, the Hokwait band of Chemehuevi lived in Ivanpah Valley, while the Kauyaichit and Timipashauwagotsit resided primarily in the Providence Mountains. The Mokwat bands lived in the Kingston Mountains, while the Yagat had villages in Amargoso. Finally, the Moviat band lived near the Mojave on Cottonwood Island in the middle of the Colorado River. Language, culture, religion, ceremony, and family connected the diverse bands of Chemehuevi. They lived with each other from time to time, conducted ceremony, celebrated births and deaths, traded, hunted, gathered, and intermarried together. But they remained separate, independent groups with great freedom to determine their own lives and activities. All of these things tied the bands in a quasi-union, particularly familial and spiritual, which brought them together in the open deserts and rocky mountains of southeastern California, western Arizona, and southern Nevada.[34]

Chemehuevi claimed much of the Mojave Desert as their home, hunting, gathering, and farming selective areas around the Bristol, Cady, Chuckwalla, Granite, Old Woman, Palen, Providence, San Bernardino, Soda, and Tehachapi Mountains. The present routes of Interstate 15 and Interstates 10 and 40 in eastern California generally mark some of the boundaries of Chemehuevi country. The people also inhabited select portions of the Colorado River Valley from the present region surrounding Lake Mead to the city of Blythe, California. Chemehuevi established villages along the east and west banks of the Colorado River from Boulder City to Fort Mojave, the west side of the river across from Lake Havasu City, and the region below the Bill Williams River to Blythe. Past and contemporary Chemehuevi view the Panamint Range as a magical, powerful place. Several songs and stories originate from this sacred site. Today's Chemehuevi still consider the Panamint Mountains sacred ground and a storied landscape.[35]

Chemehuevi sang many types of songs, including those describing the real property belonging to leadership people within a particular Chemehuevi group. Individuals *owned* songs, and owning songs meant owning land. Chemehuevi usually passed down songs from father to son, although a father could give a song to a daughter, brother, cousin, son-in-law, wife, or friend. The song belonged to a person and that person could pass ownership of the song to another.[36] In the nineteenth century and earlier, these songs indicated the property of individuals, and other Indians did not violate the ownership of land without reprisals by the owner. Chemehuevi used songs as oral deeds to real estate. Chemehuevi law validated song deeds, which to Chemehuevi were as binding as written deeds. By owning a song, the person owned the land about which the song described. This included plant, animals, and water resources. Chemehuevi elder and historian George Laird once explained to his wife, anthropologist Carobeth Laird, that Chemehuevi literally owned land and they did so through their songs.[37] Chemehuevi elders like Gertrude Hanks Leivas, Betty Cornelius, Larry Eddy, and Joe Mike Benitez corroborate Laird's statement, saying to own the song meant owning the land.[38] The songs speak of "my land," but Chemehuevi no longer sing these songs because governments and white settlers took Indian lands, ignoring Native ownership through oral deeds.[39]

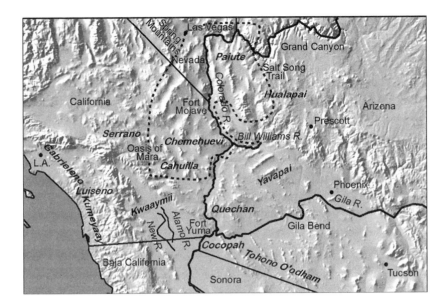

This map depicts the larger territory once used by Chemehuevi hunters, traders, and travelers as they set out across the deserts and mountains of western portion of the Southwest. The Chemehuevi earned a reputation as great travelers, meeting new people and pragmatically learning from others. The map offers some of the key tribes, towns, and places found within the Chemehuevi landscape, a huge territory they shared with many other indigenous people. Map by Robert Johnson, University of California–Riverside.

Chemehuevi country encompassed a huge geographical area that included nine biotic communities, including desert springs.[40] Throughout the Mojave and Colorado Deserts, natural springs occur in several sites, including those at Cornfield Spring, Piute Creek, Saratoga Springs, Ash Meadows, Pahrump Valley, and many others. Chemehuevi established permanent and semipermanent villages at sites with water resources, and leaders owning songs about the area claimed private ownership of the water, land, and other resources in the area. Visitors could drink the water at the spring, but they could not remain in the area and claim it without conflict. Chemehuevi leaders held oral titles to the land, which belonged to the person who owned the song describing the area. Diverse plants grew near the springs, including bulrush, mesquite, willow, yucca, screwbean, cottonwood, cattail, tule, juncus, and others. The Chemehuevi people traveled a good deal, first on foot and then on horseback. They traveled to trade, hunt, and gather, and they knew how to find desert and mountain springs. Because of intermarriage, they often had relatives living among groups residing by springs. In 1928 anthropologist Isabel Kelly visited many of the Chemehuevi villages around springs and provided a map of some Chemehuevi villages in the Mojave Desert. To navigate the desert and find water sources, people developed song maps they used to find the sites. Their survival depended on this knowledge, which elders taught children who taught their children. This was also true of Chemehuevi people living near desert washes, which provided habitat for such plants as golden bush, paperbag bush, and matchweed as well as most of the larger trees just mentioned except cottonwoods.[41]

Chemehuevi country also included desert dunes and alkali sinks. Sandy dunes occur in various spots throughout the Mojave and Colorado Deserts, including the Kelso Dunes, Devil's Playground, and Dumont Dunes. Dry lakes appear in low elevations from one thousand to twenty-five hundred feet above sea level. Only a few plants grow on the dunes and their fringes, including rice grass, wild rhubarb, and panic grass. Snakes and lizards venture onto the dunes, and desert foxes sometimes hunt kangaroo rats there, but larger mammals generally avoid the dunes. Indigenous people generally lived on the fringes of dry lakes and playas that seasonally filled with water during rains and spring snow runoffs. Although the environment sounds harsh, it provided excellent seasonal habitat for reptiles, birds, mammals, and plants that are salt tolerant, such as iodine bush, salt bush, hop-sage, bud sagebrush, matchweed, arrowweed, fluff grass, and others. Sites such as Soda Springs offered good hunting areas for round-tailed ground squirrels, white-tailed antelope, ground squirrel, wood rats, kangaroo rats, grasshopper mice, cottontails, jackrabbits, and a variety of birds and reptiles.[42]

Chemehuevi also knew creosote bush scrub and yucca woodlands communities. The biotic community of creosote bush is most common within the Mojave and Colorado Deserts. Valley floors and low bajadas (dry geographical areas at the base of alluvial fans from mountains consisting of sediment brought down from the mountains by wind and water) that averaged three to eight inches of rain per year, supported silver, pencil, and buckhorn cholla as well as barrel cactus and prickly pear cactus. Yucca and cactus provided food in the form of stalks, leaves, and fruit. In addition, the biotic community sustained salt, thorn, burro, and brittle brushes. Blue sage and Mojave yucca also grew within the community, which is home to many animals, including wood rats, kangaroo rats, white-tailed antelope, ground squirrel, round-tailed ground squirrel, pocket mice, grasshopper mice, cactus mice, jackrabbits, and cottontails. Chemehuevi had preferred foods, but they ate mice, rats, and squirrels, roasting them as they would rabbit and antelope. Larger mammals (such as the bobcat, coyote, badger, and kit fox) live in this desert community, but Chemehuevi rarely ate these mammals. They hunted and ate Gambel's quail, chuckwalla, and desert tortoise. Other plants and animals live in the yucca woodland communities that dot the deserts. Chemehuevi ate some of the plants and animals from the yucca woodlands, and they used other natural resources for medicine, clothing, and tools.[43]

Yucca generally thrives in desert elevations from four thousand to six thousand feet above sea level, where precipitation averages six to ten inches each year.[44] Some of the major plants include fleshy fruited yucca, Mojave yucca, Mormon tea, bud sagebrush, saltbush, blackbush, buckwheat, winterfat, hopsage, goldenbush, and others. The yucca woodland biotic region of the Mojave and Colorado Deserts also supports many varieties of cactus, including beavertail, barrel, hedgehog, and varieties of cholla. Deer, galleta, dropseed, and fluff grasses exist in the area as well as the large Joshua trees. Many animals make the yucca woodland their homes, including cactus mice, deer mice, canyon mice, grasshopper mice, pocket mice, kangaroo rats, ground squirrels, and pronghorns, often called antelope. The community is home to coyotes, bobcats, badgers, kit foxes, cottontails, jackrabbits, desert tortoise, and bighorn sheep. Numerous varieties of birds and reptiles live in the yucca woodland environment.[45] The plants and animals in all the biotic areas used by Chemehuevi in the past became part of the natural "community," gifts from the Creator. They remain so today among those people who have a spiritual connection with cultural places, plants, and animals. Chemehuevi songs about deer, rats, bighorns, and other animals commemorate the connection of the people and their natural environment. Salt Songs continue to provide this function among the people today.

The last two biotic communities found within Chemehuevi territory are located at the highest elevations found in the desert regions. The piñon-juniper woodlands enjoy annual precipitation of eight to twelve inches of rain and snow a year. Elevations of five thousand to eight thousand feet are the region's high mountains, receiving more rain and snow. At upper higher elevations, Chemehuevi found piñon, turbinella oak, and juniper trees that produced edible seeds. Other plants included serviceberries, manzanita, Great Basin sage, buckbush, desert mountain mahogany, barberry, Apache plume, coffeeberry, mountain rose, snowberry, and Mormon tea.[46] Desert bighorn sheep, mule deer, gray fox, bobcat, mountain lions, coyotes, wood rats, canyon mice, deer mice, piñon, mice, rock squirrel, and Panamint chipmunk lived in higher elevations.

The last biological communities within Chemehuevi country are the fir-pine forest region and Bristlecone pine forest, which only occur in southern Nevada in the Spring Mountains, the origin place of Chemehuevi people. The mountain rises up out of the desert like a great rocky ship, a sacred mountain complex filled with power. Chemehuevi also believed that some animals—especially rattlesnakes, deer, and bighorns—had spiritual "power" given to them by the Creator. From the east looking west, an outline of Ocean Woman appears along the mountain ridges to the west. During a camp in the Spring Mountains on October 6, 2012, an anonymous Southern Paiute scholar explained that the bighorn are medicine people, shamans, that have great power often sought by Chemehuevi and Southern Paiute. Charleston Peak emerges in the Spring Mountains, ranging in height from 7,500 to 11,500 feet above sea level, where the annual precipitation of snow and rain averages twelve to twenty-four inches. Yellow pine, white fir, bristlecone pine, lodgepole pine, quaking aspen, Utah juniper, dwarf maple, and piñon pines grow within the community along with barberries, serviceberries, mountain mahogany, cream bush, currants, mountain roses, blackberries, and blue elderberries. Mountain lions, bobcats, bighorns, deer, golden-mantled ground squirrels, rock squirrels, porcupines, Palmer's chipmunks, pack rats, wood rats, and varieties of mice, birds, and reptiles inhabit higher elevations in the Spring Mountains.[47]

Many contemporary Chemehuevi believe that plants and animals of all these biological regions belong to the Chemehuevi and Southern Paiute community. Ocean Woman brought plants and animals to life, and they existed alongside humans for generations, providing life to Chemehuevi. Modern people consider them sacred, a part of the Chemehuevi world tied to landscapes, flora, and fauna. Non-Natives often think of "community" as human communities, but Chemehuevi community includes people, plants, places, animals, rivers, springs, clouds, rocks, mountains, and other natural phenomena. The natural landscape is part of the community; by extension, any material item made from natural items—such as arrows, awls, bows, bowls, baskets, knives, lances, and other objects—are part of the community complex. Chemehuevi men and women made deer hide shirts, moccasins, feathered headdresses, bone awls, baskets, bows, jewelry, metates, manos, arrowheads, and homes from elements of the Chemehuevi community. Chemehuevi still view community in this broader framework.

Chemehuevi divided themselves into three large groups, including the Tantivaitsiwi (or Southern Chemehuevi), the Tantiitsiwi (or Northern Chemehuevi), and the Tiiraniwiwi (or Desert Chemehuevi). The Mojave River served as the dividing line between the Northern and Southern groups. Desert Chemehuevi lived west of the Colorado River in the Mojave and Colorado Deserts, hunting and gathering and conducting limited farming. Desert dwellers included families of the Twenty-Nine Palms Band of Chemehuevi at the Oasis of Mara near the present-day town of Twentynine Palms, California. The springs found at the Oasis of Mara offered this Chemehuevi band and their Serrano neighbors sufficient water to farm. Today, Paul and Jane Smith, proprietors of the Twentynine Palm Inn, farm the same space as the Indian garden. It produces a wealth of fruits and vegetables, just as it had for the Indian people when they lived at the Oasis of Mara.

Historically Chemehuevi marked their territories with songs. Although people no longer sing personal songs about territories, many Chemehuevi are familiar with a body of Salt Songs. Most contemporary Chemehuevi know about Salt Songs that singers would share at funerals and memorial ceremonies. Today, Salt Songs tell a story that links landscapes with the sacred. The songs begin in a cave on the Bill Williams River of western Arizona, where two women received a charge to travel vast distances into western Arizona, southern Utah/Nevada, and south into eastern California. Salt Songs delineate much of Chemehuevi and Southern Paiute territory. Chemehuevi past and present consider Salt Songs sacred and communal. Other Indians sang Salt Songs, including Cocopah, Hopi, Tohono O'odham, Hualapai, and Apache. When Chemehuevi Pearl Eddy attended Sherman Institute, an off-reservation boarding school, a Hualapai girl shocked Pearl by singing Salt Songs. Pearl remembered saying, "Hey, what are you doing singing my songs?" She learned that Hualapai sing Salt Songs too, although theirs end in the Pacific Ocean where people cry, making the water salty.[48]

Chemehuevi consider Deer and Bighorn Sheep Songs hereditary songs owned by families. The songs conveyed territorial rights to individuals. The songs travel, describing specific mountains, valleys, caves, springs, water tanks, plants, and animals. Deer and Mountain Sheep Songs offer oral maps to one's property. Songs provided an acknowledgment of the animals about which the songs center. A Mountain Sheep Song might tell of the east side of the Old Woman Mountains on the desert floor far from the base of the mountain, explaining how the elevation and environment changes as the hunter moves west. The song may speak of a broad sweeping plain from the desert floor into some rocky outcroppings. At the base of the mountains, palo verde, mesquite, and smoke trees live in profusion with many varieties of cactus and creosote. However, the farther west the hunter traveled, the higher the elevation became and

The Southern Paiute landscape of Arizona, California, Nevada, and Utah contains many petroglyphs and pictographs. Chemehuevi elders say the "Little People" made the rock etchings, and rock art often depict dreams, maps, trails, and natural elements of the environment. This is a photograph of an indigenous etching of a bighorn sheep, a traditional source of food. Chemehuevi people consider the animals spiritual and powerful. Photograph by Clifford E. Trafzer.

the more the desert vegetation gave way to barren, rocky ravines that took the hunter up the side of the mountain into juniper and piñon trees, a place where a watering hole might be found where animals drink.[49]

The mountain trail along the top of the Old Woman Mountains led a hypothetical hunter along a well-worn animal trail moving up and down along the mountaintop. For miles a hunter traveled through rocks and canyons, piñons and junipers, where deer and mountain sheep abound, living in the foliage that dotted the mountaintop. In a distance to the north, the round head of a rock figure appeared at a lower elevation. The rock formation appeared like a woman climbing a great mountain, thus the name Old Woman Mountain. The sides of the steep mountains gave way to abrupt cliffs leading to the desert floor. The song offers a visual in words of the grand expanse of a valley to the east, the direction of the rising sun, the famous Chemehuevi Valley, and the Colorado River. The song described the land owned by the singer and established a relationship between the hunter and the hunted. Men sang Deer and Mountain Sheep Songs in preparation for the hunt, and sometimes hunters lost consciousness and dreamed of the number of animals the men would kill the next day.[50]

Some of the songs capture the excitement of the hunt, the racing of the hunter and the quick movement of the animals. Songs sometimes tell of killing animals, the sounds and smell of the kill, the last motion of the dying animals. Chemehuevi verse allowed the singers to repeat the songs many times. Some Chemehuevi owned special ritual songs, but others could use or borrow them in secular gatherings intended to entertain.[51] Chemehuevi and their Southern Paiute neighbors sang Mountain Sheep Songs, Deer Songs, and Salt Songs during the Yagapi, or Mourning Ceremony.[52] Chemehuevi might also share these sacred songs during the funeral or Mourning Ceremony of a Cahuilla, Hualapai, Luiseño, Mojave, Quechan, or Serrano. Most often, Chemehuevi singers used gourd rattles, but the people also made other music with cane flutes, wooden flutes, bullroarers, and basket instruments they beat or scraped. Chemehuevi people still sing Salt Songs at funerals and memorial services.

Larry Eddy, Betty Cornelius, Matthew Hanks Leivas, Vivienne Jake, and others revitalized the songs in the late twentieth and early twenty-first centuries. They spearheaded the Salt Song Project with financial support from the Native American Land Conservancy and the Theresa A. Mike Foundation, a nonprofit organization developed out of the Twenty-Nine Palms Tribe to support educational scholarships and research. The Salt Song Project identifies a sacred trail of Nüwü people through song and brings singers together with young people to sing about the holy landscape. Tribal elders share Salt Songs with young people, teaching them songs and cultural knowledge by taking them to special sites, places of power, where the songs describe particular spots. Young people hear the Salt Songs every time they attend a traditional funeral or memorial service. When Larry Eddy leads in the singing, he always takes time to remind people: "The Creator told us, 'I am going to teach you these songs, but before I teach these songs, I'm going to break your heart." Nüwüvi people sing the Salt Songs at funerals, and Eddy's reference focuses on the loss of loved ones, breaking the hearts of the loved ones each time he sings the sacred songs.[53]

Chemehuevi sing many songs, including Quail, Day Owl, Skunk, Bear, and Bird Songs. Many years ago, Chemehuevi began singing Bird Songs, perhaps learning these from their Cahuilla friends. Bird Songs came to the Nüwü, and Chemehuevi quickly learned the beautiful music of their neighbors and continue to sing Bird Songs today. Larry Eddy sings Bird Songs, even though he is best known as the leading Salt Song singer. He grew up on the Colorado River Indian Reservation in the Parker Valley, going to school with many indigenous people who sang Bird Songs. During his life, people would gather at someone's home to sing these Bird Songs. Eddy would listen and therefore he learned the songs.[54]

During the eighteenth, nineteenth, and twentieth centuries, Chemehuevi gathered under a single roof on cold desert nights to entertain themselves with songs. They played games with sticks, dice, and strings. They played a ring and pin game, attempting to place an object tied with a string over a pin. With a swing of a hand and a wrist, they tossed the object into the air, hoping to have it slip over the hand-held object. Men played peon, a fast-action guessing game that requires players to be quick and agile with their hands, bodies, and minds. The game peon includes power songs intended to bring a player luck. Cahuilla, Chemehuevi, Kumeyaay, Kwaaymii, Luiseño, Mojave, Quechan, and other Indians still play peon. Players usually engage in the game in the evening, often playing throughout the night and betting heavily on participants. Chemehuevi sing special hand game songs, calling on their power to enter the game and help them outsmart their opponents. Chemehuevi culture includes a liberal amount of gambling, which emerged at the beginning of Creation, not in recent years with the advent of Indian gaming. Chemehuevi bet goods, money, and animals on foot races, horse races, spear-ring tosses, and archery matches. Many of these events included songs sung by men, women, and children, all woven into the fabric of the Chemehuevi way.[55] Chemehuevi songs belong to a sacred complex kept by many people today who sing and tell stories, bringing the past forward into the contemporary circle of Chemehuevi life.

Chemehuevi were great runners, and they earned a reputation as superior runners that some say could fly. Other Native Americans and newcomers noticed the ability of Chemehuevi to run fast. Even Father Francisco Garces, the first non-Indian to write about the people, commented on Chemehuevi runners on February 26, 1776.[56] When Chemehuevi groups planned important events, families and villages sent out special runners who ran from village to village over large geographical areas carrying the *tapitcapi,* or knotted string.[57] The number of knots indicated the number of nights before a ceremony began, and runners would inform villagers that the host had invited them to a ceremony at a given place.

In December 1999 the Twenty-Nine Palms Tribe held a *yagapi*, inviting people from Arizona, California, Nevada, Utah, Washington, and other states to attend. The tribe held the memorial ceremony in honor of Theresa Andrea Mike on the Torres-Martinez Reservation, inviting singers from the Colorado River Indian Reservation and the Chemehuevi Reservation as well as singers from the Las Vegas, Moapa, Shivwits, Kiabab, and other Paiute reservations. Singers sang ancient Salt Songs, while a few dancers celebrated the life of Theresa Mike. The family did not ask runners to spread the word about the ceremony. The Mike family used telephones and e-mail to alert people within the individual Chemehuevi and Southern Paiute villages. In the past, people would run from house to house, announcing the *yagapi*. Numerous people would attend the wakes and memorials, keeping alive a sacred tradition.[58]

Chemehuevi elders point out that runners maintained an important place in traditional culture for their ability to run fast and even teleport. Written documents kept by anthropologist John Harrington tell of flying runners, and contemporary Chemehuevi (such as Matthew Hanks Leivas, June Hanks Leivas, Joe Benitez, and others) tell of amazing runners with the knotted string who could fly.[59] A select group of Chemehuevi runners were not ordinary runners. Chemehuevi people considered them a special "class" within each Chemehuevi community—young men who found joy in running and knew the land intimately. This enabled them to race great distances in their bare feet over deserts and mountains using the shortest routes. They ate small amounts of chia for energy, and they drank little water. These runners traveled great distances in short amounts of time. They knew the desert springs and places where water could be found trapped in deep depressions in the rocks. Chemehuevi elder George Laird, now deceased, once told his wife, anthropologist and author Carobeth Laird, that "all of them were lean, strong, beautiful, and remarkably swift."[60] In interviews on September 10 and 17, 1997, Chemehuevi elder Joe Mike Benitez explained that "runners traveled in the old way."[61] He stated that past generations of Chemehuevi elders, including his mother, Susie Mike, believed that runners could fly.

Carobeth Laird stated that a runner "went alone" and "used his secret method," which she believed was a way of teleportation.[62] Chemehuevi elder George Laird provided a detailed example of Kaawia, or Rat Penis, who traveled from Cottonwood Island on the Colorado River to Yuma: "They watched him run away from the camp in a long, easy lope and disappear over the sand dune." The young men, including Laird himself, followed Rat Penis, following "his tracks up to and over the crest of the dune to the point where they had lost sight of him. The tracks continued on, but now they were different. They looked as if he was 'just staggering along,' taking giant steps, his feet touching

Quechan people live south of Chemehuevi along the Colorado River at Fort Yuma. Tribal scholars Barbara Levy and Edith White shared oral histories about the positive relationship of their people with Chemehuevi.

Both indigenous people used the landscape on both sides of the Colorado River and had traded with one another since ancient times. Photograph by Clifford E. Trafzer.

the ground at long, irregular intervals, leaving prints that became further and further apart and lighter and lighter on the sand."[63]

Neither Laird nor any of his comrades saw Rat Penis fly, but they believed that he had flown on his trip to Yuma. After the runner left Cottonwood Island, villagers learned that he had arrived in Yuma that very day—a distance of approximately 250 miles.[64] John Harrington, the famous anthropologist, corroborated Native American accounts of runners flying. Harrington interviewed thousands of Native people over the course of many years. In one account, he reported that Chemehuevi elders followed a runner across the sand until the runner's tracks appeared no longer. It looked as though the runner had made larger and larger strides, leaving his footprints in the sand until the imprint of his feet no longer appeared. Chemehuevi of the past and present believe that traditional runners could fly. This belief remains among many Chemehuevi people today.[65]

In the past, community tribal leaders and families used Chemehuevi runners to communicate with diverse people over large geographical areas. Today, Chemehuevi use many forms of communication to convey events, including word of mouth, the U.S. Post Office, faxes, e-mails, telephones, and others. Chemehuevi leaders announced Mourning Ceremonies as well as the Suupaaruwapi, or Winter Gathering. Winter Gatherings once brought many minor and high chiefs (who spoke a special and unique language) together with their respective families and bands. Winter Gatherings gave leaders opportunities to communicate with each other and families a chance to visit and renew old friendships. Gatherings also gave young people an opportunity to get to know one another or make marriage plans, with the permission of elders who made sure the couple was not too closely related. Modern gatherings draw large numbers of people, including non-Indians interested in knowing more about Chemehuevi culture and peoples. During the twentieth century, Chemehuevi among the Twenty-Nine Palms Band introduced the contemporary Pow Wow complex, a tradition common to the Great Lakes and Plains Indian tribes but not to the Chemehuevi or most people of California and the American Southwest. In 1997 members of the Twenty-Nine Palms Tribe hosted their first Winter Gathering, inviting Native American traditional and fancy dancers. They invited Indian Country and non-Indians to join them on their reservation in Coachella, California, to enjoy the dancing and singing competitions.[66]

During past centuries, California Indians hosted big times when many diverse people came together to celebrate. In Southern California, Cahuilla, Cupeño, Kumeyaay, Serrano, Luiseño, and others often held "fiestas"—social gatherings named after the Spanish tradition of parties. Indian singers, dancers, musicians, healers, and gamblers participated in fiestas, particularly on or near reservations. Cahuilla elder Katherine Saubel once explained that every year she could hear someone singing miles south of her home on the Morongo Indian Reservation. "I would hear singing in the wind down where Interstate 10 runs today," she said. "I would hear that singing and so would others, so we would go down there to find out who was singing. It was a group of people from other reservations that came to sing for us. They had come in wagons with horses and a number of people would be on the wagon singing. That was our invitation to come to their reservation for the fiesta." Saubel explained that the people of Morongo always took food down to the singers, lunch or supper or snacks. That way, the people communicated a future fiesta.[67]

Agents and superintendents of the Office of Indian Affairs hated the fiestas and worried that Native political leaders of the Mission Indian Federation would stir up trouble against the federal government for the many grievances they held, particularly the theft of land and resources the Federation felt should be reimbursed to the tribes. Agents, often Christians, disliked Indian gambling, drinking, and Indian doctoring. Chemehuevi and all the other tribal people played peon games or elaborate hand games of skill in guessing accompanied by song and betting. Chemehuevi participated in fiestas on several different reservations in Arizona, California, and Nevada. During the late nineteenth and early twentieth centuries, agents of the U.S. government tried to destroy the fiestas on the reservations, arguing that too many people had sexual liaisons, drank too much alcohol, and gambled away their earnings. Christian ministers, priests, and teachers working among the tribes joined the condemnation of fiestas. They universally disliked the hosting tribes giving away gifts to other Indians, and field nurse Florence McClintock even admonished and harshly scolded a woman on the Torres-Martinez Reservation for buying manufactured cloth to give away rather than medicine for her children. The Cahuilla woman responded by laughing in McClintock's face.[68] Gift giving played an important role in Native American societies, and Chemehuevi were (and are) generous people, sharing food with visitors and researchers.

Fiestas and Winter Gatherings were social events that provided Southern Paiute *puhwaganti*—an opportunity to address the physical, spiritual, and mental health needs of the people. Non-Chemehuevi often call *puhwaganti* shaman, medicine men, and witch doctors—terms the Chemehuevi rarely used in the past but might be used by some today. For Chemehuevi people, *puhwaganti* were people of high status with the ability to tap into the healing energy and direct healing into the bodies of patients. In 2007, Chemehuevi elder Larry Eddy explained that his grandfather was a *puhwaganti* and had great healing power. A researcher asked him, "What was your grandfather's familiar?" Eddy reluctantly told of his grandfather calling his familiar that lived in the mountains. "You would think that a familiar would come right to the doctor when he needed to doctor but that was not so." Eddy watched his grandfather call his familiar, and during the interview Eddy bent down, grabbing at the ground as if he tried to catch a dodging puppy. Then Eddy motioned with one hand as if he had captured the animal, saying, "Once he got a hold of his familiar, then he could do the healing." Bats from the mountains proved to be his grandfather's familiar, which gave him the power to heal others.[69]

Both men and women could receive power to heal. Many kinds of specialized Indian doctors existed among the Chemehuevi, including doctors that could mend arrow wounds, fight skin irritations and infections, set broken bones, extract and heal bullet wounds, treat organs or gastrointestinal illness, and eradicate spiritual sickness caused by witchcraft or violations of Chemehuevi law, like transgressing-against-marriage laws. All Chemehuevi *puhwaganti* had power or they could not practice medicine. Unlike Western medicine doctors who learned doctoring through formal education, Chemehuevi doctors received their abilities as a gift from the Creator and further developed their expertise over time. A person could not fake being a doctor because spiritual forces could make them ill or kill them. Chemehuevi *puhwaganti* could not abuse their healing gifts, like publicly opening medicine bundles at county fairs or "demonstrating" for court audiences.[70]

Special women served as birthing doctors or midwives, helping mothers with prenatal concerns and postpartum issues. They also treated babies and helped families in numerous ways. Spiritual doctors knew a great deal about many forms of doctoring, but the *puhwaganti* had spiritual power, the highest level of medical ability. Chemehuevi doctors, like the Cahuilla Indian *puls*, received a gift of doctoring. A person might learn some aspects of doctoring from other medicine people—like herbal medicine—but spirits gave humans the highest level of doctoring. Thus spirits gave the *puhwaganti* gifts of healing, the power of which came to medicine people through dreams, visions, and direct meetings through a spiritual experience that endowed the person with power. Chemehuevi honored and feared the *puhwaganti* because of their ability to heal and do harm. This duality of power, so common throughout the world, enabled medicine men and women to use their power in positive or negative ways, either preserving life or taking it.

In October 2007 tribal elder Larry Eddy offered some details about Chemehuevi medicine, disease causation, and healing: "As a young kid, I used to go here, go there with my grandfather. He was a healer. He was a doctor and lots of people came to him for different cures and he performed cures and I, as a little kid, I witnessed a few of those things."[71] Patients came to Eddy's grandfather and gathered outside his home late into the night when the Indian doctor sang and prayed to bring his familiar to him. "I remember . . . he sang his songs, and they all sat around outside."[72] Eddy's grandfather, like all Indian doctors, "had

Chemehuevi and Mojave people both used this style of housing. Chemehuevi *puhwaganti,* or medicine people, performed healing ceremonies in this style of lodge. Notice the granary basket to the far left and the pottery olla next to it. The people depicted have gathered melons and other plant foods. Men, women, and children enjoyed great freedom in a large natural environment. From Lieutenant Amiel Weeks Whipple, during the railroad survey near the Thirty-Fifth Parallel, "Reports of Explorations and Surveys, to Ascertain the Most Practicable and Economical Route for a Railroad from the Mississippi River to the Pacific Ocean, January 31, 1851," *Senate Executive Document* 78, Thirty-Third Congress, Second Session, 1856 (Washington, D.C.: Beverley Tucker Printers).

a spirit, an animal friend." No one could "see that animal but him. He calls to that animal through his songs. He can do this, sing and sing, and when that animal arrives, he knows that he's going to save that person. Until that animal gets there, he doesn't really put on his power. That's hard to express or understand or hard to know. He'd sing and sing until the red hawk eagle got there."[73] Indian doctors "called and they called and that helper wherever he was, he heard that song. He could hear it for miles and he heads in the direction to that doctor. When he gets there, then the doctor knows, well, 'I'm going to save this guy.'" Eddy explained that the familiar "would play around the sick person" and the doctor had to capture the familiar. "But as soon as he got enough, the doctor would grab him. And once he had his familiar in his hand or by him and captured him, this is when that healing power would be transferred to him, to the doctor, to the patient. That's how they healed." Only after the Indian doctor has captured his familiar and had the power following would he invite the patients to enter the lodge and get healed.[74]

Chemehuevi doctors carried *poros,* long staffs with a curved hook at the top. These wooden objects had great power, which Indian doctors used in curing rituals. Ownership of a *poro* or medicine staff exists today, indicating one's high position within the community. However, modern medicine people are very discreet, never bragging about their power but simply helping anyone who asks them for healing.[75] Every *puhwaganti* had at least one spirit helper or familiar called a *tutuguuvi*, which lived in the sacred mountain range in the northwestern corner of the Colorado Desert.[76] Mountain lions, bats, lizards, packrats, rattlesnakes, mice, and birds are among Chemehuevi familiars, and the healing spirit might direct any one of them, or another source (stones, plants, clouds, water, spiders, etc.), to bring power to the medicine person. Indian doctors called on their familiar, and once they had it in hand, performed their healing. Although Eddy did not volunteer the information, other Chemehuevi elders reported that his grandfather was a famous healer who called on a bat for his power.[77] In addition to healing physical ailments, Chemehuevi doctors dealt skillfully with mind-body maladies, treating people with "spirit sickness" brought on by "witchcraft," broken spiritual laws, or evil thoughts and deeds. Among Quechan, a god named Kumastamho gave Joe Homer power to cure tuberculosis. No doubt Chemehuevi had comparable tuberculosis doctors who treated people of the dreaded bacterial disease.[78] Chemehuevi doctors treated patients in their homes, in ceremonial houses, or in special power places, particularly caves.

Before the twentieth century, Chemehuevi medicine people often treated ill patients in sacred caves, including those where doctors received songs, prayers, familiars, and powers. At the dawn of the twenty-first century, Chemehuevi of the Twenty-Nine Palms and Chemehuevi Reservations have preserved a cave found within a granite outcropping on the northern end of the Old Woman Mountains. Working through the Native American Land Conservancy, a nonprofit organization established by the Twenty-Nine Palms Tribe in 1998, the conservancy has purchased and preserved approximately twenty-five hundred acres in the Mojave Desert. After frustrating negotiations, the Synod of Southern California and Hawai'i of the Presbyterian Church, the

Girl Scouts, the Boy Scouts, the Casa Colina Rehabilitation Center, and Thomas Askew sold the land to the conservancy. Since 2000, under the able leadership of Director Kurt Russo and his board, the Native American Land Conservancy has established a cultural and natural sanctuary at the Old Woman Mountain Preserve. The preserve has become a learning landscape for some people, especially Native American children, and a healing landscape for Native and non-Native people alike.[79]

The cave in the Old Woman Mountain Preserve holds special meaning to Chemehuevi, Mojave, and other Native Americans. The cave contains unique pictographs, black and orange in color, and the entire setting indicates a place of power where Indian doctors and patients held all-night ceremonies and looked east toward the Turtle Mountains, the Chemehuevi Valley, and the Colorado River. Tribal chair Dean Mike and his wife, Theresa Mike, became personally involved in the development of the Old Woman Mountain Preserve, and they supported Dr. Kurt Russo in his writing of a large grant to U.S. Fish and Wildlife to provide baseline studies of the flora and fauna of the Old Woman Mountains. Russo successfully raised nearly a million dollars in grants, which the conservancy used to hire scientists from the University of California and San Bernardino County Museum to study the plants and animals of the Old Woman Mountains. Dr. Jim Andre wrote a lengthy and detailed study of plants on the preserve. Other scholars from the San Bernardino Museum researched the animals on the preserve. Russo composed a marvelous book that used some of the findings of the flora and fauna studies. The Native American Land Conservancy published Russo's innovative book, *In the Land of Three Peaks: The Old Woman Mountain Preserve.*[80]

Chemehuevi believe that animate and inanimate power resides at the Old Woman Mountain Preserve. For them, it is a place of power, put there at the time of Creation. Chemehuevi say they are "Paleo Indians" and used a vast landscape often said to belong to ancient Patayan people, including lands now part of the Old Woman Mountains and southwestern Arizona. In an essay on ethnogenesis, contemporary Chemehuevi and ancestral Numic people argue that "all Southern Paiute bands have their traditional homelands in Arizona, Utah, Nevada, and California. We came from nowhere else. These are our homelands. This is where the Creator put us. We, the Paiute people, have stories, songs, and memory going back hundreds and thousands of years, passed down from generation to generation. This land knows our people and the memory of us always being here."[81] Thus Chemehuevi and other Nüwü say: "We have been here since Creation. We are the Paleo Indian, the Frémont, the Pueblos, the

Virgin Anasazi, and today we are called in the English Language Southern Paiutes."[82] Asserting their innate sovereignty, Chemehuevi and all Nüwü say: "No
one has the right to tell us who we are, and that is only for us to say."[83] Since
ancient times, Chemehuevi had villages in the Mojave Desert and along the
Colorado River. In the eighteenth and nineteenth century, Chemehuevi drove
"Land Mojave" from the region and established more villages in the desert.
They set up more villages in the high desert and foothills of the mountains in
the late eighteenth or early nineteenth century.

For many years before the twentieth century, Chemehuevi used surrounding materials from the natural environment to make different kinds of houses.
Like many Native peoples, they used materials such as rock, earth, poles, and
brush, but because of the transitory nature of their lives, they made homes
they could assemble and dismantle with ease. Chemehuevi often used caves
for temporary shelters, but they made four basic kinds of *kani,* or shelters.[84]
The *tivikyani,* or earthen home, offered the most substantial form of dwelling.[85]
Chemehuevi used four poles made of willow, cottonwood, or mesquite, set in
a rectangle with two rows of brush tying each side between posts. The people
used mud in between the brush, creating mud and thatch walls approximately
three feet thick. They used poles for the roof, adding arrowweed sticks to cover
the roof and packing a layer of mud on top of the arrowweed.

In the early twentieth century, Chemehuevi elder and teacher Gertrude
Hanks Leivas grew up in a *tivikyani* at Chemehuevi Valley located on the west
side of the Colorado River across from present-day Lake Havasu City.[86] Chemehuevi made a less permanent lodge called a *samarókwa*, which they built like
a *wickiup* made of brush. Chemehuevi used long, thin, young willow branches
to form the lodge. They drove each willow sapling into the earth in the form of
a circle, bending each sapling and tying it to the opposite branch. In this way
they created a dome structure, approximately five or six feet high in the middle.
Chemehuevi covered the lodge with brush, particularly sage or arrowweed.[87]
The people also created a wigwam type of home, the *tcuupikyani*, leaning short
poles together to a point. The people made this lodge rapidly, using cottonwood
or willows, tying bunches of grass together to lean against the poles. The lodge
shed most water and could last weeks. Chemehuevi made a fourth home style
called the *takagani* or *havagani*, usually supported by four poles vertically (or
more if desired) and poles running across the top horizontally. The people used
brush, willows, arrowweed, tules, or other available material on the top of
the open-sided lodge as a shade shelter. Today, Chemehuevi use the *havagani*
during wakes and memorials, singing all night under the lodge and burning it

in the morning. Although Chemehuevi rarely used sweat lodges, some contemporary people, including Joe Mike Benitez, build and use sweat lodges. Most contemporary Chemehuevi live in modern homes with gabled roofs and four or more sides. But they have knowledge of the old lodges, which they re-create for ceremony, exhibits, or special events.[88]

Chemehuevi used temporary homes while traveling, trading, hunting, and gathering. In the past, the people practiced seasonal rounds, moving from place to place to gather or hunt. Because Chemehuevi traveled to hunt and gather food, some Americans in the nineteenth century often referred to Chemehuevi, Paiute, and their neighbors as "diggers"—a pejorative term.[89] Labeling Chemehuevi and other Southern Paiute people "digger" enabled newcomers to express their superiority, and white settlers purposely denigrated Chemehuevi to lessen their impact on the environment. Pioneers argued that since Chemehuevi grazed the landscape like animals, the Indian people had no permanent places and therefore could live anywhere except lands desired by white settlers. Unfounded descriptions of Chemehuevi led textbook companies and uninformed authors to portray the Nüwü as primitive "savages" without intelligence and rational ability. Chemehuevi knew the deserts and mountains. They hunted, gathered, farmed, and traded with great intelligence. Chemehuevi navigated their environment with skill and foresight, maintaining a robust culture for thousands of years before newcomers arrived in California, the Southwest, and the Great Basin. They had farmed while living in the deserts of Arizona, California, Nevada, and Utah, but their farming developed further after they cultivated along the Colorado River. Chemehuevi continued their yearly cycle of seasonal rounds into the twentieth century, but the use of this migration pattern lessened in the twentieth century as the people took jobs to survive.[90]

Chemehuevi enriched their own culture by interacting a great deal with other tribes and intermarrying with members of other nations. From many experiences over thousands of years, they created their own unique and rich culture, which included the creation of beautiful baskets.[91] Women made some of the finest Native baskets in California and some of the most beautiful of baskets found around the world. Unlike other tribes in Southern California that used juncus, Chemehuevi women sewed their baskets with willow, devil's claw, and other desert plant fibers. Some women wove designs into baskets, others painted designs on burden baskets, triangular trays, storage baskets, and conical hats.[92] Chemehuevi made water jug baskets to carry as canteens, although they also used the stomach of animals for the same purpose. They coated water jug baskets with tar or pitch to make them waterproof. Chemehuevi generally roasted meat and fowl, but they also seared some meats and vegetables in strong cooking baskets by placing hot rocks in the basket and stirring the contents until they cooked.[93]

Chemehuevi cooked most of their foods over coals removed from an open fire. They either laid the meat on coals or dug a pit or oven, cooking food in a covered pit overnight or longer. Women generally cooked foods outside their homes but inside a circular lean-to attached to the home.[94] During a Learning Landscape program of the Native American Land Conservancy in 2010 in the Old Woman Mountain Preserve, Matthew Hanks Leivas cooked chicken for the group on bare coals, and he provided ground mesquite beans that students formed into small cakes that they cooked on rocks in the sun. Chemehuevi today know of the old ways of cooking and use these techniques on special occasions. Contemporary Chemehuevi also use earthen ovens to cook meat and vegetable foods, including venison, agave, and yucca. Some contemporary people cook agave and yucca in pits, eating the insides of the stalks. They eat yucca flowers and cactus flowers and leaves. Many Chemehuevi still eat ground mesquite beans and chia—natural foods they consider delicacies and energy foods. However, the daily diet of most Chemehuevi is comparable to that of most Americans, although no grocery stores exist on the Twenty-Nine Palms or Chemehuevi Reservations. This forces the people to travel off the reservation to buy food where they pay sales taxes, just like every other American.

When Chemehuevi traveled to hunt, gather, and trade, they wore different kinds and amounts of clothing, depending on the weather, time of year, and elevation. Before the twentieth century, Chemehuevi wore breechcloths, skirts, and little else during the summer. At one time, they made most clothing from animal skins, although they also used plant fibers to weave some clothing articles. After the arrival of white settlers, people began using manufactured cloth to make their clothing, sometimes making clothing from the material of flour sacks. When the Chemehuevi traveled into the Spring Mountains or moved about in the desert during the winter months, they wore buckskin clothing. Men wore long buckskin skirts, while women dressed in skirts made of buckskin or plant fiber. Men and women alike often traveled barefoot, but women made rugged, ankle-high leather moccasins. Women also made knee-high moccasins with tough leather soles that could be worn over rocky terrain and through snow. In the past, Chemehuevi men and women wore hides and pelts as blankets, and they had a flare for fashion and art, painting buckskins red, blue, and yellow. They decorated clothing, blankets, baskets, bows, arrows, leather containers, cradleboards, possible bags, and other items.[95]

Like modern Chemehuevi, men and women also beautified their bodies with earrings, nose rings, and tattoos. Chemehuevi living at Twenty-Nine Palms generally did not tattoo or pierce their bodies as much as their relatives living along the Colorado River. Women often parted their hair down the middle of their heads, and they generally wore bangs. Men sometimes wore their hair long and loose in a similar fashion as women, but at other times they tied their hair on top of their heads using leather strips and small sticks. For ceremony, Chemehuevi males, especially ceremonial leaders, wore headdresses with a cap of netting or full leather to which makers tied many varieties of feathers, including those of eagle, hawk, quail, and others. The Twenty-Nine Palms Tribe has preserved and displayed the headdress of a medicine man, a bonnet filled with feathers situated in a circle surrounding the netted cap. It contains red cloth and leather twine, tying the feathers to the cap.[96] Chemehuevi never wore war bonnets like those found among tribes from the Great Plains, Rocky Mountains, or Columbia Plateau.[97] But like other Native Americans throughout North America, Chemehuevi used elements of their natural environment to create their material culture. They also traded for some goods found within their possession, but Chemehuevi masterfully used materials from their desert environment.[98]

One Chemehuevi elder reported to Carobeth Laird that white men think "the desert is a wasteland," but to the Chemehuevi, the arid desert and mountains provide "a supermarket."[99] In 1997, Chemehuevi elder Joe Mike Benitez echoed this sentiment, stating that Chemehuevi knew the earth so well that they could find food anywhere in the Mojave and Colorado Deserts.[100] The finest work on the use of desert plants has been researched and written by Cahuilla elder and scholar Katherine Saubel and her longtime colleague Lowell Bean. Their work is largely the basis of this short discussion of native desert plants, and it is an authoritative study of plants used by Native peoples of the desert regions. They point out that although desert people, including Chemehuevi, hunted year-round, providing some meat for their families, the people gathered most of their traditional foods from the deserts and mountains. Saubel offered new details about plant use in her book with Eric Elliott, 'Isill Héqwas Wáxish: A Dried Coyote's Tail.[101] The authors provide details about desert fruits, seeds, and vegetables that formed the basis of Native diets, and the volume emphasizes the people's expertise in using desert foods without depleting various species.[102]

In the spring, Chemehuevi families sought agave, a food source also known as the mescal plant. Chemehuevi gathered great quantities of agave, creating large roasting pits to cook the inner leaves, stalks, and flowers. After baking agave underground, people ate the inner leaves and heart of the plant—a delicious and nutritious meal that desert people still enjoy. Chemehuevi ate the leaves of the plant called "live forever," and they gathered numerous flower buds of cacti, including jumping, bull, buckhorn, barrel, and pencil cholla—the latter of which they made into a tasty soup.[103] The people gathered buds of the Joshua tree and ate raw and ground seeds of this and other plants. Contemporary Chemehuevi continue to gather and eat the flowers and stalk of the yucca, boiling the bitterness from the flowers until they had the consistency of cooked pasta. In the spring, between April and May, Chemehuevi also gathered and ate the young fruit pods of the Mojave yucca, which they then roasted in hot coals. Chemehuevi still gather, prepare, and eat desert foods or "Indian" food.[104]

Chemehuevi ate the flowering ends (either raw or cooked) of soft flag, taking the roots during the summer months and pounding them into a meal.[105] The people ate the leaves of cabbage and prince's plume, which also had leaves like those of cabbage. Chemehuevi and their neighbors gathered rice grass, mentzelia, and immature mesquite beans.[106] The people ingeniously gathered the root or "potato" of the tule plant when water had receded sufficiently.[107] Chemehuevi planted corn, squash, melons, beans, sunflowers, and wheat in the spring. Some people continue to cultivate gardens along the Colorado River, supplementing them by hunting game.[108]

Chemehuevi ingeniously hunted and consumed a variety of animals. They called deer *tëhiya*, and most deer lived in specific ranges owned by individuals; however, they were often hunted by groups of men accompanied by the owner. Deer lived in "scattered islands of Upper Sonoran Zone vegetation," usually in ranges about five thousand feet above sea level, where juniper, sage, and piñon grew. Deer were particularly fond of grazing on waxy bitterbrush, Utah juniper, and big sage, although they also ate yucca and agave leaves. Nüwü hunted *naqa,* or mountain sheep, and *menteatsi,* or bighorn lambs. Like the deer ranges, individual Chemehuevi owned the bighorn ranges. The bighorn sheep grazed along the creosote regions of the Mojave and Colorado Deserts, but the bighorns primarily resided in the rocky reaches of the mountains, where they could find pockets of water and shade in the crevices, cliffs, and outcroppings. In higher elevations, bighorns found shade under piñons, junipers, firs, and other trees.[109]

Chemehuevi hunters generally did not carry an intact carcass back to camp, because of the animal's weight and the lack of horses before the nineteenth century. For this reason, the men skinned the animal, dressing it out in the mountains, cutting it into pieces, and hanging it in a tree. If the hunter was alone when he killed his prey, he returned to camp to report the location of the meat. Other villagers ran off to bring in the kill, carrying it home in nets. If Chemehuevi organized a group hunt, the leader directed the hunt, and the men returned to their village packing the kill. The hunter who killed the animal provided for the entire group, further cutting up the meat and giving it to others. The hunter making the kill generally took the animal hide but gave away all the meat, because sharing was the law among the people. That is not to say that the hunter never partook of his own kill; many people cooked the meat and shared it with the hunter. The hunter ate his own kill and likely ate the blood as well. Chemehuevi carefully preserved the animal's blood, boiling it into a mush or roasting it after it had coagulated. In lean times, Chemehuevi also ate the hides, but they always broke open the larger bones, eating the rich marrow.[110]

With dead falls, traps, bows and arrows, throwing sticks, and rocks, Chemehuevi hunted ducks, geese, mourning doves (*hiyovi*), and Gambel's quail (*kakara*). The chuckwalla, or *tcagwara,* was another important animal eaten by Chemehuevi, an important food source mentioned in traditional narratives as a friend of deer and mountain sheep. Chuckwalla is an herbivorous, large desert lizard with a thick, light-colored body which at full-growth measures over a foot long. Chemehuevi hunted the chuckwallas during the hottest part of the day near cliffs and slopes, as they prefer the lower elevations.[111] The people also ate the *aya,* or desert tortoise—a delicious food that once existed in many parts of Chemehuevi territory. The tortoise was once numerous, but today they are endangered because of tanks at Fort Irwin, the Twentynine Palms Marine Base, and off-road vehicles. Desert tortoises lived primarily in the low, sandy regions of the desert but could also live in other regions of the desert. Chemehuevi people cut the tortoise meat from the shell and cooked it inside the inner bark of cedar trees. They toasted the meat on glowing coals or laid the live animal on hot coals, roasting it in the shell. Despite the fact that the people cooked and ate tortoises, it was (and is) considered a sacred animal to the Chemehuevi but threatened by human's modern activities in the Mojave Desert. As a result, the Twenty-Nine Palms Tribe and the Native American Land Conservancy has applied for grants to the U.S. Fish and Wildlife Service to restore the desert tortoise on the Old Woman Mountain Preserve. With expert help of biologists, the tribe plans to establish a preserve for the desert tortoise and release healthy animals into the Mojave Desert.[112]

Chemehuevi hunted cottontails, black-tailed jackrabbits, ground squirrels, and wood rats with bows and arrows as well as throwing sticks. Sometimes the people organized group hunts, driving the animals into an enclosed area and clubbing them to death. Chemehuevi harvested rabbits and wood rats in traps, at times setting fire to an area to drive them into the open. Chemehuevi used a hunting crook (wooden staff) to probe a hole. If the hunter located the animal, he either used the crooked end of the staff to pull out the animal or the pointed part of the stick to twist into the hide of the animal before pulling it out.[113] In this fashion, Chemehuevi hunted three varieties of ground squirrels as well as chipmunks, gophers, mice, and kangaroo rats. In times of scarcity, Chemehuevi ate numerous other small animals, including lizards, snakes, horned toads, grasshoppers, crickets, worms, grubs, and others. Some authors, including those writing textbooks, have denigrated Southern Paiute peoples for eating such animals. In this manner, observers, explorers, settlers, scholars, and others have furthered the stereotype created by non-Natives that the so-called "digger" Indians were a low-class, uncivilized, subhuman group of "savages" who ranged and grazed the desert like animals, grubbing out a living by eating the lowest forms of plant and animal life.[114] To the contrary, whenever possible, Chemehuevi and other Paiute people ate the best plant and animal foods, but they ingeniously consumed available food resources biologically beneficial to their bodies. The people ate stewed snake and lizard at times, adding the boiled meat to other seeds and vegetables to form a nutritious meal, far better for their bodies than modern manufactured foods. In these and other ways, the Chemehuevi thrived in their desert and mountain environments. As John Wesley Powell once stated: "I am told by the Indians that snakes are sometimes used for food but I never witnessed it myself."[115]

During the hot summer months, past Chemehuevi people hunted small game, including rabbits, ground squirrels, mice, rats, reptiles, and birds. However, they farmed a great deal because "the Nüwü people were great farmers and have been since ancient times."[116] They also gathered mesquite beans, screw beans, and Indian rice grass. Chemehuevi elder Gertrude Hanks Leivas reported that in the early twentieth century, each summer her mother made a delicious drink from mesquite beans that children loved.[117] The people gathered seeds from chia, catclaw, devil's claw, ironwood, bulrush, native sunflower, and others.[118] They ate evening primrose, tasty mustard, serviceberries, desert currants, fleshy yucca fruit, beavertail cactus fruit and leaves, thornbush berries, wild grapes, and more. Chemehuevi traveled into the mountains to gather piñon nuts and juniper fruit, both of which they used to make bread and mush.[119]

Chemehuevi stored a good deal of plant and animal foods for winter. They stored seeds, pods, nuts, and other foods in large baskets or granaries, setting them up on their roofs or on stilts to keep mice and rats from their large storage baskets.[120] Early travelers and explorers provided written accounts of the Chemehuevi economic way of life. In 1878, naturalist Edward Palmer reported that the Paiute people called corn *ahweaph*, and that it had "been grown by the Indians since the recollection of the oldest person among them." Palmer stated that corn grown by Chemehuevi and their Paiute neighbors grew "from two and a half to three feet high and is cultivated by the Indians on the river bottoms, maturing in sixty or seventy days." The low-growing corn looked more like a bush than the tall corn stalks known in the Midwest and eastern United States, and the ears came "out of the stalk five or six inches from the ground."[121]

To many Chemehuevi, particularly those living along the Colorado River, corn was a staple.[122] In 1854 German artist of Native Americans and explorer in the American West Baldwin Möhausen stated that the Indians living on Paiute Creek "cultivate their fields of maize and wheat."[123] That same year, Möhausen served as an artist for Lieutenant Amiel Weeks Whipple on an expedition to the Colorado River. Whipple reported meeting Chemehuevi who raised crops in "rich soil" that "contains stubble of wheat and corn." The Indians living in that village also raised melons and squash.[124] In 1857 a Southern Paiute chief named Que-o-gan took explorer George Armstrong on a tour of his fields, showing the white man "the main irrigating ditch which was to convey the water from the river on his land, which I found to be a half a mile long, four feet wide and four feet deep, and had been dug principally through the gravel bed with wooden spades." Armstrong noted that Chemehuevi people farmed "small patches of land in their rude manner of cultivating the soil."[125] With the use of irrigation ditches or watering by hand, Chemehuevi raised a variety of crops, including some crops introduced by non-Indians. For example, Chemehuevi learned from other tribes to raise wheat, watermelons (an African plant), potatoes (an American crop but not native to California), carrots, beets, turnips, parsnips, and non-native sunflowers. John Wesley Powell reported that the Southern Paiute "mode of living is principally on rabbits, lizards, snakes, sunflower seeds, flag-rots, and pine-tree nuts."[126] Chemehuevi were particularly fond of "jackrabbits, cotton-tail rabbits, and quails." They also hunted wood rats, kangaroo rats, white-footed mice, and a large lizard known as the chuckwalla. However, most families relied "mainly on various indigenous food-plants."[127]

In the fall, Chemehuevi harvested crops and stored them.[128] Native foods provided nutrition and a spiritual connection with desert plants and animals. Indian food offered biologically appropriate nutrition that helped ward off disease and infection, and the destruction of native food sources made people more susceptible to infection brought by white settlers and Indians. Measles, smallpox, chickenpox, colds, tuberculosis, pneumonia, influenza, and other disease eventually spread across the desert, killing white settlers and Indians alike, although written records of cases and deaths caused by new bacteria and viruses do not exist for Native Americans, except neophytes in the missions or on reservations after 1924. Emotions of contemporary people discussing disease and death attest to the devastation brought by bacterial viruses. The loss of native foods did not cause infections, but the lack of Indian foods made infection easier to develop among tribal people.

In addition to the skill of finding nutritious food, Chemehuevi demonstrated their ingenuity through their arts. Chemehuevi artisans are known as experts in the tanning of hides with which they create beautifully made clothing, bags, quivers, sheaths, and other items. In the past, Chemehuevi men made two types of bows, including the small, powerful war bow that many people prized throughout California, the Great Basin, and the Southwest. Some Chemehuevi still make bows and arrows in the old way. Chemehuevi once made enchanting rock sketches, placing their thoughts, dreams, and ideas into a form of art that delights viewers today. The people still enjoy the innovative art of modern Chemehuevi just as they treasure contemporary people who can sing and tell stories. In addition to their stories, a few Chemehuevi still make baskets and far more create modern music or play the Indian flute. Chemehuevi men, women, and children still make gourd rattles and drums, sometimes raising their voices in song. Chemehuevi sing ancient songs and create modern ones. Matthew Hanks Leivas sings both ancient and modern songs, including an original selection he wrote and performed about the place of the Chemehuevi environment in modern society.[129] Although Leivas sings in Chemehuevi, the translation below offers the essence of his song:

What have you done?
What have you done, Whiteman?
What have you done?
What have you done, Whiteman?
You've hurt the Land.
You've hurt the Water
You've hurt the Mountains.
You've hurt the People
You haven't listened.
You haven't heard.

You haven't seen.
You don't understand.
All of our Nations are sick.
Whitemen are sick.
All the Nüwüvi are sick.
By this Bad Spirit, All the people are sick!
Listen, Listen.
We are speaking the truth.
We are speaking from the Heart.
How are we going to help Mother Earth?[130]

Leivas sings in his Native language and in English. He writes in both languages as well.[131] His song addresses non-Indians who deal with the Nüwüvi environment in harmful ways, reflecting silently on the past relationship of Nüwü with the earth, animals, plants, places, and peoples. The new song tells of Native sovereignty—given to the people at the beginning of time—the loss of Native land, the destruction of nature, the decline of animal and plant populations, and of human perseverance and survival. The song indicates that Nüwüvi people and non-Indians are physically, spiritually, and mentally ill because of the negative treatment of the environment. Chemehuevi are nothing if not survivors. And they are survivors of a contact period with non-Indians that brought many dangerous and difficult changes that will forever affect their quality of life. It began with the arrival of the Spanish and accelerated with the arrival of newcomers from the United States. Chemehuevi did not live in a utopia before 1775 and the arrival of the Spanish in their homelands, but they lived in relative peace with the Halchidhoma, Hualapai, Mojave, Quechan, Yavapai, and others of the region. The arrival of Euro-American newcomers to the river and deserts situated the people in harm's way. The Euro-American invasion and resettlement of indigenous lands of the Great Basin, California, and the Southwest brought new challenges to the Nüwü, but they survived invasion, resettlement, and the reservation system set up to confine and control Chemehuevi people.[132]

CHAPTER 2

Invading and Defaming
the Chemehuevi

ALTHOUGH THE SPANISH EXPLORED PARTS OF CALIFORNIA AND THE Southwest during the seventeenth and eighteenth centuries, Spanish soldiers, civilians, and missionaries never established a permanent colony in Alta California until 1769. Spaniards never built a presidio, mission, or pueblo in Chemehuevi country. Still, the arrival of Spanish settlers in New Mexico, Arizona, and California foreshadowed many changes that altered Chemehuevi people and places, foretelling the coming of other newcomers. Settlers from Spain, Mexico, and the United States provided new challenges for the Chemehuevi, but the people carefully navigated their relations with newcomers to ensure their survival. The ability to survive, adapt, and acculturate while maintaining tribal sovereignty and distinct ethnic culture remained significant characteristics of Chemehuevi people. Nüwüvi people had always been an adaptive people, adopting new ways and landscapes. For the most part, the Chemehuevi befriended other people and used their humor and interpersonal skills to deal with others. Long before the arrival of newcomers, the Chemehuevi developed positive relationships with many Native Americans and developed a desire for travel and adventure, walking and later riding horses great distances to meet and learn from other Indians.

Chemehuevi travel, trade, and exploration in the past enabled them to cope with dramatic changes brought by newcomers. Using old and new trails, Chemehuevi men, women, and children had traveled extensively, engaging many diverse indigenous peoples. In her essay "Reconstructing Southern Pai-

ute–Chemehuevi Trails in the Mojave Desert of Southern Nevada and California: Ethnographic Perspectives from the 1930s," noted anthropologist Catherine S. Fowler stated that human beings "are perhaps by nature wanderers
and explorers. How else to find natural resources, establish good places to live
and work, meet, greet and trade with neighbors, and ultimately claim and hold
places?"[1] When Chemehuevi families and bands started out on journeys, they
often stopped at shrines or cairns to deposit stones, twigs, plant material, and
other offerings. The people prayed for successful trips. When they found no
older shrines, they started new ones. Today, these shrines appear on the landscape near trails. Because their ancestors used the shrines and trails, contemporary Chemehuevi consider these and other cultural resources sacred features
that developers should not destroy and Indians should not mitigate.[2]

As the Chemehuevi people moved away from the Spring Mountains into
present-day Arizona, California, Nevada, and Utah, they entered diverse landscapes that provided them ample opportunities to explore, trade, meet new
people, and expand their knowledge of areas and people near and far from their
old villages. By exploring novel places, they found old trails and used them to
investigate and meet interesting people, expanding their farming and trading.
They learned about good hunting and gathering areas, and they found power
places in the deserts and mountains they used in their own spiritual lives. As
Chemehuevi traveled to far-off areas, they mapped them through song and
story, adding to their body of knowledge about the landscape. They added
place-names to their vocabularies describing sites they found while interacting
with Mojave, Quechan, Yavapai, and others.[3]

Long before Christopher Columbus sailed into the Caribbean, the Chemehuevi people had explored thousands of miles away from their creation mountain. The Chemehuevi were well established in the Great Basin, California, the
Southwest, and Mexico long before Hernando de Alarcón and Melchior Díaz
entered the lands of present-day Baja and Alta California.[4] Spanish explorers
of the early sixteenth century never met Chemehuevi people, and they did not
immediately influence them. However, Spanish explorers claimed lands once
the sole domain of indigenous people and inadvertently spread viruses and
bacteria. Nüwüvi people had little dealings with these newcomers, although
some traded for manufactured items, livestock, and other goods either directly
or indirectly. By the sixteenth century, the Chemehuevi had traded with numerous Native Americans, including the Apache, Havasupai, Hopi, Hualapai,
Mojave, Navajo, Paiute, Quechan, Ute, and Yavapai. Chemehuevi had also initi-

ated commerce with people along their way to the Pacific Coast, trading with the Cahuilla, Cocopah, Cupeño, Kumeyaay, Kwaaymii, Luiseño, Paipai, Serrano, Tongva, and others. Once the Spanish settled in Alta California in 1769, Nüwü people learned a great deal about the newcomers and how they treated indigenous people through missions, pueblos, and forced labor programs. Not content to remain on the California coast or in villages along the Rio Grande, Spanish settlers, soldiers, and slavers expanded into Indian Country to exploit natural and human resources. And once the Spanish established their mission system, they sent soldiers to remote areas to kidnap indigenous women and children to force them into missions, ranchos, and pueblos. After Spanish soldiers forced Serrano from the western Mojave Desert, Chemehuevi moved in larger numbers north of the San Bernardino and San Gabriel Mountains, often living and intermarrying with Serrano and other Indians.[5]

Chemehuevi people forged strong relationships with the people of the Pacific Coast, traveling west along the Mojave River and south along the Paiute Trail. In Chemehuevi oral narratives, the people originated from Ocean Woman who came out of the sea to create the earth, and the people maintained a relationship with the Pacific Ocean, the place where Coyote had sexual relations with Louse. Many diverse bands of Southern Paiute and Shoshone lived north of Chemehuevi people, and the people continued their close relationship with other Nüwü and Shoshone people, owing to familial, ceremonial, religious, and trade relationships. The Chemehuevi also had a close relationship with Yuman-speaking peoples along the Colorado River, including the Cocopah, Halchidhoma, Mojave, and Quechan. Too often, scholars have emphasized the animosities between Yuman and Uto-Aztecan–speaking people rather than the positive interaction of the people.[6]

In 1540 new people from Spain entered California and the Southwest by way of present-day Mexico. The Chemehuevi likely learned from other indigenous people that white men with beards and one black man had traveled through Texas and New Mexico on their way north in 1538 and 1539.[7] The Chemehuevi learned of Spaniards from other Indians, and they knew of Indians and Spaniards moving through the Southwest in 1540, led by Francisco Vasquez de Coronado. Given the novelty of Spanish explorers and Native Americans from Mexico, the Chemehuevi learned of Coronado's journey to Hawikuh near present-day Zuni, New Mexico. The expedition took Coronado and other branches of his Spanish army into the Southwest, including one visiting the south rim of the Grand Canyon. Diverse Native people did not live in isolation, and such exciting reports of newcomers reached the ears of many Southern Paiute. Some Southern Paiute living in Northern Arizona may well have seen the Spanish newcomers and reported their findings to others.[8]

Coronado made his way north and east along the present boundary between Arizona and New Mexico. In support of his expedition, soldiers led by Hernando de Alarcón traveled up the Colorado River through Cocopah and Quechan Indian country. Most likely, Alarcón arrived at the junction of the Gila and Colorado Rivers near present-day Yuma, Arizona, where he erected a cross bearing the message that he had come that far and had buried letters at the base of the cross. Not long after Alarcón returned to the Gulf of Baja California to board his ships bound for Acapulco, Melchior Díaz arrived in Quechan country, located south of the Chemehuevi people.[9] By 1540, Quechan had apparently learned of Coronado's attacks on Zuni and other Indians in New Mexico and moved aggressively against Díaz. They told him to leave. Quechan planned an attack, forcing the Spaniards to ford the great river and move into Baja California. Once the Quechan learned of Coronado's attack on Zuni Pueblo, they rose in rebellion against the Spanish, forcing Díaz west into present-day Baja California. Chemehuevi people knew of the Spanish in Quechan country, but Spanish activities occurred south of the Chemehuevi.[10] Still, these Spanish expeditions brought newcomers into contact with numerous indigenous people.

In 1542, Spanish explorer Juan Rodriquez Cabrillo landed in San Diego Harbor, where he engaged the Kumeyaay. Not long after, Cabrillo fought the Chumash above present-day Los Angeles.[11] Certainly the well-traveled Chemehuevi learned from Native peoples along the Pacific Coast of these new men. And in 1604 other Indians told them of Don Juan de Oñate, perhaps through direct contact since the explorer likely met Chemehuevi on his expedition up the Colorado River. Spanish soldiers traveled down the Bill Williams River into Chemehuevi territory and along the Colorado River before turning south to the Gulf of Baja California. Oñate named the various tribes he met, including the Amacava (Mojave), Bahacecha, Coahuana, Cocopah, Ozara, Tlaglli, and Tlalliguamaya. Most likely, Spanish met the Chemehuevi and the Amacava (Mojave).[12] Although Native Americans met the Spanish in the sixteenth and seventeenth centuries, Spaniards did not colonize Alta California until 1769, when Father Junípero Serra and Gaspar de Portolá entered Kumeyaay Indian country at a place the Spanish called San Diego de Alcala, not far from the Native village of Cosoy.[13]

The arrival of Spanish missionaries and soldiers into the heart of Kumeyaay country stirred the minds and souls of all indigenous people, including

Heinrich Bauduin Möllhausen created this painting of two Mojave men and one woman. He made the illustration when he traveled with a party of topographical engineers assigned to survey the railroad route along the Thirty-Fifth Parallel. Note the strong, healthy appearance of the people and the child. Mojave lived in close proximity to Chemehuevi, sometimes as friends and sometimes as enemies. From Lieutenant Amiel Weeks Whipple, during the railroad survey near the Thirty-Fifth Parallel, "Reports of Explorations and Surveys, to Ascertain the Most Practicable and Economical Route for a Railroad from the Mississippi River to the Pacific Ocean, January 31, 1851," *Senate Executive Document* 78, Thirty-Third Congress, Second Session, 1856 (Washington, D.C.: Beverley Tucker Printers).

Chemehuevi people. For the first time, a truly foreign people moved into an area previously inhabited only by Native Americans. Spaniards claimed land by Right of Discovery and Right of War, asserting European principles of entering lands belonging to non-Christians and laying claim to them in the name of Christ and their King. Without permission from Native people, Spaniards resettled Indian land, claiming Kumeyaay country as their own. Spanish Christians considered themselves "superior" people, commissioned by God to inhabit "heathen" lands. Spaniards intended to remain in the region, claiming that Christianity was their primary goal but desiring gold, subjects, and souls. Spaniards never established missions, presidios, or pueblos in Chemehuevi lands, yet Spanish settlement of California indirectly affected Chemehuevi people. Father

Junípero Serra and Captain Gaspar de Portolá laid the foundation for future incursions into California, the Great Basin, and the Southwest.[14]

Although early Spanish expeditions invaded portions of California and the Southwest, few made contact with Southern Paiute or Chemehuevi. Nevertheless, in hindsight, contemporary Chemehuevi people understand the devastation brought by Euro-American newcomers. One contemporary Chemehuevi offered the most dramatic view of non-Indian explorers, saying, "If I had been alive when the first white people came into our country and if I had knowledge of the meaning of their explorations, I would have killed every last one of them from the outset."[15] This person mirrors an extreme view of the non-Native invasion of the region, but tribal elders today offer many negative views of the arrival of newcomers into their homelands. The invasion altered Chemehuevi life in many ways, but the people met the challenges and survived. Apparently, the Nüwü had few contacts with Spanish settlers along the Río Grande during the sixteenth century, but within a short time, Spaniards expanded into the Great Basin looking for riches, including Indian slaves they sold on the auction blocks of New Mexico, including Santa Fe, Albuquerque, and Belen.

With time, Spanish soldiers and settlers used the ancient Paiute Trail the newcomers renamed the Old Spanish Trail that led directly into the lands of the Nüwü. As some Spanish people penetrated the Indian Country of Arizona, Nevada, and Utah from the east, others entered Southern Paiute country from the west. In 1769 the Sacred Expedition of Junípero Serra arrived in San Diego under the protection of Gaspar de Portolá. In the years that followed, Catholic missionaries established twenty-one missions near the Pacific Coast but not in Chemehuevi lands. Spanish newcomers influenced the Chemehuevi and other Nüwü people by introducing manufactured trade goods, livestock, new seeds, diseases, and ideas that likely reached Chemehuevi. With time, the long reach of the Catholic Church influenced many indigenous communities, including the Chemehuevi and Southern Paiute. But during the late eighteenth century, Spanish influences among the Chemehuevi proved minor.[16]

The first recorded contact between the Spanish and the Chemehuevi occurred in 1776, when Spaniards visited villages of Southern Paiute peoples living north of the Chemehuevi. On October 10, 1776, a band of twenty Paiute met Father Silvestre Vélez de Escalante and Father Francisco Atanasio Domínquez just north of present-day Cedar City, Utah. Spaniards met other bands of Paiute on the expedition, reporting the people enjoyed "very good piñon nuts, dates [yucca fruit], and some little sacks of maize." Escalante offered some negative reports of the people that "dress very poorly, and eat grass seeds, hares, piñon nuts in season, and dates." Although he went on to say that one group planted no crops, this is contradicted in other reports. Southern Paiute, like their Chemehuevi relatives to the south, practiced agriculture and used "irrigation ditches."[17] In the same year as Fathers Domínquez and Escalante made their *entradas*, Father Francisco Tomás Garcés traveled north from the Quechan country near Yuma Crossing and visited Chemehuevi, recording another encounter between Chemehuevi and Spanish.[18]

In 1771, Father Garcés left his headquarters at Mission San Xavier del Bac among the Tohono O'odham (Papago) near present-day Tucson, Arizona, on an exploring expedition down the Gila River to its confluence with the Colorado River. At present-day Yuma Crossing, Garcés met Quechan Indians who indicated to the priests that they knew of Spaniards on the Pacific Coast of California. Encouraged, Garcés crossed the Colorado, traveling as far as Signal Peak (Wispa or Little Wispa, meaning Eagle Mountain) near present-day Calexico, California, where he climbed the mountain, peered off to the northwest across the Colorado Desert, and theorized that the Pacific Coast was not far away. These observations influenced his first meeting with Chemehuevi. Garcés believed that if he traveled a route parallel to the Laguna Mountains of San Diego County and crossed them, he could locate Father Serra's California missions. He was correct, of course, but did not know it at the time. Garcés did not continue to the coast, choosing to return to San Xavier del Bac and visit the presidio captain at Tubac, located south of Bac.[19]

The travels of Garcés and presidio commander Captain Juan Bautista de Anza had direct implications for Chemehuevi and the Yuman-speaking people, including the Cocopah, Halchidhoma, Kwaaymii, Maricopa, Mojave, Quechan, and others. The Spanish *entradas* brought many newcomers to Indian Country, foreshadowing non-Indian claims to Native lands, destruction of food and water resources, spread of infectious diseases, introduction of Christianity, and establishment of European and later American political, economic, legal, and social institutions that proved detrimental to the Chemehuevi and all indigenous people of California, the Great Basin, and the Southwest.

When Garcés returned to Mission San Xavier del Bac, he visited Juan Bautista de Anza, an experienced soldier who had spent his life on the frontiers of northern Mexico. He served as the presidio captain at Tubac, Arizona, and Garcés convinced him that the Spanish could establish a land route from Sonora to the Pacific Ocean by way of the Colorado River through the Yuma Crossing. The route ran through the Sonoran and Colorado Deserts, just south of Chemehuevi villages on the Colorado River. However, Spanish invasions of Arizona,

California, and New Mexico affected Chemehuevi life. According to contemporary Chemehuevi scholar Matthew Hanks Leivas, Spanish missionaries brought economic chaos to the lives of many indigenous people with whom Chemehuevi traded, and when the Nüwü traded, they sometimes received pathogens they took back to their people, especially measles, mumps, chicken pox, pneumonia, influenza, colds, and the dreaded smallpox. In addition, as the number of neophytes declined within the missions, Spanish soldiers entered the desert to kidnap people to replenish Indians within the religious institutions.[20] Apache Indians delayed Anza's planned expedition to open a Spanish road from present-day Tucson, Arizona, to San Gabriel, California. For more than two years, Anza and his leather-jacket soldiers fought effective Apache warriors.

Between 1771 and 1773, Apache Indians engaged Spaniards so often that Anza could not launch his expedition until 1774. In that year, and with Tohono O'odham scouts, Anza and Garcés traveled across El Camino del Diablo (the Devil's Highway), an arid and ancient Native road running along the present international border on the north side of the Arizona-Sonora border. The party traveled through lands of Tohono O'odham, who knew the route across the desert patina and *tinajas,* or water holes. The expedition traveled on an ancient Native trail from southern Arizona to the Gila River and along the trail into present-day Yuma, Arizona. They met the first large village of Sunflower Eaters east of Yuma, and many more villages as they made their way toward the two distinctive hills overlooking the Colorado River. Initially, the Spanish had positive relations with Quechan. The people helped the Spanish cross the Colorado River and showed the trail south of the Imperial Sand Dunes and northwest along the New River and across the Colorado Desert. With the expert help of Quechan and Eastern Kumeyaay (Kamiia or Kwaaymii) scouts, the Spanish arrived safely in the Los Angeles Basin.[21] They traveled to Mission San Gabriel, becoming the first Spaniards to open a land route from Sonora to the California coast. Of course, Indians had used the route for hundreds of years, and Chemehuevi people had used these and other trails on trading expedition for thousands of years. But the "Gila Trail" was for the Spanish. Garcés split off from Anza's main party in 1774, hoping to travel to the Spanish missions of New Mexico. He crossed the Colorado River and entered Arizona, traveling as far as the Tulkapaya or Yavapai villages in west-central Arizona. Garcés then decided to return to San Xavier del Bac, never reaching New Mexico.[22]

In the fall of 1775, Anza led a new and longer expedition to California. With 240 emigrants from present-day Mexico, Anza traveled north from Mission San

Xavier del Bac to the Gila River before turning southwest along the stream to present-day Yuma. Garcés joined Anza on this *entrada*, going as far as the Yuma Crossing. Once again the Spaniards had positive relations with the Quechan, owing primarily to their cordial relationship with one headman, a man the Spaniards called Chief Salvador Palma. Anza continued the journey across the Colorado River, retracing his earlier trek across the Colorado Desert into the Santa Rosa Mountains, sacred mountains to the Chemehuevi, Cahuilla, Mojave, and Quechan. Ultimately, the Spanish settlers made their way north to Monterey, California, and on to San Francisco Bay, where they became the first non-Natives to settle among Ohlone Indians. Meanwhile, Garcés remained among the Quechan to begin a small mission of logs and adobe, a church he christened Purísima de la Concepcíon. Garcés ultimately left the Quechan to explore other areas, including Chemehuevi homelands of the Mojave Desert. He traveled north on the California side of the Colorado River through lands of the Halchidhoma Indians and into the Mojave Desert.[23]

On February 26, 1776, Chemehuevi met the priest and his guides at a spring not far from the river. "I met some 40 persons of the Chemebet nation," he wrote, offering the first written account about Chemehuevi people. When the Chemehuevi saw the priest, six of them "on a hill came down as soon as we called them." Garcés reported that the men ran "with the speed of a deer, and regaled me with a very good mescal." The Spaniard described the people, saying that "the garb of these Indians is, Apáche moccasins [*zapatos*], shirt of antelope skin [*vistido de gamuza*], white headdress like a cap [*gorra blanca á modo de solidéo*] with a bunch of those very curious feathers which certain birds [Gambel's quails] of this country have in their crest."[24] He also mentioned the people "all carried a crook besides their weapons," the crook being used to pull a rabbit, squirrel, or other small animal from its burrow.[25]

The priest correctly stated that the Chemehuevi were "the most swift-footed of any I have seen." He noted that the Chemehuevi "nation inhabits the territory that there is between the Beñemé, a tract of land very scant of water, following thence the border of the Río Colorado on the northern side as fast as . . . the Yuta nation, of whom they give much information."[26] Garcés and his fellow Spaniards treasured knowledge about the friendships and animosities among Indian nations, knowing that by recording the disposition of the tribes among each other, they could exploit Indian alliances and animosities much easier, dividing people to kill each other. The priest learned the close relationship of the Chemehuevi people with the Southern Paiute, Mojave, Quechan, and others. Garcés reported the Chemehuevi got along well with the Mojave and Apache Tejua (possibly western Apache or Tewa people). However, the Spaniard reported that the Chemehuevi were "enemies of the Comanches and Moquis [Hopi]."[27]

The priest recognized the uniqueness of Chemehuevi culture from the Yuman-speaking river tribes. The Chemehuevi language was "distinct from all the nations of the river." Garcés recognized that Chemehuevi women created exquisite basketry.[28] Chemehuevi meeting Garcés treated the priest with respect and kindness, and as a result, the Spaniard wrote that Chemehuevi "conducted themselves with me most beautifully; by no means were they thievish or troublesome, but rather quite considerate."[29] Garcés met other Chemehuevi on this *entrada*, but left no other detailed account. Still, his first impressions did not denigrate Chemehuevi people like those of latter-day explorers and travelers. Father Garcés described Chemehuevi character and clothing correctly, and his accounts closely parallel the sketch made in 1857 by H. B. Möllhausen published in Joseph Christmas Ives's "Report upon the Colorado River of the West," written in 1861.[30] Furthermore, the priest's descriptions of Chemehuevi personalities provided precise information since Chemehuevi people have always been known throughout Indian Country as hospitable, curious, adaptive, and generous—unless, of course, newcomers provoked them. Finally, Garcés recognized the ability of Chemehuevi to run extremely fast. Other Indians often commented that Chemehuevi people could run as fast as or faster than many desert animals. In the 1970s Quechan elders Lee Emerson and Henry DeCorse spoke about the great Chemehuevi runners who lived in the deserts to the north. Many contemporary Indian people know of the great desert runners among the Chemehuevi.[31]

Fray Garcés left the first written account of Chemehuevi people, but his encounter with the tribe did not lead to Spanish settlement of the Chemehuevi homelands. In fact, the Spanish mission system remained isolated along the California Coast and the junction of the Colorado and Gila Rivers, where Garcés nurtured the Missions of La Purisma de la Concepcíon and San Pablo y San Pedro de Bicuñer. Chemehuevi people watched with interest as the Spanish moved into Indian Country, establishing missions, presidios, and pueblos among the Ajachemen, Chumash, Kumeyaay, Luiseño, Quechan, Tongva Gabrieliño, and others. Chemehuevi traders frequented all of these California tribes as well as the Pueblo of New Mexico.[32] In California the Chumash, Kumeyaay, and others revolted against Spanish rule. In 1781 the Quechan and Tohono O'odham revolted against the Spanish at Yuma Crossing. Indians killed Garcés, three other priests, Spanish settlers, and soldiers.[33] The uprising forced the Spanish to abandon their missions, settlements, and fort near the Yuma Crossing. The Chemehuevi likely knew of Spanish culture through communication, direct contact, trade, policies, and disease brought by the Spanish.[34]

Chemehuevi people acquired new items from the Spanish, including watermelons, cantaloupes, and wheat seeds. They acquired metal knives, tomahawks, axes, needles, cloth, beads, pots, pans, and other material items. Importantly, through trade Chemehuevi people acquired firearms, horses, mules, cattle, and sheep from the Spanish. During the eighteenth and nineteenth centuries, the Chemehuevi adopted horses but did not develop a horse culture like Native Americans of the Great Plains and Northwest Plateau, where people had lots of natural forage for horses and other livestock. In the late months of 1819, Lieutenant Gabriel Moraga left the coastal region of California to lead fifty soldiers down the Mojave River in an attack against hostile Mojave. He passed through Chemehuevi lands near present-day Soda Lake and the Kelso Dunes, but the diary of Father Joaquín Pasqual Nuez, the chronicler of the expedition, adds little about the Chemehuevi.[35] However, Spanish traders used the Spanish Trail that passed Southern Paiute and Chemehuevi villages and camps, bringing the people into more direct contact with Mexican traders and American travelers. The Old Spanish Trail ran north of most Chemehuevi but introduced Paiute people to Spanish and later newcomers.

The Chemehuevi likely learned more about Spaniards from other Native Americans. This is also the way Chemehuevi first learned of Americans from the United States traveling through the West. Fur trappers and Indian traders invaded Chemehuevi and Paiute country before the arrival of officials of the U.S. government. Jedediah Strong Smith met Chemehuevi and other Southern Paiute on his excursions into California and the Great Basin. Smith became the first non-Native to link the routes of Escalante and Garcés. If he met any people who were distinctly Chemehuevi on his two trips to and through their homelands, he left no written record of the meetings. He did record information on Southern Paiute people but did not mention the Chemehuevi specifically. In 1826, Smith made his first journey into Southern Paiute country, traveling south from the Great Salt Lake, trading with Utes before meeting a band of Southern Paiute near present-day Saint George, Utah. At the confluence of the Virgin River and Santa Clara Creek, he met Southern Paiute. Smith called the people "Pa-Utches" and noted that they "raise some little corn and pumpkins."[36] Of course, these Paiute were related to Chemehuevi living farther south and they reported on Smith's expedition.

In his journal Smith claimed that the area was "nearly destitute of game of any description except a few hares," but later observers disagreed, and so did Paiute who knew how and when to hunt this part of the Great Basin. Smith recorded accurately that the Paiute made beautiful rabbit skin robes, marble pipes, and flint knives. Southern Paiute people received Smith in friendship and dealt with him without fear. From southern Utah, Smith edged his way south, ultimately locating the Colorado River and following it south to the Mojave villages on the eastern side of the Colorado. At this time, the Chemehuevi had villages on and near Cottonwood Island above the Mojave and west of Mojave at Chemehuevi Valley, California. The Mojave reception of Smith matched that of the Paiute, as the Mojave generously shared corn, wheat, melons, watermelons, and other crops with the white man.[37] The Mojave proved friendly at first but relations changed with time.

From the Mojave villages, Smith traveled west into the Mojave Desert near the 35th Parallel, the homeland of Chemehuevi. Again, Smith did not record meeting Chemehuevi people. In 1827 he returned to the Mojave villages, but this time the Mojave resisted him. Perhaps Mojave had received intelligence from other Indians, warning them of American newcomers, but any other explanation of Mojave hostility remains a mystery. From the Colorado River, Smith traveled west along the Mojave River, near present-day Soda Lake. Smith finally noted Chemehuevi people in his journal, reporting that he found "2 Indian lodges" belonging to the "Pauch," Smith's word for Southern Paiute. The two parties traded beads, knives, and cloth for Indian horses, water containers (water baskets), and cane grass candy. The American said little else about the Chemehuevi, except they proved friendly, cordial, and helpful. Smith had experienced some difficulties during his second visit with Mojave, but Chemehuevi treated him with friendship.[38] Smith's interaction with Chemehuevi offers greater evidence of Chemehuevi hospitality and disposition to get along with newcomers.

Although historians recognize that Smith had traveled more widely in the American West than any other American of his time, he left no lasting impression among the Chemehuevi or other Southern Paiute. During the course of the research for this work, not one contemporary Chemehuevi mentioned their people meeting with Smith. But Smith had come in peace, and he had acted in good faith with the people, offering no cause for alarm. In the years to come, other newcomers from the United States became hostile, breaking Native laws, killing, stealing, and insulting the people. Some non-Natives captured Chemehuevi and Southern Paiute slaves, while others dealt with

Southern Paiute in aggressive ways, sometimes killing men, women, and children. Historian Brendan Lindsay has addressed American aggression against Native Americans in general in his book *Murder State: California's Native American Genocide, 1846–1873*. In his chapter on immigrant guides, Lindsay demonstrates that American writers continually warned settlers of hostile Indians, encouraging newcomers to arm themselves with pistols, rifles, and large quantities of ammunition.[39] Americans generally had little experience dealing directly with Native Americans, but Eastern and Midwestern immigrants grew up hearing one-sided horror stories about savage fiends, red devils, and barbarians. Americans moved west with warped and inaccurate perceptions of "generic" Indians, and they liberally employed preemptive strikes against Native Americans, following in the aggressive traditions of American pioneers in the Eastern Woodlands.[40]

As a result of preemptive aggression against the Chemehuevi and Southern Paiute, Chemehuevi people became wary of non-Natives and more carefully dealt with the newcomers. In fact, while Smith made a peaceful expedition through Paiute and Chemehuevi lands in 1826, another American named James Ohio Pattie trapped down the Gila River to its confluence with the Colorado before moving north to the Mojave villages. While traveling the well-worn Indian trail on the north side of Gila River, dubbed the Gila Trail by Americans, a route well-traveled by American Indians for generations, Pattie killed a Tohono O'odham. When a Mojave man asked for one of Pattie's horses for food in payment for the beaver pelts the American had taken, Pattie refused, whereupon the Mojave killed the horse with a lance. Pattie shot the man to death, creating widespread anger among the Chemehuevi, Hualapai, and Mojave.[41]

Pattie met Chemehuevi people during his expedition.[42] When Pattie moved northeast into the lands of the Shivwits Band of the Southern Paiute, they acted preemptively, using their war bows to shoot fire arrows at Pattie, who had killed at least two Native Americans in the deserts to the south. Chemehuevi people used their weapons to inform the American trappers that the people did not want him near their homes.[43] Pattie's expedition among the Chemehuevi and Southern Paiute was unremarkable, except that it served as a lesson to the Southern Paiute to be cautious of Americans. Pattie began a tradition among Americans to leave written reports casting all Native Americans in a negative light. White Americans often wrote highly inflammatory, derogatory, and racist remarks about Chemehuevi people in an effort to defame them. Reports after Pattie's expedition generally began offering racialized, negative images of the Chemehuevi and other Southern Paiute.

As the survey expedition of Lieutenant Amiel Weeks Whipple crossed the Colorado River near present-day Needles, California, Heinrich Bauduin Möllhausen painted a group of Mojave people helping explorers cross the Colorado River. Notice the group crossing where the river was shallow and wide with an island in between the two channels of the river. Whipple had posed with three men, one woman, and a child. The painting emphasizes the people decorated with paint, tattoos, and feathers. From Lieutenant Amiel Weeks Whipple, "Reports of Explorations and Surveys, to Ascertain the Most Practicable and Economical Route for a Railroad from the Mississippi River to the Pacific Ocean, January 31, 1851," *Senate Executive Document* 78, Thirty-third Congress, Second Session (Washington, D.C.: Beverley Tucker Printers, 1856).

Negative written records in English made it easier for non-Indians to exploit or kill Nüwü people and, later, to steal their lands outright through "legal" means created by newcomers. American explorers, soldiers, and those who followed in their wake created a new image of Chemehuevi and Paiute people contrary to Native American (and Spanish) images of the Chemehuevi as affable, friendly, and astute traders who related well with other human beings. Non-Indian trappers and traders wrote pejorative records denigrating the Southern Paiute. American trapper George Yount commented that the people were "the lowest and most degraded of all the savage hordes."[44] According to Yount, who met Paiute in 1830, the people ran around like unorganized wild animals nearly "nakid" and had so few words they had to speak in the sign. Yount recorded that the "thieving" people ate "many kinds of grass" because they fed themselves "like cattle." What was worse, Yount wrote the people loved "to be covered with lice because they appropriated these for food."[45] Yount's colleague, William Wolfskill, reported that all Southern Paiute—including Chemehuevi people—were "apparently the lowest species of humanity, approaching the monkey."[46]

Thus non-Indians used the power of written words to create an uncivilized image of Chemehuevi and other Southern Paiute as subhuman animals that lived day to day without thought, planning, or foresight. Trappers wanted the reading public to accept their "facts" that the Chemehuevi people lived hand to mouth, enjoying lice as a food source and grazing like cattle on grass, roots, snakes, rats, lizards, ants, cockroaches, larva, and other unappealing foods. While the Chemehuevi ate many diverse foods, they did so as part of the well-established, functional economic system that had worked well for them and nourished their bodies since the Pleistocene era. Their diet made them healthy and contributed to their survival in the arid West. Wolfskill's statement about all Southern Paiute being more "monkey" than human added a natural progression for racialized views of the Chemehuevi and Southern Paiute as "diggers." Some white Americans theorized that African Americans were more monkey than human, and Wolfskill pushed this concept, connecting or comparing the Chemehuevi and Southern Paiute to African Americans. The statement that these Indian people were "the lowest species of humanity" advanced so white Americans felt comfortable and justified in labeling Chemehuevi the pejorative term "diggers."

Such unfair and inaccurate portrayals of Southern Paiute people accelerated after Yount's and Wolfskill's visit, as other non-Indians added to the negative image of Chemehuevi people. In 1839, Thomas Jefferson Farnham, frontier author and explorer of the West, traveled briefly through Paiute country at a time when many Chemehuevi people still lived north of the Mojave. Farnham wrote that they were "the most degraded and least intellectual Indians known to the trappers" and that they wore "no clothing of any description—built no shelters." Like Yount and Wolfskill, Farnham used elements of the Native diet to denigrate Southern Paiute people, reporting they ate "roots, lizards, and snails" while storing "nothing for future wants." Farnham offered false information, but since he provided a written account, non-Indian readers and some scholars accepted the writings as authoritative. Over the years historians have accepted written accounts as historical and accurate, simply because a person put their assertions to paper. Too often, scholars of Native Americans have not listened to and learned from contemporary Native Americans. Like all sources, historians have to critically assess Indian oral accounts, but many times they simply ignore contemporary people and create their histories from documents written by newcomers. Toward the end of his life, Chief Joseph's nephew, Yellow Wolf, remarked about written accounts of Nez Perce history. "As for the white man," Yellow Wolf said to rancher L. V. McWhorter, they "told their side of the story, told it to please themselves."

Contemporary Chemehuevi and other Southern Paiute people disagree with Wolfskill, Yount, Farnham, and other white writers. Offering another interpretation of their ancestors, they remind people generally that Nüwü people had lived in the Great Basin since the Pleistocene era and had survived successfully many climate changes and complex relationships with the earth, the environment, relatives, and other tribes across a huge geographic area. They survived by ingenious food acquisitions. Chemehuevi and Southern Paiute people gathered many varieties of seeds, fruits, and vegetables. They hunted deer, bighorn sheep, rabbits, and other game. They stored their foods in baskets and ate from these stores throughout the year. Farnham emphasized that the people ate roots and lizards, the diet of "diggers." But Chemehuevi and Southern Paiute people ate chuckwalla, lizards, and many varieties of edible roots, just as Europeans and Americans ate potatoes, carrots, beets, and other crops that grew as roots. Farnham used a portion of their diet to degrade the people. Social studies and history textbooks have recently portrayed California Indians in a similar manner—an inaccuracy that some publishers have not bothered to correct.[47]

Farnham incorrectly portrayed Chemehuevi people as "the most degraded and least intellectual Indians known to trappers" who ate "roots, lizards, and snails." He stated that the Paiute people had no housing and no foresight to set up for winter. He intended his words to be heavily charged against Paiute, but he offered false statements and derogatory statements about the people. Since the nineteenth century, others have repeated these statements as true and authoritative. Most outrageous, Farnham claimed that in times of want, the people dug "holes in the form of ovens in the steep sides of the sand hills," which they heated with fires until they could "deposit themselves in" the holes to "hibernate [sic]." The American reported that the people went fast asleep in these holes, just like animals, "until the weather permits them to go abroad again and hunt for food."[48] As a matter of fact, the Paiute including Chemehuevi dug holes, built fires, and tossed soil on the fire, retiring on cold nights

Two indigenous people use a log and reed raft to ferry the Colorado River. Chemehuevi, Cocopah, Mojave, Quechan, and other Native Americans living along the river constructed rafts like this to cross the river. They used poles to push off sand bars and rocks, using the current of the stream to help push them across the water. Notice the dog on the raft. Families had many dogs as pets, exterminators of vermin, and early alarms for approaching enemy. In 1858, Heinrich Bauduin Möllhausen made this drawing. From Lieutenant Joseph Christmas Ives, "Report upon the Colorado River of the West," *Report of the Secretary of War, 1861*, in *Senate Executive Document*, Thirty-sixth Congress, First Session (Washington, D.C.: Government Printing Office, 1861).

on top of the site, which kept them warm. This technique provided warmth to the people, but neither Chemehuevi nor Southern Paiute people hibernated in holes like animals. Farnham used a half-truth to make the people look inferior, uncivilized, and animal-like rather than highly intelligent and practical. Not all of Farnham's comments created racialized distinctions. He provided some accurate accounts of seed gathering, food preparation, snares, bows, and other activities. But he added to the negative stereotype of Southern Paiute people, one made worse by the famed Catholic priest, explorer, and writer Father Pierre J. DeSmet, who in 1845 wrote that all Southern Paiute, including the Chemehuevi, were the lowest forms of humans on earth. "Probably in all the world," the priest wrote, "there is not another people more wretched, more disreputable, or more poverty-stricken."[49]

DeSmet claimed that all Southern Paiute ate other humans. He wrote: "Reliable persons have informed me that they eat the bodies of their near relatives and that sometimes they even eat their own children." Labeling Indians cannibals offered another means by which newcomers denigrated indigenous peoples with false rumors. The consequence of such written slander and inaccurate information appears in some historical works today, especially in social studies and history textbooks teachers rely on. Although DeSmet had no evidence that Southern Paiute were cannibals, he eagerly spread harmful hearsay through his writings and likely through oral communications. He justified his missionary endeavors among Southern Paiute by asserting that Indians deserved pity, because they were a "poor, forsaken people" who were better off when non-Indians captured their children, enslaved them, and gave "them religious instructions."[50] DeSmet and other missionaries rationalized their actions with the belief that they lived to serve God by bringing Christ and civilization to Native Americans. DeSmet's writings affirm his view that Chemehuevi and Southern Paiute people needed both (Christ and "civilization"), whether they realized this "fact" or not. Christians in other parts of the world read such reports and took them at face value.

In the absence of any rebuttal by Native Americans or their advocates in the English language, the missionary argument proved persuasive. After all, DeSmet was a highly educated priest. Other Christians read such treatises and believed them as well, sending their own missionaries to save Southern Paiute. DeSmet offered other false information. He claimed the people ate wretched and "evil-smelling" grain, and ate human flesh."[51] Other newcomers matched DeSmet's inflammatory statements. They too actively sought to defame all Southern Paiute people. In 1851, U.S. soldier James A. Bennett added to the negative image of Paiute people, stating that Southern Paiute people were "known as Ant Eaters or Root Diggers." Americans developed the term "digger" to describe Paiute people. This pejorative term became widely used, an invention of non-Indians.[52]

Many travelers remarked about slavery among the Chemehuevi and other Southern Paiute. Before white contact, some Native Americans stole slaves from other tribes, especially during war. The concept of slavery emerged in Native America just as it did in most places on earth. However, Chemehuevi and Southern Paiute people did not sell their own people into slavery, especially their women and children. Non-Indians expanded the slave trade, capturing and selling people, justifying slavery by arguing that Native women and children were far better off living with civilized white people who would bring Christianity to heathens. Ute Chief Walkara considered the Southern Paiute to be enemies, and he joined in the slave trade, taking Nüwüvi women and children for the trade.[53]

In 1851, James Bennett wrote in his diary that slave traders brought "Ant Eaters or Root Diggers" to Santa Fe each spring to sell as slaves.[54] Two years later, Lieutenant Edward Fitzgerald Beale commented that annually "expeditions are fitted out in New Mexico to trade with the Pah-Utahs for their children."[55] Even the legendary scout Christopher "Kit" Carson purchased a twelve- to fourteen-year-old Paiute boy for forty dollars, a common practice among non-Indians living in New Mexico before the American Civil War. Some observers, including Utah Indian agent Garland Hurt, stated that some Southern Paiute willingly "sell their children to the Utahs for a few trinkets or a bit of clothing."[56] Some Paiute may have sold their children, but evidence is thin for such assertions since Nüwüvi people have a spiritual obligation to care for children as directed by the Creator. To break that law could put the entire Southern Paiute population in jeopardy, as this is the way the Nüwü world worked.[57] On the other hand, the so-called Old Spanish Trail ended in Los Angeles, where New Mexican traders arrived with a long tradition of buying and selling Indian slaves. As historian George Phillips pointed out: "The New Mexicans also participated in a slave trade that extended throughout the Southwest." He provided an example of a Paiute girl exchanged for livestock. The newcomers traded in humans and extended that tradition throughout California and the Southwest.[58]

Contemporary Southern Paiute people deny they sold their children.[59] Slave traders spread rumors that the people sold their own children but their word remains suspect. They justified the sale of other humans by deflecting the practice onto the Southern Paiute, as if the slave traders had continued a well-established practice. Chemehuevi and Southern Paiute neighbors treasured their families, a common theme throughout Paiute history and pervasive in Paiute culture. Family members within a community would not have allowed a person to sell another family member, an unthinkable and unsubstantiated concept fabricated by slavers. Reporting sales of Chemehuevi and Southern Paiute to Hurt, slavers eased their consciences or took the sting out of human trafficking, particularly women and children, by claiming Paiute sold their own people. Perhaps rogue Paiute traders sold their own people, but such transactions, if they occurred at all, happened independent of communities and Paiute leaders. By the 1850s the slave trade around the world had come under considerable criticism, and shifting the blame to the Indians (just as slavers did in Africa and China) helped the slavers justify their activities. Contemporary Chemehuevi elder Joe Benitez stated that the suggestions that Chemehuevi parents sold their own children was absurd and patently false—the product of white men wanting to create a poor image of Southern Paiute people.[60]

John C. Frémont, Kit Carson, Charles Preuss, and other famous American explorers traveled through Chemehuevi land, but they did not leave detailed accounts of their interactions with the people. However, in 1844, Frémont met a hostile group of Paiute near the Virgin River where a party of "diggers" killed one of Frémont's men using a bow and arrow. Anthropologist Robert Euler has argued that the Paiute likely killed the man because he tried to prevent them from killing a horse for food, since the party located a missing horse with an arrow in it. The label of "digger" and the hostile nature of Paiute people toward Americans contributed to a broader, non-Native image of Chemehuevi and other Southern Paiute as "a poor, treacherous, and dangerous race of people. Stealing animals at night, & shooting them from the bluff & high points during the day."[61] This hostile and dangerous image of the people dogged them from the 1840s into the twentieth century and, in some quarters, continues today. Subtle racism exists in border towns adjacent to reservations and among other peoples who know little about Chemehuevi and Southern Paiute people. Such accounts contribute to today's racialized society.[62]

In 1846 the United States and Mexico engaged in a war over the boundary of Texas and the ownership of California and the Southwest. Neither Mexico nor the United States recognized the land, grazing, mineral, and water rights of tribal people in Arizona, California, Colorado, Nevada, New Mexico, Texas, and Utah. Chemehuevi people had ancestral rights to the land that they had inhabited and used since the Pleistocene era. Since Spain had claimed the vast region of California and the Southwest, and Mexico had assumed this claim, the United States ultimately claimed the Chemehuevi land by right of war, treaty, and purchase. Initially Mexico refused to negotiate the sale of land to the United States. After the United States elected President James K. Polk, the two countries declared war. The U.S. Army invaded Texas along the Rio Grande, lands claimed by Mexico and the United States. Meanwhile, Mexican troops moved north to the great river to challenge the United States. All remained quiet until Mexican troops crossed the Rio Grande, engaged American dragoons, and killed some of them. The United States claimed: "American blood has been shed on American soil." Mexico and the United States declared war, and the conflict had a significant influence on the course of Chemehuevi history.[63]

Nüwü people, including the Chemehuevi, adored their children, and contemporary elders claim their people never sold their own children into slavery. Tribal teachers taught children through the oral tradition, repeating stories and lessons about literature, econom- ics, science, history, and art many timesuntil children understood their lessons. This photograph by Edward Curtis, "Chemehuevi Boy with Painted Face," offers a snapshot of a young boy. Gerald Smith Collection, A. K. Smiley Library, Redlands, California.

When the war between the United States and Mexico commenced, U.S. Colonel John C. Frémont moved his troops into California. Colonel Stephen Watts Kearny led a large army, including a contingency of Mormons, into the Southwest. Once Kearny secured New Mexico, he took a small force southwest and followed the Gila Trail to Yuma Crossing and northwest into California. Kearny's journey took him into the heart of Cahuilla, Cupeño, Kumeyaay, Luiseño, and Quechan country, but the Chemehuevi knew of the war and movement of newcomers. Indeed, Chemehuevi interaction with American trappers had given them an understanding of the people crossing into their land. When Kearny left Santa Fe, he ordered Colonel Alexander W. Doniphan to attack the Navajos or negotiate a treaty with the Diné people. Kearny also ordered Captain Philip St. George Cooke to lead the Mormon Battalion across the Southwest to establish a wagon road for future generations to follow on their way west.[64]

While Mormon leader Brigham Young led the original saints to Salt Lake City, the Mormon Battalion scouted new lands to settle in Southern California. In time, Mormons missionized several groups of Southern Paiute and shared their doctrines with many others, including some Chemehuevi. Mormon policy toward Indians reflected that of the mainstream "liberal" Americans who felt Native Americans were uncivilized, savage, and degraded individuals who deserved an opportunity to become enlightened, religious, civilized, and hard working. In a word, "diggers" deserved to become like white people. Mormon missionaries set out to "uplift" Indian people, because Native Americans held a special place in Mormon theology as a lost tribe of Israel that had ventured out of the holy land of the Middle East and resettled in the Western Hemisphere. It is doubtful that many Chemehuevi or their Southern Paiute relatives understood this element of Mormon belief, and even fewer would have found merit in this part of Mormon dogma.[65]

During the California Gold Rush and its aftermath in the 1850s, most Chemehuevi experienced little contact with non-Native peoples. Some Americans traveled the Old Spanish Trail through Ute and Paiute country in Utah and Nevada, and others continued westward along the Mojave River Trail, running through the Mojave Desert. Yet most Chemehuevi chose to stay clear of emigrants. As a result, few accounts are available regarding the interaction of Chemehuevi people with non-Native travelers. One account, however, spoke clearly about Chemehuevi people during the decade of the 1850s. In June 1855 a group of Mormon missionaries "found about 50 Indians (Piedes) on the Colorado, in a perfect state of nudity, except breechcloths." In 1856 missionaries reported that "two Paiute Indians from the vicinity of the Iats [Mojave Indians] came on a visit." Mormons noted Chemehuevi warriors used poisoned arrows and flint points, which they "made by having a rattlesnake bite a piece of deer's liver, and then bury it in the ground, and when it becomes putrid enough, they take it out and dry it, and when they go to use it, they steep it in water or rub it into the arrows."[66]

No doubt Chemehuevi and other Southern Paiute stole from whites and killed livestock for food. Unsavory reports by travelers helped further a negative image of uncivilized Chemehuevi and other California Indians. In fact, many words and events that seem unrelated to Chemehuevi people significantly affected their lives. When a group of Maidu Indians and whites working for John Sutter discovered gold at Coloma along the American River in 1848, the California Gold Rush commenced. Most writers of the Gold Rush era and its aftermath presented it as a grand American epic. Many historical works offer the Gold Rush as a positive event in American history, a turning point in which sourdough miners worked the rich placers of the Sierra foothills to make life better for all humankind. But the Gold Rush and other mining ventures had a significant and negative impact on Native Americans throughout California, including the Chemehuevi. The Gold Rush brought thousands of non-Natives to California, young white males eager to get rich, and some used the 35th Parallel Route that generally ran near the route of present-day Interstate 40.

The old road took travelers heading west through Hualapai country of Peach Springs and Kingman, into the desert to the Colorado River at Needles, and west into the Mojave Desert—the home of many Chemehuevi. Very few travelers mentioned the Chemehuevi of the Mojave Desert, in part because the people "run from us like wild deer."[67] More likely, Chemehuevi people kept their distance from settlers. Simply put, most Chemehuevi avoided white people because they did not trust them. From the time of Father Garcés, many non-Indians had proven themselves to be dangerous characters that might harm Chemehuevi people through attack, theft, or disease. By the 1840s and 1850s, many Chemehuevi chose to avoid white soldiers, miners, and emigrants. As a result, not one "of these 1849 journals mentioned any Indians west of the Muddy River–Las Vegas area" because the Chemehuevi people "generally avoided interaction with the whites along the trail."[68] Southern Paiute kept their distance.

In 1851 the Chemehuevi made an effort largely to avoid Captain Lorenzo Sitgreaves, when the American soldier traveled through northern Arizona, eventually arriving at the Mojave villages on the Colorado River. He likely met or saw signs of Chemehuevi living south of the Mojave, but if so, he made no mention of them. From the Mojave villages, Sitgreaves traveled south to Yuma Crossing, where he hoped to find a thriving Fort Yuma. At the time his party was distressed from its long desert journey. Instead, he found that Major Samuel P. Heintzelman had temporarily withdrawn most troops to San Diego, leaving Lieutenant Thomas W. Sweeney in charge of a few men.[69] Sitgreaves had no knowledge of the desert and became hungry and destitute. Because of his own condition, Sitgreaves provided few details about his journey south along the Colorado River; he made no mention of the Chemehuevi. Two years later, Francois Xavier Aubrey, a Santa Fe trader, traveled east along the Mojave River Trail, but like Sitgreaves, he did not mention meeting Chemehuevi.[70] However, in 1854, Lieutenant Amiel Weeks Whipple traveled west through central Arizona and "entered the fine valley of the Chemehuevi Indians."[71]

Whipple wrote that the Chemehuevi were a "band of the great Pai-ute (Pah-Utch) nation, but live separate and distinct from the mountain robbers." Whipple theorized that the Chemehuevi had about "two hundred warriors" and in their fertile soil they grew "beans, squashes, maize, and wheat." He reported correctly that most of the Chemehuevi villages were on "the west bank of the river" and were spread out over a vast area, or "considerable space" as he put it.[72] The space included a route west of the Mojave villages of the Colorado River along the Mojave River to present-day Soda Lake, leading to the Tejón Pass. A little over twenty miles from the Colorado River, Whipple found "Pai-Ute Creek," where Chemehuevi had been farming some wheat and corn in a small sink that had filled with water during the spring. He mentioned that the people lived in small lodges, where the rinds of melons and squashes appeared all around the village. However, none of the people occupied the village at the time; they were likely on a hunting or gathering journey across the Mojave Desert.[73]

Lieutenant Joseph Christmas Ives accompanied Whipple as second-in-command and at one point surprised a Southern Paiute village, sending inhabitants in every direction. Ives provided little information about the people, except to say that in their haste they left bows, arrows, clothing, cooking utensils, and baskets. The famed German artist Heinrich Bauduin Möllhausen also accompanied the expedition and stopped at the western end of Soda Lake long enough to observe that the Chemehuevi lived on very little in the middle of what he considered a bleak desert. Like other travelers, he emphasized that the people ate snakes, lizards, frogs, and roots, making no mention of rabbits, bighorns, deer, and a host of fruits and vegetables that the German would not have recognized or been able to cultivate, gather, prepare, or store. He noted that his

The Chemehuevi shared an extensive area with other Nüwü people. This photograph offers a view of the Sheep Mountains, a mountain range east of the Spring Mountains of southern Nevada. Chemehuevi people hunted in this area and gathered piñons in the Las Vegas Mountains farther east. The Paiute landscape is diverse, filled with rugged and beautiful terrain, colorful plants found on the desert floors, talus slopes, and rugged mountains. The landscape includes lands below sea level and mountains over ten thousand feet high, inclusive of evergreen trees. It offered Chemehuevi and other Nüwü a wealth of plant and animal foods as well as many spiritual sites. Photograph by Clifford E. Trafzer.

party feared an attack by Chemehuevi who might "come in the night and kill some of our mules with arrows."[74] People throughout the West recognized the Chemehuevi people as great runners and travelers who used their feet (not horses) for transportation. The people preferred to eat horses, although once they had sufficient food and livestock, they also rode horses.[75]

Whipple, Ives, Möllhausen, and other observers often mentioned that the Chemehuevi lived in the heart of the Mojave Desert, near precious springs. They raised crops in or near the washes, sinks, and natural springs that provide life to people, plants, and animals.[76] Explorers also recorded that the Chemehuevi lived north, south, and west of the Mojave villages, particularly on the west bank of the Colorado River in Chemehuevi Valley. Some of the people also lived along the Bill Williams River east of the Mojave and used this lush and fertile desert waterway for hunting and gathering. Writing from Fort Yuma at the confluence of the Colorado and Gila Rivers, Major Samuel Peter Heintzelman corroborated that the Chemehuevi lived in these places, saying "the Chi-mi-hua-hua . . . live in the mountains on the right [west] bank of the Colorado, two days journey, or about sixty miles above the post." The major wrote that the Quechan lived south of Paiute people, the Mojave to the north, the Yavapai to the east, and the Cahuilla to the west. Heintzelman mentioned that the Chemehuevi were related to the Cahuilla, at least by language and friendship. Chemehuevi married Cahuilla and were related to other desert tribes through marriage.[77]

In 1848 the United States concluded its war with Mexico, which ended with the Treaty of Guadalupe Hidalgo. As a result of the war and the treaty, the United States claimed Arizona, California, Nevada, and the remainder of the Mexican Cession, including Chemehuevi land. Of course, the Chemehuevi knew little, if anything, of the American claim, and as a sovereign people they would not have recognized that claim even if they had known. Native Americans "owned" their lands, not Spain or Mexico. Still, the arrival of American newcomers forever affected the people of the river and deserts. By 1850, when California became a state, the United States had had a lengthy relationship with Indian tribes and had developed national Indian policies based on treaties, wars, removals, and segregation of First Nations people onto specified lands designated as Indian territories or reserves. Between 1851 and 1852, federal officials negotiated eighteen treaties affecting 139 California tribes, but the government did not include the Chemehuevi in the treaties. It would have mattered little, however, since the U.S. Senate refused to ratify the treaties, which would have guaranteed some land base for many California tribes.[78]

Like the other tribes of Arizona, California, and Nevada, the Chemehuevi had no formal relationship with the United States. As a result, the people could not "legally" secure for themselves their traditional territory. The Chemehuevi knew little, if anything, about the legal systems of the United States or how the newcomers dealt with indigenous peoples. They had little idea that the newcomers jeopardized their lives and property because of American claims to Arizona, California, and Nevada. However, the Chemehuevi people knew about the movement of white men near and through their lands and the potential for trading with them for manufactured items. Chemehuevi experienced their first prolonged contact with whites in 1858, when two American exploring expeditions crossed Chemehuevi territory from east to west and from north to south. In January 1858, Lieutenant Edward Fitzgerald Beale led the United States Camel Corps across the Southwest. Chemehuevi marveled at the sight

At Red Rock Gate on the Colorado River, Heinrich Bauduin Möllhausen drew a picture of the high cliffs along the Colorado River and three indigenous people crossing the river in a canoe. The Chemehuevi used poles and canoes but usually used rafts and logs to cross the river. They remain "river people" today, and the Chemehuevi Tribe operates a ferry across the Colorado River from Lake Havasu Landing to Lake Havasu City. From Lieutenant Joseph Christmas Ives, "Report upon the Colorado River of the West," in *Report of the Secretary of War, 1861*, in Senate Executive Document, Thirty-sixth Congress, First Session (Washington, D.C.: Government Printing Office, 1861).

of white men ferrying camels across the Colorado River aboard the steamboat *General Jessup*. Both the steamboat and the camels were new to the Chemehuevi and must have caused a great deal of discussion and humor as runners raced from village to village spreading the news of their arrival.[79]

Not long after the camels marched west across the Mojave Desert on their way to Fort Tejón, California, another exploring expedition made its way up the Colorado River into Chemehuevi country. Between January and March 1858, Lieutenant Joseph Christmas Ives explored the Colorado River from Fort Yuma north. Between the mouth of the Colorado River at the Gulf of Baja California and Fort Yuma, Ives met several Cocopah Indians, but the lieutenant did not spend a great deal of time with the Cocopah as he moved pell-mell up the swift stream. Ives guided his little steamboat, the *Explorer*, up the river above Fort

Yuma past Chemehuevi and Mojave villages. On his trip north to the Black Canyon, the present-day site of Hoover Dam, Ives met several Chemehuevi and Mojave. In his "Report upon the Colorado River of the West," Ives made note of several Chemehuevi he met.[80] On January 23 a small band "belonging to a tribe called the Chemehuevi came into camp." This group of people lived along the Colorado River south of the mouth of the Bill Williams River "in the valley adjoining that which we are now traversing, but are altogether different in appearance and character from the other Colorado [River] Indians." Ives described the Chemehuevi he met as having "small figures, and some of them delicate, nicely-cut features, with little of the Indian physiognomy."[81]

These Chemehuevi did not fear Ives or his party. They had spent sufficient time with the Americans so that Ives could comment that the Chemehuevi people "are a wandering race, and travel great distances on hunting and predatory excursions." He remarked that Chemehuevi men, women, and children "wear sandals and hunting shirts of buckskin, and carry tastefully-made quivers of the same material." As for Chemehuevi character, Ives stated that he thought the people to be "notorious rogues, and have a peculiar cunning, elfish expression, which is a sufficient certificate of their rascality." When Ives caught one of the Chemehuevi men trying "to cheat me while fulfilling a bargain for a deerskin," the Chemehuevi became "highly amused" by the humor of the situation.[82] The Chemehuevi trader exhibited the sense of humor noted by Chemehuevi elder Patrick Lyttle during an interview with James Sandos and Larry Burgess. "We are always joking with people and language," Lyttle asserted.[83] Twenty-Nine Palms chair and tribal elder Dean Mike and his cousin, Joe Benitez, offered similar views in interviews. "We are always joking around with each other," Joe explained. "And we poke fun at ourselves and others," Dean added. Both of them laughed as they made their points.[84] The Chemehuevi people Ives met playfully tried to outwit Americans, and laughed at Ives, his men, and his curious contraption: the smoke belching, steam-driven *Explorer*.

Chemehuevi watched Ives guide the *Explorer* up the river and found great humor in the effort the Americans made to navigate the swift-flowing stream. "This slow progress," Ives noted, "has been a source of intense satisfaction and fun to the spectators on the banks." He remarked that his "sharp witted friends, the Chemehuevi, seem to have exclusive possession of the upper end of the valley" and have "watched with great curiosity for the long-expected boat."[85] As Ives fought the currents of the Colorado, the Chemehuevi "regarded our method of ascending the river with unaffected contempt." Chemehuevi told the two Quechan scouts accompanying Ives—Mariano and Capitan—that the

American "mode of locomotion" proved inferior to that of Indians. "They can foot it on the shore, or pole along a raft upon the river without interruption," Ives reported, "and that we should spend days in doing what they can accomplish in half as many hours, strikes them as unaccountably stupid."[86]

These Chemehuevi exhibited a "gleeful consciousness of superiority at all events" associated with the Americans, "which keeps them in excellent humor." Chemehuevi men, women, and children laughed as the *Explorer* struggled upriver, but when the steamboat became stuck on a sandbar, "our troubles occasioned them unqualified delight." This was particularly true when Ives and his party "tried in vain to get through one place after another, and every time she ran aground a peal of laughter would ring from the bank." After having fun at Ives's expense, Chemehuevi began running along the riverbank and pointing out the best routes to navigate to avoid sand bars. However, when Captain Robinson ignored an elderly woman's advice, her "benevolence" became "rage, and with clenched fists and flaming eyes she followed along the bank, screaming at the captain." She must have thought Captain Robinson quite the fool, not heeding her sage advice.[87]

Each evening after Ives made camp, Chemehuevi men, women, and children visited the Americans "in great numbers." On one of these occasions, "a chief of apparently some importance" came into camp to talk with Ives, likely speaking to the Paiute in sign language and some Spanish. Ives had heard of the famous Chemehuevi runners from indigenous people on the Colorado River, so he "prevailed upon him to send a runner to Fort Yuma for the mail." They haggled over the price for such an endeavor before striking a bargain that was suitable to both parties. When one of "the Indian runners was satisfied," he agreed to run south along the Colorado River to Fort Yuma, rest for one day, and spend the next three days running upstream to meet the *Explorer* and its crew. Although Ives complained that the Chemehuevi runner drove a hard bargain, the lieutenant wrote respectfully that Chemehuevi always kept their word. He knew that the runner would do exactly as he said that he would, noting: "After once making an agreement, I have never known one of them to recede from it, and punctually at the time appointed he came for the package."[88]

The Chemehuevi runner raced south with Ives's reports and letters. The runner returned from Fort Yuma seven days later with letters for the lieutenant and his men, just as he said he would.[89] Like other military officers in years to come, Ives remarked glowingly on the honest character of Chemehuevi people. In fact, he extended the compliment to other Native peoples as well. "We have had such agreeable intercourse with the Colorado Indians that it is pleasant to be able to notice one good quality in them," Ives wrote on January 17 from Mojave Valley. The white man recorded that it "is the exactitude with which they fulfill an agreement" that separates the Chemehuevi and their neighbors from other peoples of the world. "On several occasions," Ives stated, "this has been called to our attention, and I am disposed to give them all credit for so honorable a characteristic."[90] In contrast to the negative writings of Farnham, Wolfskill, and DeSmet, other whites recorded that the Chemehuevi were among the most honest of people. Today the Chemehuevi people continue their reputation for their integrity and personal and communal commitment to others.

The Chemehuevi navigated the Colorado River in dugout canoes and rafts. On his journey up the Colorado River above the Bill Williams River, Ives reported that he met "two Chemehuevi, with their wives, children, and household effects, paddling towards the valley below, on rafts made by tying together bundles of reeds." The Chemehuevi made reed boats out of tule, cutting large reeds and stacking them in great piles before using yucca string to tie the reeds into bundles. Then the Chemehuevi placed the lengthy reed bundles next to each other, creating a raft-type of craft with the back, side, and bow tilted slightly upward to prevent quantities of water entering the hull.

Not far above the Bill Williams River, a region located north of present-day Parker Dam and within Lake Havasu, the *Explorer* began to make good time under a full head of steam, passing Chemehuevi villages without incident. The Chemehuevi "drew their rafts into a little cave when they saw us coming, and peered out at the steamboat, as it went puffing by, with an amusing expression of bewilderment and awe."[91] Once again, Ives recorded the Chemehuevi's sense of humor, which has always characterized—and continues to characterize—the people. Chemehuevi families likely had seen the steamboat *General Jessup* on its maiden voyage up the Colorado a few weeks before, but even if they had, the sight of the smoke-belching tiny *Explorer* would have made quite a sight. The Chemehuevi must have wondered about the nature of white people who created such strange technologies.

The Chemehuevi living along the Colorado River raised crops of "beans and corn, with occasional watermelons and pumpkins." Like their Mojave and Quechan neighbors, the Chemehuevi depended on the "annual overflow of the river" for their irrigation. Ives reported that "with little labor," the people could raise "an abundant supply of provisions for the year, which they improvidently consume."[92] In a prophetic manner, Ives noted that with a sophisticated "system of irrigation and an improved method of agriculture," the region surrounding the lower Colorado River "would make the valley far more productive." How-

Lieutenant Ives and his men reconstructed a small steamboat named the *Explorer* at the mouth of the Colorado River. Heinrich Bauduin Möllhausen provided this detailed pen and ink sketch of the *Explorer* as it made its way through Chemehuevi country.

From Lieutenant Joseph Christmas Ives, "Report upon the Colorado River of the West," in *Report of the Secretary of War, 1861*, in Senate Executive Document, Thirty-sixth Congress, First Session (Washington, D.C.: Government Printing Office, 1861).

ever, he added, "it is not certain that it could never be a profitable place for white settlements."[93] Of course, the lieutenant was correct regarding his first assertion; these lands had once belonged solely to the Chemehuevi, Cahuilla, and Mojave, but with time Americans would create agribusinesses along the river. Lands previously farmed by Chemehuevi and their neighbors became highly productive farms generating millions of dollars for newcomers. Unfortunately for the Chemehuevi and their neighbors, Native peoples lost nearly all of their traditional lands and control of river water. Indian lands in Arizona, California, and Nevada have made non-Natives wealthy through the advanced agricultural methods and subsidized irrigation systems brought to the region by the U.S. government and implemented by hard-working, farsighted farmers.

However, before non-Native peoples rushed to the lower Colorado River region to claim and develop Indian lands through extensive irrigation systems, whites invaded the area to exploit mineral riches found in the mountains towering above both sides of the Colorado River. All American explorers had speculated about the presence of gold, silver, and other mineral wealth to be found in the area, which miners found. The Chemehuevi people lived on land filled with billions of dollars worth of water, copper, gold, silver, and other minerals—a fact recognized early by American explorers. On January 31, 1858, Ives recorded that his men inspected "the rugged face of the Riverside mountain" that "the rays of the setting sun" illuminated with "tints of purple, blue, brown, almond, and rose color." While the sun cast its evening light on the crevices and hollows of the mountain, one "Dr. Newberry found, in this mountain, indications of the presence of gold, silver, lead, iron, and copper, and discovered veins resembling the gold-bearing rocks of California."[94] Newberry's prophecy proved correct. Prospectors found gold there. Ives remarked that the mountains might contain "stores of treasure, which the close proximity of water transportation would greatly enhance in value."[95] Just a few years after Ives explored the region, miners swarmed the lower Colorado River area in the 1860s, prospecting on lands claimed by the Chemehuevi and Mojave and introducing the people to dangerous disease, financial greed, and greater tensions. Miners ignored aboriginal rights, and governments encouraged development at the expense of Indian rights.

Before the 1860s the Chemehuevi and Mojave lived in close proximity to each other, and they generally maintained peaceful relationships with one another. Ives remarked that the "Mojaves preserve constant friendly relations with the Chemehuevis and Yumas [Quechan], and were allied with the latter in the attack upon the Pimas and Maricopas" of southern Arizona.[96] The Chemehuevi also got along well with their Northern Paiute neighbors and relatives, although Ives recorded on March 31, 1858, that he had received "constant warnings to exercise precaution" because "bad Pai-utes are prowling about." He worried about Paiute relatives of the Chemehuevi, because the Indians, Ives believed, were under the influence of Mormons who disliked the United States. Ives reported that he had learned from Mojave that the Paiute "intended to destroy our party as soon as it should enter their territory," but this was more likely a rumor unsupported by fact.[97] Such an attack never materialized, but persecuted Mormons may well have warned Paiute about the U.S. Army and the threat of white resettlement of millions of acres of Indian lands.

CHAPTER 3

War, Resistance, and Survival

THE 1850S INAUGURATED A TURBULENT AND DEADLY TIME FOR IN-digenous people of California, the Great Basin, and the Southwest. The United States consolidated its new territory secured from Mexico during the war and as a consequence of the 1848 Treaty of Guadalupe Hidalgo. The "Mexican Cession" included a vast area that encompassed much of present-day Arizona, New Mexico, Utah, Nevada, Colorado, and California. Within the boundaries of this fresh acquisition lived numerous Native American tribes and groups. Chemehuevi people had enjoyed watching camels and steamboats pass through their country, but they became concerned when soldiers built forts, white settlers traveled through the region, and miners arrived to dig for precious metals. Emigrants used ancient Indian trails along the Gila, Virgin, and Mojave Rivers. The presence of government soldiers, agents, surveyors, and settlers forced Indian people into innovative relationships with civilian, military, and government officials who had experience dealing with Native Americans in other parts of the United States and acted to benefit themselves, not Native Americans. During the 1850s the federal government still executed its policies of forced removal of American Indians—a policy that the United States had followed since the American Revolution and made official in 1830 with the Removal Act. Eventually the government forcefully removed tribes to reservations and tried to dictate policies to sovereign indigenous people, including the Chemehuevi.[1]

The United States introduced the Chemehuevi and all other Native Americans to American Indian policies of treaties, written "agreements" between sovereign nations that guided the relationship and boundaries of Native and non-Native peoples. Between 1784, when the United States created its first treaty with Native Americans, and 1831, when Chief Justice John Marshall and the U.S. Supreme Court ruled that Indian tribes were "Domestic Dependent Nations," the government dealt with Indian tribes as foreign powers. The United States continued creating treaties with Native nations to liquidate Indian title to lands and resources. The federal government also negotiated treaties to encourage peaceful relations and to allow non-Indians rights-of-way across Indian lands. The government regulated the Indian trade, a very lucrative business in past centuries. Sometimes treaties ended wars between the U.S. Army and Indian nations, but more often the government ratified treaties as "legal" documents to take Indian land and resources desired by non-Native peoples. In this way the United States established boundaries between the "citizens" of the United States and the Native Americans who were not national citizens until 1924, and not citizens of Arizona and New Mexico until the 1940s.[2] All these policies significantly influenced Chemehuevi life and history, but few Native Americans living in the 1850s fully understood the impact of American settlement and policies designed to benefit newcomers and limit the land, resources, and sovereignty of indigenous people.

During the 1850s the United States embarked on a novel element of Indian policy known as reservations, and the government established the first modern reservation system at Fort Tejón, California. Prior to the mid-nineteenth century, the United States drew upon the experiences of Great Britain by recognizing Indian Country or "Indian territory"—lands separating Indians from non-Indians. From time to time, Indian nations in the eastern United States secured for themselves a small portion of land known as reserves, but by the 1850s the government had extinguished Indian title to nearly all Native lands east of the Mississippi River. By the time Americans took control of California and the Southwest, the government had years of experience dealing with tribes. White settlers and government officials had little interest in allowing Indians to dominate land and resources in the new acquisition. Generally in the other western territories, tensions often arose between the U.S. Army and local militia forces, especially over the question of Indian policy.

The same occurred in Arizona, Colorado, Idaho, Nevada, New Mexico, Oregon, Utah, and Washington. The U.S. Army claimed superiority over territorial militia forces, but time and again territorial militias and legislatures challenged the Army, causing conflicts with Native Americans. However, throughout much of California the U.S. Army allowed local militia forces to rule supreme when dealing with Indian nations, and the results proved disastrous for many people who experienced a genocide perpetrated by pioneers.[3] During the 1850s few immigrants chose to settle along the Colorado River or in the Mojave Desert. The discovery of gold, silver, and other minerals in the 1860s brought many miners who disregarded Indian rights and demanded protection against angry indigenous people.

In January 1848, Indian workers at the Maidu village of Koloma found gold as they dug a millrace from the American River to Sutter's mill. Head of the construction party building a sawmill, James Marshall shared the news with others, and soon the gold discovery of 1848 in California's Sierra Nevada Mountains caused a sensational international gold rush. Although miners found most of the initial gold deposits in northern and central California, Indians living in every corner of California felt the impact of the Gold Rush. This included the Southern Paiute and other Indian people of Southern California. California Native populations declined rapidly after the gold discovery from roughly one hundred thousand Indians in 1848 to approximately thirty thousand by the 1860s. This number continued to decline throughout the nineteenth century.[4] Indigenous populations declined primarily by murder, but the drop also resulted from diseases brought by Americans, Australians, Chileans, Chinese, Europeans, Mexicans, and other gold seekers. Native Americans had little immunity to measles, colds, influenza, and smallpox. The population also declined as a result of outright killings, kidnapping, and slavery, particularly in Northern California, where newspapers documented Indian hunts, rapes, and murders.[5]

Indian people throughout Southern California experienced killings, kidnapping, and slavery. They faced a constant flow of newcomers to and through their lands during the 1850s. Along the lower Colorado River, gold seekers crossed the river in large numbers on their way to the California gold fields. The Chemehuevi people lived north of the Quechan Indians, but they learned of conflicts between Quechan people and white newcomers that led to violence. To capitalize on the gold rush and to earn money, enterprising Quechan hired an Irishman named Callahan to operate a ferry for them. The Quechan competed with a ferryman named Able Lincoln but in a friendly manner until outlaws rode into Yuma Crossing. Emigrants along the 32nd Parallel Route, often called the Gila Trail, crossed the Colorado River at Yuma Crossing in large numbers. Lincoln and the Quechan made large sums of money, a fact noted by a gang of outlaws led by John Joel Glanton and his band of Indian scalp hunters. Glanton and his men muscled their way into the ferry business, forcing Lincoln to relinquish sole ownership of his ferry and encouraging the Quechan to quit their ferry. Glanton's men murdered Callahan who had operated the Indian ferry and cut the Indian ferry loose, allowing it to float downriver.

When a Quechan delegation complained to Glanton about the murder and the loss of their ferry, Glanton attacked them, striking some of them with a wooden club. The Quechan waited patiently until Glanton's men brought a keg of whiskey from San Diego, and after most of Glanton's men were drunk, they attacked, killing all but two of the white men, who at the time were cutting poles for their ferry. The two men proceeded to walk across the Colorado Desert and report the attack to government authorities in San Diego, California.[6] All of these events transpired south of Chemehuevi territory, but the conflict had implications for all Native Americans in the region. Immigrants, ferries, competition for resources, and the arrival of troops signaled dramatic changes for the Chemehuevi, Kwaaymii, Kumeyaay, Mojave, Quechan, and other indigenous groups. The struggle for control of land, resources, and self-determination that began in the 1850s grew dramatically in the late nineteenth century. The U.S. Army soon flexed its might, establishing Fort Yuma, Fort Mojave, and sending patrols to protect emigrants—not Indians.

The Chemehuevi people knew about the Glanton killings. News of the events traveled quickly by Indian runners. However, the Chemehuevi likely did not understand the full implication of Quechan killing Americans, especially an outlaw gang that had caused trouble. The killing of white men struck fear into the newcomers, and several young white men volunteered to punish the indigenous culprits. White people held the Quechan responsible. Newcomers wanted revenge. For white settlers the Quechan had to be punished. The Glanton killings brought militia forces and the U.S. Army to Quechan territory, where warriors held their own against militia forces. The Quechan Indians initially fought troops under Major Samuel Peter Heintzelman, but within a year Heintzelman had terrorized several Quechan villages and continued to press a scorched-earth campaign against the people.

The Army established Fort Yuma on the California side of the Colorado River at its junction with the Gila, the present site of the Fort Yuma Indian Reservation. From this base, troops initiated the scorched-earth campaign against the Quechan in the Yuma, Gila, and Bard Valleys of the lower Colorado River. During the final campaign Heintzelman led his troops north toward a prominent mountain called Picacho, a great and holy mountain for the Quechan, just south of Chemehuevi along the Colorado River. Quechan leader Huttamines engaged the troops, but after a short firefight the Quechan leader sued for peace, making an agreement with Heintzelman that allowed the Indians and

In 1857, Lieutenant William H. Emory led an expedition across the Southwest to survey the U.S.–Mexican boundary. Carl Victor Schott, a German artist from Stuttgart, served as the illustrator of the expedition. He painted the Sunflower Eaters, a group of Quechan Indians living east of present-day Yuma, Arizona, along the Gila River. Sunflower Eaters resided south of the Chemehuevi people. The two groups had a friendly relationship, often trading with one another. From Lieutenant William H. Emory, "Report of the United States and Mexican Boundary Survey," in *House Executive Document*, Thirty-fourth Congress, First Session (Washington, D.C.: Government Printing Office, 1857–1859).

soldiers to live peacefully in the Quechan homeland. The two parties concluded an agreement that Heintzelman wrote in his small journal, but it was not a formal Indian treaty sent to the U.S. Senate or the president. The agreement between two sovereigns allowed the people to coexist on the Colorado River. The Chemehuevi, Cocopah, Kumeyaay, Mojave, Yavapai, and others took note of what happened between the Quechan and the U.S. Army, no doubt contemplating its meaning to their people. Clearly a major change had come into the region with the arrival of American troops accompanied by settlers, miners, merchants, and budding towns.[7]

No direct evidence links the Chemehuevi with events between the Quechan and the Army. But Chemehuevi runners surely informed the people of hostilities and the construction of Fort Yuma. The Chemehuevi and the Quechan were two distinct people but good friends. In 1857, Heintzelman wrote Major E. D. Townsend that the "Chi-mi-hua-hua . . . live in the mountains on the right bank of the Colorado, two days journey, or about sixty miles above the post." The major noted correctly that the Chemehuevi people lived near the Mojave with the Quechan living to their south. Heintzelman noted the Yavapai lived east of the Chemehuevi and "Cah-willas" to the west. An observant soldier, Heintzelman recorded the location of other Indians and their disposition toward other Native peoples as a means to control or regulate Indian actions along the river. He used information about other tribes to help control events.[8]

In 1853, Lieutenant Amiel Weeks Whipple found Chemehuevi people living north of the Quechan along the Colorado River, noting that most of them lived in "the fine valley of the Chemehuevi Indians."[9] Lieutenant Whipple found Chemehuevi people living in large numbers on the west bank of the Colorado River in the fertile Chemehuevi Valley, in California across the river from present-day Lake Havasu City. The United States destroyed this Chemehuevi homeland when the government built Parker Dam, flooding the entire valley with the waters of Lake Havasu. Whipple found the people in their valley where they farmed, hunted, and gathered. He characterized them correctly as "a band of the great Pai-ute ('Pah-Utah') nation, but live separate and distinct from the mountain robbers." Whipple reported the village at Chemehuevi Valley "contains probably two hundred warriors—short, but robust and well formed, with regular features, and a pleasing air of activity and intelligence." Chemehuevi people lived in the valley with villages found "mostly on the west bank of the river [the California side of the river]." The people treated Whipple "kindly, and flooded our camp with a portion of the surplus produce of their fields for trade." The American explorer mentioned that the "principal articles of traffic

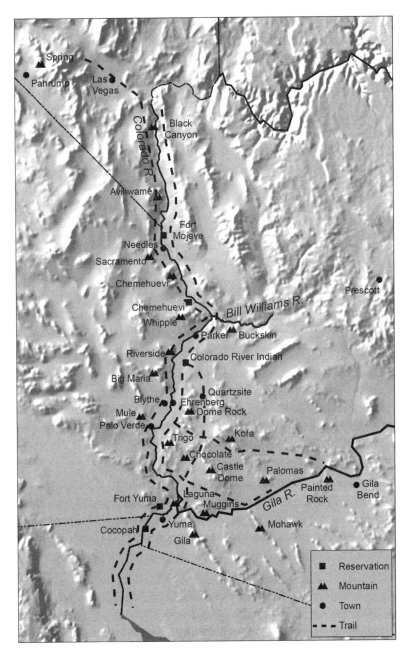

This map illustrates the key trails used by the Chemehuevi on both sides of the Colorado River as well as trade routes into southwestern Arizona, where Chemehuevi hunted, gathered, and engaged other indigenous people in commerce. Map by Robert Johnson, University of California–Riverside.

were beans, squashes, maize, and wheat—the latter usually ground to flour."

Whipple estimated the Chemehuevi in the valley "possess a tract of about thirty square miles." In a prophetic statement, Lieutenant Whipple praised the grandeur and fertility of the Colorado River region, noting that the "valley of the Rio Colorado forms a distinguishing feature in the topography of the western portion of the continent." The valley "itself affords a large extent of fertile bottom-land, which may be perfectly irrigated and easily cultivated."[10] He found the soil "superior" in quality, stating that the land the "Indians now cultivate so abundantly" was perfect because "the soil and climate are remarkably adapted to the cultivation of cotton, sugar-cane, and rice." Whipple had "no doubt that the valley of the Colorado is destined, at some future day, to be divided into plantations, supporting a numerous population." Although he did not say so, he meant a non-Native population and he was correct. Today non-Indians control a vast region of what was once owned by the Chemehuevi, Quechan, and Mojave—very productive agricultural land fed by irrigation water from the Colorado River. Today indigenous people live on reservations bordering the river, but non-Indians own the profitable "plantations" and support a huge population beyond that envisioned by Whipple in the 1850s.[11]

Many non-Native people passing through Chemehuevi country noted the people generally got along well with the Paiute farther north, the Hualapai and Havasupai to the east, and the Mojave neighbors living close by all of the Chemehuevi villages along the Colorado River. The Chemehuevi had positive relations with other Native people in the region. According to Chemehuevi elder Joe Benitez, the Chemehuevi lived in harmony with the Mojave living in the Mojave Desert and Colorado River Valley. Mojave warriors did not fight Chemehuevi people. In fact, Mojave had friendly relations with Southern Paiute for years through trade and farming. The Chemehuevi had villages north, west, and south of the Mojave country along the Colorado River.[12] A positive economic and social confluence existed between the people. Chemehuevi Salt Song singer Matthew Hanks Leivas confirmed this observation, pointing out that the Mojave always outnumbered the Chemehuevi, but the two people primarily had amicable relations.[13]

In 1860, Captain A. S. Burton stated that a small "portion of the Pah-Utahs, called the Chi-mi-way-wahs, live in the mountains near the Colorado River, between the Mojave and Yuma countries." Burton referred to Chemehuevi people living in the Blythe area on both sides of the river. He pointed out that the Chemehuevi were "intimate friends of the Mojave and are in constant commu-

During the Ives expedition up the Colorado River in 1857–1858, the explorers met numerous Chemehuevi. Ives wrote glowingly of their honesty and the remarkable ability of Chemehuevi runners to run great distances to deliver messages. Heinrich Bauduin Möllhausen created this work of two Chemehuevi men and a woman with child. Notice the baby's cradleboard with the woven shade piece to protect the child from the sun, and the two types of bows carried by the men, including the long hunting bow in the center and the smaller war bow carried by the man on the right. From Lieutenant Joseph Christmas Ives, "Report upon the Colorado River of the West," in *Report of the Secretary of War, 1861,* in *Senate Executive Document*, Thirty-sixth Congress, First Session (Washington, D.C.: Government Printing Office, 1861).

nication with the Pah-Utah Indians of the Salt Lake country."[14] Other Chemehuevi lived north of the Mojave on Cottonwood Island, while still others lived in Chemehuevi Valley west of most Mojave until 1865, when the government created the Colorado River Indian Reservation. In that year Jacob Hamblin visited Cottonwood Island and the Chemehuevi villages there, noting that some Mojave also lived there. The two groups enjoyed friendly relations for many years.[15] However, at times Mojave and Chemehuevi people fought each other, attacking one another especially in the Mojave Desert. The Chemehuevi generally maintained friendly relations with the River Mojave, but at times they fought Land Mojave living west of the Colorado River.

Some Chemehuevi and Mojave intermarried, creating familial relationships between the two groups. Each tribe maintained its own sovereignty and identity but found common ground to live near one another. Equally important, the two groups shared cultural elements with each other, learning from the rich cultures of each people. The Chemehuevi people learned Mojave Bird Songs, while some Mojave singers sang Salt Songs. The Chemehuevi acquired some elements of Mojave mourning ceremonies, and some Chemehuevi cremated their dead like the Mojave. Mojave families invited the Chemehuevi to sing Salt Songs in honor of their dead, since it was considered inappropriate in the past for the people to sing Bird Songs at funerals.[16] The Cahuilla Indians also invited Salt Song singers to sing at funerals and memorials—highly significant ceremonies of the past and present. Perhaps the close relationship between the Mojave and the Chemehuevi would have continued had it not been for the arrival of white settlers and the U.S. Army. During the late 1850s, the Mojave became more and more alarmed over the arrival of white pioneers north and south of them, challenging their control of Mojave land and food supplies. Only a few immigrants traveled through Mojave homelands until 1858, but after that, an increasing number of settlers and soldiers passed through. Indigenous people worried about the ill effects of non-Indians whose animals ate native foods, disrupted animal habitat, and introduced disease. Mojave and Chemehuevi people knew the Army had attacked the Quechan and established Fort Yuma in 1851. They worried about their own fate in dealing with these newcomers.

Horses, mules, oxen, and people depleted native natural resources, threatening the well-being of Indian people. Settlers brought smallpox, measles, influenza, whooping cough, and the common cold—diseases that killed Chemehuevi and Quechan people as early as the 1780s. Often settlers did not intentionally introduce diseases, but sickness and death was the harvest of these diseases. In 1857, Lieutenant Edward Fitzgerald Beale had opened a wagon road across the 35th Parallel. Immigrant guides encouraged white settlers to use the new trail that cut through Mojave and Chemehuevi country.[17] In 1858 the first large emigrant party used Beale's Wagon Road, entering Mojave country without permission of local Native leaders. Mojave warriors attacked the wagon train, keeping up a siege until the white settlers retreated. The settlers returned to Albuquerque, New Mexico, where they reported the attack to government officials. When Secretary of War Jefferson Davis learned of the attack, he ordered General Newman Clarke, commander of the Pacific Department, to establish a military post on the Colorado River near Beale's Crossing.[18]

The United States planned a new fort in the heart of Mojave country, and the Army intended to dominate Mojave and Chemehuevi country, just as Heintzelman had done at Fort Yuma in his dealings with the Quechan. The Army established frontier posts to control indigenous people and to protect whites, not Native Americans. The Army served as one institution designed to take power from Indian people for the benefit of newcomers. This was a common practice of the U.S. Army, a policy followed in California and Arizona. In December 1858, Colonel William Hoffman left Los Angeles with a company of dragoons on their way to Mojave country. Under orders from General Clarke, Hoffman and his soldiers traveled east across the Mojave Desert on their way to the river with instructions to find a suitable site for a fort. The soldiers reached the Colorado River and surveyed the area for a possible building. The Mojave watched, waited, and then harassed the soldiers. Then Mojave warriors attacked. On January 9, 1859, Mojave warriors and soldiers clashed in a brief but deadly fight. The Indians fought primarily with war clubs, bows, and arrows, while the soldiers used firearms. According to soldiers, the Mojave lost approximately twelve men. According to Tcatc, granddaughter of the great Mojave leader Chief Irataba, "The Mohave had war with the Whites at Akawak'heyo:v. The Whites were using firearms and killed nearly half of the Mohave men who were in the battle."[19] Hoffman returned to Los Angeles to report the incident, and General Clarke ordered him back to Mojave country with seven companies of soldiers, enough to fight the Mojave and build the fort.[20]

Two companies of the troops traveled overland to the Colorado River, riding directly into Mojave and Chemehuevi country. The other five companies journeyed across the Colorado Desert to Fort Yuma. In the heart of Quechan country, the troops regrouped before moving up the Colorado River, penetrating the home of the Chemehuevi and the Mojave from the south. When Hoffman arrived in April 1859 with over seven hundred soldiers, the Mojave offered no overt resistance.[21] Hoffman and his troops prepared for battle, but the Mojave chose not to resist. Hoffman reported that several Mojave chiefs visited him and said that the Americans were welcome. "They said the country was mine," Hoffman wrote, but either the interpreter got the message wrong or the colonel made this up. Under no circumstances would the leaders simply hand over their land to white men, even to so many bluecoat soldiers. They likely expressed peace and friendship. Hoffman claimed that Mojave headmen told him to "do what I pleased with it [meaning the land]." The Mojave did not surrender their land, but Hoffman knew the power of the written word, so he made this erroneous claim of Mojave ceding their land. Because the Mojave initially offered no hostile resistance, Hoffman withdrew with most of the troops, returning to Los Angeles. He left Major Lewis Armistead in charge of two companies of infantry and ordered them to build Fort Mojave on the eastern bank of the Colorado River in present-day Arizona.[22]

In 1859 the United States began construction of a military post in the heart of the Mojave homeland, not far from Chemehuevi villages. The fort became a symbol of the United States and an affront to the First Nations of the Colorado River. The United States established the fort to guard the emigrant trail along the 35th Parallel through Mojave country. It was built to protect white people rather than Indians or indigenous rights. With the military post came some elements of white culture, including domestic animals, trade goods, whiskey, prostitution, and attitudes of superiority by whites over Native people. An uneasy truce existed between soldiers and Mojave, but the Mojave were not sufficiently armed or prepared to remove the Americans. Such discussion within Mojave communities would have been natural, and the increased tensions within the villages and among the Mojave people most likely contributed to growing tensions between the Mojave and Chemehuevi. The Chemehuevi lived sufficiently far from Fort Mojave so that they did not have to deal with soldiers on a regular basis. The tension between Mojave and Chemehuevi people during the 1860s originated from newcomers overrunning the land and dictating policies. Mojave warriors—great and powerful warriors ordained by dreams and spiritual power to protect their people—had lost an embarrassing and costly battle. Mojave warriors, men, and women had died, and U.S. soldiers had assumed leadership roles in Mojave country. Similar developments occurred at Fort Yuma, San Diego, Los Angeles, and other outlying Native communities. Tensions developed intertribally and intratribally.

Chemehuevi people learned of the interaction of whites with Indians living in the deserts and mountains of the Colorado Desert, Coachella Valley, the San Bernardino Mountains, the San Jacinto Mountains, the Santa Rosa Range, and the Pacific Coast. In fact, as early as the 1810s, the Los Angeles, California, census reported twelve Chemehuevi living in the small town of Los Angeles, California—the largest group of indigenous people recorded living there. The fact that Chemehuevi lived in Los Angeles demonstrates the range of travel and communication of the Chemehuevi people.[23] From the Cahuilla and Serrano, Chemehuevi people likely learned about the large number of immigrants

Irataba, the man on the left, led one group of Mojave people. He fought American soldiers and witnessed the deaths of many Mojave warriors in the ill-fated fight. In the 1860s, Irataba led many Mojave to the Parker Valley onto the newly established Colorado River Indian Reservation, created on March 3, 1865. From Lieutenant Joseph Christmas Ives, "Report upon the Colorado River of the West," in *Report of the Secretary of War, 1861*, in *Senate Executive Document*, Thirty-sixth Congress, First Session (Washington, D.C.: Government Printing Office, 1861).

moving into former Indian lands. This included settlements of Mormons in San Bernardino, Yucaipa, and other inland areas where settlers found fine farming and grazing lands. White Americans traveled through the desert and mountain passes of Cahuilla, Kumeyaay, Kwaaymii, and Luiseño country, invading Native villages and bringing sickness. Emigrants and their animals destroyed native plants and animals, causing food shortages. The mere presence of whites posed a threat to Indian people who knew that white resettlement of their lands would have a negative impact on their lives.

The Chemehuevi learned from the Cahuilla three distinct views about the American invasion. Most Indians, regardless of their opinion, regretted the invasion and settlement of non-Natives in California but felt relatively powerless to check the flow of whites. Other Indians, led by Cahuilla leader Juan Antonío, believed that the best strategy was coexistence and cooperation with whites. They felt the best way to preserve tribal sovereignty and self-determination within traditional leaders and communities included working with the newcomers. Another view held that Native Americans should rise up in a general rebellion against the Americans and drive them from California. Cupeño-Quechan leader Antonío Garra represented the hostile view, and he encouraged the support of Cahuilla, Cupeño, Luiseño, Quechan, Serrano, and others to join him in a grand war against the United States and American settlers. After killing a few whites near Warner Springs, Cahuilla chief Juan Antonío captured Antonío Garra and turned him over to American authorities, who tried and convicted Garra and his associates.[24] American soldiers made Garra dig his own grave before shooting him to death in a cemetery located in Old Town San Diego. Garra remained composed and defiant to the end. He represented Indian leaders throughout Southern California, past and present.[25] Juan Antonío cared little for Americans, but his actions attempted to preserve people and Native sovereignty.

Chemehuevi and other Indians in the region knew of Garra's fate, and many people consider Garra a patriot who resisted American encroachment. The Chemehuevi people never joined the so-called Garra Revolt, but they had no interest in being ruled by white foreigners. They learned that American occupation of California had caused increased tensions between the Cahuilla and the Luiseño. In January 1847, Cahuilla chief Juan Antonío and his followers attacked and killed thirty-eight Luiseño and Cupeño near Temecula, California, creating a serious rift between Cahuilla and Luiseño people.[26] The capture and subsequent execution of Antonío Garra added to intertribal tensions among Native people in Southern California. This same type of uneasiness contributed to the rift between the Mojave and Chemehuevi after 1859, when the U.S. Army forced its way into Mojave and Chemehuevi land. Although the Chemehuevi had to deal with white Americans at Fort Mojave and Fort Yuma as well as miners, merchants, traders, and steamboat crews along the Colorado River, the United States could not keep the Chemehuevi under their thumb.

The Chemehuevi and Mojave traded with white men, and they sometimes worked for steamboat companies or independent miners, cutting wood and providing food for travelers, but initially they had relatively little contact with the white newcomers. Many Indians experienced the market economy for the first time in the 1850s and 1860s, working for wages and trade items rather than living solely by subsistence. Some Chemehuevi and their Southern Paiute brothers and sisters dealt with travelers and traders along the well-established Indian trail—a route whites called the Old Spanish Trail—from New Mexico, Utah, Arizona, Nevada, and California. This ancient road meandered along the Mojave River of eastern California, where the Serrano and Chemehuevi people once had villages. In the past, Spanish troops had captured neophytes for the San Fernando and San Gabriel missions.[27] The Chemehuevi had moved into some of these village sites in the Mojave Desert, expanding their domain over a vast area above the San Bernardino Mountains. The route along the Mojave River witnessed increased travel by non-Natives during the 1850s.

Not long after the United States built Fort Mojave, tensions increased considerably between the Chemehuevi and the Mojave. In addition to the difficulties brought to the area by the U.S. Army, new conflicts developed from both tribes' interaction with white miners, traders, freighters, and soldiers. After Joseph Ives's expedition, steamboats began moving up and down the Colorado River, bringing miners, soldiers, settlers, travelers, and traders into Chemehuevi and Mojave countries. In fact, the Colorado Steam Navigation Company established a port town called Ehrenberg on the eastern side of the Colorado River near Chemehuevi villages, located near Ehrenberg and the Palo Verde Valley of California.[28] The Army built Fort Mojave above the present-day site of Needles, California, and with the new institution came whiskey peddlers, freighters, and unscrupulous traders. Some miners—particularly those seasoned by years of mining in the Cascade and Sierra Nevada Mountains of western California—brought with them a deep racial hatred of indigenous people. This development further racialized conditions in California. In northern and central California, miners had murdered or kidnapped thousands of Native men, women, and children in a terrible genocide that dramatically reduced the number of Native California Indians. Some miners who helped bring about this drastic reduction in Native people moved to the mines of southeastern California and southwestern Arizona, the home of most Chemehuevi people. Miners, traders, soldiers, and settlers brought increased social chaos and racialization, which flowed over into Mojave-Chemehuevi relations.[29]

During the early 1860s some Chemehuevi attacked miners prospecting in the mountains surrounding their country. Chemehuevi warriors also struck freighters, stages, and travelers moving east and west across the desert between central Arizona and San Bernardino, California. Major hostilities between Chemehuevi people and white Americans preceded overt hostilities between the Chemehuevi and Mojave. Chemehuevi and their Paiute relatives struck at whites moving into and through their lands to encourage the invaders to leave.

The Chemehuevi rightfully feared Americans would claim Indian lands and resettle Natives, whether or not tribes agreed to surrender their homelands. This had happened to Cahuilla, Luiseño, Quechan, Serrano, and other California Indians during the 1850s, and in Arizona, whites had taken lands owned by Apache, Maricopa, Navajo, Pima, Tohono O'odham, and other tribes. The Chemehuevi knew that whites would one day want their land as well, and some Chemehuevi reacted by attacking white people.[30]

Chemehuevi living along the Colorado River and Mojave occupying nearby areas generally maintained cordial relations during the eighteenth and nineteenth centuries. Out of necessity, Chemehuevi living along the river were careful not to incite or offend their neighbors. Mojave warriors had earned excellent reputations as great fighters. Other Indians considered Chemehuevi fine fighters as well, but they had developed diplomatic skills, trying to live in peace with other people. For the Mojave, the Chemehuevi villages had served as a buffer between the Mojave and their enemies. If warring parties ventured into the region, they first passed through the Chemehuevi, who fought the invaders and warned the Mojave of the encroaching enemy. However, Chemehuevi people considered the Mojave dangerous foes.[31]

In 1934 anthropologist Richard Van Valkenburgh interviewed a ninety-year-old Chemehuevi elder named Mukewiune. Born in 1844 near El Dorado Canyon fifteen years before the U.S. Army built Fort Mojave, Mukewiune and her son, George Snyder, provided Van Valkenburgh a detailed story of Chemehuevi destroying the Turat Aiyet, or Land Mojave, living west of the Chemehuevi in the eastern Mojave Desert, near Old Woman Mountain.[32] Mukewiune was emphatic that the Mojave "had always been the foes of her people, and had been removed from Parker in 1934 'because there were too many Aiyet [Mojave] around.'" She traced the origin of her racialized hatred of the Mojave, whom she considered not "good at mountain fighting," to hiring "Yavapai to do their fighting." As a young child, Mukewiune, her sister, and her family had been attacked by a Yavapai war party that had killed Mukewiune's sister.[33]

Angered at the Mojave who had enlisted the Yavapai, the Chemehuevi sought revenge against the vulnerable Desert Mojave. According to Mukewiune's son, George Snyder, he heard the following account from his mother, who had heard it from her grandmother. During the 1770s or 1780s, Chemehuevi warriors had exterminated the Turat Aiyet, or Land Mojave. In 1934, Mukewiune reported, "there are none of them now. Our people killed them all off. They lived from the New York Mountains to near the sinks of the Mojave River. They spoke almost like the River Mohave, and burned their dead, but wore sheepskin, and lived like the Chemehuevi."[34] Most of the Land Mojave "lived below Danby, in the Old Woman Mountains." Mukewiune's grandmother had reported that the struggle between the Land Mojave and the Chemehuevi began when a group of "Chemehuevi men were out hunting mountain sheep in the mountains that are just east of Goffs [eastern California in the Mojave Desert]." While the men hunted, they heard a loud cry from a woman who had climbed a great volcanic butte to sound the alarm. When the men rushed toward her, they called out asking what was wrong. The woman explained that the women, children, and elders had been attacked by Land Mojave. "The Land Mohave," she said, "have come to our camp and have stolen women and killed children." She also reported that Land Mojave warriors had taken the wife of a chief, a woman who was pregnant with their first child.[35]

The hunting party and the woman rushed back to their village. The woman had reported accurately. After holding a brief council, the men "decided to go right after the Land Mohave."[36] Chemehuevi warriors "caught up with them at their camp," where they found that the Mojave were "roasting the head-man's wife over the fire." According to Mukewiune's account, the Mojave had roasted the woman and her unborn child alive and sang victoriously at the time the Chemehuevi arrived. "They're done, they're done," sang the Land Mojave, referring to the woman and her unborn child. According to the Chemehuevi account, the Land Mojave had cut "some of the woman's flesh" and were "try-ing to eat some" of it, perhaps in a ritual manner to defile the Chemehuevi.[37] There is no mention that the Mojave actually consumed any part of the woman, but Chemehuevi warriors did not wait to see. In a flash they rushed into com-bat. "There was a short fight, and the Land Mohave fled" the battlefield.[38] The Chemehuevi did not break off the fight but chased their enemies to "a spring in the mountains near Goffs." Unable to run any farther, the Mojave drank from the spring and turned to face their enemy. They stood in a single line, backs to the spring. The Chemehuevi had run a long distance and needed water, so the Mojave stood their ground, hoping to prevent the Chemehuevi from drinking. When the Chemehuevi reached the Mojave, the chief who had lost his wife gave the order to "keep going," so the Chemehuevi attacked the Mojave again. In close combat, the Chemehuevi used their powerful mesquite and mountain sheep horn bows before using their own war clubs in fierce hand-to-hand com-bat, scattering "the Land Mohave again."[39]

The Land Mojave, refreshed from drinking at the spring, raced south on foot toward a cave near Danby, California. The Mojave took refuge inside the cave, believing that the Chemehuevi would give up the chase. They were wrong.

Chemehuevi warriors raced after the Mojave and tracked them to the cave. They likely hurled insults at their enemies as they gathered wood, brush, and grasses with the intent of smoking Mojave warriors from the cave. When the Land Mojave refused to come out, the Chemehuevi lit the brush, causing a great deal of smoke inside the cave. "Some never came out," according to Mukewiune and her son, George Snyder, and those Mojave died of smoke inhalation. When the others came out, the Chemehuevi took no prisoners, killing every one of the Land Mojave in this party. Not satisfied with this revenge, the Chemehuevi chief, whose name was not provided by Van Valkenburgh's consultants, ordered his men to "get rid of all the Land Mohave."[40] The Chemehuevi living in the eastern Mojave Desert decided on a war of extermination against all Land Mojave, and to this end, they began a well-planned, systematic hunt of Mojave, killing them wherever they found them. The Chemehuevi killed men, women, and children "from the Turtle Range to Clark's Mountain."[41]

Several Land Mojave lived near Old Woman Mountain approximately forty miles west of the Colorado River, and Chemehuevi fought their last campaigns against Land Mojave in the Old Woman Range, a special landscape to the Mojave and Chemehuevi and the site of a sacred cave filled with many fine painted pictographs. The Chemehuevi believed Little People had created the pictographs long ago.[42] In retaliation against the Mojave, Chemehuevi warriors "cleaned out the whole works," killing every Land Mojave except a leader named Tavavits, who "made a short cut across the desert from the Old Woman Mountains to the Stepladder Mountains, traveling from there to the River Mojave villages near Needles. Chemehuevi warriors nearly caught him, but the agile Mojave outran them. Tavavits escaped. The Chemehuevi killed Land Mojave and expanded onto their former homeland, particularly in the area of Old Woman Mountain, where Chemehucvi families established a village.[43]

Sometime between 1835 and 1850, Mojave living along the Colorado River decided to strike Chemehuevi villages (and perhaps their Serrano neighbors) living west of the river in villages near Newberry Springs north of the San Bernardino Mountains. According to Chemehuevi consultant Julian Booth, Mojave marched west across the desert and attacked. Chemehuevi people mustered a force to fight them, but they lost the battle. The Mojave reportedly killed every Chemehuevi warrior except Moha, who was taken back to the river and ultimately married Chigquata. On another occasion, River Mojave attacked Chemehuevi living near Needles, but like the Mojave attack at Newberry Springs, no one left accounts of the cause of the conflict. Moreover, contemporary members of the Twenty-Nine Palms Band of Chemehuevi have no memory of the causes of these conflicts, except to agree that the Mojave became enemies of Chemehuevi people, especially after the arrival of white Americans.[44] On yet another occasion, a Mojave war party led by a Yavapai, often identified as an Apache, attacked Chemehuevi living in Chemehuevi Valley. A Chemehuevi scout and lookout named Loco Tom watched as Mojave approached, concealing himself in rocks on the side of a mountain. He had time to spread the alarm, and Chemehuevi warriors prepared for war. Knowing the terrain of their precious valley, the Chemehuevi set up an ambush at the mouth of Chemehuevi Valley. As Mojave entered the valley, the Chemehuevi set their trap, attacked, and defeated the Mojave warriors, killing several enemies.[45] The Chemehuevi generally enjoyed a positive relationship with most neighboring Indians, including the Mojave and the Hualapai of west-central Arizona. Now and then during the nineteenth century, Hualapai lived temporarily along the Colorado River in close proximity with bands of Chemehuevi. However, on at least one occasion, Chemehuevi "fought Walapai near the Cord Ranch." Chemehuevi warriors lost the conflict and the lives of twenty to thirty men, a huge kill count for the day and a drain on the small Chemehuevi population of approximately fifteen hundred people.[46]

During the late 1850s, the Chemehuevi may have contributed to tensions between themselves and the Mojave by poking fun at their neighbors for losing the fight against the U.S. Army and allowing soldiers to live at Fort Mojave. No concrete evidence exists to support the theory, but Chemehuevi may have teased Mojave for permitting miners, freighters, and traders to travel through their homelands.[47] Historically, the Chemehuevi had earned a reputation for teasing and joking, and they may have made the Mojave the butt of their stories, perhaps contributing to hostilities. For their part, the Mojave may have contributed to the growing tensions between themselves and the Chemehuevi. Since the late 1820s, the Mojave had lived in relative peace with the Chemehuevi, who had served as a human buffer to potential Mojave enemies. Mojave warriors could have tired of Chemehuevi neighbors and relations. After the arrival of American troops, the Mojave may have decided to assert their position as the dominant and more numerous tribe in the region. The Chemehuevi had established positive relations with Americans. It is plausible that the Mojave decided to reestablish themselves as the central indigenous power along the Colorado River above the Quechan. In part, the war resulted from white presence and power in the area that harmed the Mojave. Since the great Mojave nation with its renowned warriors could not challenge the United States, perhaps they directed their ill will toward the ever-growing and expanding

Chemehuevi people. In any case, in the 1860s war broke out between Mojave and Chemehuevi people, which led to the creation of a separate Chemehuevi group that became the Twenty-Nine Palms Tribe.

Within the Indian communities of the Colorado River, many interpretations of the war's causation exist today. Chemehuevi Matthew Hanks Leivas has argued that the war began when Mojave killed some innocent Chemehuevi, while Chemehuevi elder Joe Benitez stated that he is not certain who drew the first blood.[48] Other contemporary accounts exist through oral histories about the origin of the conflict, but in 1903 anthropologist Alfred L. Kroeber provided an account that offers a Mojave view of the war. In 1973 coauthors Clifton Kroeber and Alfred Kroeber produced an outstanding work on the Chemehuevi-Mojave War, although most of the testimony is one-sided from Mojave consultants. In 1903 a Mojave named Chooksa homar narrated several stories about the Mojave and Chemehuevi wars of the 1860s to Kroeber through another Mojave named Quichnailk, or Jack Jones Sr. Kroeber considered Quichnailk an extremely reliable interpreter who represented the words and story of Chooksa homar with great accuracy. Included in Chooksa homar's fascinating accounts is a discussion of the Mojave War with Chemehuevi between 1864 and 1867. Chooksa homar provides a contemporary account and an early Mojave perspective of events during the war. The accounts offer insight into some of the conflict.[49]

Chemehuevi of the Twenty-Nine Palms Tribe find the Chemehuevi-Mojave War significant for many reasons, since the two groups had lived in relative peace for several years and had learned from each other's culture and language. More important, the war caused conservative Chemehuevi people to leave their villages along the Colorado River and establish a permanent life for themselves in the Mojave Desert. At the same time of the conflict, Congress created the Colorado River Indian Reservation and expected Mojave and Chemehuevi people to live together in peace on the reservation. The Chemehuevi disliked the idea of removal to a reservation controlled by white agents from the United States. Some Chemehuevi refused the reservation and moved away to rule themselves. For many generations Chemehuevi people had lived autonomously in the deserts and mountains on both sides of the Colorado River, traveling freely to other Native communities to hunt, gather, and trade. The Chemehuevi intimately knew the Mojave Desert, including important hunting areas, gathering places, sacred caves, and precious water holes. Several Chemehuevi people owned hunting songs and lived near the life-giving springs of the Mojave Desert, raising crops. However, after the Chemehuevi-Mojave War, other Chemehuevi people moved permanently to village sites in the Mojave Desert. The war caused a serious break in Mojave-Chemehuevi relations that remains a reality in the social, political, and cultural confluence of the two peoples in the twenty-first century. Neither the Chemehuevi nor the Mojave can point to any single, definitive cause of the difficulties, but they both agree that the war brought death, destruction, and diaspora that forever changed their histories and relationships.

Chooksa homar suggested that war began because "the Chemehuevi turned bad" and "they thought they could whip" the Mojave.[50] Such a statement might indicate that the Chemehuevi had verbally harassed the Mojave. They may have challenged the Mojave in other ways, but if so, they had taunted dangerous people with excellent warriors, skilled at destroying Native American opponents and taking scalps. The Chemehuevi had witnessed this firsthand when "the Mohave and the Yuma drove the remnants of the Halchidhoma and Kohuana eastward into the Pima villages on the middle Gila."[51] The Chemehuevi people well knew that the Mojave had turned against the Halchidhoma, so it would have been dangerous for the Chemehuevi to challenge the Mojave through overt military action. Still, this is exactly what Chooksa homar told Kroeber: the Chemehuevi had attacked and killed a Mojave woman. This was a Mojave interpretation about the origin of the war. No comparable Chemehuevi account exists. According to Chooksa homar, two Chemehuevi men visited a Mojave village where they found an unarmed woman processing seeds. Without provocation, the Mojave asserted, the Chemehuevi murdered her. When her husband learned of the death, he reportedly told the commander of Fort Mojave about the murder and the officer told the Mojave to pursue the Chemehuevi.[52]

The Mojave husband had little reason to complain to the officer at Fort Mojave or ask permission, because Mojave warriors had acted voluntarily against their enemies for hundreds of years without seeking a foreigner's permission. The Mojave had been (and continue to be) sovereign people, and they looked no further than their own authority to act. The man may have gone to Fort Mojave for Native help or trade items, necessary for his manhunt. Perhaps he mentioned the incident to the soldiers, but for a warrior to seek permission seems unlikely, except to inform the soldier that Mojave warriors would act in concert against the Chemehuevi, not the soldiers. If he did, a major change had occurred within the Mojave community. Perhaps the interpreter misunderstood the conversation. More significant, the officer reportedly told the Mojave to run down the culprits. This may have been the case, since officers of the U.S. Army sometimes encouraged conflicts between different indigenous groups as a strategy to destabilize Native American people. In this way Indians kept busy killing each other rather than Americans, making it easier for representatives of the United States to control Indian people and their lands. According to Chooksa homar, not long after the woman's death, a Mojave killed a Chemehuevi man who "came alone" into the villages.[53]

This may or may not have been in retaliation of the woman's death, although Chooksa homar is not clear about this. Chooksa homar stated that after this death, Mojave leader Aratêve (Yartav or Irataba) summoned one hundred warriors to accompany him to the Chemehuevi villages on Cottonwood Island to attack the unsuspecting people living there in the middle of the Colorado River. The Chemehuevi learned of the impending attack and left the village. By the time the Mojave war party reached the island, the Chemehuevi had moved into the mountains. Most likely, the Chemehuevi traveled into the desert mountains to prepare for war against their former friends. Clearly, for an entire village to vacate, the people had to have had warning, but they took sufficient goods and weapons to fight. The Chemehuevi had good reason to leave their homes. Rumors, threats, and suggestions of war between the two peoples swirled about the entire region.[54]

Aratêve and his men pursued the Chemehuevi into the mountains, while at the same time a party of Mojave warriors attacked Chemehuevi living in Chemehuevi Valley on the west side of the Colorado River. When the Mojave found a group of Chemehuevi living in the mountains north of Fort Mojave, they pretended to come in peace. Dressed in "a tasseled suit and a big hat he had got in Washington," Aratêve told the Chemehuevi that he had no interest in fighting, only friendship. Apparently the Chemehuevi leadership did not believe him. They already knew that hostilities had commenced. As Aratêve turned to leave, a Chemehuevi warrior fired an arrow at him. A fight ensued in the north, and the Mojave killed one Chemehuevi. This was Chooksa homar's version of the fight. He also reported that while Mojave warriors tracked the Chemehuevi north of the fort, another group of Mojave operated south of the post on the California side of the river near Palo Verde Valley, not far from present-day Blythe, California. In the south, the Mojave found the Chemehuevi had left the Chemehuevi Valley and moved into the mountains. Like their relatives to the north, Chemehuevi from the valley had learned that the two people had initiated a general war, so they had left their homes, seeking refuge in their mountain retreats. A Mojave war party followed the Chemehuevi and fought a battle with them. According the Chooksa homar, Chemehuevi warriors killed one Mojave. Therefore, if Chooksa homar's version of the opening events of the war is correct, both sides suffered the death of one warrior, but the war had just begun and already an innocent Mojave woman had died.[55]

Van Valkenburgh provided a Chemehuevi account of the Chemehuevi war with the Mojave, one that is suggestive of a possible causation for the conflict between the two peoples. Chemehuevi elder Mukewiune provided another account of Chemehuevi fighting Mojave. She told Van Valkenburgh that two Chemehuevi women had left their homes near Union Gap above Fort Mojave to gather willow for making baskets near the site of Hardyville. A group of Mojave captured the women, abused them, stripped them naked, and impaled them on sharp sticks, leaving them to die slowly. When the Paiute women were absent too long, Warap, the brother of one of the women, traveled south and found them dead, still hanging on the sticks upon which they had been placed. Warap used *umpahapuhup,* or knotted strings, to summon Indians to gather and have a council of war.[56] Chemehuevi runners raced across the Mojave Desert and beyond with the knotted strings, and Paiute Indians as far away as the Monos living north of Bishop, California, responded to the call. Warap met representatives from many bands of Paiute near the Ivanpah Mountains, and they planned on a course of war. At the announcement of war, the Paiute shot bullets and arrows into the air. One of the arrows struck a friendly warrior, which was a sign that they should not go to war. Some of the people returned to their homes, but most of them moved forward against the Mojave.[57]

A Chemehuevi war chief named Chacar (the father of Tom Painter) led the Chemehuevi war party down the Colorado River on the west bank until they reached Cottonwood Island. They crossed the river early one morning and continued their journey south on the east bank of the Colorado. According to Mukewiune, the Chemehuevi war party passed within sight of Fort Mojave, and the American soldiers reportedly came out to cheer them on, encouraging the Chemehuevi to kill the Mojave. An advance party of Chemehuevi scouts returned to the main body of warriors, telling them that the Mojave had camped only a few miles away. Chemehuevi scouts reported that the Mojave were "all together, singing, smoking, and dancing . . . getting ready to fight."[58] Apparently the Mojave warriors did not know that the Chemehuevi were so close, because the Chemehuevi warriors made a surprise attack, killing all of the Mojave warriors in that party. Some of the Chemehuevi wanted to continue their campaign, moving south to strike other villages, but other warriors desired to go home. The Chemehuevi agreed that they would end the fighting for now and come back another day, but Mukewiune reported that although "they went planning to come back later, . . . they never got together again."[59]

After these brief but deadly encounters, most of the outright fighting ended for a short time. Still, tensions remained high between Chemehuevi and Mojave people, and some Chemehuevi refused to return to their villages near the

Several Chemehuevi people lived in villages located on Cottonwood Island in the middle of the Colorado River above present-day Needles, California. In 1858, Heinrich Bauduin Möllhausen made this pen and ink sketch of Chemehuevi setting up a poled structure in the river.

From Lieutenant Joseph Christmas Ives, "Report upon the Colorado River of the West," in *Report of the Secretary of War, 1861*, in *Senate Executive Document*, Thirty-sixth Congress, First Session (Washington, D.C.: Government Printing Office, 1861).

Colorado River. During the conflict the Chemehuevi who had once lived peacefully on Cottonwood Island, along the Bill Williams River, south of the Mojave in Palo Verde Valley, and in Chemehuevi Valley, left the river region, moving to villages and camps occupied by their relatives living in the Mojave Desert of Arizona, California, and Nevada. They also moved into the nearby mountains, where they had long hunted and had established temporary camps. The Chemehuevi knew where to find water in the mountains and desert springs, so they relocated to familiar lands along the river to live in the heart of the desert. However, once the fighting died down, some Chemehuevi returned to their former villages along the Colorado River but carefully guarded their people against renewed attacks. Some of the most conservative Chemehuevi, perhaps the most hostile of the various bands, remained in the deserts and mountains away from the river. Some Chemehuevi even moved into the Coachella Valley to live with and near Cahuilla Indians. This was clearly the case for those of the large Mike family, who had once inhabited and worked in the Coachella Valley but who made a new home for themselves at the Oasis of Mara—commonly called Twenty-Nine Palms.[60]

According to Chooksa homar, the relationship between the Mojave and Chemehuevi remained peaceful until 1866, when a Chemehuevi leader named Oenyô-hiv'auve visited Fort Mojave to tell his Mojave neighbors and the soldiers that his people wanted peace. The Chemehuevi leader lied, if the Mojave chronicler Chooksa homar's report is accurate, and returned to his people to gather a force bent on attacking the Mojave. Two months later, Chemehuevi attacked the Mojave villages near present-day Topock, Arizona, south of Needles. However, it is unclear which leader led the Chemehuevi warriors, or if the same Chemehuevi who had professed peace was involved. Chooksa homar thought there was a connection, but the leadership of the hostile Chemehuevi is unclear. During the Battle of Topock, Chemehuevi warriors stood and fought the Mojave, killing two men and two women as well as cutting a portion of scalps from the heads of two Mojave boys while they were still alive. The fight continued in the surrounding area, and the Chemehuevi won the battle.[61]

In 1867 some Chemehuevi people moved back to their homes in the Chemehuevi Valley and Palo Verde Valley near present-day Blythe, California, perhaps believing the Mojave no longer threatened their security. Perhaps the Chemehuevi believed themselves strong enough to resist a Mojave attack. The Chemehuevi people maintained caution, but Mojave detected them living along the Colorado River and decided to make a reconnaissance of the valley. Two Mojave visited one group of Chemehuevi, saying they desired peace. According to Chooksa homar, Mojave used the occasion to determine the strength of those Chemehuevi who had returned. Not long after this visit, a party of Mojave attacked Chemehuevi living in Chemehuevi Valley on the California side of the Colorado River. The Mojave reached "the Chemehuevi houses at daylight" and surprised the people living there. Several Chemehuevi had decided to live in the valley during the daytime, but each night they retreated to nearby mountains to sleep away from their villages. As a result, Mojave did not hurt those Chemehuevi who had taken precaution, but those who remained in the village at night suffered a fatal attack. The Mojave managed to kill four Chemehuevi men and capture an elderly woman and a child. They also captured a young woman, "but the younger woman was angry, refused to come along, bit and kicked when they took her by the hand, threw sand and sticks." So the Mojave killed her.[62]

As the *Explorer* steamed north of the Bill Williams River, the explorers passed Chemehuevi Valley on the California side of the Colorado River. Just north of the valley, the Chemehuevi Mountains jut up into the sky, offering a stunning scene. Heinrich Bauduin Möllhausen sketched Grand Mesa of the Chemehuevi Valley.

Notice the beaver on a log in the river. From Lieutenant Joseph Christmas Ives, "Report upon the Colorado River of the West," in *Report of the Secretary of War, 1861,* in *Senate Executive Document,* Thirty-sixth Congress, First Session (Washington, D.C.: Government Printing Office, 1861).

Still another group of Chemehuevi people left Chemehuevi Valley and moved south to a place on the California side of the river, adjacent to present-day Parker, Arizona. Apaily-kmaO'e led this band of Chemehuevi people. The Chemehuevi had lived in the area before but had abandoned their village sites because of the war. Not far away on the Arizona side of the river lived a Mojave leader named Itsiyêre-Oume, who told his people that the "Chemehuevi think they only are men. Others are men too." He proclaimed himself a warrior and promised to attack the Chemehuevi.[63] For the Mojave to become warriors, they had to dream of warrior power, and failure in battle would indicate the leader had not actually experienced the dream. This account does not reveal whether the young man had dreamed his war power. The Mojave moved across the Colorado River to the Chemehuevi village, and the Chemehuevi learned of their approach. Rather than retreating to safety, Chemehuevi warriors prepared to

fight. The Mojave approached the village as Chemehuevi warriors armed and
positioned themselves for battle.

Chemehuevi often fought like Apache warriors rather than Mojave people,
who stood and fought hand to hand. As the attack unfolded, Chemehuevi took
position in the rocks between their village and the Mojave. The Chemehuevi
fought a frontal assault before backing up into the mountains to take advantage of the terrain. According to Chooksa homar, the Mojave killed four or five
Chemehuevi, but he did not record whether any Mojave died in the conflict.
The Indians fought a fierce battle with bows, arrows, lances, and war clubs. The
Mojave leader and Chemehuevi leader both received arrow wounds, but they
refused to stop fighting. The battle eventually ended in a draw after both sides
became exhausted. The Chemehuevi returned to their village and the Mojave
took boats east across the Colorado River to their village. Both Chemehuevi
and Mojave continued the larger war but on different fronts.[64] The conflict between the two tribes continued throughout the 1860s and deep into the 1870s.
Tensions between the two people still exist today, and elders remember the
Chemehuevi-Mojave War as a "recent" event. The struggle was a watershed in
the history of the Twenty-Nine Palms Tribe. The conflict led to the voluntary
removal of some Chemehuevi families west of the Oasis of Mara, where they
resettled an old Serrano village site.

The conflict between the Chemehuevi and the Mojave was not the only
source of irritation for the Chemehuevi and their Southern Paiute neighbors.
The Chemehuevi people had to contend with the movement of U.S. Army troops
that crisscrossed their lands in east-west and north-south directions. Sometimes the interaction between the troops and Indians proved satisfactory for
both people, but other times trouble arose in varying degrees. Superintendents
of the Office of Indian Affairs wanted the Chemehuevi to move to the newly created Colorado River Indian Reservation. Few Chemehuevi wanted to surrender
to life on a reservation, and the people of Twenty-Nine Palms opposed living on
the reservation, preferring to reside in the desert. In addition, the Chemehuevi
and other Southern Paiute had to contend with civilian merchants, traders, and
freighters. In July 1870, Captain W. R. Johnson hauled supplies in a number
of wagons from present-day Kingman, Arizona, to Hardyville on the Colorado
River, where he abandoned his "wagons and rigged up a pack train." On his way
to Las Vegas, Nevada, Johnson encountered Indians who killed two of his cattle
for food. He negotiated a settlement with a chief, receiving eighteen dollars for
the two animals, but he reported having "more trouble with Pahutes" along the
trail.[65] Several Chemehuevi and Southern Paiute groups had to contend with

white people traveling over their homelands, allowing their animals to graze on Indian resources and introducing many changes, including disease. Like other Indians, the Chemehuevi people felt the pressure of white expansion and Mojave attacks.

In 1871 a group of Southern Paiute in Death Valley met Lieutenant Daniel W. Lockwood, who was on his way to Tucson, Arizona. In the desert he met "quite a number" of Chemehuevi and other Southern Paiute numbering about two hundred who moved in a seasonal round gathering foods while also cultivating the soil.[66] Lieutenant D. A. Lyle made a similar observation about other Southern Paiute, noting that they had "small patches of ground here which they irrigate and cultivate during the seasons." Specifically, Lyle commented that the Indians near "Pah-rimp Valley, and around Cottonwood and Las Vegas, raise . . . corn, melons, squashes, and gather large quantities of wild grapes." He made no mention of hostilities, although American soldiers, freighters, miners, and settlers continually feared the Southern Paiute, particularly the Chemehuevi, who were skilled trackers and warriors. During the 1870s white people recorded only one disturbing altercation that involved a Chemehuevi, and this event touched the life of a single Chemehuevi rather than a large number of the people.[67]

On September 28, 1872, the *Arizona Citizen* reported an Indian attack on a stagecoach near Wickenburg, Arizona. The stage heading to California carried the United States Mail, employees, as well as Frederick Loring, Frederick Shohomm, P. M. Hamel, W. G. Salmon, C. S. Adams, William Kruger, and Mollie Shepard. "Apache-Mojave" attacked the stage, pinning down the driver and passengers. Most likely these Apache-Mojave were Yavapai, Yuman-speaking peoples of central Arizona who had adopted the ways of the Apache and intermarried with the Apache people at San Carlos, White Mountain, Camp Verde, and others. Kruger and Shepard managed to escape on horseback, although the Indians pursued them a short while. The Indians killed the others, and the Army chased the raiders, finally confronting some of the attackers. One of the raiders was "Chemahueva Jim," who reportedly was "a very bad Indian, who speaks English." Chemahueva Jim could not be coaxed into a council with whites, but some of the others did and died as a result.[68]

Nothing further is known of Chemahueva Jim and his exploits, although his attack of the stage may have been induced by a general hatred of white men who had rapidly invaded Indian Country, offering a real threat to Native peoples throughout California and the Southwest. Chemehuevi like Jim had reacted to the white invasion and their troubles with the Mojave in many different ways. Some of them left the river for good, establishing themselves as Desert Chemehuevi. Others returned to the river regions to live but kept their distance from the Mojave unless the government forced them to interact with Mojave living at Fort Mojave or the newly created Colorado River Indian Reservation, near Parker, Arizona. To some degree, the Chemehuevi, always an adaptive people, acculturated aspects of white culture. Many Chemehuevi changed their dress, preferring to wear clothing like whites, cowboy hats, boots, and belts. Many Chemehuevi adopted firearms, using guns and rifles effectively. They bought guns and ammunition with cash money earned from wage labor. Chemehuevi rather quickly became part of the market economy, often taking part-time jobs with the steamboat companies, miners, freighters, and farmers in the Coachella Valley and Banning Pass.[69] Although they acculturated in these ways, they did not assimilate into white society. In 1872, Indian agent G. W. Ingalls of the Southern Nevada Agency wrote that the government had provided little "in the way of education or civilization" to the Southern Paiute, including "the Chimewawas, in Arizona," and in 1873, special agent John G. Ames failed to mention Chemehuevi at all when he surveyed the condition of Indians within the newly formed Mission Indian Agency, which included Chemehuevi at Twenty-Nine Palms. More than likely, Ames had failed to travel to Twenty-Nine Palms or to the Colorado River to visit the Chemehuevi people, who were considered part of his agency.[70]

Written records during the remainder of the 1870s provide little evidence of overt resistance by the Chemehuevi to white encroachment, but like so many Indian people, they harbored resentment against white soldiers, traders, miners, and settlers. They resented American agents working for the Office of Indian Affairs and American officers of the U.S. Army. Still, the Chemehuevi people largely checked their aggression against the United States in the 1870s, but the next decade opened with a conflict between the two nations. In 1880, Colonel O. B. Wilcox, the commander of the Military Department of Arizona, remarked in his report that a conflict had "occurred among the Chimejuevis, which threatened to become serious."[71] Wilcox referred to an unfortunate event on the Colorado River involving the Chemehuevi that nearly erupted into full-scale war and had implications far beyond that of the principals involved in the controversy. On the surface the event along the Colorado River involved only a few hostile Chemehuevi and a white man, but a detailed look by anthropologist and scholar George Roth suggests something much deeper.

By 1880 the Chemehuevi people lived once again in Palo Verde Valley of the Colorado River, near present-day Blythe, California, some miles south of the Colorado River Indian Reservation. This group of Chemehuevi lived in peace with the Mojave who resided north of them on the Colorado River and with a few white people settling in the region. However, they lived off the reservation and worked for an engineer named Oliver P. Calloway, who created hostility among several Chemehuevi. In partnership with Thomas Blythe of the Colorado River Irrigation Company, in 1875 Calloway and Blythe filed a claim for forty thousand acres using the Swamp Act as their mechanism to obtain the land. Calloway and Blythe claimed Chemehuevi land and their village sites. Between 1877 and 1880, Calloway constructed an irrigation canal in the heart of Chemehuevi country to support a large-scale agricultural enterprise. Approximately twelve Chemehuevi and a few Mojave worked on the project. At one point over the years, some unspecified disturbance caused Calloway to ask the U.S. Army for military support, but generally the Indians and engineer worked well together. Agents and superintendents of the Office of Indian Affairs approved of Chemehuevi living off the reservation to work for non-Indians as laborers and thus join in the market economy. But Calloway created his own trouble with the Chemehuevi, since many Indians believed he had fathered a child by a Chemehuevi woman but would not own up to his actions. This possibly strained relations for a time.[72]

According to Chemehuevi and Mojave accounts, the struggle erupted into a major event when an unnamed mixed-blood Chemehuevi harassed a full-blood Chemehuevi named Aapanapih (White Clay Lightening Flash), some say by knocking a cigarette from his mouth. The full-blood hit the boy, and Calloway—who may have been the boy's father—intervened to help the boy by shooting the Chemehuevi. At that point a Chemehuevi named Big Bill Williams and another Chemehuevi man stabbed Calloway to death. Indian recollections make no mention of alcohol use, but white accounts state that the Chemehuevi men had been drinking. These white accounts further claimed that a few intoxicated Chemehuevi men had reportedly tried to enter Calloway's home, and Calloway shot and killed Aapanapih, who was the son of a Chemehuevi chief living in the Palo Verde Valley. The other Chemehuevi, Big Bill Williams, stabbed Calloway, assisted by an unidentified Chemehuevi man. An investor in the irrigation business, John H. West, two Mojave laborers, and an agency employer named Porter reportedly witnessed Calloway's killing. After the violence, the Chemehuevi men reportedly ransacked Calloway's house, stole several items (including guns and ammunition), and burned their own homes in the Palo Verde Valley before retreating north to the Turtle Mountains, where they set up camp near Mopah Springs and Mopah Peak in the Turtle Mountains of eastern California.[73]

Learning of the killings and the trouble in the Palo Verde Valley, the Chemehuevi living in Chemehuevi Valley, California, and those residing on the Arizona side of the river also moved west into the mountains and the desert. The Chemehuevi defiantly held the mountain lair, sending a message to threaten every white person living along the river. Through their runners, these Chemehuevi made it clear that the agency was particularly vulnerable to attack if soldiers challenged them. Indian agent Henry R. Mallory urged whites not to cross to the west bank of the river because it was not safe, and the U.S. Army established a special military district in the area under Colonel Redwood Price while summoning soldiers from Fort Mojave, Fort Yuma, Fort Whipple (Prescott, Arizona), and the Presidio of San Diego. When a Mojave peace delegation under Asuket visited the Chemehuevi, they returned with word "that the agency would be attacked that night by the Chim-e-hue-vas if soldiers were sent up after them."[74]

Agents and soldiers estimated that the Chemehuevi could muster between 80 and 150 warriors as well as women who were "good fighters."[75] Perhaps more important to Chemehuevi security, warriors occupied a natural fortress in the mountains that they knew intimately. From the high ground in the Turtle Mountains, the Chemehuevi could hold off a superior military force for some time, especially with the number of Winchester and Spencer rifles the warriors had accumulated, along with a large quantity of ammunition. Colonel Price and Agent Mallory worked cooperatively to negotiate a peace. Agent Mallory sent Settuma, a prominent Mojave leader, to arrange a peace council with sixteen Chemehuevi warriors at the agency, and although they agreed to meet, they refused to surrender the two men accused of killing Calloway. The two parties had a conference at the agency, which provided both parties an opportunity to express their points of view.

To their credit, neither Price nor Mallory attempted to detain any of the Chemehuevi, unlike other Americans like Lieutenant Bascom, who treacherously held Indian leaders after luring them into their camps on the pretense of peace talks. The council concluded with no concrete results and the Chemehuevi left the agency, stopping by the headquarters of the irrigation project to ask for their jobs back. Officials there refused to hire them so long as the two killers remained at large. This attempt at obtaining their former employment may have had a touch of Chemehuevi humor attached to it, but it also indicates that the Chemehuevi men had suffered from their exile. They needed cash money to buy the items they had become increasingly dependent on. They likely needed food, clothing, blankets, and other goods they had grown to enjoy as a result of their labor and participation in the market economy. Because of the Calloway affair, many Chemehuevi had abandoned their supplies as well as their new way of life—a transition from their traditional cultural and economic ways to day labor, trade, and purchases of material goods from non-Indians. They had had to flee their homes rapidly, and they had had little time to hunt, gather, or trade for food necessary to sustain the people. The conflict had cut them off from both their traditional and new economies.[76]

In the 1860s and 1870s the Office of Indian Affairs tried to force the Chemehuevi to live on the Colorado River Indian Reservation. Mojave Indians controlled the reservation. Some Chemehuevi moved onto the reservation. Several more Chemehuevi drifted off the reservation, traveling west across the river to Chemehuevi Valley, south to Blythe or Ehrenberg, or moved east along the Bill Williams River. Indian agents knew the Chemehuevi had reestablished themselves in the Chemehuevi Valley, and for the most part allowed them to remain across the river where they could raise their own crops and fend for themselves—away from white people and their Mojave neighbors. This saved the Army and agency time and money, always a significant consideration for federal officials working in Indian Country. During the late nineteenth and early twentieth centuries, Chemehuevi lived on and off the reservation, just as they do today. In addition, they moved about the Colorado River—including the Palo Verde and Blythe areas—and west to the Coachella Valley and Banning Pass, where they found employment as cowboys, freighters, maids, cooks, and farm workers. However, the Chemehuevi people had no trust lands or reservations of their own. They lived on their own, including those at Twenty-Nine Palms.[77]

Historian George Roth maintained that while some Chemehuevi joined the market economy as laborers and worked in cooperation with many whites, the Mojave did not rapidly adopt "civilian dress" and did not join in the market economy to the same extent as the Chemehuevi. However, the Mojave had a land base recognized by the United States, while the Chemehuevi had no lands of their own recognized by the federal government (although the government wanted them to move onto the Colorado River Reservation with the Mojave). The Chemehuevi did not want to move onto reservations, especially the people of the Twenty-Nine Palms group. The Chemehuevi had to find work to survive economically, apart from government rationing. They seemed more inclined to work away from government agents, traveling great distances on foot to find work on ranches and farms. The Chemehuevi had always been great travelers and fighters. And they continued to use resourceful traits to secure a better standard of living for their families, while holding onto their language, culture, and beliefs. The people acculturated to the extent that they chose to do so, drawing on their personal and tribal sovereignty to deal with a rapidly changing world.

However, they did not assimilate but continued to live as independent people despite losing thousands of acres of rich farmland along the Colorado River Valley as well as the vast and beautiful reaches of the Mojave and Colorado Deserts that had once been their domain.[78]

By the end of the 1880s the Chemehuevi people understood that the white invasion had changed forever their ancient life of farming, hunting, and gathering on their own terms. Non-Indians took control of former Indian lands, and both civilians and military men significantly influenced their lives, attempting to dictate policies through the Departments of War, Interior, and State. Private capital financed farming and ranching enterprises along the Colorado River, taking the most fertile areas and operating businesses that provided more capital for future investments. Non-Indians quickly took control of water resources, knowing that the future of any population living in the Southwest depended on water. The Chemehuevi people lost their landed estates as well as water, mineral, and legal rights. They had no say in the development and use of their former homelands. True, the Mojave claimed all Chemehuevi lands. The Mojave argued that they had only allowed the Chemehuevi to use Mojave land despite the fact the Chemehuevi had an ancient, lengthy association with the river and adjacent lands. The Chemehuevi also held onto their spiritual beliefs, sovereignty, and language. They learned some English and Spanish to survive, but they held onto their culture.

At the end of the 1880s and the beginning of 1890s, some Chemehuevi joined the Ghost Dance and its derivatives. Wovoka, the Ghost Dance Prophet, continued a religious revitalization among the Paiute and Shoshone that had begun in the 1870s. Like his father, Tavivo, before him, Wovoka had a religious experience that transformed his life and those around him. He reported he had passed away to the Land Above, where he met the Creator who told him to return to earth and prepare the people for the day when the world would turn over and Indians would once again live in the old way.[79] "God told him he must go back and tell his people they must be good and love one another, have no quarreling, and live in peace with the whites; they must work, and not lie or steal; that they must put away all the old practices that savored of war." The people would one day "be reunited with their friends in this other world, where there would be no more death or sickness or old age." The Paiute Prophet promised this in accordance with knowledge he had gained during his visit with the Creator, provided the people obeyed the instructions of the Almighty and Wovoka. The Creator instructed Wovoka to do "the dance which he was commanded to bring back to his people"—a dance to be held "for five consecutive days each time" so that the people "would secure this happiness to themselves and hasten the event."[80] Wovoka taught the people to dance and sing five consecutive nights, which caused them to become weak and appear ghostly as they danced all night long.

Some Chemehuevi people joined the Ghost Dance religion, praying for a better day for Indian people. When these Chemehuevi first heard of Wovoka's revelations, "they sent delegates to the messiah and in all probability took up the Ghost dance." In fact, several Southern Paiute and Chemehuevi groups joined in the religion. Contemporary people still practice the Circle Dance, which derives from the Ghost Dance. Several principles of the Ghost Dance continue today among some Chemehuevi people. American explorer John Wesley Powell noted: "The Chemehuevi, being a branch of the Paiute and in constant communication with them, undoubtedly had the dance and the doctrine."[81] Some Chemehuevi people participated in the Ghost Dance but others held onto old beliefs. According to Dean Mike, chair of the Twenty-Nine Palms Band of Mission Indians, his great-grandfather, William Mike, opposed the Ghost Dance as nontraditional. William Mike wanted to continue the old religion and did not want his people practicing new religion.[82]

The leader of the Chemehuevi at Twenty-Nine Palms, William Mike, was of "an old time mind" and he held onto the old ways of the Chemehuevi people, not the new Ghost Dance religion. Both traditional religious beliefs and Ghost Dance offered a form of resistance, traditionalism, and survival. During the Chemehuevi-Mojave War the Mike family had moved to Twenty-Nine Palms to continue their way of life far from the reach of most white men, particularly agents, traders, and soldiers. The Oasis of Mara was also some distance from the Mojave. At the Oasis of Mara, which white people ultimately named Twenty-Nine Palms, Jim and William Mike and their band of Chemehuevi forged a new life, one based on that which the people had long known during their earlier days in the Chemehuevi Valley. They farmed the Oasis lands, hunted, gathered, and traded.

During the 1870s and 1880s Chemehuevi people who remained living along the Colorado River continued to struggle with Mojave, white bureaucrats, and soldiers, but the Twenty-Nine Palms Band found a great deal of freedom, seclusion, and self-determination at their desert oasis. They maintained a life with far fewer threats to their well-being—physically, spiritually, and mentally. After the 1860s the Twenty-Nine Palms Band faced the future with measured optimism and resolved to maintain their isolation from white influences. They did not want to live on a reservation or become government Indians. They did not want to become Christians or follow the dictates of Indian agents. The Cheme-huevi of Twenty-Nine Palms wanted to preserve their sovereignty and hold onto their freedom and independence. In the desert they felt they could retain their language, culture, and way of life. For a short time, they succeeded.[83]

CHAPTER 4

The Chemehuevi at
Twenty-Nine Palms

IN THE HEART OF THE MOJAVE DESERT, ABOUT A HUNDRED MILES
west of the Colorado River, a group of Chemehuevi established a new life.
During the 1860s and the Chemehuevi-Mojave War, Chemehuevi people estab-
lished a permanent residence at the present-day town of Twentynine Palms,
California. Indians called the place Mara, or Mar-rah, meaning Little Spring,
Much Grass.[1] The Serrano Indians had lived at the oasis for hundreds of years.
Traveling bands of Chemehuevi people had camped at the Oasis of Mara many
times in their past, as they walked and, later, rode horses from the Colorado
River to the Pacific Coast to trade, hunt, gather, and visit friends and relatives. Nüwü from the Colorado River traveled west to the Little San Bernardino
Mountains, the San Bernardino Mountains, and the San Gabriel Mountains
to hunt bighorn sheep, deer, and antelope. Joshua Tree National Park now
controls much of this land, preserving the landscape and wildlife. Chemehuevi
had also entered the mountains to gather "piñon" after receiving permission
from their friends, the Mamaytam Maarrenga'yam, or Serrano people of the
desert and mountains.[2]

When war between the Chemehuevi and Mojave became intense, most
Chemehuevi people retreated and regrouped in the mountains and desert valleys west of the Colorado River, but near the river. No record exists about the
discussions among Chemehuevi men and women of the Twenty-Nine Palms
group about the best course of action, but contemporary Chemehuevi elder Joe
Mike Benitez argued that some of the people talked the matter over and decided

that the Oasis of Mara offered a safe and sound place for the people—away from the Mojave, Indian agents, and reservation life. Benitez argued that once the elders made this decision, those Chemehuevi who agreed with the plan accompanied their leaders into the desert to the oasis and those who did not determined their own course of action. The leadership included Joe's relatives.[3]

Few records exist describing the initial movement and settlement of the Chemehuevi from the river to the oasis, but through oral accounts and limited written records, it is clear that only a few families initially moved to Twenty-Nine Palms in the 1860s, numbering between thirty and fifty people. Most likely a few people moved to the oasis first and others followed. Accounts by miners and travelers suggests as much. The limited census data provided by the Office of Indian Affairs in the 1890s offered the names of some of the people living at Twenty-Nine Palms nearly three decades later, but the number of people and their names varied from year to year. The change of names and numbers suggests that agents at the Malki or Morongo Indian Reservation did not travel into the Mojave Desert and the Oasis of Mara to visit the Chemehuevi and Serrano directly. Instead, they relied on travelers to provide census information. The census data suggests a mobile population that came into and out of a fluid indigenous community, which was very much in keeping with Chemehuevi traditions of traveling, hunting, gathering, and trading.[4]

The Chemehuevi did not enter virgin territory in the 1860s, for they knew that Mamytam Maarrenga'yam Serrano Indians had a well-established village at the oasis. According to Serrano elder Dorothy Ramon, Serrano of Twenty-Nine Palms had established "a great ceremonial site for Indians" and a sacred ceremonial house, "where shaman sang, conducted yearly renewal ceremonies, and held funerals and memorials."[5] After the 1860s, Chemehuevi leaders Jim and William Mike established their own ceremonial house and shared songs and ceremony with Serrano people. William Mike earned a reputation as a superior ceremonial leader and medicine man. He became a man of great power, healing people and helping others as a ceremonial and civilian leader. Outsiders called him a chief, an honor he earned among his own people and the larger indigenous world of Arizona, California, Nevada, and Utah.[6]

Oral tradition suggests that when the Chemehuevi arrived at the Serrano village in the 1860s, Serrano residents had abandoned the site. Some sources suggest that the Serrano had fled their home because of a smallpox epidemic, and documents confirm that in the early 1860s smallpox decimated several Native nations in Arizona, California, Nevada and beyond, taking the lives of untold number of people, including the famous Cahuilla Indian leader Juan

Antonío.[7] When the Chemehuevi first arrived at the oasis, the Serrano had abandoned the site temporarily, so the Chemehuevi took up residence without opposition or permission. After a short time, however, the Serrano Band returned to Twenty-Nine Palms. The two groups worked out an agreement to live together in peace at the oasis, and from roughly 1865 to 1909 the Serrano and the Chemehuevi lived together in peace and without significant conflict.[8]

In fact, the people thought of themselves as relatives, learning each other's traditions and languages. Some people intermarried. Still, they also guarded their own cultures, maintaining their tribal identity. Thus the Chemehuevi and the Serrano people worked together, but they also kept separate spheres. In the early twentieth century, Jim and William Mike led the Chemehuevi of Twenty-Nine Palms, establishing their own village political unit that evolved into a tribe, but one that kept its close relationship with other Southern Paiute. Members of this group recognized they were part of the larger Southern Paiute community and, at the same time, maintained and preserved their own sovereignty, establishing a tribal identity through ethnogenesis. At the same time and in the same village, Jim Pine, or Akuuki, led the Serrano. Both Pine and the Mikes served their people as civil leaders and medicine men, and Jim Pine's influence extended to Mission Creek, Malki (renamed Morongo), and Palm Springs.[9]

No records exist describing the agreement between the Chemehuevi and the Serrano at Twenty-Nine Palms, but the two people worked out an amicable accommodation to live with each other. It is most likely they discussed the matter during a traditional council meeting in the village Big House or Ceremonial House. They likely shared tobacco, an act of friendship and prayer. Together men and women participated, discussing the issue that had arisen. The two peoples spoke distinct languages. "Chemehuevi men would talk" and "they spoke Serrano."[10] They also communicated some concepts through sign language. No doubt the Serrano had heard of the fighting between the Chemehuevi and the Mojave, and it may not have been a great surprise to them that the Chemehuevi had removed to the oasis, some distance from their old enemies and away from the newly created reservation. Both people had traditions of holding councils that included men and women, so they would have discussed the matter within and outside of the council. Generally men took the lead in council discussions, but women shared their opinions formally and within the family structure. Men led the Big House or Ceremonial House, but women had influence within the communities. In the late nineteenth and early twentieth centuries, Chemehuevi, Serrano, and other indigenous people were far more open to women participating in politics than white Americans. All the regional tribes valued the opinions and views of their women (and still do).[11]

Whatever the particulars, in the end the Serrano and the Chemehuevi agreed to live side by side at the oasis, sharing land, resources, and space. The Serrano and the Chemehuevi shared a large communal garden and the water to keep it alive. Families had their own small gardens, but the oasis water and communal garden offered a central element of the village. Today, Paul and Jane Smith own the property where the people once lived, and they continue to use the Indian garden as part of the Twentynine Palms Inn and Restaurant. Non-Natives writing the history of the region remarked often about the cordial relationship between the Serrano and the Chemehuevi at Twenty-Nine Palms. In fact, indigenous people intermarried and learned each other's language. In the early twentieth century, Serrano chief Jim Pine led his people and also influenced the Chemehuevi. Serrano elder Dorothy Ramon stated that "her mother was a Chemehuevi."[12] In contemporary literature authors identify Jim and Matilda (a Cahuilla woman) Pine as a Chemehuevi, not a Serrano, but this information is incorrect.

The people had much to gain by sharing the oasis. The Chemehuevi and Serrano could live comfortably at the oasis far removed from whites living at the Colorado River, Coachella, San Bernardino, San Fernando, Los Angeles, and San Jacinto valleys. They could live in their sanctuary some distance from the soldiers stationed at Fort Mojave and Fort Yuma as well as the reservations in the Coachella Valley and the Colorado River Indian Reservation. They could live free of Indian agents, reservations, and the Mojave. The Chemehuevi and Serrano at the oasis in the Western Mojave Desert isolated themselves from the most hostile Indians, white settlers, and government officials. If threatened, they could depend on each other for protection against aggressors. Most important, they respected the sovereignty and religious practices of the other. As a result of their close relationship, the Chemehuevi and Serrano at Twenty-Nine Palms shared a strong sense of community. They shared a division of labor, especially in planting, weeding, watering, and harvesting their garden, and they enjoyed their own tribal identity while cooperating with each other in a dynamic relationship.

The Chemehuevi and Serrano believed Twenty-Nine Palms to be a sacred place, a spiritual, giving, and affirming place where life thrived in the middle of the Mojave Desert. For them, a spirit filled the oasis and surrounding area and contemporary people say that spirit remains at the Oasis of Mara.[13] In every direction and at all times of the day and night, Twenty-Nine Palms reflected an

Chemehuevi people made many types of houses, including an A-frame home pictured here in Chemehuevi Valley. They made this home from log poles and arrowweed, a common and prolific plant growing along the banks and washes of the Chemehuevi landscape. The long, straight wood of the arrowweed is pliable when first cut, but with time it becomes extremely hard, dense, and strong. Chemehuevi people issued arrowweed for arrows, roofing, and thatching in their homes. Gerald Smith Collection, A. K. Smiley Library, Redlands, California.

ever-changing body, like the living body of Ocean Woman. The oasis developed from a fissure in the earth, creating a natural repository for underground water at the base of mountains, which collected water that seeped to the earth's surface. The oasis once enjoyed more water than it does today, water that appeared on the surface in small puddles and ponds, providing a nourishing habitat for humans, plants, and animals. Lush grasses once grew wild along the length of the oasis for approximately a mile. Tall Washington palm trees, native to California and Arizona, sprang up at the oasis, sending their roots deep inside the earth for nourishing water. Palm trees, mesquites, grasses, cane, creosote, and other plants made the oasis a welcome place for Native Americans crossing the Mojave Desert from the four cardinal directions.[14]

From the oasis and surrounding area, people could see for miles, particularly to the east, west, and north. This dramatic view remains intact today.

Mountains rise up in every direction surrounding Twenty-Nine Palms. To the north, the Cady and Bristol Mountains stand out like ships on a calm desert sea. The Sheep Hole Mountains rise up out of the desert to the east, quickly changing shapes and colors with the movement of the sun. Indeed, mountains stand watch over the oasis, animating an enchanting landscape. To the south, the Little San Bernardino Mountains rise up quickly from the village site, today the home of Joshua Tree National Park, a place of good hunting and gathering, a place filled with caves, rock art, and desert life. Mountains hovered above Twenty-Nine Palms like great sentinels keeping watch over the swaying palms and the Indian village that once graced the area. To the west, the direction of colorful sunsets, the greater San Bernardino and San Gabriel Mountains stand out like pilots pointing the way for westward travelers to the Pacific. Nearly every day, the sun shines brightly above the town of Twentynine Palms, with occasional clouds passing by and throwing shadows on the mountains, slopes, and desert floor. Rain remains scarce in the area, but the skies can open with torrential downpours that quickly fill the washes and flood the rocky and sandy soil. Many desert travelers used the Oasis of Mara on their way across the desert to and from the Pacific Ocean. In the winter, snow cloaks the great mountains to the south and west. The mountains and surrounding foothills supported healthy populations of deer, antelope, bear, mountain lions, and mountain sheep. In the late nineteenth and early twentieth centuries, the desert and mountains teemed with life, and the Chemehuevi of Twenty-Nine Palms preferred this place to any other on earth.[15]

In 1855 the United States authorized its first survey of the desert regions near Twenty-Nine Palms. Colonel Henry Washington made the first survey, but his notes and calculations on the site are sparse. In his official survey report Washington remarked that he found a small Indian village and a "cluster of cabbage palmettos," which in 1879, Professor H. Wendland named *Washingtonia filifera* after President George Washington—not Colonel Washington.[16] In 1856, U.S. government surveyor A. P. Green made another official survey of Twenty-Nine Palms, writing that there were "a few Indian huts" and that the people used "the leaf of the Palm tree for making baskets, hats, etc."[17] Green also commented in his report that "some 26 fine large palm trees in Sec. 33 from which the springs take their name, Palm Springs." White people originally called the oasis site Palm Springs, while the Indians living there called it Mara.[18]

Both of these Americans conducted surveys of Twenty-Nine Palms before the Chemehuevi people took up permanent residence at the oasis. However, even though the Serrano lived at the oasis when the surveyors passed through,

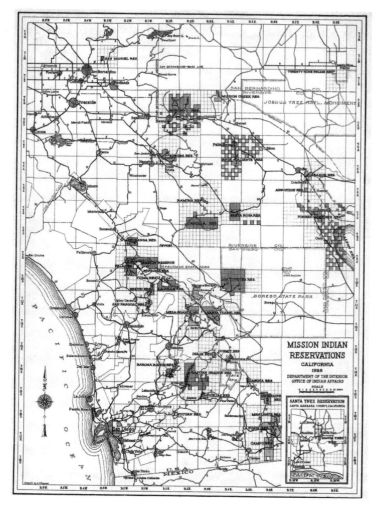

In the 1870s the Office of Indian Affairs created the Mission Indian Agency, which included twenty-nine Indian reservations in Southern California. The agency included the Twenty-Nine Palms Indian Reservation in the town of Twentynine Palms and the Cabazon Indian Reservation, where the Indian Office enrolled the Chemehuevi. In 1938 the Department of Interior, Office of Indian Affairs, created this map of the Mission Indian Agency and the reservations found within the agency. Map provided by Robert Przeklasa, University of California–Riverside.

these white observers had little to say about the Native inhabitants of Twenty-Nine Palms who owned the original claim to the region.[19] By the early 1870s miners, freighters, and other non-Natives passing through the Mojave Desert referred to the site as Twenty-Nine Palms—the name perhaps originating from Tom Coover and his party who visited the site in 1873 "looking for pasture for cattle, horses and sheep." After this visit to the oasis, the place "was supposed to be called Twentynine Palms after that." Non-Natives began calling the Chemehuevi and Serrano village by the name of Twenty-Nine Palms. During the late nineteenth century, the name became a permanent place name usually spelled "Twentynine Palms" on maps, signs, and official places within the state. Today the city uses the spelling of "Twentynine Palms," while the tribe prefers "Twenty-Nine," thus creating minor confusion regarding the spelling of the place. Indians continued to call the site Mara, but non-Indians determined the name of this traditional Native landmark.[20] None of the first surveyors of Twenty-Nine Palms wrote detailed accounts of Native people or the Indian village located north of the oasis and northwest of the present-day Twentynine Palms Inn. Still, Serrano Indians, known as the Vanyume Band of people, lived there throughout the era of early government surveys. The Serrano had several headmen over the years, but after the 1860s, Akuuki, or Jim Pine, became the most notable Serrano leader at Twenty-Nine Palms. His relations today are on the Morongo Indian Reservation near Banning, California.[21]

The Chemehuevi and Serrano both knew the region of Twenty-Nine Palms intimately and harvested a host of plant foods from the Mojave Desert. They shared these resources, in a close-knit community, but they focused on different work. According to one source, the Serrano enjoyed hunting while the Chemehuevi conducted most of the farming at the oasis.[22] This is in keeping with a strong agricultural tradition of the Southern Paiute people. This observation fits well with prior information about the Chemehuevi and other Southern Paiute who were (and are) great farmers. It was natural for the Twenty-Nine Palms Chemehuevi to lead the communal farming at the oasis. However, in 1856, A. P. Green had noted that the land "near the spring" had "the appearance of having been cultivated by the Indians."[23] Clearly the Serrano people had farmed the land near the oasis before the Chemehuevi arrived in the 1860s, but the extent of their cultivation is unknown. Green also mentioned the Indian homes at Twenty-Nine Palms as well as the fact that Serrano women made baskets from "the leaf of the Palm tree." The Indians used palm leaves in much the same manner as the Native Hawai'ian, Tahitian, Samoan, Filipino, and other Native people of the Pacific Basin. The Serrano, and later the Chemehuevi, used the "growth of cane" growing near the oasis to "make arrows for their bows."[24]

Before the arrival of the Chemehuevi in the 1860s, the Serrano had raised corn, squash, and beans. They encouraged the growth of other useful plants, and they raised gourds for their major musical instrument: the rattle. The people fostered the growth of native plants, particularly palms, tobacco, smoke trees, mesquites, and grains like chia. Along with produce of indigenous horticulture, they ate palm date fruit that grew on the native palms. Tobacco, a sacred plant used in prayers, rituals, and ceremonies, grew under the nurturing of the Native people. The Serrano and the Chemehuevi both hunted a host of large and small game animals, and each group farmed. In their distant past and over many years, the Chemehuevi had enjoyed a great deal of experience raising crops before moving to Twenty-Nine Palms. They brought with them an in-depth knowledge of desert agriculture, farming the bottomlands of the Chemehuevi Valley, Blythe, and desert springs. The Chemehuevi used their knowledge at Twenty-Nine Palms, further developing agriculture and irrigation, thus enhancing the garden in the fertile soil on the north side of the oasis, just east of the village site.

After moving to the oasis, Chemehuevi elders, including Carroita and Neitta, better known as Jim and Mary Mike, expanded the Indian garden at Twenty-Nine Palms. Jim and Mary are often found in the historical literature as Jim and Mary Boniface, but contemporary members of the tribe and family insist that the family name had always been Mike, not Boniface.[25] In any case, the Chemehuevi expanded farming at the small community, using water from the oasis to irrigate their crops, and they produced a bounty of fruits and vegetables. Today, employees of the Twentynine Palms Inn cultivate the same garden, providing excellent fresh fruits and vegetables for their guests. They point out that the location of the garden today is where the Chemehuevi and Serrano cultivated the first native garden.[26] At Twenty-Nine Palms, the Chemehuevi raised corn, beans, squash, watermelons, cantaloupe, apricots, peaches, pears, plums, and other soft fruit suitable in the desert environment.[27] With seeds brought from the Chemehuevi Valley or bought in Indio, Coachella, Palm Springs, or Banning, the Chemehuevi people planted many edible plants. Because of their association with farmers in the Banning Pass and Coachella Valley, the Chemehuevi introduced peaches, plums, apricots, and other soft fruit to the oasis. They may have introduced date palms and citrus, but no written records exist to confirm this. The fertile soil, hot weather, and availability of water fostered agriculture, and the people took advantage of these

Jim and Matilda Pine joined William Mike in the leadership responsibilities at the Indian village at the Oasis of Mara. The Serrano people at the village followed Pine and considered him their *keeka,* or leader. When the people left the village in 1909, Jim and Matilda Pine moved to the Mission Creek Reservation, and after the Indian Office destroyed that reservation, the Pines and their relatives moved to the Morongo Reservation. Descendants of the Pine family reside today on the Morongo Reservation. Photograph provided by Richard Hanks.

circumstances to enhance their lives with food for their own consumption and for sale.

The Chemehuevi and Serrano built their village north of the oasis, where approximately forty-five to fifty Indians lived in 1870, living in traditional native homes suited for the desert environment.[28] The village contained little homes made of small logs, branches, palm leaves, and mud. The people created a frame of vertical and horizontal posts and used branches horizontally to tie the structure together with palm, agave, or yucca cordage. People packed mud between the branches to create the sides of the home and used branches, cane, and palm leaves for the roof, packing it with a layer of adobe. The Chemehuevi built their homes to be very worthy, providing a cool chamber in the summer and a warm room in the winter. The people slept in their homes in the winter, but most slept outdoors during the hot summer months, often under a brush arbor. In the summer they set up log and brush arbors, which during the day afforded them shade from the searing sun and at night a place to sleep. The Chemehuevi and Serrano at Twenty-Nine Palms nearly always cooked outside, spending most of their time outdoors, living and working in the sun. They enjoyed the cool waters of a small pond situated near the village, a pond that varied in size depending on the amount of water seeping up from the aquifer and the amount of rain and runoff in the area. The pond provided water for irrigation and a unique ecological habitat for butterflies, mammals, reptiles, birds, and plants. The Indians hunted small game at the oasis and gathered some plants growing close to their homes. The people hunted and ate desert tortoise but not to the edge of extinction, which the creatures face today.

In 1892 an account reported that an elderly Chemehuevi man named Chepeven, approximately a hundred years old (born in 1792), moved about the oasis every day with his bow and arrows, shooting game birds and other small animals that he gave to Native families to cook and eat.[29] Many game birds used the pond, including ducks, geese, doves, and quails. These birds constituted an important part of the Native diet. In addition, the village at Twenty-Nine Palms placed these Chemehuevi and Serrano in the heart of excellent hunting-and-gathering territory. Large groves of mesquites, nourished by water from mountain runoff, existed to the south, west, and east of the oasis, providing nutritious beans and a habitat for rabbits, squirrels, deer, quail, and other animals. The area included yucca, agave, cactus, ironwood, and other nutritious plants. A single mesquite tree produced approximately ten bushels of unshelled mesquite beans that the Chemehuevi found more appealing than corn.[30] South of the village, on lands now part of the Joshua Tree National Park, the Chemehuevi and Serrano hunted deer, rabbits, and bighorn sheep. These and other natural foods provided subsistence for indigenous people of Twenty-Nine Palms.

Chemehuevi living at Twenty-Nine Palms enjoyed a strong Native economy that satisfied both Chemehuevi and Serrano for several years. However, non-Indians introduced them to many useful manufactured items. The Chemehuevi, the great travelers and traders of the desert Southwest, traded excess furs, feathers, fruits, vegetables, and meats for items brought by non-Native people, including pots, pans, picks, powder, knives, axes, hoes, shovels, bullets, and guns. Chemehuevi and Serrano people bought these items with money earned from selling some of the most unique and artful baskets in the world, but they had few markets for their baskets in the middle of the Mojave Desert.[31] While the Kumeyaay of southern San Diego County, Luiseño of northern San Diego County, Cahuilla of Morongo and Palm Springs, Serrano of San Bernardino

County, and others found markets for their baskets, the Chemehuevi and Serrano of Twenty-Nine Palms had a more difficult time finding markets near their home. Unlike many Indian people living in the western part of the United States, the Chemehuevi and Serrano had no railroad depots or major roadways near their homes where tourists purchased Indian art. Stages and wagons drove through Twenty-Nine Palms, stopping to enjoy the water and shade offered by the oasis, but few people purchased baskets or other hand-made goods, even though Chemehuevi and Serrano women made some of the most masterful baskets found in the world. However, when the people of Twenty-Nine Palms traveled south to towns, they sold and traded some of their baskets. They also sold their art and tools to anthropologists purchasing for museums located around the world. In this way they earned some cash to buy cloth, coffee, sugar, flour, beans, and other staples.

William Mike's widowed mother-in-law, Surda, was a noted basket maker. In 1900 she lived with William and his wife, Maria, at Twenty-Nine Palms. In addition, a Serrano elder named Allesandro became famous for his ability to braid horsehair hatbands, belts, and bracelets as well as rawhide bridles, ropes, reins, and other leather items. Like other indigenous artisans, Surda and Allesandro traded and sold their art, but they enjoyed a small, limited market for their goods, sharing them with other Indians and white Americans.[32]

Because of their isolation and desire to live some distance from the main trails traveled by non-Indians, the people at Twenty-Nine Palms entered the market economy slowly and cautiously. During the late nineteenth century, some Chemehuevi worked part-time jobs as laborers for miners, freighters, surveyors, ranchers, and farmers. They did so to earn cash for items they wanted to buy from white merchants, including food, seeds, guns, ammunition, horses, farm tools, pots, pans, clothing, blankets, knives, hatches, axes, beads, cloth, and manufactured items that the people could not otherwise obtain. Soldiers and emigrants introduced the Chemehuevi to some of these items when they lived in Chemehuevi Valley, and after moving into the Mojave Desert, the Indians desired to own and use them at Twenty-Nine Palms. As a result, some Chemehuevi worked with miners combing the desert washes and mountains for gold and other precious metals. Few non-Natives traveling through the Mojave Desert and oasis at Twenty-Nine Palms during the late nineteenth century left records of their exploits. Several miners visited the desert surrounding Twenty-Nine Palms in the late nineteenth century looking for a gold strike. Cowboys grazed cattle in Twenty-Nine Palms, and freighters drove their teams through the area, allowing them to graze on native plants. Most of these individuals were uneducated men who had little reason to record their adventures and observations of Indians. Early miners and freighters had common knowledge of the desert and its peoples, keeping mental notes of people and places but not writing down their observations. As a result, few personal accounts of miners prospecting near Twenty-Nine Palms exist, particularly in the years after the California Gold Rush.[33]

Initially miners in California concentrated their efforts in the northern part of the state, where they found the greatest deposits of gold.[34] In the 1850s and 1860s some prospectors searched for gold in western Arizona, eastern California, and southern Nevada, particularly near the Colorado River. White miners tramped through the Mojave and Colorado Deserts prospecting for gold, locating some mines in the heart of Chemehuevi country along the Colorado River. Even Major Samuel P. Heintzelman, the first commander of Fort Yuma, engaged in prospecting.[35] Many others followed his example, but the activities of these miners were often cloaked in secrecy. Miners had no interest in announcing their activities or locations to anyone. Some miners hired Indians as guides, cooks, and laborers, including a Chemehuevi named George Laird. He provided one of the few—if not the only—accounts by a Chemehuevi about his work for white miners. Chemehuevi elder George Laird gave an oral history to his wife, anthropologist Carobeth Laird, who included his account in her book *The Chemehuevis*. When George turned twelve years old, he worked for three miners in the desert. The miners had built a one-room shack with a lean-to near a well, and they prospected nearby mountains.

George cleaned and cooked for the sourdough miners, preparing food for them to take to the mountains each day and providing an evening meal when they returned each day. He also cared for their livestock, feeding and watering them, generally keeping the animals in good condition for his employers. In the evening he unloaded the ore the miners brought back, and he spent his days coaxing a mule to walk around and around an *arrastre*, which ground the ore into small particles. George worked for these miners one Christmas when the white men raised a few glasses of whiskey to celebrate the day. The miners became very intoxicated. According to George, each man had committed murder at least once, and while they were drunk, they started talking about death, dying, and ghosts. In the middle of the night, while telling ghost stories about the dead, a face appeared in the window of the shack, and everyone became frightened. The "ghost" disappeared and George retired. The next day he tracked the ghost and found a Mexican man—likely another miner—who had died from thirst and exposure. George quit his job after the miners decided that they should conduct some claim jumping, acts that resulted in violence. George wanted no part in the crime, so he rode back to the Colorado River to rejoin his people.[36] Other Chemehuevi from Twenty-Nine Palms worked for miners, but details have not emerged in the written record.

Miners influenced the lives of Chemehuevi living at Twenty-Nine Palms.[37] According to Maude Russell, the former local historian of the oasis, the first miners prospected the mountains around Twenty-Nine Palms in 1873, and after "gold was first discovered prospectors came in from all around the country, until the mining industry became very active."[38] Frank Sabathe, a Frenchman, became one of the first miners to prospect in the area surrounding Twenty-Nine Palms, but Russell provided no details regarding his relationship with Indians. In her writings about Twenty-Nine Palms, Russell offered general information about Death Valley Scotty (Walter Scott), Bill Keyes, and various mines in the area. However, she offered no information regarding the relationship of miners with the Indians at Twenty-Nine Palms. Nevertheless, she provided a little information on the region's mines during the 1870s and 1880s.[39]

Jim McHaney, an early miner of the Mojave Desert, began prospecting at Twenty-Nine Palms in 1888, and he spent his life in the region, often working with his brother, Bill. These men discovered and worked the Desert Queen Mine, a site that Indians had long known about because it included a cave ancient Indians had marked with rock art. All around the area, Indian people had placed sacred sticks, holy objects that indicated they considered the place special. Some of the people may have used the sticks to ward off evil or bad spirits that could harm, sicken, or kill Indians. Spirit sticks have a haunting look, perhaps intended to fend off negative forces. Furthermore, Indians may have blessed the sticks before setting them out to face unseen power that threatened Indian people. The sticks also protect sites, and many exist today in the archives of Joshua Tree National Park.

Cahuilla, Chemehuevi, and Serrano knew about the cave at the Desert Queen Mine, but apparently they placed little value on the gold ore found within the cave. However, in the twentieth century, Indians used quartz rocks they found in this and other mines to adorn the top of graves with quartz rocks that they had obtained from outcroppings of white quartz. These rocks have power, and people honored their dead with them. Chemehuevi elder Jim Ticup (Waterman) once visited the Desert Queen Mine with Bill McHaney. Ticup had a reputation among white people as a dangerous man, one who reportedly had "killed a lot of white men" in his younger days. Indians throughout the desert held the Ticup family in high esteem, so McHaney took the famous leader to assess the mine. After seeing the gold ore, Jim Ticup told McHaney that the Indians knew of a mountain of that rock, "enough for many white men."[40] The Chemehuevi leader took the miners "to the place where the gold was supposed to be." It was a large hill, and McHaney went to work digging for treasure. "Bill dug there for thirty-five years," according to Maude Russell, "but he never found any gold." Jim Ticup had likely played a practical joke on Bill McHaney, one that provided hours of humor for Chemehuevi and Serrano—a joke that lasted for over thirty-five years.[41] The practical joke offers another insight into and example of Chemehuevi humor.

Apparently the Chemehuevi and Serrano had no interest in gold, at least originally. But once they realized gold's value among whites, Indians mined some gold. According to Malki Indian agent Clara True, who visited the oasis in 1909, William Mike "had a mining claim out several miles drive from the water hole." True explained that the ore "samples he brought me assayed as good gold bearing stuff," but she also noted "that an Indian could not file on a mining claim." She offered to file the claim on William's behalf and to that end asked Horace Bryan to travel with William "to his location and put up a notice of Mike's claim." True never detailed the location of Mike's mine and never reported if she filed a formal claim for the Chemehuevi. In her correspondence True stated that she had no idea about the location of the mine, even though she had visited it with William Mike and Horace Bryan to set up the sign. In a letter written thirty-three years after her visit, True described the clear and beautiful day she visited the mine. A "bluebird fluttered about" and it was "very, very blue." She remembered William Mike commenting to her that "there had to be water near there or the bird couldn't stay."

Agent True mentioned that William "Mike was so sincere in his belief that he had something" special at the mine, but that he never developed it because "Mike was killed not long after" their visit to the Chemehuevi's mine. In a work about a Chemehuevi named Willie Boy, coauthors James A. Sandos and Larry E. Burgess suggested that "the mountain was sacred to him and he wanted to protect it for spiritual purposes," not material gain. This may be so, since William Mike was a holy man among his people. But in addition, True had firsthand knowledge that William Mike wanted to make a gold strike, which represents his knowledge of mineral wealth and how it could benefit his people. By the early twentieth century, he understood the power of gold and cash money. He worked as a laborer to make money to buy items available through merchants and traders. William Mike's lure of gold was very real, even if the mountain held sacred meaning to him and his people.[42]

John Wilson, better known as Chuckawalla Wilson (or Quartz Wilson), came to the oasis in 1884 and remained. He knew all of the Chemehuevi and Serrano families and individuals, and he got along well with his Native neighbors. Like many miners, Wilson liked to drink, and he bootlegged liquor to Indians during the late nineteenth and early twentieth centuries. Unfortunately, little information about his economic or social relationship with the Chemehuevi and Serrano at Twenty-Nine Palms has survived, although when the first Indian agent visited the oasis in 1909, she found Wilson with a supply of whiskey that True said he planned to sell to Native people. At the time of his capture, Wilson was hauling whiskey to Twenty-Nine Palms. Generally, Wilson worked as a miner, not a freighter, but the easy money made by selling bootleg whiskey enticed him into the liquor trade with Indians.[43]

To bring goods to the oasis, freighting companies drove wagons across the Mojave Desert, and a stage line ran small stagecoaches called mud wagons through the region, transporting passengers and freight. In 1895 or 1896 a stage ran from Garnet, California, to Twenty-Nine Palms, introducing the area to a system of transportation that proved an alternative to travel by foot, horseback, or wagons. All of the commerce to and through the Indian village at Twenty-Nine Palms contributed to the ill health of the Chemehuevi, because non-Native passengers and employees introduced Indian people to colds, influenza, smallpox, chickenpox, mumps, and other pathogens. Improved and more frequent transportation systems to the village increased the market economy for Indians, but it came at a great cost, because more whites moved into the area. Interest in the area also grew because of the availability of water. With every new visitor or resident came greater exposure to bacteria and viruses that created sickness and death among the indigenous inhabitants of Twenty-Nine Palms.[44]

Contact with whites influenced the Indian population at Twenty-Nine Palms. No one really knows the base population of Chemehuevi and Serrano living along the Colorado River or in the Mojave and Colorado Deserts during the eighteenth or nineteenth centuries. Reliable census data for the Chemehuevi did not exist until the late nineteenth century, and even then, the data is suspect. At the time of the United States–Mexico War of 1846, approximately twenty-five hundred Chemehuevi lived in a vast and unexplored region of the Colorado River and surrounding deserts. Far more Southern Paiute lived north of Fort Mojave. In 1863, Charles D. Poston, superintendent of Indian Affairs for Arizona, estimated the population of the Chemehuevi at somewhere between two thousand and twenty-five hundred, but by 1866 another estimate stated their numbers had dwindled to a thousand to fifteen hundred people.[45]

In 1903 the *Handbook of American Indians North of Mexico* reported the number of Chemehuevi had dropped to about three hundred on the Colorado River Reservation, not counting Chemehuevi living off the reservation or with their Southern Paiute relatives at Pahrump, Moapa, or Las Vegas. Dent provided no estimate of the number of Chemehuevi and Serrano at Twenty-Nine Palms.[46]

In 1892 miner Chuckawalla Wilson estimated the Indian population at the oasis at forty-five to fifty people. Visitors to the oasis often identified all of the Indians as Chemehuevi, because Chemehuevi outnumbered Serrano. Even Jim Pine had Chemehuevi blood. Before the 1860s Serrano had composed nearly all of the inhabitants of the Oasis of Mara, although the people married other Indians, including Cahuilla and other visitors. After the Chemehuevi-Mojave War of the 1860s, however, more Chemehuevi from the Chemehuevi Valley and Mojave Desert moved to the oasis. By the 1890s several elderly single Indians— Southern Paiute or Chemehuevi—had made Twenty-Nine Palms their home. Many people moved off the desert because of the death of their relatives from smallpox and other infectious diseases. The Office of Indian Affairs through the Mission Indian Agency did not conduct a census of Chemehuevi people until 1890, when Superintendent Horatio N. Rust authorized an accounting of the people at Twenty-Nine Palms. According to the first census, only twenty-one Indians participated in the census by the Office of Indian Affairs, providing the names of the Arenas family, the Olds family, and the Waterman [Ticup] family.[47] The names included people unfamiliar to contemporary Chemehuevi, most likely Paiute from the desert living at the oasis.

Although the Mike family had lived at the oasis since the 1860s, agency officials did not record the names of any member of the Mike family, not Jim or William, the leaders. Contemporary elders have suggested that their family may have traveled to the Banning Pass to work at the Gilman Ranch or crossed the Little San Bernardino Mountains to the Coachella Valley, where they worked in the fields or traded goods with Indians or non-Indians. Contemporary Chemehuevi elders had never heard of the Arenas family at the oasis, although the Arenas family is a prominent Cahuilla family on the Agua Caliente and Cahuilla Reservations. Contemporary Chemehuevi had never heard of the Old family. Both Joe Benitez and Dean Mike agreed that the Watermans were Chemehuevi, although they were known by the Native name of Ticup. Both Benitez and Mike questioned the accuracy of the first years of census data, suggesting that an agent may not have traveled to the oasis to take the census but had relied on information provided by other people so that he or she could fulfill the assignment to record a census.[48] They pointed out that for years Jim Mike, also known as Jim Boniface, had led the Chemehuevi at Twenty-Nine Palms. He and his wife, Maria (Mary), as well as their numerous children, should have been on the census of 1890. During the 1890s, Jim Mike was in his eighties. William Mike and Maria also lived at the oasis at the time. William was Jim's younger brother and had grown up to be a prominent medicine man, a holy person of power who led the ceremonies. The Chemehuevi called the Mike family the Timtimmon family (also written as Timpemoningtite or Timpingmoneytite). In the Paiute language, Jim had been given the name of Carriota, or Courinote, and the Chemehuevi called his wife Nietta.[49]

Jim had led the Timtimmon family from the Colorado River to Coachella Valley and then to the oasis of Twenty-Nine Palms during the 1860s. At the time he was in his fifties, a man of sufficient age, vitality, and influence to lead the group. Jim and Maria had a number of children, including Jeff Boniface (who took the name Boniface, after the St. Boniface Catholic Indian School in Banning, California), Billy Mike (the grandfather of Jennifer Mike Estima), and Minnie (or Annie). When shown the census of 1890, contemporary Chemehuevi elder Jennifer Mike pointed out that since the government agent had not included Jim and Maria on the census, the government had also not identified her grandfather, Billy Mike, and her grandmother, Nellie Holmes, as well as Nellie's family. Jennifer Mike agreed with Dean Mike and Joe Benitez that the first census of the Twenty-Nine Palms people is incomplete and inaccurate. She also agreed with the other two elders that the census of 1892 is not much better, recording that only twenty-one Indians lived at the oasis. This census conflicted with an estimate made by Chuckawalla Wilson, who lived at the oasis and estimated that between forty-five and fifty Indians lived at Twenty-Nine Palms.[50]

In 1894 the Office of Indian Affairs provided a much shorter census but one that appears more accurate, although the names of Jim and Maria Mike do not appear on this census. Agent Francisco Estudillo recorded that William and Maria Mike resided at Twenty-Nine Palms and the census recorded their ages as sixty and forty-five, respectively, which Chemehuevi leaders today believe are incorrect ages because William Mike was about sixty-five years old in 1909 when he was murdered. The census suggested that William was born in 1834, but the family believes he was born in either 1844 or 1845. In any case, his life represents an amazing era of Chemehuevi history—from his birth during the transition from Mexican rule of California to the American invasion of 1846–1847. William was twenty years old and a strong young warrior when the Chemehuevi and Mojave fought their war. He likely fought in the war with his older brother, Jim Mike, and their neighbor, Jim Ticup. They likely formed a

This is the only known photograph of William and Maria Mike at the Indian village of Twenty-Nine Palms. The illustration shows William's Ceremonial House on the right and his home located behind the three people. The Chemehuevi situated their village on the north side of the oasis near the present-day Twentynine Palms Inn. Maria is holding Dorothy Mike, the youngest daughter of William and Maria Mike. Photograph provided by Richard Hanks.

permanent bond during the war. In any case the war significantly influenced all three men and their families, who moved to Twenty-Nine Palms. Between the 1860s and 1900 these three Chemehuevi leaders and their people witnessed dramatic change as white miners, freighters, stage drivers, soldiers, and settlers invaded Chemehuevi country and forever altered the way of life the people had known. In his lifetime William Mike saw traditional life diminish in importance, particularly in terms of economics. Wage labor, unknown to most Chemehuevi before the 1850s, became a major part of Chemehuevi life for many people by 1900. Many more changes occurred as the twentieth century progressed.

Like the life of William Mike, the lives of all Indians living at Twenty-Nine Palms changed significantly over time. Jim and Matilda Pine led the Serrano at the oasis, and in 1894 the census recorded their ages as sixty-five and fifty, respectively. The ages were approximations by the census taker. Although the agent does not record any children belonging to William and Maria Mike, they had several children born in the 1880s and 1890s who lived at the oasis and were among the forty-five to fifty people mentioned by the miner, Chuckawalla Wilson. Jim and Matilda Pine had children as well, but the agent recorded no children associated with the couple.[51] In 1894 agent Francisco Estudillo recorded the presence of the Rameriz family at Twenty-Nine Palms, including the head of the family, Pancho, his son, Marcus, and daughter, Jacinta. Agent Estudillo also recorded the first names of another family, including Jacinto and his wife, Carlota. They had a son of thirteen named Berdugo, but the agent did not offer the last name of this family. Today no tribal elder has been able to identify this family.[52] Like too many Chemehuevi families, all members of the Rodriguez family disappear from the records and most likely died out, moved away to live as Hispanics, or returned to the river taking a new name. The number of Chemehuevi of the Twenty-Nine Palms Tribe declined over time, which makes the survival of modern people almost a miracle.

The census data recorded at Twenty-Nine Palms in the 1890s coincides with Native American oral traditions. Three leadership families emerge from the data, which generally is unclear about the number of children, grandchildren, or relatives at the oasis in any one year. The censuses are sketchy. Jim and Matilda Pine led one of the prominent Indian families. Jim's mother gave birth in 1840, and he carried the name of Courinote, although later in life, Serrano called him Akuuki, meaning "ancestor."[53] He led the Serrano at Twenty-Nine Palms, although he was closely tied to the other leadership families of Jim and William Mike. Jim Pine shared civil and spiritual leadership responsibilities with the Mikes.[54] Jim Pine "was a distant relative" of Serrano from the San Manuel, Mission Creek, and Morongo Reservations.[55] His father "was a Mamaytam Marrenga'yam Serrano," but "his mother was a Chemehuevi."[56] Non-Indians often mistook Jim Pine for a Chemehuevi because he spoke both Serrano and Chemehuevi.

Jim Pine also knew the Cahuilla language, which he spoke with his wife, Matilda, who was Serrano and Cahuilla. Matilda could also converse in the Cahuilla, Chemehuevi, and Serrano languages. Serrano people called Jim's wife Mathilde, but written documents identify her as Matilda. She was born in 1844 when her mother, Coyote, gave birth to Matilda.[57] Jim and Matilda married in 1880, and they reportedly had a total of fourteen children, although only two boys, named Juanito and Juan, and a girl, named Teresa, survived any length of time. Their twelve other children died in infancy or early childhood, since one report simply stated that they "had a number of children, all of whom died young." The Pines buried all their children in the Indian cemetery at Twenty-Nine Palms.[58] Non-Indians reported that Jim Pine was a good hunter, while Matilda and her mother, Coyote, were accomplished basket makers. When the people moved from the oasis in 1909, the Pines moved to Mission Creek but ultimately lived with friends and relatives on the Agua Caliente Reservation, where Jim's loved ones buried him in the Indian cemetery at Palm Springs.[59]

Jim and Maria (or Mary) Mike became another notable leadership family at Twenty-Nine Palms. Indians called them Carriota, and his wife, Nietta. They began a large extended family that included three boys and two girls. The boys included Billy Mike, grandfather of Jennifer Mike, and not to be confused with William Mike, Bob Boniface, and Jeff Boniface. No one is certain about the origin of the Boniface name, but Joe Benitez believed it came from children attending Saint Boniface Indian School in Banning, California. The girls included Annie (also known as Minnie) and Lucy. Annie married Joe Pachecco, a member of a Chemehuevi family that settled at Twenty-Nine Palms after the others had moved in 1910 to the Cabazon Reservation. Billy Mike married Nellie Holms (later known as Nellie Morongo), the daughter of Frank and Maria Holms.[60] Nellie's family originated among the Chemehuevi living in the Mojave Desert, but they had moved to the Chemehuevi Valley when Nellie was a girl, relocating later to Twenty-Nine Palms. Bill and Nellie had two girls, including Mary and Lucy. Mary married Isaac Morongo, while Lucy first married Marcus Pete and, later, Joseph Saubel. Lucy and Marcus had three children, including Elizabeth, Marcus, and Jennifer. Of the three, Jennifer has become a leader of the Twenty-Nine Palms Tribe. Her daughter, Courtney, has long served on the tribal council. Jennifer's grandparents, Bill and Nellie Mike, made a good life for themselves at Twenty-Nine Palms, but they ultimately moved to Banning, where they found work, particularly on various ranches, including the Gilman Ranch in Banning. In 1908, Randolph Mason took Bill and Nellie's photograph while they worked at the Gilman Ranch, but their lives fell apart when a wagon jarred a rifle loose, causing it to discharge into Bill's body. Bill Mike died of the gunshot wound, and Nellie became a young widow with children. Ultimately she married Tom Morongo, a prominent leader on the Morongo Indian Reservation. They raised their children on the Morongo Reservation, where Nellie's children and grandchildren grew up.[61]

William and Maria Mike headed another prominent family at Twenty-Nine Palms. Some details about these and other Indian families are found in the census data collected by the Mission Indian Agency. The censuses of 1894, 1895, and 1896 are almost identical, although the ages of everyone increased.[62] It is likely that Agent Estudillo simply copied these censuses from the year of 1894 to save time and expense. According to the 1895 census, seven adults and six children lived at Twenty-Nine Palms, and the agent recorded the same number in 1896. This data represents an undercounting to be sure. Indeed, in 1909 when agent Clara True, the first agent to make the trip to Twenty-Nine Palms, visited the village, she counted twenty-nine Chemehuevi and Serrano living at the oasis.[63] Certainly, in the 1890s more than thirteen Indian people lived at the oasis at Twenty-Nine Palms.

Of all the censuses of Twenty-Nine Palms during the late nineteenth century, the census of 1897 is the most striking. It indicates that twenty-seven people lived at the oasis, including six separate families. Most interesting, the census of 1897 provides the names of widows and widowers who ranged in age from eighty to ninety-three. Their names vary from Coyote (Matilda Pine's mother) and Wilepa, female and male, ninety-three and ninety years of age, respectively, to Josepha and Joe Privan, eighty-eight and eighty years of age. The census of 1897 contains more names than any other census of the nineteenth century and includes several elderly people who may have died between 1897 and 1900. In addition, other younger and middle-aged people not listed on the census of 1897 likely moved to live at the Mission Creek, Morongo, Agua Caliente, or San Manuel reservations, where they could find work on nearby ranches. They may also have moved to the high desert near present-day Victorville or Palmdale. All told, the census of 1897 offered the names of twenty-seven people, including fifteen males and twelve females. Although there names are known, little is known about the various people who once lived at the oasis, except for the families of Jim Ticup (Waterman), Jim Pine, Jim Mike, and William Mike. However, because the families at the oasis produced so many children, the superintendents of the Mission Indian Agency wished to have them educated at Sherman Institute, Saint Boniface, or one of the other government schools where the government could assimilate them into white society and teach them trades to make them productive workers.[64]

It is likely that some of the widows and widowers in the census of 1897 were Chemehuevi from different desert groups who had lost their spouses and families. They moved to Twenty-Nine Palms to spend their remaining days with other Chemehuevi people.[65] These people only appeared on one census, and the elderly people likely died and were buried at the Indian cemetery at Twenty-Nine Palms or they moved away. Before the 1870s and 1880s the Indians had buried bodies of their loved ones all about the area of the oasis. Before this, the Indians made their burials "at various places, wherever the families decided, so the entire oasis is undoubtedly full of the graves of Indians." In the 1870s and 1880s, before Jim Pine became the Serrano leader at the oasis, he established a cemetery west of the village, a short walk from the palm trees. He began burying residents of Twenty-Nine Palms in the Indian cemetery after "his very old aunt" named "Patri" passed away. The exact date is unknown, but Chemehuevi and Serrano people used this cemetery for years after Patri's death.[66]

Chemehuevi and Serrano people jointly conceived of the cemetery as a sacred place, the final resting place of their loved ones. Before this, Serrano and Chemehuevi people buried their dead all along the oasis, and the elders feared whites would build on these graves, disturbing the dead. Jim Pine created a designated burial ground because non-Natives had moved into the region and began using different areas around the oasis where the people had once buried their dead. He set aside a spot not far from a shallow wash that ran down from the foothills of the mountains within walking distance of the village. Today, the spot is adjacent to Adobe Road that leads south of the city of Twenty-Nine Palms to the northwestern corner of the Twenty-Nine Palms Indian Reservation, near the town of Twentynine Palms. When Pine created the cemetery, the government had not yet established a reservation, but the reservation recognized by the United States in the 1890s did not include the lands encompassed in the cemetery. The people set aside the cemetery to protect the remains of their loved ones, and they honored the dead at the time of burial and in memorial services or "doings" conducted a year after the burial.

Chemehuevi and Serrano people also marked the graves of their loved ones with small white quartz. "These Chemehuevi Indians," wrote Maud Russell, "marked their graves by strewing flat white stones over them." She felt that the Indians chose rocks to mark the graves because the stones "could not easily be displaced by either wind or floods." White people reportedly created the first wooden headboards to mark the graves of their Indian friends, and by the early twentieth century, "miners and prospectors" cut headboards and placed them at the head of the graves.[67] When Indian agent Clara True visited the oasis in 1909, Jim and Matilda Pine took her to the cemetery to show her "the tiny graves which he and Matilda had covered with colored pebbles." Jim and Matilda had lost several children, including two boys they buried in the cemetery (one had shot himself accidentally with a 22-caliber rifle and another had been kicked and killed by a horse). "Every morning of my stay," Agent True wrote, "I could hear Jim and Matilda crooning at the little graves, about the time of sunrise."[68]

After 1910 the Chemehuevi and Serrano who had left Twenty-Nine Palms sometimes returned to the cemetery to pay their respects to the dead. "After the Indians left this reservation," Russell wrote, "occasionally one would come, who was, I think, a son of the old Chief [Little Mike or Lily Mike], and give some care to his graves." So many people had died and had been buried in the cemetery that Lily Mike and other Native people periodically tended the graves. Contemporary Chemehuevi people return to the cemetery at Twenty-Nine Palms to pause and pray for friends and relatives. In the summer of 2005,

Lily Mike's grandson, Dean Mike, returned to the cemetery to tend the graves and consider future preservation measures. The Southern Pacific Railroad had purchased the cemetery in the nineteenth century but conveyed it to the government, which in turn asked the city of Twenty-Nine Palms to care for and protect the remains of Chemehuevi and Serrano buried in the old desert cemetery.[69] Dean Mike, Joe Mike Benitez, Jennifer Mike, Matthew Leivas, and other contemporary Chemehuevi people and their families are familiar with the cemetery at Twenty-Nine Palms and consider it a sacred place that must be protected and preserved. However, none of the contemporary people from the Twenty-Nine Palms Tribe are certain of how many Chemehuevi and Serrano are buried in the cemetery. Furthermore, they do not know if the remains and patrimony of their ancestors all rest within the boundaries of the cemetery. Dean Mike and Joe Benitez have speculated that the cemetery may be larger than today's established boundaries. More graves and funeral objects may be buried immediately outside of the area designated as the cemetery.[70]

In 1909 two men attempted to determine the number of people buried at the cemetery at Twenty-Nine Palms. Henry Pablo, a Serrano from the Morongo Reservation, and Ben de Crevecoeur, a storyteller from Banning, California, visited the cemetery. They estimated that the cemetery held between fifty and sixty graves, but they could not determine how many bodies had been laid to rest in the burial area. Contemporary Chemehuevi people believe that more graves exist in the cemetery and the area surrounding the current boundaries of the Indian cemetery. The National Park Service may find additional graves during construction projects near the oasis. Chemehuevi people today know the names of some of the persons buried in the cemetery, but most of them are not known and the location of the remains of certain people in the Indian cemetery at Twenty-Nine Palms is unknown.[71]

Some of the men, women, and children buried in the Indian cemetery at Twenty-Nine Palms died of diseases brought to the area by non-Native people. Unfortunately, the Native elders who lived at Twenty-Nine Palms had no written language and left no written accounts of diseases and epidemics. The Indians left a few oral accounts of diseases, but specifics about the various diseases and their effects upon the Chemehuevi at Twenty-Nine Palms are few. More is known about the diseases through the emotional responses provided today from contemporary Chemehuevi elders and other Native people who remember that "White Man's Diseases" or "Traveling Disease" killed many Indians and greatly reduced the Native population. Some specifics about diseases among the people at Twenty-Nine Palms exist in written records of non-Natives who

lived at the oasis or were familiar with conditions there. The oldest recorded epidemic was the "black measles" that "reached this oasis and east to the Colorado
River." This "black measles" epidemic was likely smallpox that swept through
California, emerging in Los Angeles in the 1860s on its way east into Arizona.[72]
Smallpox returned to the desert Southwest in 1877 and 1878, and Chemehuevi
people living along the Colorado River reportedly fled into the mountains and
deserts west of the river to escape the dreadful disease. It is not clear whether
the disease reached Twenty-Nine Palms in the late 1870s, but the people living
at the oasis continued to have a close association with river people. It is quite
probable that some Desert Chemehuevi contracted smallpox from their friends
and relatives along the river.[73]

Among virgin populations, like that of the Chemehuevi and Serrano, smallpox proved extremely lethal, indiscriminately killing men, women, and children
who had little or no biological immunity to smallpox. The virus attacked their
bodies aggressively, causing violent eruptions of the skin while destroying the
body from within. According to one account: "One droplet of exhaled moisture
from the lungs of an infected individual contained a thousand more smallpox
viruses than the minimum necessary to produce the disease in someone else."
The disease was highly contagious, and it caused large black pox to form on
the skin or inside the body's orifices, including eyes, nose, mouth, anus, and
genitals.[74] Smallpox is excruciatingly painful, and the people died in agony
while their loved ones became exposed to the contagion, spreading it to others.
In addition to smallpox, common cold viruses, influenza, pneumonia, measles,
whooping cough, and other diseases reached the Chemehuevi and Serrano at
Twenty-Nine Palms, contributing to deaths among the people. While little is
recorded about most diseases that affected the Chemehuevi and Serrano at
Twenty-Nine Palms, the fact that tuberculosis infected the people of the oasis
is fairly well documented.

Tuberculosis infected Chemehuevi and Serrano Indians, especially during
the 1890s when white miners and other non-Natives arrived at the oasis, either
bringing the bacterial disease with them or encouraging tubercular patients
to live at Twenty-Nine Palms where the hot, dry, clean climate offered a possible cure. White people living or working along the Colorado River and at the
oasis exposed Chemehuevi people to tuberculosis before the 1890s. American
Indian students attending off-reservation boarding schools returned home with
tuberculosis and spread the infection among family and friends. However, the
disease does not appear to have greatly affected the lives of the Chemehuevi
at Twenty-Nine Palms until the early 1900s, although accurate data on deaths

within the Mission Indian Agency did not appear until 1924, when the agency began collecting death data that tracks disease.

In 1903, Mr. and Mrs. Eaton hired a mixed-blood Indian named Pete Domac to drive a freight wagon from Banning to Twenty-Nine Palms to supply their mine in the Dale District. In 1903 the Eatons hired a woman named Mrs. Whallon to cook and clean for them at their mining camp. On one of his trips from Banning, Domac brought Whallon and her young daughter to Twenty-Nine Palms. Whallon had taken the position in large part to bring her daughter to the hot, dry climate of the Mojave Desert to cure her tuberculosis. Domac, Whallon, and her daughter, Maria Eleanor Whallon, arrived at Twenty-Nine Palms and spent the night in the Old Adobe—a structure built years before and used by many travelers over the years. According to Maud Russell, "The mother thought the desert country would help the girl," but the first night at the Old Adobe brought death to her. Ben de Crevecoeur, Chuckawalla Wilson, and either John Thurston or John Burt reportedly helped build a casket and dig a grave for the girl near the palm trees, where they buried her. Although no account links this girl's death to the Chemehuevi, the Whallon girl provides a concrete example of a person introducing tuberculosis to the area and its people. Indians may well have been exposed to tuberculosis when meeting the visitors or attending the girl's funeral. Moreover, Mrs. Whallon and other whites with whom the people had contact may have had tuberculosis, quietly infecting the Indians without knowledge of doing so.[75]

Whallon was not the only non-Native who brought tuberculosis to Twenty-Nine Palms. Thousands of non-Indians sought relief from consumption by moving to the deserts of Southern California, and these individuals unwittingly introduced tuberculosis to Indian people. One of the tubercular patients who brought his disease to Twenty-Nine Palms was a man identified as Preacher Aldridge from Santa Ana, California.[76] "The preacher came here for his health," Russell wrote, "being induced to do so by a fellow townsman" named "Mr. Halesworth, who came out here in 1888, and bought the Carlisle Mine." William Campbell, the famous archaeologist of the Mojave Desert region, also moved to Twenty-Nine Palms because he was "in poor health." Campbell and his wife originally lived in a tent pitched near the Old Adobe before they moved to the small non-Native community.[77] Their home remains a cultural site today, a reminder of scholarship and the deadly disease.

Native American oral histories offer general information regarding Indians contracting tuberculosis, but one well-documented case exists today. During the 1910s a Chemehuevi cowboy named Joe Pachecco married the young daughter of Jim Mike. Her name was Tomachi, but whites called her either Annie or Minnie. Joe and Tomachi had two children, including Harlie and John. Joe was such an accomplished cowhand that owners of the Barker and Shay Ranch in Banning offered him a job, so Joe and Tomachi moved from the Chemehuevi village at Twenty-Nine Palms to Banning. Joe and Tomachi lived in Banning during the 1910s and 1920s. Joe contracted tuberculosis, but the disease remained dormant until the 1920s, when it took over his life. He continued to ride for Barker and Shay, although with difficulty. He became generally ill and coughed a great deal. Over a period of time, he became weak, often coughing blood and losing weight. In 1922, Joe Pachecco died of tuberculosis in Banning, about sixty miles southwest of his home at Twenty-Nine Palms.[78]

Among the Indians of Southern California, tuberculosis was an insidious killer, usually taking the lives of the very young and people ages fifteen to twenty-eight. In an environment where the disease spread easily within a virgin soil population, infants and babies often contracted tuberculosis. Medical doctors, nurses, and lay people had difficulty detecting tuberculosis, because it often appeared more like influenza or pneumonia. In the early twentieth century, no X-rays existed, thus making early detection nearly impossible. Tuberculosis often killed very rapidly. In infants and babies, the disease attacked the child's brain or the lining of the brain, causing what was once described as meningitis tuberculosis. In these cases the brain and the membrane surrounding it became infected, often killing the child. No one knows how many infants and babies died this way in the tiny communities of the Mojave and Colorado Deserts, but by the mid-1890s, when the government conducted its first censuses, agents listed few children. In part, agents failed to mention children known to have lived at Twenty-Nine Palms at the time, but also mothers bore few children and those born during this era lived in jeopardy because of the spread of tuberculosis, gastrointestinal disorders, pneumonia, and other infectious diseases. With few natural immunities to colds, flu, pneumonia, gastrointestinal disorders, tuberculosis, and other infectious diseases, Chemehuevi and many other indigenous people, but especially babies and young people, died. The Chemehuevi living in remote desert communities died without the notice of agents and other non-Natives. Although families and communities recorded these deaths in their memories, they left no written accounts of the deaths.[79] Indians and scholars know that Native Americans died of diseases, but no one recorded the extent of these deaths until 1924, when the Mission Indian Agency began recording death registers.

The non-Native world also did not know of the deaths of Indian children resulting from malnutrition. With the growth of the white population in the desert, non-Natives and their livestock depleted and altered the natural plant and animal habitat of the fragile desert environment. Horses, burros, cattle, and sheep ate many of the same plant foods as Chemehuevi people, including mesquites, screw beans, chia, and many varieties of grain. In addition, soldiers, miners, freighters, and travelers used firearms to shoot game animals, depleting the population of deer, antelope, rabbits, and bighorn sheep. As a result, native food supplies became unpredictable and sometimes dangerously low, placing nursing mothers at a disadvantage and depriving infants and babies of basic nutrition. An unknown number of infants and babies died of diseases brought by non-Natives and malnutrition brought on by depleted food supplies caused by the invasion of outsiders.[80]

Illnesses became more common after the arrival of non-Natives. In the Chemehuevi way, traditional healers played a significant role in every community. People with power, like William Mike, healed others and often led communities in civil as well as religious affairs. Sometimes this same person led the people during wars, having gained military experience through battles with other Indians, conflicts with settlers, soldiers, and freighters. However, medicine people played a central role within all Native communities in Southern California. They healed others, but this became extremely difficult when patients contracted illnesses caused by bacteria and viruses. Traditional medicine men and women worked to eliminate spirit sickness that affected the health of patients, and Native Americans had great confidence in the abilities of their healers to bring patients back into balance and eliminate the negative effects of spirit sickness.

Like others within their communities, medicine people had an in-depth knowledge of medicinal plants, psychology, and basic medical procedures such as setting broken bones, stopping venal and arterial bleeding, and other basic techniques. However, they had difficulty dealing with tuberculosis, pneumonia, colds, influenza, and other illnesses.[81] Thus when Old Jim Ticup (Waterman) became ill, the family asked a medicine man reportedly named Black Bill to doctor the elder. Unfortunately, Ticup died as a result of his illness. According to one account by Ben de Crevecoeur, the shaman failed to heal Ticup, and Ticup's family avenged the death by murdering him. This tale is suspect. Chemehuevi people rarely if ever practiced revenge murders resulting from the failure of medicine people. Maud Russell maintained that Ticup "was accidentally killed while hunting, when his horse slipped on a rock and both fell over a cliff, near Victorville." She suggested that Ticup died from the accident, not disease, but she included de Crevecoeur's version of events in her story about Black Bill. Contemporary Native elders reject the notion of killing medicine men, and not one person interviewed had ever heard of Chemehuevi killing Black Bill near Mission Creek.[82] De Crevecoeur earned a reputation as a storyteller, not a scholar or historian. He spread tales harmful to the people and their culture.

In his account given to Maud Russell, de Crevecoeur argued that "it was a law among the Indians that should a Medicine Man fail to effect a cure, particularly should the patient be a distinguished person, the eldest son of the patient must execute the doctor, along with his entire family, and all animals thereto belonging, including even the dogs and cats." In de Crevecoeur's account, Black Bill and his Chemehuevi family fled to Mission Creek, the home of Serrano people, where the medicine man lived "in a secluded place north of the Mission Creek Reservation." De Crevecoeur maintained that "it was there that Hank and Jim [Ticup] found them" and murdered them according to "Indian ways." He further argued that Chemehuevi and other "Indians did not look upon this as murder, but merely as an execution under the law. The white man who created this story stated "that he had always supposed that Jim was the elder of the two brothers [Jim Ticup's sons], but Hank spoke as if he had done the killing, or at least a part of it."[83]

It is possible that Hank Ticup toyed with de Crevecoeur's mind by spinning him a story that had more to do with Chemehuevi humor than reality. But it is also possible that de Crevecoeur concocted the story to provide Maud Russell with copy for the *Desert Spotlight*. The white man had a well-established reputation as one who would stretch the truth to form a negative story, and he likely made up the tale of Black Bill.[84] The story fits representations made by other whites interested in denigrating medicine people and sensationalizing the murder of medicine men who failed to cure, which did occur in some tribes. This particular story fits the national preoccupation and belief that Native Americans were savage, crude, barbaric, and uncivilized—particularly in reference to powerful medicine people. Contemporary Chemehuevi people know of no tradition among their people of executing medicine people for failure to cure. Moreover, Katherine Siva Saubel, an elder historian and holy person among Cahuilla Indians who lived on the Morongo Indian Reservation for years, said that she had never heard an elder speak of this specific event or of any tradition among indigenous people living near or within the Mojave or Colorado Deserts of executing a medicine man. She believed that de Crevecoeur had fabricated the story. Contemporary Chemehuevi agree. In like fashion, Serrano-Cahuilla elder Pauline Murillo had never heard of Chemehuevi people or any other Southern California tribe having the tradition of killing a medicine person, and she had never heard of this incident. Her father had been a medicine man and had lost patients without ever fearing retribution. Similarly, Chemehuevi elder Dean Mike had never heard of such a tradition among his people, and he believed that de Crevecoeur had fabricated the story.[85]

De Crevecoeur's misrepresentation of the Ticup family may have been followed by other accusations about the Ticup family. Despite the fact that whites and Indians living near the oasis at Twenty-Nine Palms tended to interact well with each other, another white man contended that the elder Jim Ticup had greatly disliked white people. A settler named Phil Sullivan told Russell that Ticup was "an angel to Indians, he hated white people."[86] This may or may not have been true. Certainly Ticup had lived near and interacted with miners for years. To date, no written document or oral history has been produced demonstrating that Ticup hated whites, although Sullivan claimed that when Ticup was a young man he had fought white people, perhaps attacking soldiers, freighters, and miners entering Chemehuevi territory in the Mojave Desert. Ticup may also have fought in the Chemehuevi-Mojave War in the 1860s. The characterization of Ticup as a hater of whites may or may not have been correct, because in his youth Ticup could have been a warrior who opposed the migration of white settlers through the deserts and mountains of Arizona, California, and Nevada. Most written documents suggest that the Chemehuevi living at Twenty-Nine Palms were peaceful and that the small white community at Twenty-Nine Palms lived separately but peacefully. During the late nineteenth century, Chemehuevi and Serrano people situated their village at the west end of the oasis, but one time they had lived all along the tree line of the oasis. Although the Indians and whites lived in close proximity and became somewhat friendly and dependent on each other, they still lived separate lives. Records kept by whites do not provide many details about the Indian community, in part because few whites lived at Twenty-Nine Palms before 1910, and many of those living at the east end of the oasis were busy mining, freighting, and ranching— not making ethnographical notes about their Native neighbors. Furthermore, many non-Natives living at Twenty-Nine Palms were not very literate and likely wrote few letters, diaries, or other accounts of their relationships with Indian people. If they did, the documents have not surfaced.[87]

Few records about the Native community at Twenty-Nine Palms are available, and those available have to be pieced together carefully. From contem-

porary Native accounts, the Indian community at Twenty-Nine Palms generally cooperated as one with joint meetings and discussions regarding various
decisions. However, when a matter pertained only to the Chemehuevi people,
they met among themselves to resolve the matter. The same held true for the
Serrano people. For example, when U.S. government ultimately encouraged
the Chemehuevi and Serrano people to move from the oasis, the two groups
made their own determination about their course of action and future location.
The Serrano did not move with the Chemehuevi to the Cabazon Reservation
near present-day Indio, California. Instead, they moved to the Mission Creek
Reservation to live with other Serrano and Cahuilla. In this case, as in others,
each group exerted tribal sovereignty and autonomy. Each group enjoyed its
own independence, and leaders within each group decided on the actions affecting their people. Of course, they consulted with the men and women of
the group to discuss matters in a democratic manner, but in the end neither
Chemehuevi nor Serrano told the other group what to do. Each group maintained its own political sovereignty—a treasured and ancient tradition among
both people. Government officials of the Mission Indian Agency did not like
the fact that the Chemehuevi lived so far from the other agencies and wanted
them to move into the Banning Pass or the Coachella Valley, where agents could
better control their activities.[88]

Although Indian people at Twenty-Nine Palms identified with their particular tribe or group, they also understood the importance of families within
tribal structures at the oasis. They did not have a "clan" system like other tribes,
but they adhered strongly to familial affiliations. Family connections proved
highly important among Chemehuevi and Serrano people, because their marriage laws required males and females not be too closely related.[89] As a result,
different people within the communities became experts at determining who
was related to whom, how closely, and as a result of what particular relationships between people. According to Chemehuevi elder Adrian Fisher, "People
back then kept track of who were your relatives, who you could and could not
marry."[90] During the late nineteenth and early twentieth centuries, families
kept their own oral traditions regarding familial relationships and history, particularly the Mike family, the key leadership family among the Chemehuevi of
Twenty-Nine Palms.[91]

Contemporary members of the Mike family know a great deal about tribal
events and familial relationships of the early twentieth century. In the late
nineteenth and early twentieth century, William Mike and several Chemehuevi
people at Twenty-Nine Palms would travel to Banning each summer to work in

the fruit and olive orchards. According to curators at the Gilman Ranch, Riverside County Park, Gilman hired William Mike each year to act as a foreman of the Indians working at the ranch. For several summers William Mike and members of his family—as well as other Chemehuevi and Serrano families—camped in the trees east of Gillman's ranch house and spent the late summer picking fruit for cash wages.[92] William Mike had earned a reputation as a hard worker and efficient foreman. He spoke several languages and worked well with Cahuilla, Chemehuevi, Serrano, and other Indians seeking work at the Gilman Ranch.[93] He did not drink alcohol, and he embodied the positive qualities of elder Chemehuevi leaders. Although William Mike had acculturated to the point of wearing western clothing and working part of the year for wages, he maintained a good deal of his Chemehuevi culture, particularly his religion and social structure. He had memories of ancient ways, and while living close to and with non-Indians, he applied the old knowledge to his present situation. He led the people in their ethnogenesis, as they changed in order to survive in the modern world controlled by newcomers. At the same time, they maintained central elements of culture, language, religion, and political sovereignty. William Mike was careful not to break Chemehuevi law, and he followed tribal traditions with great care and concern.[94]

In 1909 he was the leader of the Chemehuevi at Twenty-Nine Palms Band when Indian Agent Clara True visited the oasis. True became the first known Indian agent to travel from her headquarters on the Morongo Reservation to the oasis at Twenty-Nine Palms. She interacted well with Chemehuevi and Serrano people, and she asked them to relocate out of the desert, offering them land at Morongo or Palm Springs. The agent wanted the people living closer to the agency headquarters near Banning. Neither William Mike nor Jim Pine volunteered to move. The people wanted to remain in the middle of the Mojave Desert separated from non-Natives.[95] They worked for white ranchers and traveled across the Little San Bernardino Mountains to work in Banning, Indio, and other places within the Coachella Valley. Working in the Banning Pass and the Coachella Valley brought Chemehuevi people into greater contact with Cahuilla people, and some Chemehuevi adopted elements of Cahuilla culture and intermarried with the people. This contact brought some Chemehuevi into greater political awareness, which blossomed into their participation with the Cahuilla people in the Mission Indian Federation—an intertribal sovereignty organization—to fight for Indian rights and self-rule.

Despite working with Cahuilla in the Coachella Valley, the Chemehuevi did not want to live in the area because of too many white settlers. Officials of the Office of Indian Affairs attempted to convince the Chemehuevi to move, but the tribe's leadership remained steadfast in their desire to remain in the Mojave Desert, far removed from numerous white people. In 1909, Agent True made the greatest attempt to convince the people to move, as the Indian Office wanted them out of the desert to better control them. William Mike and Jim Pine refused to move. The people collectively held this position, refusing to move, until tragic events later that year led to an agreement by the people to relocate for cultural reasons, not economic or political incentives.

While True remained at the Oasis of Twenty-Nine Palms, she had a surveyor mark the boundaries for a Chemehuevi Reservation, including a large portion of that land near the Indian settlement and the water. Some years later, she learned that neither the state nor the federal government would recognize the reservation boundary she had established because the boundaries did not match those granted the people in 1895 through an Executive Order.[96] The state of California had claimed the land in 1875 and sold it to the Southern Pacific Railroad Company. True did not know this. Neither did members of the Twenty-Nine Palms Tribe. However, fearing government officials might attempt to remove them from their homelands, as they had the Cupeño people from Warner Springs, members of the Twenty-Nine Palms Tribe became active in political resistance. This eventually developed into their participation in the Mission Indian Federation, an intertribal American Indian sovereignty group that supported Indian control of their own affairs without government interference. The children of William Mike, members of a strong leadership family, were among the first to join the Federation in 1919, participating long into the twentieth century to protect Chemehuevi rights. Their lives at the oasis took a dramatic turn shortly after the visit of Agent True. These events turned the tribe's attention away from political matters to familial, cultural, and legal issues that forever changed the tribe and its people.[97]

CHAPTER 5

Unvanished Americans

AT ONE TIME NATIVE AMERICANS OWNED ALL OF THE LAND AND RE-
sources of North, Central, and South America. The Chemehuevi owned a huge
geographical area, including the western side of the Colorado River Valley, the
eastern side of the river near Ehrenberg, the Bill Williams River, and most of
the western Mojave. Spanish, Mexican, and American people and their governments sought to liquidate Indian title to the land, and in the hope of doing so,
created a negative racialized image of Native Americans as hunters and gather-
ers, despite the fact that the Chemehuevi had farmed the land for thousands of
years. European newcomers and lawmakers often argued that Indians should
rightfully give up the land to God's chosen people, the followers of Christ, who
would develop the land, turning it into bountiful farms. Generally speaking,
English law recognized that indigenous people had a natural right to the land,
but they also believed the first owners had a right to surrender title of the land
through written agreements. English settlers, and later the United States, believed that they had a "legal" right to extinguish title to Native lands by written
agreements or treaties. Europeans and Americans used many techniques to
"buy" Indian land, and they used "right of war" to extinguish title to millions
of acres. By the time the United States created the state of California, national
and state governments had become skilled at "legally" taking Indian lands.
Although the Chemehuevi people of Twenty-Nine Palms may have heard something of American dealings regarding the land, they could not have anticipated
the full impact of the American invasion, survey, and resettlement of Arizona,
California, and the Great Basin.

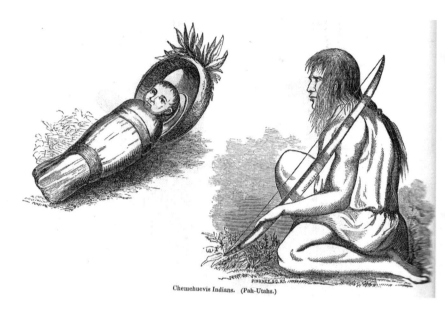

Chemehuevis Indians.　(Pah-Utahs.)

In 1853 and 1854, Lieutenant Amiel Weeks Whipple of the U.S. Army Corps of Engineers led a survey party along the Thirty-Fifth Parallel, crossing the Colorado River in the Mojave Valley. The party met many Mojave, but they also traded with friendly Chemehuevi. Heinrich Bauduin Möllhausen sketched this drawing of a Chemehuevi warrior carrying a short war bow. He is wearing leather buckskin clothing, common among the Chemehuevi men, women, and children who often traded in skins. They were great hunters of the deserts and mountains of Arizona, California, Nevada, and Utah. Lieutenant Amiel Weeks Whipple, during the railroad survey near the Thirty-Fifth Parallel, "Reports of Explorations and Surveys, to Ascertain the Most Practicable and Economical Route for a Railroad from the Mississippi River to the Pacific Ocean, January 31, 1851," *Senate Executive Document 78*, Thirty-third Congress, Second Session (Washington, D.C.: Beverley Tucker Printers, 1856).

The Serrano people lived at the Oasis of Mara before Chemehuevi settlement. These two distinct groups worked out an amicable agreement to live in peace at Twenty-Nine Palms after the 1860s without confirming details in writing. The Chemehuevi and Serrano made a binding oral pact to live together, which both groups honored from the 1860s through the 1910s. Even before Chemehuevi people left the Colorado River to live permanently at the oasis, the U.S. government had sent a surveyor to mark the lands surrounding the oasis and assign the landscape English, not Native, names. In 1855, Colonel Henry Washington made the first survey of the Twenty-Nine Palms area, and on July 23, 1856, the U.S. government recorded the Indian village at Twenty-Nine Palms at the Southwest One-quarter of Section 33 of Township One West, Range Nine East, San Bernardino Baseline and Meridian as an "Indian Reservation." Accordingly, in 1856 the United States labeled the Serrano village at Twenty-Nine Palms as a reservation. But the federal government ignored its own survey and the plat designated in 1856, yielding to the state of California in 1875, allowing the state to claim the "Indian Reservation."

Not long after the state of California claimed the Oasis of Mara, the state transferred ownership of the oasis to the Southern Pacific Railroad for an undisclosed amount. The state sold the Indian village of the Chemehuevi and Serrano without the consent of the indigenous owners of the oasis. The Indians had a natural right to their land but lost it because of an unscrupulous act of state authorities. No records have come to light detailing this action, but given the close connection of California state government to the "Big Four of California railroading," it is plausible that railroad surveyors had identified the water at Twenty-Nine Palms as a necessary source for the Southern Pacific Company. If the railroad had attempted to buy the oasis from the Chemehuevi and Serrano, the Indians would have refused the sale of their homeland. But since the state claimed the land as part of its holdings, the Indians had no say in any "legal sale." Without the knowledge or consent of the Serrano or Chemehuevi, the state of California claimed the entire Oasis of Mara in 1875, making a legal claim to the Indian village and the Native cemetery.[1]

It is clear from the 1856 plat that both state and federal officials knew from government surveys that Indians lived in a village at the oasis, but officials ignored the natural right of the people to their land. Equally important, governmental officials stole the water—the clear, pure, and plentiful water of the oasis that the Indians owned and used daily. Non-Indians wanted to capture, control, and pump the precious water. In the minds of the Chemehuevi and Serrano, their people actually owned the land and the water at Twenty-Nine Palms, because both peoples owned songs about the land and the water. Salt Songs had traveled through Twenty-Nine Palms, and the songs reference land and water, a highly significant indigenous resource. The people did not simply use the land. They believed in private ownership of real property and resources. They had no written deeds of ownership, but they had songs of ownership and the word of many non-Indians that passed through the area who knew of the village and the water rights. The Chemehuevi and Serrano people owned the oasis without American-style documentation, but the state of California did not recognize this form of inherent Indian ownership. The state's non-Native inhabitants certainly would have scoffed at the idea of land ownership evidenced by "ownership" of a song. The state's grab of Chemehuevi and Serrano land also violated American, English, and Native American law that recognized that Indians had a natural right to their land.

The action by California, the United States, and the Southern Pacific Railroad to take this Indian land and home site fits appropriately into the historical period. From its inception, the state of California had violated Indian rights and lives, allowing state, county, and city officials to steal Indian land and resources, kidnap Indian women and children, exploit the Native population, and kill Indian people indiscriminately. Federal officials did not take a prominent role in California's affairs, allowing state and local officials to deal directly with Indians in their own ways, regardless of the impact on Native peoples. In so doing, California often dealt with Native Americans in a brutal fashion. State and local governments and organizations ignored Indian rights, and between 1850 and 1880 many citizens of California called for the outright extermination of Indians—sometimes participating in the killing of men, women, and children simply because they were Indians. It became commonplace for local and state officials as well as private citizens to confiscate Indian land and resources without making formal agreements or treaties. The state did not follow American rule of law, making its move without consultation or authority.[2]

The Chemehuevi people did not participate in the Treaty of Temecula, and they had nothing to do with initial negotiations by federal officials to create some of the early reservations in Southern California in the 1870s and 1880s. However, the Chemehuevi people became significantly influenced by the federal reservation system in 1890, even though they knew little or nothing about the federal legislation that affected them so profoundly. On January 12, 1890, President Benjamin Harrison signed into law "an Act for the Relief of the Mission Indians in the State of California." The new federal law instructed the secretary of the interior to "appoint three disinterested persons as commissioners to arrange a just and satisfactory settlement of the Mission Indians residing in the State of California, upon reservations which shall be secured to them." Although the president was to appoint "disinterested" persons, he selected men who had been interested in the reform of Indian affairs for many years. President Harrison chose three excellent men who had the best interests of Indian people at heart and made Indian welfare a major goal of their work. One of these men was Albert K. Smiley, a Quaker and former schoolteacher who owned a commercially successful resort in New York at Lake Mohonk. Smiley had lived in Redlands, California, since 1889, and he had addressed several issues facing Southern California Indians at annual gatherings of the Indian Rights

Association that had met at Lake Mohonk. Harrison asked Smiley to head the Mission Indian Commission, better known today as the Smiley Commission.[3]

President Harrison also appointed Professor Charles Painter and Michigan Supreme Court Justice Joseph B. Moore. Of the two, Painter enjoyed a much broader reputation. He was a famous scholar and member of the Indian Rights Association of Philadelphia. Like Smiley, Painter knew Southern California and its original people, having made three trips to the region to meet the people and study the condition of the tribes. He had intimate knowledge of some of the tribes, particularly the Cahuilla, Kumeyaay, Luiseño, and Serrano, but like his fellow commissioners, Painter knew little about the Chemehuevi. All three of the commissioners were dedicated to the work ahead of them, and they took their appointments seriously, working hard to resolve the fact that few Indians in Southern California had a legal patent to their land. At one time Indian people in Southern California had owned a vast territory of oceanfront property, inland valleys, mountains, and deserts. The Spanish and Mexican people who had moved into California threatened Native ownership of some traditional lands, but the arrival of white Americans from the United States fully challenged Native rights to their property, resources, and freedoms. As a result, the Native peoples of California had secured for themselves only minute portions of their former lands. The Chemehuevi had once used the entire Mojave Desert from the northern slopes of the San Bernardino Mountains to the Tehachapi Mountains and from the western end of the Mojave Desert to the Colorado River. The Chemehuevi people had lived along the Colorado River from Black Canyon, not far from present-day Las Vegas, Nevada, south to Blythe, California, and the Palo Verde Valley. Chemehuevi territory had once existed in the Colorado and Mojave Deserts, but by 1890 much had changed. The government ignored Chemehuevi land rights along the western bank of the Colorado River, urging the people to move to the river's eastern bank onto the Colorado River Indian Reservation. Some Chemehuevi moved but others refused. Like the Chemehuevi of the Chemehuevi Valley of California, the Chemehuevi living at the oasis of Twenty-Nine Palms wanted to remain in their homeland. In 1891 the Smiley Commission addressed some of the land issues of this group.[4]

The president and Congress instructed the Mission Indian Commission to examine Indian lands in Southern California and select "a reservation for each band or village of the Mission Indians." Under the terms of the bill passed in 1890, the commission had to consider the "occupation and possession" of lands inhabited by the Indians, and the officials were to recommend reservations "sufficient in extent to meet their just requirements." The federal government

Commissioner A. K. Smiley led the effort to establish several new reservations in Southern California through the Mission Indian Commission. In 1891 and 1892 commissioners visited the tribes and negotiated revised boundary lines for all the reservations of the Mission Indian Agency, at times creating reservations recognized by the United States where none had existed before. Treaties were not used to create these reservations, but presidents used Executive Orders to establish all the reservations in Southern California. Photograph Collection, A. K. Smiley Library, Redlands, California.

asked the commission to recommend what was in the best interest of Southern California Indians, including the Twenty-Nine Palms Band, but the government did not empower the commission to purchase or sell lands. Smiley, Painter, and Moore could recommend the purchase of lands, but they had no funds to do so. Under the terms of the law, the commissioners hoped to create reservations and define their boundaries so that the government would hold these lands in trust on behalf of Indians for twenty-five years. The commissioners planned for the day when the U.S. government would allot these new reservations into individual parcels so that Indians could enjoy private ownership of their land. The commission's work in 1890 occurred at the very time that reformers and policy makers within the United States set about to allot most reservations, breaking up reservations into private ownership by Indians and selling excess lands to non-Indians, thus destroying reservations. The work of the commission may appear contrary to government policy, but the government planned to create the reservations and fairly quickly allot the lands to provide faster assimilation of the people. At the time, this was the process in the United States.[5]

The commission's work became critical to the creation and preservation of legal land titles for many Indian people in Southern California. Some tribes had reservations with government-recognized boundaries, but most did not. Because most tribes in Southern California had only a few "legal" titles to their remaining homeland, the Smiley Commission set about to create reservations so that Indians would have clear boundaries and patents to their lands. In this way federal, state, and local governments would understand the boundaries of Indian lands, and in theory keep unwanted settlers off Indian land—thus reducing conflict. This was important given the fact that before the 1890s, government surveyors had "floated" boundaries of reservations, moving them about to suit themselves, their friends, and local interests. Furthermore, the boundaries of the reservations established in the 1870s had never been surveyed carefully, and Indians often found that the government had not included their villages, productive lands, and water reserves within the reservation boundaries. White squatters had invaded some reservations, and some whites had challenged Indian ownership of Indian lands at San Manuel, Morongo, Mesa Grande, Captain Grande, Palm Springs, Warner Springs, Temecula, and other sites that had been inhabited for generations by Indian people. Years before the creation of the Mission Indian Commission, Indian reformer Helen Hunt Jackson had stated that "there is no possibility of protecting these Indians . . . [without] determining, re-surveying, rounding out, and distinctly marking their reservations already existing." She advocated hiring competent, independent surveyors who could not be swayed or corrupted by local white interests.[6] Jackson sought the removal of white squatters from reservations, the same people who had "wrested" from Indians their "fields and settlements."[7] When Indians learned of the Mission Indian Commission, most leaders willingly conferred with the commissioners in the hope of resolving land, water, and boundary disputes. William Mike, the Chemehuevi leader of the Twenty-Nine Palms Band of Chemehuevi, met one of the commissioners at a conference held at the oasis.[8]

The commissioners divided their work, traveling throughout Southern California visiting the Indians one or more times on their lands and in hotels. The commissioners had the power to recommend the expulsion of non-Indians from Indian lands, but they could not enforce their recommendations or actually remove squatters from Indian lands, or pay claims to clear titles. Commissioners could recommend compensation for non-Natives who had placed improvements on Indian land, but the government would have to authorize these payments. Commissioner Smiley wrote that all Indians living in Southern California, including the Chemehuevi, had suffered from "the depressing effect of the continued uncertainty of the extent of land which may eventually become theirs by allotment, restricted as it must be in many cases by the limited area of arable land." The Chemehuevi at Twenty-Nine Palms had a grasp of the entire landscape and considered it theirs. But they shared the mountains and desert with non-Natives, particularly miners and freighters who passed through the region. Most miners, freighters, and traders rarely remained in the area for any length of time. Still, knowing the way white people divided up the land and claimed it, Chemehuevi people lived with "the uncertainty of boundaries and of the tenure of land until these are established by surveys and by law." Smiley and his colleagues looked forward to a time when the government acted to end the "delay of years, during which the rights of both whites and Indians had remained undefined, and those of the Indians undefended." This condition had existed since Mexico ceded California to the United States in 1848 and had resulted in "conflicting claims and bitter feelings." The government intended for the work of the Smiley Commission in 1891 to end the ambiguity of land titles among Indians and whites in Southern California.[9]

With enthusiasm and energy, the commission began its work in March 1891, meeting first with the San Manuel Band of Mission Indians. The Serrano at San Manuel were Yuhaviatam, or the People of the Pine Trees, and Pakuuma, or Santos Manuel, was their leader. In 1915, Santos Manuel told anthropologist John P. Harrington that his mother was Chemehuevi. A few other Chemehuevi married into the tribe that shared the resources of the San Bernardino Mountains with Southern Paiutes and others who gathered acorns and piñons on the north side of the great range. However, white settlers in the mountains and in San Bernardino had used the conflict between Chemehuevi and whites as an excuse to launch a thirty-two-day campaign against the Serrano that had driven Santos Manuel and his Yuhaviatam into the San Bernardino Valley. The Serrano had settled in the foothills of the mountains near present-day Highland. But like the Chemehuevi people, they had no clear title to their land.[10]

As a result, they eagerly met the Smiley Commission and settled on the boundaries of their future reservation. Like many Native peoples, they believed that their agreement with the Smiley Commission in 1891 constituted a completion of the reservation agreement, but they did not receive their patent on the land through Executive Order until August 31, 1893. Smiley kept a sketchy diary of his dealing with the Indians with whom he met, and it is clear from this diary that he never traveled to Twenty-Nine Palms to visit the Chemehuevi people.[11] However, Commissioner Painter visited the Indian village at Twenty-Nine Palms to confer with the villagers. In her masterful work on Indian reformer Helen Hunt Jackson, scholar Valerie Sherer Mathes has pointed out that Commissioner Painter worked throughout the hot summer of 1891, making a "difficult fifty-mile journey on horseback from Indio . . . [to] a small, old Indian settlement at Twenty-Nine Palms." He found a village "with good water and land." Painter believed that the land "needed to be protected."[12] So Painter arranged to create a reservation at Twenty-Nine Palms for the Chemehuevi and Serrano people.

In their final report, the commissioners wrote that they had talked to "Chemehuevi Mike," William Mike or Jim Mike, the two Chemehuevi leaders of the tribe. Painter had spoken to either William Mike or his brother Jim Mike, both of who were Chemehuevi and known as Chemehuevi Mike.[13] According to the commissioners, the Chemehuevi at Twenty-Nine Palms "have plenty of water and can be comfortable here." They noted the tribe had "plenty of water and can be comfortable here." In addition, they stated that at the Oasis of Mara, the Chemehuevi would have "sufficient tillable land for their needs, and the balance of the land proposed is valuable grazing land."[14]

The commissioner reports offer significant insights as noted by Painter and other commissioners. Perhaps most important, as a body of governmental representatives, the commissioners recognized the Chemehuevi's and the Serrano's right to their own lands. These lands were not a gift from the federal government, because the Indians had inhabited the region for some time. Painter recognized this fact in his comments, and he championed the right of the Indian people to keep for themselves a portion of the land that they had owned for years. Second, Painter had learned from his visit with the people that Chemehuevi and Serrano living at Twenty-Nine Palms reveled in their seclusion and distance from non-Native populations along the Colorado River, Banning Pass, and Coachella Valley. Although the Chemehuevi had worked in the Coachella Valley for years and had a well-worn trail running between Twenty-Nine Palms and Indio, as well as Banning, most Chemehuevi people living at the oasis preferred living in isolation. These desert dwellers could only exist in the middle of the Mojave Desert because of the precious pools of water at the site, a special spot they shared with Desert Serrano. Without the water, the Indians could not live at Twenty-Nine Palms, and Painter and his fellow commissioners readily recognized this important fact. Third, Commissioner Painter saw firsthand that the Chemehuevi at Twenty-Nine Palms were farmers, noting that they tilled the soil. For many generations, Chemehuevi living in a number of locations in Arizona, California, and Nevada had practiced some farming. The food they raised supplemented their hunting and gathering, but the Chemehuevi at Twenty-Nine Palms could not farm the fertile desert floor without water. The commission recognized this, commenting that the people had "plenty of water," but the Executive Order creating the Twenty-Nine Palms Reservation at the Oasis of Mara did not include the water or good pasture that had been used by indigenous people for generations before the arrival of American settlers and governments.[15]

Finally, the commissioners realized that Chemehuevi people at the oasis also lived by raising a few animals that grazed on native grasses growing near the water. Forage and water made stock raising possible, but the Chemehuevi people here had limited resources for their ranching of domestic animals. However, the good grazing at the oasis also attracted deer and many small animals, including bird, mammals, and reptiles, which the people killed and ate. The Smiley Commission offered an accurate account of the Chemehuevi at Twenty-Nine Palms because Commissioner Painter had braved the summer heat and made an arduous trip on horseback over the Little San Bernardino Mountains to get to the oasis. Painter confirmed that the Chemehuevi here lived in a beautiful land that had sustained about fifty people for many years. "Chemehuevi Mike" acted in good faith and believed that he had made an agreement with Painter for reservation situated at their village site at the oasis. However, this agreement, like so many made in American history, proved unfortunate because of the bad faith of California, not the federal commissioners.[16]

The Smiley Commission recommended that the U.S. government establish a reservation for the Twenty-Nine Palms Band of Mission Indians on the oasis where the people lived. Roughly between 1863 and 1891, Chemehuevi people had occupied a village at Twenty-Nine Palms, establishing their site next to their Serrano neighbors on the north side of the oasis where they took advantage of the shade provided by the towering palm trees growing at the site. Of course, the Serrano had lived at this village far longer than the Chemehuevi. Chemehuevi and Serrano people lived north of the oasis at a slightly lower elevation than the south side. In this way they enjoyed the overflow from the oasis that created a wetlands near their village site. Plants and animals in this area formed a unique biotic zone. The plants and animals living in this desert habitat provided a "food and materials market" for Chemehuevi and Serrano people. In addition, they used the water overflow to create a pond that they used to irrigate their garden. Indians had long used the oasis as their home, and the commissioners reaffirmed this in their report, recommending to the U.S. government that officials recognize the Twenty-Nine Palms Reservation at the oasis. However, between 1891 (when Smiley and his associates made their recommendation) and 1895 (when the United States issued its patent on the land through an executive order), governmental bureaucrats set up a reservation on the dry desert location in the foothills of the mountains. The land north of Mara had little vegetation except creosote and no water. The site of the "new" reservation was about a mile from the oasis but far enough away that the people could not take advantage of the natural springs, trees, grasses, or animal life that now legally belonged first to the state and then to the Southern Pacific Railroad.[17]

The government initially acted on the recommendations of the Smiley Commission, establishing the reservation at the oasis, but then they changed the boundaries. The government moved the boundary lines of reservations after the Smiley Commission had made its recommendations. This was also the case when dealing with the Cahuilla people at Agua Caliente (Palm Springs) and other sites. At Twenty-Nine Palms the federal government refused to recognize the lands of the Serrano and Chemehuevi Indians once officials of the Office of Indian Affairs learned that California had made a recent claim on the land. Furthermore, the United States had declined engaging California officials in a discussion about boundaries and Indian rights, even though federal officials knew that the Chemehuevi Indians at the oasis had inhabited the region continuously for more than thirty years and the Serrano for even more years. Instead of challenging California, the United States ordered the Indian people to move off the oasis to a desolate land devoid of the most basic necessities, particularly water.

Perhaps the Chemehuevi people would have had a chance of keeping their lands if Painter had been more involved, but he had done his best and the people had no advocate in the government other than the Smiley Commission. It was easier for the bureaucrats to accept the fact that California had claimed the region than to engage state officials. Besides, Twenty-Nine Palms was located in the far-off Mojave Desert, and the Indians numbered fewer than a hundred by this time. Federal officials found it expedient and easy to ignore Chemehuevi land and water rights. For Chemehuevi and Serrano people living at Twenty-Nine Palms, the government's decision was a death sentence. They simply could not survive on the new reservation without water. So the Chemehuevi and Serrano people asserted their sovereignty and ignored the government's order. Historian Larry Burgess put it succinctly: "Some of the lands that the Smiley Commission believed rightly belonged to certain of the reservations recommended for establishment did not become part of the final patents. Pending law suits, threats of others, and some lands occupied by whites on lands desired for reservations vexed the Commission as it sought to balance the desires of multiple parties. In some cases, after the Commission filed its report, lands were set aside and made part of a reservation that the Commission had not originally endorsed."[18] This proved the case for the Twenty-Nine Palms Tribe, which resulted in reservation lands absent of water and located away from their village at the Oasis of Mara.

The U.S. government denied the Chemehuevi and Serrano the oasis as a reservation of their own land, but the reasons for the denial are complex and not totally understood. After California joined the Union in 1850, the state government began the process of claiming various parcels of land. At first politicians within the state of California ignored the region near Twenty-Nine Palms, perhaps believing it to be a worthless desert land filled with creosote, jackrabbits, and rattlesnakes. However, as government surveyors traversed the region looking for a viable route for a transcontinental railroad, officials took note of the water at Twenty-Nine Palms. When the Big Four of California railroading considered main and spur routes for the Southern Pacific Railroad, they always considered the availability of water to be a foremost consideration. Railroads in general and the Southern Pacific in particular acted on behalf of their companies, not Native people. In fact, most railroads considered Indians impediments to the progress, commerce, and civilization that railroads offered to the developing nation. Indians stood in the way of land, water, trees, and other natural resources that white Americans could exploit. Thus, when the Southern Pacific Railroad considered expanding its enterprise in Southern California, the company wanted lands that had water, especially in desert lands where water was scarce.

Steam locomotives had to have water, and future settlers had to have water to survive in the desert. People and animals needed water to drink, and if railroads were to sell excess lands to settlers, they had to assure them of water rights. The U.S. government gave the Southern Pacific Railroad, as it had other railroads, the "public lands" that the company later sold to speculators and private individuals. However, the federal government did not give the railroad lands at Twenty-Nine Palms. The Southern Pacific Railroad did not originally "own" the land at Twenty-Nine Palms, but in 1875, at the very time the railroad was building across Southern California on its way to Yuma Crossing, the state of California claimed the oasis at Twenty-Nine Palms—of course without consulting the Chemehuevi and Serrano people who lived there. No evidence has surfaced that the officials working with the railroad influenced the state's decision to take Indian lands at Twenty-Nine Palms, but the fact that they did when the Southern Pacific was expanding its influence in the region is highly suggestive. It is possible that railroad officials influenced state officials to claim these Indian lands so that the company could buy them. In this way, the railroad would control the most important water source in the region, an area that miners hoped would produce great quantities of gold and other precious metals that rail spur lines could haul to processing plants.[19]

Among descendants of the Twenty-Nine Palms Band, not one person knew a thing about the state taking their land in 1875. However, every descendant of the first inhabitants knew that the Southern Pacific Railroad had been involved in a deal to take the land from their people, saying that the railroad "capped" their water. According to one elder, "The Southern Pacific destroyed them, capped over the water, so that they couldn't get water at 29 Palms."[20] But contemporary elders had no idea until recently that the state had confiscated their lands first before the state had conveyed the oasis to the railroad. Nevertheless, the undefined relationship between the state and Southern Pacific had a huge bearing on the creation of the first Twenty-Nine Palms Indian Reservation. Commissioner Painter had planned on the government creating a reservation for the Twenty-Nine Palms Band on the land they occupied at the oasis, and the Mission Indian Commission supported this recommendation in their document to the government. According to H. M. Critchfield, director of lands for the Office of Indian Affairs, "the original Twenty-Nine Palms Reservation was established by Executive Order of December 29, 1891 on the basis of the recommendations contained in what is known as the Smiley Report."[21]

Critchfield pointed out that the "land recommended in this report and reserved by Executive Order is described as the SW1/4 of Section 33 Twp. 1 North Range 9 East S.B.M. [San Bernardino Meridian], and the NW1/4 of Section 4 Twp. 1 South Range 9 East." Some time later, Critchfield pointed out, the government "found that the SW1/4 of Section 33 Twp. 1 North Range 9 East was included in a State selection which was approved to the State on November 15, 1875, and which was later sold by the State to a private individual." As a result, there were "no lands owned by the Indians in that Section," and the government issued a patent on the unoccupied reservation on November 11, 1895.[22] The United States originally acted on the recommendation of the Smiley Commission, setting aside the land on the oasis for the Chemehuevi and Serrano. On December 29, 1891, an Executive Order withdrew the land on the oasis for the

Twenty-Nine Palms Band, but the secretary of interior withdrew this order on February 2, 1907, when the government learned the state of California filed a formal claim with the federal land office and "the federal government approved to it on November 15, 1875."[23] As a result, the president could not set aside lands privately owned and created a reservation south of the Oasis of Mara about one mile from the village and the water source.

Commissioner Painter had assured William Mike that the government would recognize the Indian ownership of the oasis, and the Indians had believed that the United States acknowledged their ownership of their homes and village site at Twenty-Nine Palms. They did not know about the government's official maneuvers to set aside their homes for the reservation, and they did not know that the state had claimed their homeland as early as 1875—lands ultimately transferred to the Southern Pacific Railroad. As a result of legal actions, the state of California had stolen their lands and the United States acquiesced to the state's actions. Attorneys for the state of California and the United States might well argue that their actions were not illegal according to the traditions of the United States, but in accordance with Chemehuevi law—a system of law that predates that of the United States. Native Americans considered the actions of the state and the inaction of the federal government illegal. The state had stolen Chemehuevi land and the United States did nothing to correct the wrong. When the United States finally issued the patent for reservation land at Twenty-Nine Palms for the Chemehuevi and Serrano, the parcel selected was therefore not on the oasis but approximately a mile southwest of their homes in a desolate, unproductive, barren landscape of sand and rock. The waterless parcel was, in the humorous muses of Cherokee comedian Will Rogers, a place where the grass don't grow and water don't flow. The Chemehuevi Reservation created at Twenty-Nine Palms had no water, and although the government attempted to drill a deep well on the new reservation in the early twentieth century, the drillers could not find a drop of water.[24] As for the "Indian reservation" designated on the plat of 1856, the governments of the United States, California, and San Bernardino County reneged on their recognition of the site as Indian land. In 1943 this led San Bernardino county recorder Ted R. Carpenter and chief deputy of the county recorder and registrar of titles to write "that the land was never owned or possessed by the Twenty-Nine Palms Indians."[25] Of course this statement totally ignored the historical record and the natural rights of the Indians to claim title to their lands, a fact addressed years later by Little (most commonly called Lily) Mike, the eldest son of William Mike.

The Chemehuevi and Serrano people who lived at Twenty-Nine Palms and their descendants never saw it this way. They believed that the oasis and hun-

To supplement hunting and gathering, Billy Mike worked on the Gilman Ranch picking olives and fruit to earn cash to support his family. He also worked as a cowboy. While living at Twenty-Nine Palms, he married Nellie Holmes. Billy Mike died by accidental gunshot, after which Nellie married John Morongo.

Billy Mike is the grandfather of the contemporary Chemehuevi leader Jennifer Mike Estama. In 1909, Randolph W. Madison made this photograph. Special Collections and Archives, University of California–Riverside.

dreds of miles surrounding the area in every direction belonged to them. The people believed in private ownership of land and resources, and under Chemehuevi law the Indians owned the site because they owned the song associated with this place. Furthermore, the Indians had never relinquished their title to any of it. For non-Natives to properly own it, they had to have a song about the many places within the vast region. In Serrano and Chemehuevi society, the song about a particular mountain, water site, gathering area, hunting grounds, home site, and so on constituted an oral title to the land. For hundreds, if not thousands, of years the Chemehuevi, Serrano, Cahuilla, and other Southern California Indians had passed down songs about land areas from one generation to the other, and the owner of the song owned the land, water, mesquites, piñons, acorns, and other resources on the parcels of real estate. Songs usually transferred land titles from fathers to sons, but the owner of a landscape song could pass along the song—and thus the property—to a daughter, daughter-in-law, son-in-law, brother, and so on. In the late nineteenth and early twentieth centuries, Chemehuevi and Serrano people still had these songs and therefore had an oral title to a huge geographical landscape where they lived, hunted, gathered, and prayed. They owned the land, but the foreign government of the United States, California, and San Bernardino County—in essence the conquerors—did not recognize Indian ownership of the land. However, neither the Serrano nor the Chemehuevi ever surrendered their sovereign right to the land. They never transferred their ownership songs to the governments, and they never signed a treaty surrendering their lands. As a result, the Indian perspective is that the governments stole their vast territories, relegating them to a 160-acre parcel of rocks and sand where they could not live.

Between 1891 (when Professor Charles Painter visited them) and 1910 (when the Chemehuevi and Serrano left their lands at the oasis), the indigenous people remained on their land. They ignored the patent creating a new reservation on Section 4 of Township 1 South, Range 9 East, San Bernardino Meridian, on the present-day northeast corner of Base Line Avenue and Adobe Road.[26] In 1910 superintendent William T. Sullivan of the Malki Indian Agency described the land as "a worthless tract of land 65 miles from the railroad out on the desert." He noted that this circumstance resulted from an "error in survey made several years ago" that "placed this reservation on worthless land, missing the good quarter section that it was intended they should have." Apparently Sullivan was not aware that the state had taken the land in 1875 and that there had been no mistake in the surveys. Still, he commented that the Office of Indian Affairs had set out to make Section 4 more habitable for the original people of Twenty-Nine

In the late nineteenth and early twentieth centuries, Chemehuevi people took jobs as day laborers for miners, ranchers, and farmers to earn cash money. In 1909, Randolph W. Madison, a twenty-two-year-old Virginian living in Los Angeles, photographed Maria Mike and her children, including baby Dorothy and others, while they worked at the Gilman Ranch in Banning, California. Special Collections and Archives, University of California–Riverside.

Palms by "sinking a well on the section referred to and the hole is now 1300 feet deep." He had high hopes that drillers would find an artesian well that would make the land "very valuable." But the drillers found no water, and the land has never become valuable.[27]

The state of California took possession of the land at Twenty-Nine Palms without consent of the Chemehuevi or Serrano people. Government officials never asked the original owners, as they knew the people would not surrender title. The land selected for the reservation is south of the present-day town of Twentynine Palms in the foothills of the Queen Mountains. It is a parcel of desert land filled with cactus, desert plants, sun, and wind. Lizards, snakes, and desert tortoise live on the land, but neither Chemehuevi nor Serrano Indians ever lived on the site. The government's well never produced. Today the land is developed, as the Twenty-Nine Palms Tribe established an Indian casino on the site in 2014.

In the early summer of 1909 some Serrano Indians and most of the Cheme-huevi prepared to travel to Banning to work on the Gilman Ranch. To acquire cash money with which to buy material items from merchants, Chemehuevi and Serrano people worked in Banning, Palm Springs, and Indio to earn wages. They had worked in the Coachella Valley for years, but the early summer of 1909 opened with some trepidation. Before they made their way into the Banning area, they experienced a major thunderstorm. South of Twenty-Nine Palms the mountains rose in mighty dominance, a sentinel to the people and the holy mountain of William Mike. These were his hunting lands that he owned through his song. No one traveled into these mountains without William Mike or his permission to do so. During the summer a huge storm rose up over Wil-liam's mountain, a storm with lightning and crashing thunder that created "a big roar from the mountain." William Mike was "not only the chief but the Medicine man." He was a powerful spiritual leader. The mountain's roar caused him to believe that "there would be some kind of tragedy to befall him or his family because of the roar from his mountain." The elder that shared this ac-count stated that non-Indians might find the story about an omen brought to Earth through a thunderstorm "fantastic and in our present day and age and life we're not supposed to believe in such things, but they did and they really weren't surprised in any way of the tragic events which happened." Still, de-spite the storm and warning, the small band of Chemehuevi people prepared to travel to Banning for their annual work at the Gilman Ranch.[28]

William Mike and his wife, Maria, made preparations to take their family into Banning. In addition to the money, the Gilman Ranch had the added at-traction of being a cooler site to live than Twenty-Nine Palms, so William and his extended family prepared to travel to the ranch. The group included sons and daughters as well as their families. The group also included members of Jim Mike's family, including his son, Bill Mike, and his wife, Nellie Holms Mike. William's many sons and daughters prepared to travel into Banning, including Lily (Little), Jack, Sam, Albert, and Johnson. His daughters gathered the family belongings and foods in preparation of the journey to Banning. The Mike girls included Carlota and Susie as well as Dorothy, the baby of the family born earlier that year.[29] Most likely other residents of the oasis also traveled to Banning with their headman, William Mike. But a few villagers remained at Twenty-Nine Palms and watched over the place, including the elder Mrs. Ticup, whom some people knew as Mrs. Waterman, and two of her sisters or female in-laws. William Mike's journey into Banning in 1909 was not his first. For some years he had worked as a foreman of Indian laborers at the Gilman Ranch. He was a trusted employee of Gilman because he was a hard worker and he interacted well with all employees, including other Native Americans. He did not permit his family or employees to drink on the job. William Mike opposed the use of alcohol, and as a civil leader and holy man, he had power and influence.

No events of note occurred on William Mike's journey into Banning. The people traveled by foot and horseback across the sweeping desert valley past present-day Joshua Tree and south to Yucca Valley. They followed a well-worn route through the Morongo Valley to Mission Creek and from Mission Creek to Banning. Gilman Ranch had been established along a flowing creek where tall cottonwoods shaded the watercourse, providing an inviting camping area. The Gilman family always anticipated the arrival of William Mike and his band because they were good laborers and the family had not had difficulties with the Chemehuevi working for them. William's steady hand and firm management of the people provided a welcomed source of labor that the Gilmans appreciated. The Mikes always camped in the same place when working at the ranch, setting up their temporary settlement near the shaded banks of the cool stream flowing from the mountains. Their work at the ranch consisted mostly of picking fruit, but the Gilman family also called upon them to help shoe horses, trim fruit trees, gather firewood, and repair baskets used during the picking season. In fact, the Gilman family could rely on the Mikes to do a variety of jobs, because William guaranteed that the work would be done efficiently and correctly. When the Mikes first arrived at the Gilman Ranch, they found everything as they had in years past. Initially they settled into a routine of work and rest, with everyone contributing in one way or another, including Maria, who cooked for the family and watched over young Susie and baby Dorothy. Then something happened that changed the cadence of the group, forever changing their lives and serving as a watershed in Chemehuevi and Southern Paiute history—an event that Chemehuevi people still talk about today. That summer of 1909, Willie Boy, a young Chemehuevi man, arrived at the Gilman Ranch to work.[30]

CHAPTER 6

Willie, William, and Carlota

THE HISTORY OF THE TWENTY-NINE PALMS BAND OF CHEMEHUEVI and that of many other Chemehuevi is closely tied to events surrounding the killing of headman William Mike by another Chemehuevi named Willie Boy. The murder of William Mike and the subsequent death of his daughter, Carlota, are clouded in mystery and intrigue—circumstances that cannot be unraveled with great certainty. However, this much is clear from the momentous events of 1909: Willie Boy's killing of William Mike, the death of Carlota, and the sensationalism of the desert manhunt significantly altered the history of the Twenty-Nine Palms Tribe. It is a watershed moment in their history and one often discussed on and off the reservation. The murder and ensuing manhunt caused the Office of Indian Affairs to move the people from their desert homeland and urge them to relocate to the Cabazon Reservation. The violent murder caused the tribe to abandon the oasis and burn their homes. The events associated with Willie Boy left the band in disarray, causing a diaspora of the people in many directions. After the murder and removal of the people from the oasis, members of the Twenty-Nine Palms Tribe could no longer live by hunting and gathering, as their ancestors had before them. The actions of the U.S. government and local law enforcement officials forced the people to earn their living through wage labor as cowboys, farm workers, laundresses, cooks, and domestic servants. Willie Boy's murder of William Mike set into motion a series of confusing events that still challenge the mind. As a result, reconstruction of these events is difficult. This account provides Chemehuevi and Southern

Paiute voices associated with one of the most well-known historical events in Southern California.[1]

William Mike became the leader of the Chemehuevi band at Twenty-Nine Palms in 1903 after his brother, Jim Mike, passed away and the people buried Jim in the Indian cemetery at the oasis. William lived in close proximity to Akuuki, better known to whites as Jim Pine, and his wife, Matilda. He was a close friend of both. Jim Pine was a Mamaytam Maarrenga'yam, or a Twenty-Nine Palms Serrano.[2] William, Jim, and other elders living at the oasis shared leadership responsibilities. They cared for each other's children like aunts and uncles and grandparents. During the early years of the twentieth century, the people continued to hunt, gather, and farm as they had done in years past. In addition, each year some Chemehuevi and Serrano from Twenty-Nine Palms traveled to the Coachella Valley and Banning Pass to work on ranches, where they made cash money to buy desired goods, particularly manufactured goods, cloth, clothing, coffee, flour, sugar, and other staples. According to Chemehuevi elder Joe Benitez, men, women, and children followed a well-worn trail over the Little San Bernardino Mountains to the Coachella Valley, where they worked the farms located near Coachella, Indio, and Palm Springs.[3] Others traveled another trail that led from Twenty-Nine Palms to Pipes Canyon, Mission Creek, and onto the Morongo Reservation, where the people found employment at various Indian ranches, including the Gilman Ranch.

Prior to 1909, William Mike and his family had worked on the Gilman Ranch many times. Each summer they traveled to Banning where they lived in a camp established by the Indians in the large cottonwood trees lining a small creek that flowed through the ranch.[4] The Gilman family recognized William Mike's abilities as a natural leader, and because he spoke Chemehuevi, Serrano, and Cahuilla, as well as English and Spanish, the Gilman ranchers hired him to serve as a foreman for the ranch. William's primary duties included managing the Native work force, and because of his high status as a leader and his innate ability to deal well with others, he succeeded in his work at Gilman Ranch.[5]

When William traveled to Banning, California, to work at the ranch, his wife and children accompanied him. Each family member worked to benefit each other. During the harvest season, members of the Mike family worked at the Gilman Ranch picking soft fruit and olives. Their association with the Gilman Ranch led them into an association with the Saint Boniface Indian School, a Catholic boarding school for American Indian students, where some members of the Mike family attended. According to Joe Mike Benitez, the Mike family inherited the name of Boniface through their association with the Saint Boni-

Willie Boy was a Chemehuevi who had lived with his Southern Paiute relatives in Nevada as well as in the Chemehuevi Valley. Among his people, he was known as a special runner and athlete. His grandparents lived at the Oasis of Mara, where Willie moved to find a wife, falling in love with a distant cousin, Carlota Mike, thus precipitating cultural complications that led to deaths and removal from the oasis. Special Collections and Archives, University of California–Riverside.

face School. Some non-Indians called William Mike "Old Mike Boniface," and one member of Joe's extended family, Jeff, took the name Boniface . . . a name today associated with the Soboba Indian Reservation, where Jeff Boniface married and lived most of his life.

Nuns and priests at Saint Boniface School nurtured their relationship with Indian leaders like William Mike. When William Mike worked at the ranch bordering the school, he brought family members into the Banning area. In 1909 his sixteen-year-old daughter, Carlota, accompanied him and the family to Banning. Back at the oasis of Twenty-Nine Palms, months before traveling with her family to the Gilman Ranch, Carlota had fallen in love with Willie Boy, the grandson of the elder Mrs. Ticup and son of Mary Snyder. Two of Willie's aunts lived at Twenty-Nine Palms, so he had a natural connection with the place and people at the Oasis of Mara. Willie left the Chemehuevi Valley in 1909, eventually moving to Twenty-Nine Palms, where he reportedly hoped to find a wife. Once at the oasis, he fell in love with Carlota Mike, a distant cousin. During his stay at the oasis, Willie and Carlota formed a close relationship with each other. Chemehuevi elder Alberta Van Fleet once reported: "My mother used to say" that "love is hard." In other words, "love should never have happened. Never. They were too close." Willie Boy and Carlota were cousins, and the Chemehuevi people "back then kept track of who were their relatives, who you could and could not marry." She pointed out that both Willie and Carlota wanted to marry. "They wanted it, but the families couldn't let it happen." In the end "she wanted her way. He wanted his way. There had to be trouble."[6]

According to tribal law, couples had to be approximately six generations removed, and the Mike family realized that the couple was too closely related to marry. Their union would be a "sin" in the Chemehuevi belief system . . . a very high violation of the creation story and old stories that illustrated the ill effects of incest. To the Chemehuevi and all Southern Paiute, such a marriage would have constituted incest. Willie's grandmother and aunts understood the problem, so both families opposed the marriage. The couple ran away from the village at Twenty-Nine Palms, but members of both families found and separated them, including Segundo Chino, a man from the Banning Pass and of Cahuilla and Chemehuevi blood. The families separated the couple and exiled Willie to Banning, placing Carlota into the home of Jim and Matilda Pine, her Indian uncle and aunt. Willie went to work while the Pines taught Carlota tribal law and proper behavior. The Pines lectured Carlota about the old law and explained that she could not marry Willie. According to tribal elders, violating marriage laws resulted in serious consequences to the couple and to the entire community of Southern Paiute. The people shared a belief system similar to the Puritan covenant theology. The violation of one person affected the spiritual balance of all Southern Paiute, so people took care to teach proper behavior for the benefit of all Paiute. Apparently Carlota learned her lessons and dutifully traveled with her family to work at the Gilman Ranch in the summer of 1909.[7] Alberta Van Fleet pointed out that "she [Carlota] went with him once before you know, and members of both families went to get them and bring them back." Van Fleet noted that under Chemehuevi law "if they stayed together, both families would have cut them off."[8]

Traditional scolding of Carlota worked for a while. Tempers cooled with time, but William Mike was of an old-time mind, a conservative who would not tolerate the relationship between the two related parties. He watched over his daughter out of love, concerned that she follow the Chemehuevi way of being. William may have had a deeper dislike for other reasons as well. Willie Boy appears to have been an impulsive and hot-tempered young man, traits a father would not find endearing in a potential son-in-law. The young man had also reportedly followed the Ghost Dance, a new religion of the late nineteenth century born to Northern Paiute people near Bishop, California. Wovoka, the Paiute Prophet or Ghost Dance Prophet, had reintroduced the Ghost Dance among the Northern Paiute people in 1889. His father had been active in the first Ghost Dance, which had survived in a latent manner. On January 1, 1889, Wovoka experienced his own revelations from the Creator. Wovoka told anthropologist James Mooney: "I saw God, with all the people who had died long ago engaged in old time sports and all the people who had died long ago engaged in old time sports and occupations, all happy and forever young." The Creator told Wovoka to return to the people to tell them to "love one another, have no quarreling, and live in peace with whites." The Creator wanted Indian people to work, to not lie or steal. Native Americans could hasten a Native apocalypse through ceremony, dancing, and singing for five days.[9]

Willie Boy had learned the Ghost Dance from friends and relatives among Southern Paiute. The Chemehuevi spoke the same language as the Northern Paiute, with dialectical differences. Southern Paiute peoples, including the Chemehuevi, learned of the Ghost Dance movement that asked followers to pray and sing in anticipation of a Native apocalypse. The world would turn over and be renewed without the hindrance of white people. The Creator would restore plants, animals, and places to aboriginal days when people lived from the bounty of the earth without dreadful diseases and government policies.[10]

While Willie Boy likely gravitated to the Ghost Dance, William Mike—a healer, holy man, and civil leader—adhered to the Chemehuevi way. He and the people sang and danced but did not follow the new belief.

Another issue troubled William Mike. Reports spread that Willie Boy already had a wife, and William may have foreseen difficulties for Carlota in this situation. Oral histories with Willie's family do not support the rumor that Willie Boy had a wife and had secreted her away so that he could marry Carlota.[11] No doubt, however, William was concerned about a possible relationship between Carlota and Willie Boy, because the two young people were too closely related. William Mike vowed not to allow Willie and Carlota to break tribal law. The issue of tribal law involving incest emerged during the time of Creation, when tribal law first came to all Southern Paiute people, including the Chemehuevi. The people considered the laws to be sacrosanct, and leaders expected everyone to follow them without exception. But times had changed, and young people had started to question the ancient rules. The Southern Paiute explain that the incest laws of their people were closely tied to a covenant theology. If one couple broke this law, all Southern Paiute would suffer from the violation, the law being that significant. Therefore the violation of the incest laws by Willie and Carlota provided the foundation for the conflict between William Mike and Willie Boy and their families, not many of the other matters offered in newspaper or popular novel accounts. Among the Southern Paiute, the incest laws offered the key to understanding the tribal issues that precipitated the entire Willie Boy affair.[12]

Carlota had grown up at Twenty-Nine Palms, and she knew everyone in the village. She was a blossoming young woman of sixteen in 1909, certainly old enough to marry. However, she was related to nearly everyone living at Twenty-Nine Palms. As a young woman, she likely looked forward to the day when she met young men who lived away from the oasis, young men with whom she might fall in love and marry. However, in accordance with tribal law, she could only marry a man approved by her family. Carlota came from a leadership family, a class of people that adhered strongly to traditional laws and values, and her father and mother had to approve her choice of husband. In fact, they may well have had ideas of their own for Carlota's match, because elders often selected spouses for their children, regardless of the young person's wishes. Carlota became smitten with Willie Boy, and he grew interested in her as well. Willie was born and raised along the Colorado River but had also lived in the Mojave or Colorado Deserts—often with his mother, Mary Snyder. Also, he had once lived in Victorville, California.

On one occasion in 1906, Willie Boy had served a jail sentence for "disturbing the peace," but jail sentences for Indians living near white communities were common in the late nineteenth and early twentieth centuries. Local law enforcement in California often arrested Indians for the slightest alleged violation, and courts frequently forced inmates to work off their debts to society by laboring outside of the jail. In this way the state and citizens received free labor from Indians who were not citizens of Victorville, San Bernardino County, the state of California, or the United States. The government classified Willie and most Indians as "wards," and as a result, Indians had few "constitutional" rights under the law. Although some whites enjoyed labeling Willie a criminal, Chemehuevi admired him because of his running ability.[13]

Among Chemehuevi, the people best knew Willie Boy as a great runner, not a criminal. He was a seasoned athlete and spiritual man who did not drink. He ranked among the elite few of young men who "ran in the old way." Willie had earned a reputation as a great athlete, and he honed his skills as a runner with other young men who could travel great distances at breakneck speed. Elders said that when the runners traveled in the "old way," they actually took flight.[14] Noted anthropologist Peter Nabokov has argued that runners "relied on powers beyond their own abilities to help them run for war, hunting, and sport. To dodge, maintain long distances, spurt for shorter ones, to breathe correctly and transcend oneself called for a relationship with strengths and skills which were the property of animals, trails, stars, and elements."[15] Willie Boy was such a runner, and many people admired him for his unusual ability.

According to Mary Lou Brown, Patrick Lyttle, Adrian Fisher, Joe Benitez, Alberta Van Fleet, and other Chemehuevi elders, Willie Boy and Carlota fell in love with each other, and this was the root of the troubles between Willie Boy and William Mike.[16] Although past authors have written extensively about Willie Boy and William Mike's death, they failed to interview the Chemehuevi families of William Mike or Willie Boy. Historians James Sandos and Larry Burgess conducted the first extensive oral histories about Willie Boy and the Chemehuevi for their path-breaking book, *The Hunt for Willie Boy*. The book provides several key interviews, but the most pertinent is that of Chemehuevi elder Mary Lou Brown.[17]

She explained that the story of Willie Boy, William Mike, and Carlota was "a simple story."[18] Furthermore, the most significant element of the story involved love. "Whenever my mother would tell this story," Brown said, "she always began by saying, 'Love is hard.'" According to the family, Willie Boy "needed a wife, but there were no young women nearby" where he lived "with his mother [Mary Snyder] in the desert." He moved to Twenty-Nine Palms to join his grandmother

WILLIE, WILLIAM, AND CARLOTA   ✷   183

and aunts as well as to find a wife. Willie "was young and strong, so he went across the desert looking for a wife." Not long after arriving at Twenty-Nine Palms, Willie "saw his cousin, Carlota, and he wanted her." Carlota "looked back at him openly, and they both ran away together." However, because tribal incest laws forbade their relationship, members of both families "followed and found them." Elders from both families separated them and explained the problem of a relationship between these two young people. After the elders separated Willie and Carlota, Willie left the oasis and moved to Banning. The Mike family tried to reestablish their normal routine and put Carlota back into balance with tribal laws. In July 1909 the Mike family traveled to the Gilman Ranch in Banning to work. Carlota traveled with the family.[19]

When the Mike family traveled across the desert from Twenty-Nine Palms, Willie had already relocated in Banning. After the Mike family began their work at the Gilman Ranch, Willie appeared at the ranch. The Gilman family hired Willie Boy, knowing him to be an excellent worker. He likely signed on to be close to beautiful young Carlota. According to officials at the Gilman Ranch, Riverside County Park, Willie Boy roomed with the youngest son of the Gilman family. The two young men were friends, and they took up residence together.[20] Willie Boy and Carlota secretly visited with each other at the ranch, and they found moments away from their elders. They talked about reigniting their relationship. However, William and Maria Mike kept a fairly tight rein on Carlota, and they continually lectured her about keeping her distance from her cousin, Willie Boy. Chemehuevi elder Mary Lou Brown said that the elders had warned Willie that he "was not to look at her again." But "both their hearts were still restless."[21] Whether the couple prearranged a meeting on the night of September 26, 1909, is only conjecture, but they had spoken to each other and were determined to renew their relationship.

Although no one knows for certain, Carlota likely refused to marry Willie Boy without her father's permission. The couple probably decided Willie should try to talk with William Mike about taking his daughter's hand in marriage. Did this translate into an attitude of rebellion against tradition and cultural ways? Or did the couple believe that they owed it to William to explain their position before they ran off together to live as husband and wife? Given her recent education regarding incest laws, Carlota likely insisted that Willie speak to her father out of tribal respect. Whatever the motivation, Willie visited William Mike. Mary Lou Brown offered her view, saying Willie wanted to marry Carlota, "but her father was a man of power." Willie feared William Mike because he was a medicine person and a leading elder among the people. "Willie Boy got a rifle and came to see her father," Brown explained. William was a man of sixty-five years, but he was strong, robust, and fearless. In his youth, he had been a warrior fighting Mojave. Willie knew that William Mike would not receive the news well, so he carried a weapon to protect himself. No evidence exists to suggest he intended to murder the elder.[22] Willie simply feared William Mike and brought the gun to protect himself.

In his book on Willie, writer Harry Lawton claimed that Willie Boy was a drinker and was drunk when he talked to William Mike. Historians Sandos and Burgess have successfully deconstructed this myth about Willie Boy, pointing out that the rumor of his drunkenness did not emerge until after the manhunt ended in October 1909, and that the stories grew from one bottle of whiskey to two bottles of beer to half a suitcase of whiskey. Willie was a runner and athlete. He was not a drinker or alcoholic. His contemporaries did not consider Willie Boy a drinker of spirits, and he likely drank little, if at all. Employers of Willie Boy never complained of Willie drinking, and Willie did not miss work because of alcohol use or abuse. He was an athlete in great shape, and the Chemehuevi have no account of him being drunk when he visited William Mike. No credible record exists to support Lawton's assertion. Two accounts exist of Willie's meeting with William, but rumors suggesting that Willie murdered William while the elder slept are absurd.[23]

According to Mary Lou Brown, "One night Willie Boy got a rifle and came to see her [Carlota's] father." The two men "argued, and Willie Boy got mad." Willie visited William around 9:00 P.M., but the talk likely turned heated. William had previously made his views known, and he refused to budge. William believed in the old laws taught to all Southern Paiute, and the incest laws still applied. Carlota and Willie were too closely related, and William would not allow his daughter to marry. To consent would run contrary to the Chemehuevi's and William's belief systems. The couple, family, and all Paiute people would be placed in jeopardy of disease and death if the two violated the marriage laws. Thus William flatly refused to give his permission to the couple. No one knows exactly what happened, but when Willie persisted, a scuffle ensued, the rifle fired, and William was killed as the gun went off in his face. Willie ran. Brown maintained simply that "Willie Boy killed her [Carlota's] father, then he and Carlota ran away again."[24]

Whatever the details, the fact remains that the rifle discharged in William's face, and William Mike died of gunshot wound. According to some accounts, Willie Boy threatened to kill the entire Mike family unless they allowed Carlota to accompany him. Apparently no one objected to the couple running away, not even Carlota's older brothers. Willie had a rifle and had used it once. William

Mike's boys could have feared what Willie might do to the rest of the family. Moreover, the Mike family was in shock. They had lost a husband, father, and leader of the tribe. Maria Mike reportedly told Carlota to go, and her brothers did not follow the couple or immediately report the murder to authorities. The young woman and her family must have been emotionally conflicted and confused. Carlota finally had an opportunity to be with the man she loved, but he was also the man responsible for killing her father. In any case, the two fled on foot that night, heading northeast into the rugged mountains and deserts. They ran off toward The Pipes and the trail leading to the Oasis of Twenty-Nine Palms.[25]

Maria Mike and her family reportedly fled into the hills to get away from the violent scene on the night of September 26, 1909. They did not notify Indian or white policemen of the killing of William Mike until 9:00 A.M. the following morning.[26] In a letter to her sister, Ethel Gilman wrote from the Gilman Ranch that she had not "heard any more of Willie Boy," but the posse had "tracked him out west through the orchard to the railroad then on to Cabazon." She repeated the posse's rumor that Willie was "driving" Carlota toward Whitewater. Native American consultants discount the idea of Willie abusing Carlota, because they loved each other and she had willingly escaped with him. Ethel Gilman told her sister that Willie had shot Mike with "Arthur's [Gilman, son of the ranchers] rifle, for they found the shell close by" the body. Willie had killed William Mike with one shot, taking "the rifle and about 50 cartridges." She speculated that Willie would "fight for [h]is life." Ethel concluded on the sad note that the Indians had "buried Mike at Portrero."[27]

Chemehuevi elder Brown noted that after the killing, "the whites chased them, along with some of The People." On the morning of September 27 law enforcement officials formed a posse that included Joe Toutain, Ben de Crevecoeur, Wal de Crevecoeur, Charlie Reche, and others. Two notable Indian trackers joined the posse, including Segundo Chino, a Pass Cahuilla with Chemehuevi blood and brother of the famed Cahuilla Pul amnawet, Pedro Chino, and the Kumeyaay (Diegeño) John Hyde. Indian people considered Chino a reliable man of strength, stamina, and good judgment. He served the Native community at Morongo as a peace officer for years, and he had been one of the people who had found Carlota and Willie Boy when they first eloped at Twenty-Nine Palms. In September 1909, Chino became a member of the posse chasing the couple again, but this time his objectives included bringing in William's killer and returning Maria's daughter.[28] John Hyde, a Kumeyaay Indian with roots in southern California and northern Baja California, also accompanied the

Riverside, Cal., Oct. 1st, 1909

Wanted for Murder

$50.00 Reward

Willie Boy, a Chimawawa Indian. 28 years old. Height 5 feet 8 or 9 inches. Weight 150 pounds. Smooth face. Medium build. Has a scar under his chin where he was shot about three years ago, the bullet coming out of the mouth, taking out two or three teeth. Wore new black hat, dark gray coat and pants.

Willie Boy is wanted for the murder of Old Mike, an Indian, on Sept. 26, 1909, at Banning, Cal. He also shot and killed Old Mike's daughter on Sept. 30th, after forcing her to follow him 70 miles in the mountains. He was trailed to a point about 25 miles northeast of The Pipes in the San Bernardino mountains on Sept. 30, 1909, and was headed toward Daggett or Newberry. He has a 30-30 rifle with him and is a desperate man. Take no chances with him. I hold warrant for murder. Arrest and send any information to

F. P. WILSON, Sheriff.

After Willie Boy killed William Mike on September 26, 1909, members of the posse accused him of killing Carlota Mike, the woman he loved. Following her death, Riverside County offered a reward of fifty dollars for information leading to Willie's arrest. This is a photograph of the Wanted Poster for Willie Boy, preserved at the University of California–Riverside. Special Collections and Archives, University of California–Riverside.

posse.[29] He and Segundo Chino rode in front of the posse as trackers. According to newspaper accounts—not the Indian trackers—the two Native trackers found "signs" that Willie was pushing Carlota along the rocky trail, prodding her with his rifle, beating and raping her occasionally. All this, the newspapers claimed, the trackers had discerned from reading the signs—a spurious claim by the media that went unsubstantiated by the Indian trackers. In addition, reporters claimed the Indian trackers got so close to the couple that they could hear Carlota crying as Willie Boy drove her forward. However, even though

Willie and Carlota traveled on foot and the trackers on horseback, the Indian trackers never closed the gap sufficiently to capture Willie and Carlota.[30]

In reality, the trackers never got so close to the couple that they could hear Carlota's whimpers or to capture them. Accounts by James L. Carling in the *Desert Magazine* of Carlota writing in "Piute signs" that Willie planned to kill her or that "My heart is almost going . . . I will be dead soon" is just pure nonsense, created by a fanciful writer who attributed the reading of the sign to Serrano elder Jim Pine.[31] Non-Native members of the posse, newspaper companies, and inventive authors wanted to sell their stories, hence spinning accounts to please themselves and their audiences. Storytellers, liars, and writers enjoyed the limelight of sharing their purported knowledge of Native American cultures.[32] The Chemehuevi, like other indigenous people throughout the Americas, had created pictographs and petroglyphs for thousands of years, offering symbolic representations of ideas, dreams, stories, and knowledge understood by those with whom they communicated. They did not write such descriptive sentences in Chemehuevi signs since no such language existed. Storytellers had fabricated the account of Carlota, who reportedly wrote "on a smooth bit of wind-blown sand." Apparently only the Chemehuevi-Cahuilla lawman Segundo Chino could understand the message. Nonsense! The posse may have used the story to spur themselves on, and the public used it to justify the capture of Willie Boy or sensationalize the manhunt. White members of the posse and clever Western American authors created a great myth about the signs in the sand, motivated by the desire to see their names in print, sell newspapers, and validate their knowledge of American Indian culture, which proved superficial.[33]

Although members of the posse never got close enough to Willie and Carlota to capture the couple, Kumeyaay tracker Hyde got sufficiently close to fire his rifle.[34] Between September 26 and 30, Willie and Carlota led the posse on a breakneck journey across the southern border of the Mojave Desert and Coachella Valley, a rocky and rugged arid terrain composed of huge boulders. Willie and Carlota traveled on foot, while the posse moved on horseback. Still, the couple always remained in front of the posse, a tribute to their skill in running and surviving in the desert. When they left the Banning area, they crossed the Morongo Hills toward Mission Creek, a geographical area that included a small creek and a Serrano village. Willie and Carlota had traveled these trails many times in the past, and they knew the area extremely well. The couple knew where to find food and water. From the sandy desert floor and rocky hills, the route took them through a pass that separated the eastern base of the San Bernardino Mountains from the western edge of the Little San Bernardino

In 1909, Segundo Chino and John Hyde joined the posse and served as Indian trackers during the hunt for Willie Boy. Chino, an Indian policeman from the Morongo Reservation, told Juan Siva and Katherine Siva Saubel that the posse never found Willie Boy dead. Saubel reported the posse threatened Chino, telling him not to divulge the fact that they never found Willie's body. This supports the indigenous interpretation that Willie Boy survived the manhunt and lived out his life in southern Nevada among the Paiute. Special Collections and Archives, University of California–Riverside.

Mountains. The landscape remains extremely rough in this area today, with steep canyons and barren, rocky mountains dotted here and there with mesquites, palo verde, creosote, Joshua trees, and yucca.

Willie and Carlota led the posse into the foothills of the mountains to a place called The Pipes, a majestic area with huge white boulders where deer, bears, and cougars roam to this day.[35] Small streams flow from the San Bernardino Mountains during the winter and spring or during storms that visit the mountain heights in the summer. Willie knew how to obtain water and food from the abundant plant and animal life found in the area of The Pipes. The site was located on the trail to Twenty-Nine Palms, the home of Willie's grandmother, the elder Mrs. Ticup, and the family and friends of Carlota Mike. At The Pipes, Willie separated from Carlota, leaving her in the massive rocks while he moved off to hunt small game and gather such desert foods as mesquites, chia, piñon nuts, and the fruit of cactus, yucca, and Joshua tree. Chemehuevi elder Mary Lou Brown remembered that "Willie Boy hid his wife [Carlota] in a wash" and "gave her his coat, and water skin, and went for food." When Willie "came back with food," he "could not find his wife."[36]

In the early morning of September 30, 1909, John Hyde saw someone moving in the huge boulders at The Pipes. Before 7:00 A.M., Hyde could see clearly for miles around him. With the sun rising in the east, the bright light animated the entire desert at the base of the San Bernardino Mountains. In the rocks far ahead, Hyde saw a human about seventy-five to one hundred yards from him carrying a canteen and either wearing Willie's distinctive coat or carrying it. Given the evidence provided by Burgess and Sandos, Hyde likely made a terrible error. He likely thought he had spotted Willie Boy, because he could easily recognize the coat, dark skin, and black hair of the person scrambling over the rocks. He carried a modern rifle with a scope. He probably rested it on a rock to take careful aim. He fired a shot and the bullet hit its mark, dropping the person to the ground. Hyde moved quickly to reach the body while the echo of the bullet continued and faded into the rocky landscape of The Pipes. When he reached the body, he found that he had shot and mistakenly killed Carlota.

According to official accounts, mining foreman Charles Reche, who had joined the posse chasing Willie Boy, reached the body first, and Reche reported that Willie Boy had killed the girl because she had slowed his progress. By concocting this story, the posse covered up Hyde's mistake and made Willie Boy a double murderer. The public already believed the worst about Willie Boy, and members of the posse and others set about to create an image of Willie Boy as a ruthless murderer, a person who easily fit the negative image of an Indian as a savage human being without conscience, scruples, values, or intelligence—save for his animal instincts that had made him so formidable an enemy in the deserts and mountains.[37] Willie Boy had murdered William Mike. Regardless of the circumstances, the young Chemehuevi had taken the elder's life. But Willie had not murdered the woman he loved. Most likely, Hyde accidentally shot her, and the posse opted to blame Willie Boy for the deed. That is the Native American perspective. As a member of the posse, the others did not want to tarnish Hyde's reputation because a mark against Hyde was a mark against all the lawmen, so they invented the story that Willie Boy had killed his "wife."[38]

Not all people were willing to accept the posse's story. According to the coroner and his jury, the fatal bullet hit Carlota "just behind the left shoulder" and had cut its way downward through her breast." The bullet came "out through the right abdominal cavity." Scholars Sandos and Burgess investigated the death of Carlota Mike. They concluded that the wound was "consistent with the trajectory of a long-range shot." The coroner and his jury questioned the theory that Willie Boy had murdered Carlota at close range, saying that Carlota died of a "gunshot wound in the back fired by a party to the jury unknown."[39] If Willie Boy had shot Carlota with his rifle, the bullet would have moved more directly through her body. Even more important is the fact that Willie Boy loved Carlota, and all their troubles had arisen over their love for each other. After traveling miles into the desert to escape with his future wife, Willie had little cause to kill the person he loved. Still, his actions contrary to Chemehuevi culture had led to Carlota's death as well as that of William Mike, and neither the Mike family nor the general public would excuse Willie for his role in their deaths. Many Chemehuevi and Southern Paiute likely agreed with the Mike family, condemning his actions. The posse had to blame someone for Carlota's death, so they accused Willie Boy, the "savage" villain of the episode. Willie brought the calamity on himself by breaking tribal law, attempting to marry a young woman too closely related and by going to see William Mike with a weapon. White members of the posse, reporters, the Indian agent, and others joined in the condemnation of Willie Boy by circulating unsubstantiated rumors and outright lies about the young Chemehuevi that coalesced into a negative image of this young man. It reflected negatively on other Native people of the region as well. Myths created by non-Natives live on today and continue to taint the way people view Willie Boy, California Indians, and the history associated with the "last Western manhunt."[40]

The posse gave up the chase temporarily after Carlota's death, returning to Banning for supplies. They traveled back to Banning with her body, and turned over her remains to Maria Mike and her family. The Mike family mourned Carlota's death in traditional fashion. They sang Salt Songs to her honor, just days after they had sung these mourning songs for William Mike. They sang their sad songs, sending Carlota on her journey to the next world. At the same time, Willie Boy likely sang the Salt Songs, mourning his loss, honoring Carlota, and helping her make the transition to the afterlife.[41] While the Cahuilla, Chemehuevi, Serrano, and others sang, non-Indian people printed a dramatic wanted poster for Willie Boy, dated October 5, 1909, calling for his "Arrest for Double Murder." The poster described Willie Boy as a Chemehuevi man "26 years old, about 5 feet, 10 inches in height; slim built, walks and stands erect; yellowish complexion, sunken cheeks; high cheek bones; talks good English with a drawl; has a scar under chin where he has been shot and some teeth gone." The poster announced that Willie Boy had once lived in Victorville "with a half-breed American woman with two children, a girl of 10 and a boy of 2 years." Writers of the poster further claimed that Willie's common law wife had "left him because he had beaten her." They noted correctly that Willie Boy had relatives "living among the Kingston Mountains, along the Nevada state line." Although non-Indians claimed Willie had a mixed-blood wife, his relatives had no recollection of this arrangement, and no other documents of the time support this assertion. He may have had a former wife or newcomers may have created another fabrication to destroy Willie's character.[42]

Willie's life in the deserts of Southern California provided him with great knowledge of the natural environment and survival skills. He knew the area around The Pipes and that region east of Victorville in the high desert just north of the San Bernardino Mountains. This land had been the home of the Serrano and Southern Paiute, some of whom the Spanish had forced into Missions San Fernando and San Gabriel. Some Chemehuevi had moved to areas surrounding Victorville. Willie Boy had moved there to find work, and he reportedly had lived there for a short time. Certainly he was familiar with the area between The Pipes and Victorville as well as the desert and mountains between The Pipes and Twenty-Nine Palms. This was his homeland, but he also knew the Mojave Desert from the San Bernardino Mountains to the Colorado River and north to the Southern Paiute villages near Pahrump and Las Vegas, Nevada.

When the posse resumed its manhunt, they returned to The Pipes, where they picked up Willie's trail that took them to Bullion Mountain (later renamed Ruby Mountain), which was fewer than ten miles from the place where Hyde had accidentally shot Carlota. John Hyde and Segundo Chino led the posse that consisted of Wal de Crevecoeur, John Knowlin, and Charlie Reche. As the posse approached the base of Ruby Mountain, Hyde saw signs on the ground that led him to believe that Willie had made them. Most likely Willie had left the trail to lead the posse to his makeshift rock fort in the mountains. When Chino found the trail, every member of the posse dismounted to study the signs and search the rocks above for Willie Boy. The posse left their horses in the open while they climbed the rocks. Willie Boy had the posse covered and had the advantage. He had built a barricade of rocks high on Ruby Mountain where he had a commanding view of the approaching lawmen. His position at Ruby Mountain was similar to Cochise's stronghold in southeastern Arizona, the natural fortress of the great Chiricahua Apache chief. From his position Willie could see the approach of his enemies. Willie opened fire on the horses, killing three horses, wounding another, and frightening a fourth horse. If he had been the cold-blooded murderer portrayed in Western lore, he would have shot members of the posse. Chemehuevi elder Mary Lou Brown remembered the story this way: she reported that Willie Boy "found the men chasing him and shot their horses with his rifle so that they would have to run like he did." In other words, she suggested Willie enticed the posse to him where he could kill their mounts and put them on foot, just like him. Willie Boy was a great runner and he knew how to survive in the Mojave Desert. Shooting the horses of the posse was Willie's way of laying down the gauntlet, inviting the posse to come on foot to take him—if they could.[43]

The advantage rested with Willie because members of the posse—including Chino—couldn't run like Willie. "He was so much faster" than the posse and had been throughout the chase. Reche carried handcuffs in his jeans, the metal dangling from his hips and creating a reflection in the desert sun—a wonderful target that Willie Boy hit, sending a bullet into the cuffs and Reche's body. The bullet fragmented when it entered Reche's hip and thigh, causing excruciating pain. It was not a mortal wound. Reche remained in pain on the desert floor until nightfall in plain sight of Willie. The Chemehuevi man did not kill Reche. During the chaos, Hyde realized that he could not help Reche without exposing himself to Willie's rifle fire, so the Kumeyaay tracker raced off toward The Pipes on foot to sound the alarm and find help. Indian agent Clara True claimed that Willie had tried to shoot Hyde as he ran away. "John [Hyde] jumped from his cover as soon as his mind was made up," True wrote in her report. She stated that Hyde "darted across the open in range of Willie Boy's gun, narrowly escaping two shots by doubling up and jumping sidewise as only an Indian knows how to do."[44] Meanwhile, Chino tried to attack Willie from the rear, but Willie fought from his fort, keeping Chino at bay. Willie pinned down the attackers

In 1909 the Riverside County Sheriff's Department initiated a manhunt for Willie Boy, a Chemehuevi who had killed William Mike at the Gilman Ranch in Banning, California. Native American consultants argue that the person laying down by the rocks was a member of the posse, not Willie Boy. Riverside County forensic anthropologist Deborah Gray stated the body was "articulated" and showed no signs of animal or insect activity on the body, making the body in the photograph inconsistent with a corpse lying in the desert for days. Randolph W. Madison took this photograph of the posse and the purported body of Willie Boy. Special Collections and Archives, University of California–Riverside.

until dark, when the posse retreated with Reche strapped to a horse Hyde had brought back. Agent True reportedly drove her automobile "loaded with food, ammunition and emergency remedies" to help the posse. "This machine," True claimed, "was the only one which proved of any use in getting through the sand." But rescuers resorted to horses to help the posse. As the posse retreated and help arrived, some members of the posse claimed that Willie Boy shot his rifle one last time.[45] This point is highly significant.

The posse made its way back to Banning with stories that Willie had committed suicide or that Chino had shot him. This made good copy for the press and helped redeem the emasculated posse. To add evidence for the story that

Willie had fallen, either at his own hand or that of Chino's, the posse circulated stories that they were certain that Willie had died in the desert. Some people speculated that Willie Boy had died in the shootout, while others said that Willie Boy had committed suicide. Not everyone in Banning and the surrounding area believed that Willie had died, and they openly encouraged the posse to return to the desert and get their man. In the aftermath of the manhunt, local newspapers were not content to run the true story of the family tragedy. They felt compelled to exaggerate facts and defame Willie Boy's entire character. Apparently it was not titillating enough that Willie Boy had murdered his lover's father, a respected elder. Stories soon emerged that Willie Boy and Chemehuevi warriors had threatened the life of President William Howard Taft, who had planned to visit the area. Newspaper editors claimed the Indian desperado threatened the president and speculated on a Chemehuevi uprising. No evidence exists that Willie Boy or any other Indian in Southern California intended to harm the president. Like so much written about Willie Boy, the yellow journalists made up stories to sell papers. Editors suggested that since Willie had once been arrested in Victorville, the young Indian man might be inclined to assassinate the president. Other outrageous stories depicted Willie as an Indian renegade, the leader of a new Indian war. The accusations speak more about the honesty and character of editors than Willie and other indigenous people.[46]

Newsmen also began running stories depicting Willie Boy as a drunk when he had approached William Mike. Ben de Crevecoeur smeared Willie Boy's name. He and others used the "drunken Indian theme" to destroy Willie's character—a theme that played well with the non-Native audience that read newspapers and helped perpetuate stereotypes that Indians drank too much and had loose morals. Editors and storytellers depicted Willie as alcoholic, wild, dangerous, and unpredictable. Newspapers stirred up trouble by claiming that the Chemehuevi and Serrano at Twenty-Nine Palms had planned an Indian war throughout Southern California. Some reports urged law enforcement officials to round up Indians and horses, including the people at Twenty-Nine Palms. Agent True sent deputies to round up the people at Twenty-Nine Palms, but "the old women were in sympathy with the boy" and could not be found. Another account suggested that San Bernardino County sheriff John C. Ralphs had also traveled to the oasis or sent his men to round up the Chemehuevi. Even though these men could not locate Willie's aunts and grandmother—because they had "disappeared from the Palms apparently without leaving tracks"—True reported having men gather up (steal) the horses "from the Palms and taken to a ranch some thirty miles away to prevent the use of the ponies by Willie Boy."[47]

At least some of the people remained at Twenty-Nine Palms. Nellie Holmes Mike Morongo had remained at the oasis with Willie's grandmother, Mrs. Ticup, and two of his aunts.[48] Records provide confusing accounts of what happened immediately after Willie Boy held off the posse and shot Reche. Clearly the oral histories of Chemehuevi and other Indians do not always match those left in writing. No contemporary Native American consultant has ever suggested the people planned to harm the president or rise in war. The suggestion is ridiculous.

The press wanted the chase to continue, because the hunt for Willie Boy sold newspapers. So editors goaded the posse into action through their sensational words, but members of the posse were in no hurry to outfit themselves again and race back into the Mojave Desert in search of Willie Boy. They had tired of the pursuit and hardships, so they remained in Banning for some rest. They also discussed among themselves their next course of action. The posse appeared incompetent, complete failures. They greatly outnumbered Willie Boy and they traveled on horseback with supplies, weapons, and ammunition. Willie lived off the land. Yet the white posse and their Indian scouts could not capture Willie Boy and bring him back, dead or alive. The posse had walked into a trap, allowed their horses to be shot and scattered, and permitted a lone gunman to wound one of them. Rather than continuing the pursuit, the posse had retreated, given up. Perhaps most mortifying for these Western lawmen, a female Indian agent had arranged their rescue. Members of the posse had much to live down when they resumed the great and "last" Western manhunt.

Eight days after Willie Boy had ambushed the posse at Ruby Mountain, the posse returned to the mountain on October 15, 1909, and reportedly found Willie Boy's body. They claimed Willie had committed suicide with his last bullet, just as they had predicted. They provided no proof of the suicide, and no clear rationale as to why Willie Boy, the man who had single-handedly pinned down the posse and shot their horses, would suddenly kill himself. The assertion of suicide lacks convincing evidence. It defies logic. According to white accounts, Ben de Crevecoeur, not Hyde or Chino, claimed to have found Willie Boy's body. The Indian trackers who normally led the group had to remain in the rear. The white men never explained why their Indian scouts, who knew how to read the signs far better than any white man, had remained at the rear of the posse. The posse claimed that Willie Boy had removed his boot, cocked his rifle, and used his bare toe to fire the rifle into his body. In this way, the posse claimed, Willie Boy had committed suicide. We have only their word for it. Rather than bringing in Willie Boy's remains, the posse reportedly cremated his body. Their justification was that his body was swollen and rotting, and cremation was a better option than strapping his body onto a horse or using a lengthy lariat to bring in their prey. The posse claimed they used fuel found at the site to build the crematory fire, though it is questionable whether sufficient amounts of fuel existed to cremate a body.[49]

Even more amazing, the posse did not take close-up pictures of Willie's body. Randolph Madison carried a camera and readily took photographs. However, he made no clear photograph of the notorious outlaw. In Western history, photographers took close-up, detailed pictures of such outlaws as the Daltons, the Clantons, John Dillinger, and Bonnie and Clyde. Madison made no close-ups to prove that the posse had gotten their man. According to Dr. Deborah Gray, forensic scientist of the coroner's office of Riverside County, the photographs Madison had created showed a body too articulated or put together for a body dead so long. Gray suggested the arms and legs should not have been attached. Because the limbs had not fallen apart, Gray questioned whether the body shown in Madison's photos was in fact that of Willie Boy. Gray noted that Madison's photographs illustrated no sign of insect or mammal damage, which should have shown up as areas eaten away at the body. Finally, Gray pointed out that the shirt worn by the man on the ground was too clean and not torn apart by animal activity. She concluded that if the body shown in the Madison photos was a corpse, it had been dead only twenty-four hours.[50] The posse even covered the face of the large man they had photographed. Throughout the American West, lawmen commonly documented the capture, killing, and execution of notorious criminals. Lawmen often used photography to record the deaths of outlaws, including Charlie Pierce, Bitter Creek Newcomb, Tulsa Jack Blake, Sam and Billy LeRoy, Cole Estes, Dick West, Cherokee Ned Christie, and Bill Brazelton.[51]

For non-Indians the posse's story of Willie Boy taking his own life offered a dramatic, satisfying conclusion, even though it would have been better for the posse to have claimed to have killed Willie Boy outright. But the suicide story had to do, and it corroborated their earlier story to the press that they believed Willie had committed suicide or that Chino had shot him to death. The story satisfied a number of purposes: it protected the tarnished reputation of the posse; it satisfied the press; and it perpetuated the myth of the heathen "savage" who preferred the sin of suicide to a speedy trial and swift hanging. Historians Sandos and Burgess leave the conclusion up to the reader, because as a Ghost Dancer, Willie Boy could reunite with Carlota in the afterlife, returning to those days before white contact when only Indians and the natural world existed in the deserts and mountains. Indians from many tribes in Arizona, California, and Nevada claim that Willie Boy got away, lived in Nevada, and ultimately died of tuberculosis. The oral tradition of the Southern Paiute also includes a law against suicide, and Willie understood that Ocean Woman, Wolf, Coyote, and other characters of Chemehuevi Creation would have forbidden suicide. He had already violated traditional law by marrying Carlota and murdering her father, and after her death he chose life and revenge—not death.[52]

Native Americans in western Arizona, California, Nevada, and Utah have never believed that Willie committed suicide. The oral traditions of many tribal people conflict with the posse's story, particularly about Willie's alleged suicide. Since 1909, Indians have explained that Willie Boy got away and spent his life in southern Nevada, most likely in Pahrump, Nevada, close to the eastern border of California. Non-Indians have noted this Indian "tale" but gave it little or no credibility. For example, in his famous book *Willie Boy: A Desert Manhunt*, Harry Lawton wrote: "Indians have their version of the legend. They scoff at reports that Willie Boy's body was burned on the ridge at Ruby Mountain." Lawton claimed that Indians maintained that Willie "escaped into Mexico, where he married and had many children," or that Willie "passed away with tuberculosis in a Nevada sanatorium in 1933." Indeed, Lawton claimed he had interviewed Indians who "insist they heard the story of his [Willie's] escape from his own lips." Lawton further claimed that Indians felt that Willie Boy's saga "represented something, stood for some romantic cause, although they scratch their heads and lapse into silence if asked to explain."[53]

When Katherine Siva Saubel, Cahuilla elder and friend of Harry Lawton, learned that Lawton planned to write about Willie Boy, she asked him to get the story correct. She explained to Lawton that Willie had escaped and lived out his life among Paiute in Nevada. According to Indian accounts, Willie never committed suicide but ran to freedom and lived out his life in Nevada, melting into the Paiute who inhabited the region.[54] Since 1909, Indians have had their own interpretations about Willie Boy, but Lawton and other non-Indians ignored Indian accounts, and they failed to interview the Southern Paiute of Pahrump. Authors have marginalized or silenced indigenous accounts. Indians based their views on their own evidence found within their own communities, primarily oral interviews with Willie Boy, his mother, his relatives, and friends. Non-Indians chose to ignore and devalue Indian oral interviews, so the written record reflects the interpretations of whites, not Indians. As a Nez Perce chief explained: "Nobody to help us tell our side—the whites told only one side. Told it to please themselves."[55]

The Indian story is very simple, a sketch of which is found below. After Willie Boy shot and scattered the posse's ponies and held off the lawmen, he left Ruby Mountain and headed east to Twenty-Nine Palms. A well-worn Indian trail traced the desert floor from Ruby Mountain to Twenty-Nine Palms, cutting through high desert lands, broken sandy washes, and plateaus running through deep sand. For thousands of years, Indians had traveled this trail to the east and west, back and forth from the Oasis of Mara to the San Bernardino Mountains and the Pacific Ocean. Indians living in the Mojave Desert had used the trail to travel to the mountains where they gathered live oak and black oak acorns, piñon nuts, and other natural foods as well as hunted bighorn sheep and deer. Willie traveled the trail east in October 1909, a time when the landscape turns brown, although thunderstorms looming and booming over the Mojave Desert could bring torrential rains that turn the desert vegetation of creosote, cactus, and Joshua trees into dark green and brings forth yellow flowers that dot the desert floor.

Willie Boy traveled on foot, not horseback, and he moved east toward the western and northern foothills of the Little San Bernardino Mountains, probably traveling at night and in the early morning hours of October 15 and 16. A great Chemehuevi runner, he made his way rapidly along the path shaded in the morning by the tall peaks found today within the boundaries of Joshua Tree National Park. According to Chemehuevi elder Mary Lou Brown, Willie Boy "was so much faster [than the posse] that he quickly ran off."[56] And Chemehuevi elders Joe Mike Benitez and Dean Mike say that family members told them that after the fight at Ruby Mountain, Willie eluded the posse and ran east to Twenty-Nine Palms.[57]

Indian accounts indicate that Willie Boy arrived at his old home at the Oasis of Twenty-Nine Palms, where he encountered his grandmother, Mrs. Ticup (also identified in the census data as Mrs. Waterman), and his aunts. His elders gave him a cool reception because his actions had led to two deaths. By violating tribal incest laws, Willie had invited the negative events that surrounded him. Mrs. Ticup scolded Willie for his behavior. He argued with his grandmother, who tossed his rifle into the pond. After shaking his grandmother, Willie ran north into the mountains, where he hid. Eventually, he worked his way through the east Mojave Desert by way of Chemehuevi villages, where people gave him aid to help him escape. Willie had family living in the Kingston Mountains and friends at the village located in the Old Woman Mountains, located about forty miles west of the Colorado River. He worked his way to Pahrump, Nevada, to live with the Southern Paiute community there.

Many contemporary California Indians state they learned the outline of this story from members of their families or tribal elders. It is a common story, one still told throughout the Great Basin, California, Utah, and Arizona. Indians say the posse never killed Willie Boy, and the young runner never committed suicide. He vanished into the Mojave Desert and lived out his life. Native Americans say the embarrassed posse made up their story to quiet critics and satisfy a public hungry for the death of an upstart Indian. For Native Americans the indigenous version of the Willie Boy story is the "real Indian history, the truth, and the story that needed to be told."[58]

On September 15, 2000, noted Cahuilla elder Katherine Saubel stated that Segundo Chino had been a close friend of her family. Katherine knew Chino so well that she called him grandfather, and she had many conversations with the Indian tracker. According to her, Chino first confided in his friend, Juan Siva, that "we never got him; he got away."[59] Saubel heard Chino make this declaration. She claimed that Chino and Juan Siva "never lied."[60] Juan Siva's oral testimony and that of Katherine Saubel is strong, credible evidence.[61] In many cases Native Americans do not care if non-Indians believe the Indian side of their accounts. They understand how non-Natives use history to frame their own truths.[62] The Chemehuevi people feel that non-Indians tell their stories to satisfy themselves. Chemehuevi elder Alberta Van Fleet bluntly told Burgess and Sandos: "The posse never got him, you know." She maintained that Willie Boy "got away to Nevada," where he ultimately "died in a sanatorium in Loften [Laughlin, Nevada?] in 1947."[63]

Chemehuevi elder Mary Lou Brown corroborated Van Fleet, telling Sandos and Burgess that Willie's mother (Mary Snyder) moved to the Colorado River "a few years after her son died in Nevada, in a sanatorium, in 1927 or 1928." Willie's own mother reported to other Indians that her son got away from the posse, lived out his life in Nevada, and died in Nevada of tuberculosis—not by his own hand at Ruby Mountain.[64] Snyder used to visit her son and take wagonloads of goods to him, likely meeting him between the Colorado River and Pahrump.[65] Nevertheless, at the end of their book, Sandos and Burgess concluded that "Willie Boy used darkness to join Carlota by killing himself with a rifle." They write Willie "did not choose to commit suicide because the posse wore him out; he killed himself to rejoin Carlota."[66] Despite this final interpretation, Burgess and Sandos believed that Willie Boy had "no reason to surrender" because he "could have run away easily."[67] Chemehuevi people argue that Willie Boy ran away and lived several years. For them, this is the correct and truthful version, and not because they consider Willie a hero. Many

Chemehuevi people deeply disapprove of Willie Boy's actions, but prefer their version of events.

Many parts of the Willie Boy story—from Carlota's death and shootout at Ruby Mountain to Willie's death at a "sanatorium"—deserve analysis. Some accounts suggest that after Willie Boy learned that Carlota was dead and the posse returned to Banning with her body, he ran from The Pipes to Twenty-Nine Palms, where his mother and grandmother resupplied him. Then, some say, he ran west back to Ruby Mountain, not far from Pipes Canyon. This makes little sense, since Willie Boy had a rifle to hunt game and could easily live off the land. He also knew the edible plants and could find food. His most logical direction of escape lay to the east and the great expanse of the Mojave Desert, including the Mojave River's drainage where he could find water and food. No one is certain about his whereabouts during the week between Carlota's death and the posse's return to Ruby Mountain. And no one knows for certain why he remained in the region and did not flee, although he likely decided to prepare for the posse's return so he could have a showdown. They had killed Carlota and he owed them some revenge.

Clearly Willie Boy could survive living off the desert, just as his Chemehuevi people had done for generations. He really had little need for supplies, including ammunition, because he had not shot at the posse up to this point. He may have used some ammunition to hunt, but even if he had needed ammunition, there was no guarantee that any of the Chemehuevi at Twenty-Nine Palms had the correct caliber of bullets. Besides, Twenty-Nine Palms was approximately forty miles from The Pipes, depending on the route taken—quite a distance to travel to and from on foot—and for what reason? More likely, he remained near the place where Carlota had died to mourn her death, to sing Salt Songs and cry, even though the posse had taken her body back to the Morongo Reservation for burial on the reservation next to her father.[68] Willie Boy loved Carlota, and remaining at or near The Pipes to say prayers, make offerings, and consider his course of action is more in keeping with the Indian way. When confronted with this argument, Cahuilla elder Katherine Saubel said, "I've always wondered about that, too." Why would Willie Boy run all the way to Twenty-Nine Palms and then return west to Ruby Mountain? Saubel thought it quite possible that Willie Boy spent his time mourning Carlota's death. She found it quite likely that after Carlota's death, Willie built the barricade out of rocks at Ruby Mountain and lay in wait so he could ambush the posse. He likely regretted his own actions that had brought about the death of William Mike, the triggering event of the entire affair.[69]

In the late 1940s, Maud Carrico Russell, a prominent resident of Twenty-Nine Palms, interviewed Chemehuevi elder Nellie Mike Morongo. Unfortunately the text of that interview has not come to light, although Russell reported on the interview in a small newspaper or newsletter called the Twenty-Nine Palms *Desert Spotlight*.[70] Originally Nellie had married Billy Mike, the eldest son of Jim Mike, the brother of William Mike. Both Nellie and Billy were Chemehuevi and residents of Twenty-Nine Palms during the Willie Boy affair. After Billy died from an accidental gunshot wound in 1909, Nellie had married Tom Morongo. After marrying Morongo, Nellie visited Maud Russell, who told her "soon after the slaying of Mike and his little daughter, Mrs. Waterman [Ticup] was the one who got Willie Boy's gun and ammunition and threw them into the irrigation pond in order to keep Willie Boy from continuing his rampage."[71] Sandos and Burgess discounted this story, not understanding perhaps that Nellie Morongo was a significant participant in the events of 1909. She and Billy Mike lived at Twenty-Nine Palms at the time of these events, and Nellie knew all the Native participants in the story.[72] If Willie Boy left The Pipes running to Twenty-Nine Palms after Carlota's death, according to Nellie Morongo, he would have lost his rifle and could not have returned to Ruby Mountain to shoot the posse. He would have had no weapon. He therefore traveled to The Pipes to wait for the posse. He had the showdown, shooting their horses. After the posse retreated, Willie ran to the oasis.

As for Willie Boy's rifle, Jane Smith, owner of the Twenty-Nine Palms Inn, stated that when her father owned the Twentynine Palms Inn (on the site of a Chemehuevi village), he once drained the irrigation pond near the village site and found a rusty rifle buried in the mud of the pond.[73] Of course, there is no guarantee that the rifle he found had once belonged to Willie Boy, but it is suggestive. For Chemehuevi people Nellie Morongo's story has validity, as does Nellie's account that when Willie's grandmother, the elder Mrs. Ticup (Waterman), threw his rifle into the pond, Willie responded angrily. Nellie told Russell that Willie attacked his own grandmother for scolding him and destroying his gun. Nellie said, "Willie Boy 'beat her up' terribly." Russell added that the beating likely caused the old woman's death. It is difficult to discern how much of this retelling can be directly attributed to Nellie Morongo and how much Russell added with literary license, but a new scenario arises from this bit of information provided by a Chemehuevi elder and contemporary of Willie Boy and all of the people then living at Twenty-Nine Palms.[74]

If traditional Chemehuevi practices are any guide, Willie Boy followed Carlota's death by singing and praying Salt Songs in mourning. Even if he was not a

Salt Song singer, he had heard the songs every time he attended a funeral or memorial. Rather than using the cover of darkness to kill himself at Ruby Mountain and reunite with Carlota, he began his journey to Twenty-Nine Palms. Agent Clara True reported that the sheriff had rounded up some Chemehuevi and forced them into Banning, but not all of them. Authorities stole Chemehuevi horses, but they could not find some Chemehuevi, particularly the old women in "sympathy" with Willie. They had moved into the mountains temporarily, camping near water. When the sheriff came to Twenty-Nine Palms to round up their horses and force the people to move to Banning, the female elders could not be found.[75] These women included Willie Boy's aunts and grandmother, Mrs. Ticup. When Willie Boy arrived at Twenty-Nine Palms, his elders had returned. They scolded and blamed him severely for killing William Mike, a medicine man and village leader, a relative of the Ticup family, Willie's own family. They condemned Willie for breaking tribal marriage ways and running off with Carlota, indirectly causing her death. The close relationship of the families had caused the difficulty in the first place, a fact emphasized in oral testimony again and again.

The elders at Twenty-Nine Palms chastised Willie for causing the death of William Mike and his daughter, Carlota. When Mrs. Ticup had the opportunity, she threw Willie Boy's rifle into the pond. The gun represented death and destruction of Chemehuevi people, and she tossed it into the pond so that Willie could harm no other person. Then she told him to leave. Willie reportedly grabbed and shook his grandmother out of anger and frustration, but a "beating" may be extreme. If Nellie suggested that Willie's beating of Mrs. Ticup contributed to her death, then the report could be credible. In any case, Willie Boy left Twenty-Nine Palms and moved across the desert that he knew so well. According to Chemehuevi elder Joe Mike Benitez, his mother reported that the Mike family always stated that Willie got away after his fight with the posse. Joe's mother, Susie Mike, was William Mike's young daughter, a baby in 1909, but she grew up with the story told by Chemehuevi relatives and other Native Americans. Although Susie was a child at the time, she claimed that Willie Boy had an argument with Mrs. Ticup and fled the oasis at Twenty-Nine Palms, running north into the mountains, where "he lived in a cave until things cooled down" and he thought it safe to continue his journey into the Mojave Desert.[76] When the posse failed to follow him to the oasis and beyond, he ultimately decided to run across the Mojave Desert, heading northeast. No one remembered his route. He may have taken the foot trail to the Old Woman Mountains before turning north to the Providence, New York, and Ivanpah Mountains, where Chemehuevi people once had villages. From there, he traveled to the Paiute village of Pahrump, west of Las Vegas, Nevada, where he joined other Southern Paiute people.[77]

According to Indian people, Willie traveled toward the Southern Paiute villages near Pahrump, Nevada, where he lived out his life. Chemehuevi elder Joe Mike Benitez pointed out that his mother always said that Willie Boy "went to live with relatives in Paiute country."[78] According to one Southern Paiute scholar, Willie went to Pahrump because the village contained a spiritual hill that opened up the line of power and communication into the Spring Mountains, the Creation site of the Chemehuevi and all Southern Paiute. According to this scholar's account, when Willie arrived, villagers met and decided to send him away before government police invaded their village. However, the medicine people had met with Willie and learned he had come to Pahrump to be healed. He asked for help. As a result, the shaman told the people they had an obligation to help Willie Boy come back into spiritual balance. If they refused, all Paiute people would be harmed. They would share in Willie's position of living out of balance with Southern Paiute cultural ways. This argument touched the people deeply. They allowed Willie Boy to live in their community to continue his spiritual journey to correct his many wrongs from murder, incest, and elder abuse. People at Pahrump, Las Vegas, and other Paiute communities believe Willie struggled with his spiritual demons and died of a severe lung infection.[79]

Before killing William Mike, Willie had worked with Indians and non-Indians, some of whom likely carried the tubercular bacteria. In the late nineteenth and early twentieth centuries, tuberculosis was the foremost infectious disease and killer among Native Americans in the United States, and many Native and non-Native people carried the bacteria. Willie had contracted tuberculosis sometime during his life, perhaps as a child. In any case, the bacterial disease developed in his body as it did among the bodies of many indigenous people during the late nineteenth and early twentieth centuries. Sometime after the killing, Indians say Willie came down with active tuberculosis, which caused him to lose weight, become weak, and cough blood. Tuberculosis killed Willie slowly, perhaps as the result of his negative actions. The disease apparently attacked Willie's lungs, but it may have settled in other organs or tissues of his body as well. His relatives reported that Willie died in a sanatorium in 1927 or 1928, although Alberta Van Fleet suggested the date of 1947. Chemehuevi Salt Song singer Matthew Hanks Leivas places the date of Willie's death about 1928, adding: "The white people keep getting the story wrong. All of us know that

Willie Boy got away and he died at a sanatorium in Nevada about 1928. At least that's what the elders like my mother and others always said. This is the Indian history about Willie Boy."[80]

Mary Lou Brown had told Burgess and Sandos that Willie Boy had died in a sanatorium in Lofton, Nevada.[81] She may have meant Laughlin, Nevada, where he may have traveled to seek help, but one Paiute scholar suggested that Willie died in the Pahrump area of Southern Nevada. However, officials at the Nevada Historical Society reported that no sanatorium ever existed in either Lofton or Laughlin, Nevada. Officials at the historical society explained that Lofton had been a rough mining town in a remote part of Nevada where state officials had never established a sanatorium. They suggested that the Chemehuevi elders had meant Lawton, Nevada, near Sparks and Reno, where Northern Paiute lived. But Lawton, Nevada, is situated many miles from Pahrump, a long way for a sick person sought by the law to travel. Still, Paiute people used a spring in Lawton for healing and Willie may have gone north to the Reno area to take the waters of the hot springs at Lawton, Nevada. No records have come to light to support the idea. Instead, every indigenous person interviewed about Willie Boy said he died in southern Nevada. During an interview with Alfreda Mitre, then chair of the Las Vegas Paiute Tribe and relative of the Mike family, stated that everyone in the area knew that Willie Boy "lived out his life with us." She said that she had heard this account her entire life and that he died in the area, perhaps in Pahrump.[82]

No one recorded Willie's tubercular treatment, if he had any Western medical attention at all. Indian healers likely doctored him, and he may have used a hot spring. He knew the medicine people of Pahrump and the power of the Spring Mountains. He likely sought the services of Paiute doctors, since they had supported his request to live at Pahrump in the first place. Regardless, no antibiotics existed during his life to treat tuberculosis, and Indian accounts say Willie died of lung disease or tuberculosis. He likely died a troubled, unsettled man, though he had attempted to be healed at Pahrump, a spiritual entrance into the Spring Mountains.

Non-Indians often claim that Willie Boy died violently at Ruby Mountain, but Indians claim that he died of tuberculosis or some other lung ailment in southern Nevada years after 1909. Willie won the battle with lawmen only to face other monsters—those that lived inside himself: physical, mental, and spiritual monsters. In his victory over the posse, Willie Boy was not victorious. He had lost Carlota, his family, and his community. He had lost his Chemehuevi way, his personal song. He had lost his social status among the Chemehuevi, and all of these conditions haunted him.

During the entire Willie Boy affair, the Office of Indian Affairs used the killing of William Mike as an excuse to remove the Chemehuevi and Serrano people from Twenty-Nine Palms. Officials of the Mission Indian Agency had wanted them removed from the desert in the early twentieth century, because the Indian Office could not easily direct policies to Chemehuevi people with them located more than fifty miles away through the steep landscape of the San Bernardino Mountains and the deep sands of the Mojave Desert. Only a few federal officials had ever traveled to Twenty-Nine Palms to take the Indian censuses. In 1909, before the Willie Boy affair, Malki agent Clara True traveled across the desert to Twenty-Nine Palms. She recorded her trip with documents and photographs. She offered William Mike, Jim Pine, and the people "better lands" on one of the other reservations near Banning, California, but residents of Twenty-Nine Palms chose to remain on their oasis homeland.

True and other authorities encouraged Chemehuevi and Serrano people to abandon the oasis, but to no avail until Willie Boy murdered William Mike. Immediately after the killing and the initial manhunt, True asked law enforcement officials to round up Indian horses and gather up the people. In the fall of 1909, True began moving the people to the Morongo Reservation or the Mission Creek Reservation. According to Joe Benitez, after his grandfather's death, the people chose to move away from Twenty-Nine Palms, fearing the ghost of William Mike who had died so violently. People may have buried him without full honor of an all-night Mourning Ceremony with Salt Songs and prayer. According to Paiute beliefs, this may have disturbed his soul and caused him to roam on earth rather than travel on north toward the spirit world. Benitez maintained that some of the people feared the spirit of William Mike. The ghost might return to the oasis and do harm. Fear of William's ghost contributed to people to leaving Twenty-Nine Palms. Some of the people refused to move, at least initially, but ultimately Agent True had her way and the government forced the Chemehuevi and Serrano from the oasis.

Jim and Matilda Pine moved to the Mission Creek Reservation east of the Morongo Reservation. When they moved, Jim moved his Big House or Ceremonial House to Mission Creek, "where he held ceremonies." According to Serrano elder Dorothy Ramon, Cahuilla medicine men or Puls from the Patencio family and other "ceremonial officials" from the Agua Caliente Reservation traveled to Twenty-Nine Palms to move the power found within the Ceremonial House to Mission Creek.[83] Some of the residents of Twenty-Nine Palms moved to Mission Creek, but others first moved to the Morongo Reservation, not far from the Gilman Ranch and the city of Banning where they found work. Before leaving their homes at Twenty-Nine Palms, the Chemehuevi people "destroyed their huts, burning everything that could be burned." In addition, they performed a special ceremony at the home of William Mike, Carlota Mike, and the Mike family. The people "plowed, or dug up the ground, as is their custom after the death of the owner."[84] According to Joe Mike Benitez, Chemehuevi turned the soil of his grandfather's home so that the spirit of William Mike and Carlota Mike would not find familiar ground around the home. By turning the earth at the village, the people wiped out the footsteps of the deceased so they could not find their way back there and would go on to the Spirit world. In this way, the spirits would continue their journeys north to the Land of the Dead, a Chemehuevi heaven in the Milky Way. This was where they belonged, not at their former homes at the Oasis at Twenty-Nine Palms.[85]

The killing of William Mike and his daughter Carlota, and the entire Willie Boy affair, remains highly significant in contemporary society. In 1960, author Harry Lawton published *Tell Them Willie Boy Is Here*, setting off a controversy that has raged ever since among scholars, lawmen, Indians, and Western history buffs. In 1969, Universal Pictures released a full-length motion picture by the same title, which has received some notoriety because Abraham Polonsky directed and Robert Redford, Katherine Ross, Robert Blake, Barry Sullivan, and Susan Clark starred in the film. Lawton served as adviser, and the film followed much of the storyline of his book. The film portrayed Willie as a drunk, even though he was not a drinker and casts him as a rapist, murderer, and coward. Rather than committing suicide or escaping, Willie had a shootout with the sheriff. Of course, Redford's character beat Willie in the gunfight and emerged a pseudo hero. Lawton, Polonsky, and the screenwriters ignored the Native American story. "The family of William Mike remembers the events surrounding William and Carlota's death as if they occurred yesterday."[86] For them and other indigenous people, the Willie Boy affair means more than an interesting story about the last Western American manhunt. According to some scholars, the Willie Boy story is a classic example of the way Indian hating manifested itself in diverse ways.

Historians Sandos and Burgess have proven this beyond any doubt in their masterful book *The Hunt for Willie Boy*. Yet the entire episode means far more to Chemehuevi people, as it constitutes a family and tribal tragedy. The story also symbolizes Native American individual sovereignty and freedom, since

Willie outsmarted and outmaneuvered the posse, thereby making his escape. The year 1909 is a watershed moment in Chemehuevi history, because of the events surrounding the deaths of William and Carlota Mike, Willie's escape, and the entire Willie Boy affair. "The Mike family and other Indians view the Willie Boy incident as a great tragedy that few white people get right. Chemehuevi and Southern Paiute explain that the real story is one of love—not lust, liquor, and arrogance portrayed in Lawton's book and Polonsky's film."[87] The film missed its mark in terms of accuracy and paid a disservice to Chemehuevi people that they still cope with today. The film does not represent indigenous history or the long-term effects the events had on the Mike family and Chemehuevi people. The killing of William and Carlota Mike provided the federal government sufficient provocation to remove the Twenty-Nine Palms Tribe and the Serrano people from the oasis.

In 1910 the Chemehuevi people of Twenty-Nine Palms moved first to the Morongo Reservation and then to the Cabazon Reservation. The Willie Boy affair brought about the indigenous abandonment of Twenty-Nine Palms, a sacred place to Chemehuevi and Serrano people. The oasis had been their homeland and the site where they had buried their loved ones. The cemetery held special meaning to the people and remains so today. The affair also caused a diaspora of the Chemehuevi people into Banning, Palm Springs, Coachella, Indio, San Jacinto, and other towns in California where the people sought work off the reservations. The people dispersed to live temporarily on or near several reservations, including the Agua Caliente, Torres-Martinez, Cabazon, Morongo, and Soboba Reservations.[88] In addition, a few members of the Mike family, including Johnson Mike, moved to Moapa, Utah, to live among other Southern Paiute people, and their families remain there to this day. After the Chemehuevi moved from Twenty-Nine Palms, a new family of Chemehuevi moved into the oasis and lived there quietly for a few years. In 1911, Chemehuevi elder Charley Pachecco brought his family to live at Twenty-Nine Palms, including his son Joe, his wife, and two sons—John and Harlie Pachecco. This family lived and worked at the oasis until 1913, when they moved into Banning where some of their people intermarried with the Indian people living on the Morongo Reservation.[89]

By 1914 no Chemehuevi people continued to live at Twenty-Nine Palms. Their removal from the oasis of the Twenty-Nine Palms had been accomplished and the U.S. government had completed its task of clearing Chemehuevi from the Mojave Desert, relocating them into the Coachella Valley where they could become "civilized," productive members of society. The change from life in the desert to life in an ever growing and changing agricultural valley controlled by non-Natives proved a challenge for Chemehuevi people and the families. But they had faced change and adversity before, so the families set about to survive this change by finding jobs and earning a living—not through government programs, welfare, or federal assistance but through their own hard work and determination. All the while, the people maintained a strong attachment to their elders, traditions, and former lands within the vast Mojave Desert. They survived these changes, in part because of their innate ability to laugh at adversity and their tenacious attitude to move progressively and pragmatically forward.

The Chemehuevi have never forgotten their heritage at Twenty-Nine Palms and have continued to identify themselves with the oasis ever since removal. They have not forgotten the meaning of the desert landscape and its importance to their ancestors. They have not forgotten their relatives buried at Twenty-Nine Palms. In 1875 the state of California claimed the Indian land and water at the Oasis of Mara, never informing the Serrano Indians that the government had taken their land and resources without permission or compensation. Then the state sold the Chemehuevi land and water at Twenty-Nine Palms to the Southern Pacific Railroad. The state ignored the indigenous rights of the Chemehuevi and Serrano to their homelands, and they made a deal with the powerful Southern Pacific Railroad, which wanted water to operate steam engines. Without the permission of the people, the state stole Indian land that held the bones of their ancestors.

Federal, state, and local Indian policy often worked against Indian tribes, especially when non-Natives could possibly take indigenous land, water, and other resources. The United States did not recognize Indians as citizens, and governments acted on behalf of citizens and corporations, not Native Americans. Thus, when given the opportunity to steal the oasis village site and water, the state took advantage of the situation and quickly transferred title of the Oasis of Mara to the Southern Pacific Railroad company. Chemehuevi people fell victim to non-Native greed and avarice. They had to deal with newcomers who considered themselves superior to their primitive neighbors. As a result of these and other circumstances, the Chemehuevi of the Twenty-Nine Palms Tribe lost nearly all of the Mojave Desert except for a few acres located at the northern base of the mountains near the present-day town of Twentynine Palms. In 1910 the people moved from the oasis, eventually settling in the Coachella Valley.

Lily Mike, a son of William Mike, returned to the oasis on September 6, 1936, to make a claim on his former homeland. At that time, he had been a longtime member of the Mission Indian Federation, an intertribal sovereignty organization, and he used his association to reclaim his land and water at the oasis. Mike traveled to the oasis in the company of Willie Marcus and Purl Willis to the Twentynine Palms Inn, where Mike informed the owners that he was the rightful owner of the site and they had to leave. He made his point but could not follow up on the claim. In fact, the Office of Indian Affairs and the Federal Bureau of Investigation launched an investigation against Mike, Willis, and Marcus for making false statements to hotel manager Margaret Kennedy, and impersonating federal officials. Like Mike's claim, the investigation went nowhere, but it offers a window into the mind-set of the Chemehuevi of Twenty-Nine Palms who never lost their sense of "being Chemehuevi" from the oasis or believing the site still belonged to American Indian people. Like Lily Mike and his contemporaries, members of the Twenty-Nine Palms Tribe today continue their deep appreciation and cultural relationship with the Oasis of Mara. It is the home of their ancestors and the resting place of many indigenous people in the Indian cemetery on Adobe Road.[90]

CHAPTER 7

Cultural Preservation, Ethnogenesis, and Revitalization

AFTER THE DEATH OF WILLIAM AND CARLOTA MIKE, AND THE RE-moval of the Chemehuevi to the Cabazon Indian Reservation in Indio, California, the Nüwü of this tribe struggled to maintain elements of their culture. They had lost their leader, land, and direction. Many survived economically by working several jobs and acculturating to a greater degree into American society. The Chemehuevi story complements that of other indigenous people during the reservation and transitional era of Native American history. For the members of the Twenty-Nine Palms Band, life was no easy task because of the rapid changes that came along with their removal from their home, the diaspora of the people, and the influence of other tribes and non-Indians with whom they associated. Many scholars point to elements of cultural loss by tribes without considering that cultures are often dynamic and that change occurred over time. The invasion of the United States and the expansion of white America significantly influenced the course of Chemehuevi culture and all of their Nüwü relatives. After 1909 the Chemehuevi entered the market economy in greater measure as men, women, and children sought work in the Coachella Valley and Banning Pass. They found jobs as farm workers, house cleaners, ranch hands, handymen, carpenters, and other odd jobs in Palm Springs, Banning, Hemet, San Jacinto, San Bernardino, and other towns. Most people settled away from the Cabazon Reservation. As a result of work experiences and their children attending school, the people learned English and Spanish.

Leaving their homelands and the cultural security of their oasis and their families contributed to the erosion of culture and language. If they traveled alone or spent a good deal of time away from other Chemehuevi people, they had no one with whom to speak. Over time, Chemehuevi children lost touch with their language and culture, learning English, Spanish, and Cahuilla. Of course, most of these children learned some Chemehuevi, but some parents urged their children to use English so that they could advance in society, succeed in school, and compete with non-Indians. One elder explained that his mother spoke the language, attended ceremony, and participated in other cultural events, but in the mid-twentieth century she would not allow her children to participate or learn the language. To do so, the mother felt, would harm them in school and in successfully navigating the non-Indian world. This mother kept her children sequestered from indigenous culture.[1]

Over time, the Chemehuevi language became the second language for most children, while others lost their Native language altogether. This was the natural course of events given their situation, and over the years fewer and fewer Chemehuevi of the Twenty-Nine Palms Tribe spoke Chemehuevi. Some children grew up in towns and did not learn certain elements of Chemehuevi culture, particularly if their parents sent them to Saint Boniface Indian School or Sherman Institute. Yet Chemehuevi children of the mid-twentieth century retained some elements of their language and culture, and they kept a profound appreciation of traditional culture, especially the significance of family, landscape, ceremony, religion, and songs. Through ethnogenesis they kept some cultural elements alive and spent their adult lives revitalizing and enhancing components of the old culture.[2]

In 1909 members of the Twenty-Nine Palms Tribe suffered a severe cultural blow with the death of William Mike. They lost the tribe's civil authority and religious leader. He had kept Nüwü traditions, particularly the spiritual knowledge of the people. When William Mike died, no one replaced him as spiritual leader because no person had received a spiritual calling as an Indian doctor or civil leader of the band.[3] Jim Pine had shared leadership with William Mike at Twenty-Nine Palms, but Pine led the Desert Serrano. His mother had been Chemehuevi, and his wife was Cahuilla. When the people left Twenty-Nine Palms in 1909, the Serrano Indians moved to the Mission Creek Reservation rather than relocate to the Cabazon Reservation with the Chemehuevi. Jim Pine's followers and most of the people from the Mission Creek Reservation ultimately moved again to the Banning Pass on the Morongo Reservation.[4] Thus, when the Chemehuevi resettled at the Cabazon Reservation, they had no elder-leader with the leadership abilities of William Mike or Jim Pine, although William's son, Little Mike or, more commonly, Lily Mike, soon led the group.

Lily Mike and other sons of William kept some cultural elements alive, passing them on to children born into the tribe. However, as explained by contemporary leader Dean Mike, William Mike's various children had very few children of their own, and in turn their children had few children. Perhaps the trauma suffered from the violent deaths of William and Carlota influenced fertility or interest in having children. Only now are the number of children increasing.[5] The death or diaspora of Jim Mike's children and their spouses harmed cultural preservation. For example, the accidental death of Bill Mike about 1912 and the later death of Nellie Holms Mike Morongo in 1958 (better known as Nellie Morongo) likewise influenced the loss of traditional Chemehuevi culture, including Nellie's masterful basket making. The departure of Jeff Boniface (Mike) after 1934 to the Soboba Reservation and Johnson Mike to Moapa Reservation in Utah drained the group of two important cultural teachers who knew the old ways. All this happened relatively rapidly, bringing about radical cultural change for the Chemehuevi almost overnight in 1910 and 1911.

Those Chemehuevi assigned to the Cabazon Reservation and those choosing to live on the Morongo Reservation found themselves surrounded by Cahuilla Indian people. The various Cahuilla groups were the dominant Native groups of the valley, desert, mountain, and pass areas. The Cahuilla people spoke a different language but shared similar cultural ways as the Chemehuevi. Still, the two peoples enjoyed separate and distinct cultures and languages. This had been the way of many American Indian cultures throughout the Western Hemisphere, but after Chemehuevi people became closely associated with Cahuilla culture, they absorbed elements of that culture.[6] The children of William and Jim Mike maintained elements of their own culture, and children and grandchildren kept some elements of the Chemehuevi way, especially a spiritual sense of place and preservation of the larger Chemehuevi landscape. Contemporary Chemehuevi elders have explained difficulties growing up. Jennifer Mike pointed out that her grandmother, Nellie Mike Morongo, knew a great deal about Chemehuevi culture, having grown up in the Mojave Desert and living at Twenty-Nine Palms for years. Nellie never learned English and could only speak the Chemehuevi and Cahuilla languages. Jennifer Mike grew up speaking English. She could speak some Chemehuevi but had difficulty communicating in Chemehuevi with her grandmother. She learned some words and phrases as she spent a great deal of time with her grandmother, but they could not communicate deeply. Nellie could not teach the culture and language in an in-depth manner to Jennifer, and

Nellie passed away when Jennifer was a young girl. Jennifer Mike has always regretted that she could not have known the Chemehuevi language and culture better, but she has spent her life serving her tribe as a leader and teaching her children to honor and respect the ancestors, the Chemehuevi landscape, and tribal members and to preserve Chemehuevi culture.[7]

In a similar fashion, Dean Mike and his sister, June, grew up in Palm Springs, where they lived with their grandfather, Lily Mike. Except for members of their own family, they grew up knowing few Nüwü people. The vast number of indigenous people living in the Coachella Valley were Cahuilla Indians, not Chemehuevi, but the Mike family had many friends among the Cahuilla. Their mother, Jessie Mike, knew various Chemehuevi and Cahuilla Indians. She had grown up with them, and she had participated in songs and ceremony with indigenous people. As a child growing up in Palm Springs, Jessie Mike's best friend was Katherine Siva, a Cahuilla woman who became one of the most famous Native American scholars in Southern California. Jessie often participated with Katherine in Native ceremonies and social events, growing up among Native people. However, she did not want Dean or June growing up in the Indian way. Instead, Jessie stressed the importance of education to her son, encouraging him to break the cycle of poverty and learn the language and ways of white people. As a result, Dean did not grow up heavily involved in preserving Chemehuevi or Cahuilla language and culture—a fact he now laments as a leader of the Twenty-Nine Palms Band.[8]

Dean's cousin, Joe Benitez, learned a great deal about Chemehuevi culture and language from his mother, Susie Mike, one of William Mike's daughters, and his uncles. Benitez grew up on the Cabazon Reservation and other reservations nearby where Cahuilla people predominately lived. As a child, Joe spent summers and weekends in the Chemehuevi Valley and on the Colorado River Indian Reservation, but he did not live there full time. Like others who had once lived at Twenty-Nine Palms or who had relatives that had lived at the oasis, Joe learned various elements of the language and culture. But he did not grow up in Chemehuevi culture in the way of young people who had been raised years before at Twenty-Nine Palms. So many things had changed for the Chemehuevi; it is not surprising that the culture experienced by such young people as Joe, Dean, and Jennifer had greatly changed from that enjoyed by their parents and grandparents.[9]

Dean, Joe, and Jennifer experienced the process of cultural survival, revitalization, and ethnogenesis. They have led the process of preserving and re-forming their culture. Throughout their lives they have embraced the old ways of the Nüwü. As the children, grandchildren, and great-grandchildren got older, these three worked together through their families and the tribe to meet and discuss the future course of their people. Most of them now lived off the reservations in towns where they worked, although Joe often lived with his mother and stepfather on the Cabazon Reservation (his home today with Diana, his wife). They could not live as their ancestors had at Twenty-Nine Palms, but they remained connected as Chemehuevi people and families. They preserved their culture while learning new ways, and when they were in positions of power and influence, they worked harder at preserving their tribe and organizations designed to preserve and protect. Members of the Twenty-Nine Palms Tribe learned more about culture from Chemehuevi people living along the Colorado River.

For Chemehuevi people living along the Colorado River, there were greater opportunities to be raised within the culture, even though Mojave Indians lived near and constituted the majority of indigenous people living along the river. Numerous elders continued to live along the Colorado River, but only a few elders remained in the Coachella Valley. Chemehuevi people raised on the Colorado River Indian Reservation or in Chemehuevi Valley lived near Parker, Arizona, where this Nüwü community learned and continuously participated in language, song, and story together. In the late twentieth century, river people often shared their culture with Chemehuevi people living in Indio, Coachella, Rancho Mirage, Palm Springs, Banning, and other areas. Thus Chemehuevi youths growing up along the Colorado River heard several elders speaking their language daily, and they attended far more sings and ceremonies, especially Indian wakes, where the people sang Salt Songs all night. Members of the Twenty-Nine Palms Tribe attended some ceremonies on the river, but the distance was considerable, taking four hours today to travel on highways in modern vehicles.

Chemehuevi people living in the Coachella Valley generally participated in Native functions sponsored by Cahuilla people or other tribes, not Chemehuevi. As a result, the young people had different cultural experience than the Paiute on the river. This was no fault of their own, but a by-product of cultural change brought on by the American invasion and policies destructive to indigenous people. Despite this loss, members of the Twenty-Nine Palms Band kept elements of their culture and history. Many tribal members take every opportunity to learn more about the Chemehuevi way as they became older and to retain elements of their culture. They pass on what they know to the children of the tribe. However, they struggled to make a living and had little time to devote to language acquisition, storytelling, or learning the old songs. Dean and Jennifer Mike have used the success of their gaming enterprise at the Spotlight 29 Casino to support cultural revitalization. With gaming money, they have developed environmental programs and initiated cultural revitalization programs. When members of the Business Committee of the Twenty-Nine Palms Band had sufficient funds, the committee established ongoing cultural programs.[10]

In 1997 the Twenty-Nine Palms Tribe hired Dr. Marshall Cheung to write grants to establish a Tribal Environmental Protection Agency (EPA), funded by the federal Environmental Protection Agency. Since 1997, Cheung, Anne Cheung, Dr. Anthony Madrigal, Sr., Jeffrey Smith, and Anthony Madrigal, Jr., have led the cultural side of the Tribal EPA program, which included a Department of Cultural Resources that the Madrigals anchored. Once Marshall Cheung secured the first grant, he began to establish laboratories on the reservation to analyze water quality on the reservation. To this end, he established the first of several laboratories, which eventually included separate organic, inorganic, microbiological, and molecular biological laboratories—all of which Cheung operates and maintains with the help of his wife, Anne, and research assistants. Over the years Cheung has conducted many experiments dealing with water on the Twenty-Nine Palms Reservation and other Indian reservations. He has studied the water of the Salton Sea, a saltwater lake that lies within the boundaries of the Torres-Martinez Indian Reservation near Thermal, California. He also studies the influence of hormones on reproduction, particularly estrogen, which has been inadvertently placed in water systems by way of sewer systems.

The Tribal EPA of the Twenty-Nine Palms Tribe supports an Office of the Geographical Information System, established to map reservation lands and many other areas significant to the tribe, including vast regions in the Mojave and Colorado Deserts. For a time Dr. Jeffrey Smith led the development of a broader program to map habitat and cultural areas of the deserts. The Tribal EPA also supports projects to study cultural science among the Chemehuevi of Twenty-Nine Palms and to share information about Native uses and views of plants and animals with tribal members and school-aged children. In 2011 the Tribal EPA hired three Native American consultants to research and write a report on Chemehuevi use of the reservation landscape along the White Water River that runs through the reservation and on south to the Torres-Martinez Indian Reservation. This project studied flora, fauna, water, pollution, astronomy, geology, geography, earthquakes, and other scientific subjects significant to the Chemehuevi people. The staff of the Tribal EPA has won an award as the best

Tribal EPA program in Region 9 of the American West. This environmental and scientific endeavor began after the tribe established and used seed money from the Spotlight 29 Casino to develop the Tribal EPA under Anthony Madrigal, Jr., who, with the assistance of Matthew Hanks Leivas, created a dynamic study of Native plants along the Whitewater River that flows through the reservation. This unique study is the most comprehensive plant analysis conducted on the Twenty-Nine Palms Reservation.[11]

The Twenty-Nine Palms Band of Mission Indians opened the Spotlight 29 Casino in 1994, but the enterprise was not an immediate success. It took the tribe two years before the casino started making a profit. At that point the General Council composed of all adult members of the tribe and the Business Council decided that cultural revitalization must be a priority. Led by Jennifer Mike and Dean Mike, the Business Council voted to invite Cahuilla Bird Singer Luke Madrigal to lead the cultural programs for the tribe. Madrigal had learned to sing Bird Songs from noted Cahuilla elder Robert Levi and other elders of the Torres-Martinez Reservation, and Madrigal had performed Bird Songs hundreds of times by the time the Business Council of the Twenty-Nine Palms Band approached him. He had also learned an intricate Tobacco Ceremony from Saturino Torres, offering smoke to the Creator in the four directions and asking for blessings that traveled into the atmosphere to the spirits.

Throughout Indian Country, particularly in Southern California, Luke Madrigal had earned a reputation as a young cultural leader, and his family became highly valued for Native cultural and historical preservation.[12] Madrigal earned a bachelor's degree in history from the University of California–Riverside and later received his master's degree. For many years he directed the Indian Child and Family Program in Temecula, California. He and his family have shared and enlarged Cahuilla cultural revitalization, and they continue the work today. Madrigal proved an excellent choice because of his innate intelligence and sincere energy to organize cultural functions for the Twenty-Nine Palms Tribe. Madrigal executed programs that included Native people from many diverse tribes and cultures, in addition to Nüwü people. He established a relationship with the Serrano people of the San Manuel Reservation, Nüwü people of the Colorado River and Chemehuevi Indian Reservations, and Hualapai Indians of Western Arizona. Madrigal knew the Serrano people had once shared the village situated at the Oasis of Twenty-Nine Palms, so he strengthened the cultural relations of members of the Twenty-Nine Palms Tribe with several other tribal people, including local Cahuilla.[13]

Every month throughout the year 1997, members of several tribes met alternately on the Twenty-Nine Palms Reservation and the San Manuel Reservation

In 2011 the Tribal EPA of the Twenty-Nine Palms Tribe conducted an extensive study of native plants along the Whitewater River used by Chemehuevi and Cahuilla Indians. The analysis centered on indigenous plants used for foods, tools, medicines, basketry, and housing. The survey recorded invasive species on the reservation. Left to right: Matthew Hanks Leivas Sr. and Anthony Madrigal Jr. Photograph by Clifford E. Trafzer.

in San Bernardino, California. The people shared a meal provided by the host tribe and a cultural program that took many forms. Everyone enjoyed renewing old acquaintances and making new friends. Luke Madrigal served as the master of ceremonies, introducing honored guests, including tribal elders from local tribes or visiting dignitaries. Each time the tribes met for a cultural exchange, they enjoyed many different discussions, including dialogues on Chemehuevi baskets. Many people had seen the powerful baskets of Mary Snyder, the mother of Willie Boy and a specialist of depicting rattlesnake images. The group also discussed the art of bird singing. Cahuilla, Mojave, Hualapai, Cocopah, and other tribes have sung Bird Songs since the time of Creation. The Chemehuevi people have sung Bird Songs for hundreds, perhaps thousands, of years; they learned Bird Songs from Cahuilla, Mojave, and Hualapai singers. The various tribes share this song complex; the men sing with a gourd rattle and both men and women dance in a unique stylized fashion.

At the cultural nights on the Twenty-Nine Palms Reservation, Cahuilla elder Robert Levi often led the singing, and he spent a good deal of time explaining the significance of the songs. The audience joined in singing the Bird Songs they knew best, and women often honored the male singers by facing them and dancing to the songs. Levi had learned Bird Songs while growing up on the Torres-Martinez Reservation; he had also learned songs from many of the old-timers who shared their songs at cultural functions held on many different reservations. He spent his adult life revitalizing Bird Songs, singing at schools, social events, fiestas, and other settings. In addition, he taught many groups of young men how to sing and handle the power of these ancient songs. These people in turn have taught Bird Songs to their children and grandchildren. Members of the Twenty-Nine Palms Tribe incorporated greater emphasis of Bird Songs, while continuing their use of Salt Songs in sacred ceremonies, such as funerals and memorial ceremonies. Salt Songs are their death songs, and Chemehuevi of the Twenty-Nine Palms Tribe have supported the preservation of songs for many years. Matthew Hanks Leivas and Larry Eddy, with the support of Betty Cornelius and Vivienne Jake, have led the songs and ceremonies on behalf of the people of the Twenty-Nine Palms Tribe. Matthew Hanks Leivas presented songs at the cultural gatherings.

Some of the cultural gatherings focused on language preservation. Norma Vasquez taught about the Southern Paiute language. For two hours or more, at the gatherings, various Native American instructors would teach about their language. Having grown up in Chemehuevi language and culture, Vasquez presented on the Chemehuevi language. Linguistic professors at the University of Arizona provided formal education to Vasquez, which she has used to preserve and teach the language and share it with children. Vasquez presented her work at one such cultural gathering and encouraged the audience to say words and phrases. She talked at length about the importance of Native languages and their preservation by Indian people. Since the 1990s, Vasquez, as a Chemehuevi speaker living on the Colorado River Indian Reservation, continues her language work. Her lectures and presentations on the Twenty-Nine Palms Indian Reservation have demonstrated excellent teaching ability, use of language, and commitment to preservation.

On other occasions the tribe hosted programs to discuss the creation of the Native American Land Conservancy (NALC) and its purpose among indigenous people. Tom Askew, a longtime resident of the Coachella Valley, planted the seed that grew into the NALC.[14] In 1997 he requested a meeting with Theresa

Mike, director of human resources for the Twenty-Nine Palms Band of Mission Indians. In typical fashion, Theresa Mike paused in her duties to listen to Askew explain that his family owned property in the Mojave Desert near the Old Woman Mountains that he wanted returned to the Chemehuevi people who once lived there. Askew understood that Chemehuevi and Mojave people had both lived in the area for thousands of years, and he had previously offered the land to the people of the Chemehuevi Reservation. The transfer of the land had never occurred, and Askew told Theresa Mike that he wanted to offer the land to the members of the Twenty-Nine Palms Band of Mission Indians. Theresa agreed to inform her husband, chairman Dean Mike. Dean and Theresa Mike both valued historic preservation and became interested in protecting the cultural site and the property's flora and fauna. However, neither had seen the land or knew its location. Late one evening, Askew drove with the Mikes to the Old Woman Mountains, traveling east of the Coachella Valley toward Blythe, California. Before reaching Blythe, Askew turned north at Desert Center onto Highway 177, first heading northeast into the Colorado Desert, then into the Mojave Desert. The highway met State Route 62, and the adventurers traveled in two vehicles in the dark by the light of the moon. Some miles up the highway, the group turned due north onto a dirt road, which they followed for an hour across the Mojave Desert.[15]

Askew led Dean and Theresa Mike into the Old Woman Mountains, west of Ward Valley. Traveling by car, sometimes at breakneck speeds, Askew took the Mikes "into the middle of nowhere" through soft sand but always along a power line linking Interstate 10 with Interstate 40. The path took them through the heart of the Mojave Desert, where few vehicles except those with four-wheel drive ventured. Dean and Theresa tried hard not to get stuck and to keep up with Askew. After traveling on the unimproved desert road for an hour, Askew made a left turn onto another less improved desert road, where the amount of sand and dust became intense. Theresa remembers wondering where they were going and what she had gotten them into. Askew made another radical turn to the left, traveling through cactus, yucca, and creosote bushes. The silhouette of the mountains appeared along the horizon ahead, and soon the two vehicles stopped at the base of the range. The two men hiked into the mountains to a granite rock formation and up into a cave. Askew led Dean Mike to a unique "shaman's cave" located in an outcropping of the mountains where a natural cave formed in a granite deposit. Theresa Mike remembers "watching them disappear into the mountains" and "wondering if and when they would reap-

With the support of the U.S. Fish and Wildlife Foundation, the Native American Land Conservancy (NALC) sponsors Learning Landscapes in Old Woman Mountain Preserve. The NALC teaches children about flora, fauna, and cultural resources. Chemehuevi and Mojave Indians once had villages in the Old Woman Mountains, and the Twenty-Nine Palms Tribe invested funds to buy and protect the pristine preserve. This photograph depicts children and leaders hiking to the granite outcropping and site of the ancient cave. Photograph by Clifford E. Trafzer.

pear." About thirty minutes later the two men returned after exploring the cave and pondering at the eastern stretches of the desert with the mountains reflecting in the moonlight.[16]

Archaeologists had recorded the site years before, but few people knew of the site. For thousands of years, ancient Native people had used the cave. The granite floor was worn flat and had the feel of human skin oils. Ancient Native people had decorated the cave with pictographs. In other caves in California and the Great Basin, holy people had created rock art to depict their power, dreams, or origins. The cave in the Old Woman Mountain contained orange and red pictographs of many designs. They were faded and quite old, but in the darkness with only a flashlight, Dean could not make out much detail. The rock art and the atmosphere of the cave touched Dean deeply. He decided the tribe should acquire the land, not for economic exploitation but for cultural preservation.[17]

After this trip into the desert, Dean and Theresa Mike resolved to protect lands significant to Native Americans. Theresa joined her husband in the effort to preserve lands, and to this end they formed a core group from their cultural committee composed primarily of Jennifer Mike, Matthew Hanks Leivas, Joe Mike Benitez, Diana Benitez, Luke Madrigal, Kurt Russo, Anthony Madrigal, Thomas Dullien, Michael Madrigal, Thomas Estama, Clifford Trafzer, Bernie Thomas, and others.[18] The group met often in 1997 and 1998, forming bylaws and articles of incorporation to create a nonprofit organization called the Native American Land Conservancy. Between 1997 and 2000 the NALC worked diligently to raise the funds and arrange the real estate agreement to buy the Old Woman Mountain land. By 2001, Thomas Martin and Dick and Fay McClung joined in the effort, contributing to the success of the group. When the committee first met, it discussed how the NALC could best preserve the land in the Old Woman Mountains as well as other lands important to Indian people.

The Twenty-Nine Palms Tribe invested in the NALC, providing funds for an appraisal, title search, and preliminary legal work involved in forming an agreement with the owners, including Tom Askew. Although the Twenty-Nine Palms Band led the formation of the NALC, the organization was an intertribal effort to preserve and protect cultural lands, animals, plants, and sacred places. The Business Council of the Twenty-Nine Palms Tribe led the endeavor, creating a nonprofit corporation and negotiating with the Internal Revenue Service and the state of California. The IRS initially thought the tribe had established the NALC to buy lands for a business or housing endeavor, but board members convinced IRS officials that the NALC existed to preserve lands and protect those lands, plants, and animals through a sanctuary, not a business venture. The tribe worked closely with director Kurt Russo to secure a grant from the U.S. Fish and Wildlife Foundation, an organization that has supported NALC efforts. The five entities that owned the land in the Old Woman Mountains proved the greatest impediment to the NALC purchasing the preserve in the Mojave Desert. Like Tom Askew, they all wished to be paid for the land. To this end, the NALC negotiated with each group separately and began fundraising.[19]

Initially Tom Askew presented the idea of transferring the land his family owned at the Old Woman Mountains to the Twenty-Nine Palms Band. He later mentioned his grandmother had willed portions of twenty-five hundred acres to four groups, including the Boy Scouts, the Girl Scouts, the Casa Colina Rehabilitation Center, and the Upland Presbyterian Church. Askew had the largest interest in the land, but he could not sell it without the consent of the other owners. When this came to light, Askew assured the NALC board that he would deal with the other owners, strongly encouraging them to sell the land to the Native American Land Conservancy. He believed the organizations that owned portions of the land would listen to him and sell their interest to the NALC. Because none of the owners could sell the property without the consent of the others, it became imperative for the conservancy to seek an independent agreement with each of the owners.

Thus NALC members negotiated with each owner, but efforts to deal with them individually proved frustratingly futile. In a sincere effort to ask the other nonprofit organizations to donate or sell the land to the Native American Land Conservancy, the organization called a joint meeting of the owners at Casa Colina Rehabilitation Center. Some of members of the NALC board naïvely believed that since the group was dealing with other nonprofit organizations that had ignored the land for forty years, they would want to sell. Some members of the conservancy felt that since the Native American group wanted to preserve and protect land, plants, and animals for Indians and non-Indians alike, the other nonprofit organizations would willingly, if not eagerly, join in the effort—and perhaps even donate their interest. But members of the NALC learned a different side to the world of charities, nonprofits, and one Christian representative of the Presbyterian Church of Upland, California. The bottom line for these other groups was money—not conservation, protection, or preservation. The organizations wanted money for their own causes, which took precedence over the goals of the land conservancy.[20]

Meanwhile, Askew hired an attorney to represent his interest, and he asked the Business Council of the Twenty-Nine Palms Tribe to pay for his lawyer. He agreed to reimburse the tribe after the land deal succeeded, and he ultimately repaid the tribe once he had received payment for his portion of the land. He also asked for one hundred dollars an acre for the land, despite its taxable value of just twenty dollars an acre. Still, members of the NALC felt that the land was worth one hundred dollars an acre because of its cultural and biological value. The NALC board agreed to pay Askew and the other owners at the same rate of one hundred dollars per acre. At the meeting at Casa Colina, the Presbyterian Church failed to send a representative. Representatives for the Girl Scouts graciously offered to donate their 7.75 percent interest in the property to the Native American Land Conservancy, provided all the other owners at donated their share of the land. If, however, one owner received money, the Girl Scouts wanted to be paid the same amount per acre. Minutes after this proposal was delivered, the other owners announced they would not donate their property to the NALC. Representatives of the conservancy offered to purchase the land for one hundred dollars an acre. Eventually all the owners agreed to the same terms, except for the Presbyterian Church of Upland. In an attempt to resolve the impasse between the NALC and the church, the group asked board members Joe and Diana Benitez to intercede on behalf of the conservancy.[21]

The Benitezes had belonged to the Presbyterian Church for many years, and they agreed to speak with their former pastor, Stewart Wood, who knew many people within the synod of the Presbyterian Church of California and Hawai'i. Wood, an expert in conflict resolution, arranged the first meeting between some of the board members of the NALC and a representative of the church. They met in Banning, California. Theresa Mike spoke for the conservancy, explaining the cultural significance of the land at the Old Woman Mountain, particularly in terms of its spiritual meaning to Indian people. The church representative, a lay leader and former attorney, was not moved. He explained that cultural considerations of the land had no meaning to him, regardless of the church's expressed interest in dealing fairly and closely with indigenous communities that had been affected by the historical missionary zeal of Presbyterians.[22] Theresa Mike understood that Presbyterians had participated in the exploitation of the Native people, land, and resources of Hawai'i and the Pacific Northwest. She knew Presbyterian missionaries had forced themselves on the Native American peoples and the lands of the Columbia Plateau at their missions of Waiilatpu (at present-day Walla Walla, Washington) and Lapwai (Lapwai, Idaho). The representatives of the church explained that they only wanted to talk about money. The Christian representative of the Presbyterians flatly stated that he wanted a price higher than one hundred dollars per acre; he would not negotiate.[23]

In 1998 the Twenty-Nine Palms Tribe led the effort to create the Native American Land Conservancy (NALC), a nonprofit organization that protects endangered Native American sites and landscapes. The NALC promotes the preservation of threatened and endangered species and landscapes, and it supports the education of young people through Healing and Learning Landscape Experiences. The conservancy created this emblem, depicting the sun sign, desert tortoise, and bighorn sheep. Photograph by Clifford E. Trafzer.

The representative of the Upland Presbyterian Church conflicted with the position presented in a faith-based magazine article produced by Christians suggesting that U.S. Presbyterians had taken an interest in dealing more fairly with indigenous peoples around the world, that they respected the creative religious views of Native Americans. Some officials within the Presbyterian Church had advanced the idea of reconciliation with Native Americans, and Chemehuevi leader Matthew Hanks Leivas had pointed out to members of the

NALC that Presbyterians had announced that they wanted to work more closely with Indian people and understand their religious beliefs. However, the representative of the Upland Presbyterian Church had not read the article and had little, if any, interest in Native spiritual views of the earth, animals, and plants. He did not listen to Theresa Mike. Instead, he insulted the Indians who had met with him, insisting on talking money and his fiduciary responsibility to get as much money as possible for his church. In his own words: "This is my bottom line." He may have held the common opinion that all Indians are rich as a result of gaming and did not understand that the conservancy was not a tribe and held no assets. For the indigenous people in attendance, words spoken by the Presbyterian were insulting and shallow. This man represented negotiators from centuries past when non-Indians showed little respect for Native people and their beliefs. The meeting had come to an impasse. Rather than saying any more, the American Indian representatives of NALC excused themselves and left the meeting. Theresa Mike counseled patience, and her sage approach proved the correct one.[24]

Other meetings took place with Presbyterians. At one meeting at the Presbyterian Church in Redlands, California, three members of the board of directors of the NALC met with two representatives of the Presbyterian Church. Stewart Wood attended this meeting and facilitated it, just as he had the earlier meeting. Once again, Theresa Mike presented the plans of the Native American Land Conservancy to buy the land within the Old Woman Mountains to create a cultural nature sanctuary. She spoke about the healing landscape program for the benefit of Indians and non-Indians alike. She expressed the view that the conservancy wished to protect the Native American cultural resources of the Old Woman Mountains. Joe Benitez expanded on the theme, expressing the view that Christian and Native American values could join forces to protect and preserve land made by the Creator. He emphasized that the Presbyterian Church and the Native American Land Conservancy could partner to preserve and protect the earth and that the church could benefit from learning from Indian people about this special place.[25]

When members of the conservancy board had shared their ideas, they faced a startling response. A spokesman for the Upland Presbyterian Church indicated: "We don't really care about the land. It has no meaning to us. You can do with it whatever you want, but we want the money and we want more than the hundred dollars per acre you are offering." The blunt statement surprised the board members. The unenlightened attitude of this non-Indian man represented the worst in non-Native interaction with Native peoples: negative, materialistic, and anxious to take advantage of Native Americans. The church's representative stated clearly that the earth had no meaning to his people and that Native American views of the earth, plants, and animals meant nothing. Board members felt they had entered a surreal reincarnation of nineteenth-century attitudes toward American Indians. Certain members and leadership of the Presbyterian Church had historically represented the worst of a materialistic stealing of land and water, while destroying the natural wonders of Native America. Many Christians had exploited Native Americans and indigenous people around the world so that non-Natives could expand their personal wealth. It appeared to board members that the official representative of the Presbyterian Church lacked humanity, Creation, and spirit.[26]

Church representatives wanted more than the proffered one hundred dollars per acre, claiming that the land in the Old Woman Mountains was worth nearly three hundred dollars per acre. This dollar amount was based on assessed value of land adjacent to Interstates 10 and 40, not lands in the Colorado and Mojave Desert. They agreed to sell their portion of the land only for this amount, regardless of the conservancy's agreement with other owners. They appeared unconcerned that the conservancy could not afford to pay the church three times what they had offered the other owners. To most board members, purchase of the Old Woman Mountains land seemed out of reach, except for Theresa Mike. She viewed the church as a challenge to be overcome with patience. She continually reminded everyone: "It is a process. It takes time." She grew more persistent, always maintaining patience. Meanwhile, Kurt Russo, the NALC director, had heard from Charles Little, an author writing a book on sacred lands of Native Americans. Little had asked Russo about Arleco Forest in Washington state, which the Lummi Indians had raised money to preserve. During the conversation Russo mentioned the Old Woman Mountains, and Little became intrigued by the efforts of the NALC to preserve the land. Little traveled to Southern California to meet Dean and Theresa Mike and to visit the Old Woman Mountains. He was moved by the rugged landscape and cultural site. Little had been a member of the Presbyterian Church for years, and his father had been a minister. He became directly involved in the preservation effort, mustering support from many key faith-based religious organizations—people who shared a view that the Creation should hold special meaning to Christians. Joe Benitez also contacted the American Indian committee within the synod to ask for their help. Together, this group of activists encouraged the leadership of the Presbyterian Church to discuss the sale of the Old Woman Mountains with members of the Native American Land Conservancy.

At a meeting at California State University–San Bernardino the board had a lengthy conference call with leaders of the synod of the Presbyterian Church for Southern California and Hawai'i. During this meeting church representatives asked the conservancy to submit a proposal in writing to purchase the land at the Old Woman Mountains for one hundred dollars per acre. In their next meeting the board drafted this proposal and submitted it to the synod. During the first annual conference of the Native American Land Conservancy, the Presbyterian Church informed the NALC that it would sell the land to the group for one hundred dollars per acre. Some church officials joined in the first annual conference, where the NALC leadership announced its intent to purchase the land at the Old Woman Mountains and create a preserve. By the fall of 2000, the Girl Scouts and Boy Scouts of America, Casa Colina Rehabilitation Hospital, the Presbyterian Church, and Thomas Askew had all agreed to sell their portion of the land to the Native American Land Conservancy. The task of the conservancy turned to raising sufficient money to purchase the land, using the exceptional grant-writing skills of Kurt Russo. Robert Cabot, author of *Joshua Tree*, participated in the first annual conference of the Native American Land Conservancy, and he shared his special bond with the lands of the Mojave Desert. He encouraged Russo to submit a grant to the Cabot Foundation, and Russo responded with a winning proposal that brought the first funds to purchase the preserve. The board decided to use these funds for acquisition, but before committing funds to the purchase, the board asked Russo to submit a major grant to the U.S. Fish and Wildlife Foundation—a funding agency dedicated to the preservation of endangered landscapes, plants, and animals.[27]

The NALC had previously submitted a grant proposal to the Fish and Wildlife Foundation in 1999, but the agency did not initially fund the proposal at that time because the conservancy had not yet made an arrangement with the Presbyterian Church to buy their portion of the land. But with the agreement sealed between the conservancy and the church in 2000, Russo rewrote the grant and submitted it on behalf of the NALC in the summer of 2001. The conservancy requested one hundred thousand dollars . . . all to be used for acquisition—and foundation officials provided hopeful optimism about funding the request. However, not content to wait to learn if the U.S. Fish and Wildlife Foundation would fund the grant, the conservancy began discussing other ways to raise the $250,000 needed to buy the land at Old Woman Mountains. To facilitate this discussion, the Cabazon Band of Mission Indians agreed to host the conservancy for a daylong meeting of board members and friends. Approximately twenty people joined in the meeting, including two representatives of the Bighorn Institute, including Dick McClung, Fay McClung, and Tom Martin. They brought considerable experience into the Native American Land Conservancy. During the discussion Tom Martin and Dick McClung suggested hosting a golf tournament, which became the most important event of the year in terms of fund raising.[28]

The conservancy never wavered from its commitment to use the funds it had raised to purchase the land at the Old Woman Mountains, and the Twenty-Nine Palms Band of Mission Indians remained central to this purchase plan. Both the conservancy and the tribe looked forward to the day when the conservancy would manage other lands important to Indian people and protect them for all. The tribe remained committed to preserving plants, animals, and landscapes important to the Chemehuevi people, but they also worked diligently to encourage other tribes to join the conservancy to purchase lands important to Cahuilla, Luiseño, Serrano, Mojave, and other Indian people. In fact, the tribe spearheaded the conservancy as an intertribal initiative with the support of the Cahuilla and other Indians, creating a nonprofit corporation and providing funding and leadership.

The U.S. Fish and Wildlife Foundation has been a key partner in the success of the Native American Land Conservancy. Initially the foundation granted the conservancy one hundred thousand dollars to help purchase the Old Woman Mountains, which the conservancy bought in 2004. Through two separate grants, the U.S. Fish and Wildlife Foundation has also supported detailed academic studies of flora and fauna in the preserve, totaling about five hundred thousand dollars. The funds supported research projects conducted by biological scientists of the University of California, including Jim Andre, and those at the San Bernardino County Museum. These detailed studies have formed the foundation or the first baseline studies of the Old Woman Mountains. These studies will lead to future comparative projects, particularly in the area of management. Kurt Russo, executive director of the NALC, used some of the data from these studies to write a guide to the Old Woman Mountain Preserve, and he based his dissertation on research about the Mojave Desert and its people.[29] Russo wrote all the grants submitted and administered by the Twenty-Nine Palms Indian Tribe, and he plans several other grants and writing projects on behalf of the tribe and conservancy.[30] Russo led the conservancy to find federal funding, and in 2006 he received an additional $250,000 grant from the U.S. Fish and Wildlife Foundation to support further studies of the desert tortoise. These funds offer protection of the desert tortoise, which has encouraged the return of the tortoise to the preserve.[31]

In addition to the Old Woman Mountains, the Native American Land Conservancy has partnered with the Anza-Borrego State Park Association to purchase two sections of land in Horse Canyon, California. A private developer owned the former Cahuilla village site and put the land on the market. Anthony and Michael Madrigal, both members of the conservancy board, supported the purchase of the lands in Horse Canyon because the land contained the ruins of their family's village of Nacuta. The conservancy borrowed money to finance its portion of the purchase, and bought the Horse Canyon lands. The conservancy turned the land over to the Anza-Borrego State Parks to manage with an agreement that the parks would not conduct archaeological work on the village or nearby cemetery without the consent and help of Cahuilla Indians and the Native American Land Conservancy. State Parks ultimately paid the conservancy for the land and has since honored all agreements.

In a similar arrangement the Native American Land Conservancy partnered with the Trust for Public Land to purchase hundreds of acres on the eastern border of the Anza-Borrego State Park west of the Salton Sea of Southern California. The lands contain ancient Indian fish traps in the Colorado Desert east and north of the Anza-Borrego State Park. Kurt Russo worked closely with the Trust for Public Land to make the purchase through a national transportation bill that Congress passed and the president signed in the summer of 2005. The purchase of prehistoric stone structures called fish traps along the remains of ancient Lake Cahuilla constitutes a major national preservation project that the Twenty-Nine Palms Tribe and the NALC spearheaded, with the support of the Trust for Public Land. William Madrigal headed another research project to interpret lands in the eastern part of the Anza-Borrego State Park, funded by the Trust for Public Land. The NALC had hoped the purchase of new lands for the park would lead to preservation, but the governor opened up a huge portion of the cultural landscape to off-road vehicles. Unfortunately, after the gift to the State Parks, Governor Arnold Schwarzenegger turned these cultural lands over to the off-road segment of the department, rather than to cultural preservation specialists within California State Parks.[32]

The interests of the Twenty-Nine Palms Tribe in historical preservation went beyond the Native American Land Conservancy. In 1997 the Cultural Committee of the tribe began several, still ongoing projects. The tribe began an oral history project and to this end conducted multiple interviews with Dean Mike, Larry Eddy, Jane and Paul Smith, Jennifer Mike, Joe Mike Benitez, Matthew Hanks Leivas, and Gertrude Hanks Leivas.[33] Each individual offered unique information about the culture of Chemehuevi people. Several tribal elders provided details of their family's lives during the nineteenth and twentieth centuries, when the people maintained a difficult life as a result of the reservation system and intense cultural change. They explained the ways people survived as a unique ethnic group by preserving plants, animals, and lands as well as human remains that were being threatened by construction. They held onto their ceremonies, songs, and stories. They met formally and informally to preserve and protect water, land, and cultural resources. Gertrude Hanks Leivas, for example, lived through the transitional period when her family lived on the California side of the Colorado River in Chemehuevi Valley, an area largely destroyed by Parker Dam. But she remembered growing up in a traditional home made of sticks, mud, and thatch—a home where everyone spoke Chemehuevi and ate traditional foods. Although those days had ended by the time Jennifer Mike was born, she remembered her grandmother, Nellie Mike Morongo, telling her about the old life at the village of Twenty-Nine Palms. Joe Mike Benitez kept alive many stories about ancient places and people his mother had once known. Today he is a treasure of historical knowledge because he listened to and learned the old Native way through stories. Susie Mike, spent hours telling Joe about her family and life in general at the desert oasis. Dean Mike had grown up in Palm Springs, but he too remembered stories of his mother, Jessie Mike, and other family members. Together, they helped reconstruct the history of their people by sharing the oral tradition that had come down to them from friends and relatives. In this way the people participated in an ethnogenesis of their people and the reconstruction of their past through oral histories. They thus reestablished the Twenty-Nine Palms Tribe as a legal, contemporary, and cultural tribe with a past and a future.[34]

Not content to sponsor oral histories, the Business Council of the Twenty-Nine Palms Band asked Luke Madrigal, Anthony Madrigal, and Clifford Trafzer to collect historical documents for the establishment of a tribal archive, filled with documents germane to their history and culture. The tribe created its own manuscripts and archival collection with documents and photographs collected from the National Archives, Smiley Library, National Parks, Rivera Library of the University of California–Riverside, Census Data, Office of Indian Affairs, Twentynine Palms City Library, Indian Claims Commission, Twentynine Palms Historical Society, San Diego Historical Society, and other repositories. The growing collection at the reservation includes newspaper accounts of the tribe, photographs, and selections found in books and articles, including those published in the *Desert Spotlight*, a newspaper originating at the city of Twentynine Palms after the Chemehuevi moved to the Coachella Valley and Banning Pass.

The documents found in the office of the Bureau of Indian Affairs helped the tribe understand more fully how the United States had split the Twenty-Nine Palms Reservation at Coachella, California, from the Cabazon Reservation, and many documents out of the National Archives demonstrated the relationship of the Mission Indian Agency with the members of the Twenty-Nine Palms Tribe and Chemehuevi living along the Colorado River. As one elder from another reservation put it: "The Bureau of Indian Affairs did virtually nothing for some Indian people." This assertion simply reflects the tribe's view of the past Indian Office.[35]

The collection of documents and photographs has helped the tribe in many different ways as it plans for the future and deals with contemporary issues. The tribe's Business Council decided to consolidate its efforts regarding the implementation of the Native American Graves Protection and Repatriation Act with the people of the Chemehuevi Reservation. To this end, the two tribes have examined collections throughout the United States to determine if they would like to repatriate cultural patrimony. The exploration into material culture led the Twenty-Nine Palms Tribe to travel to Washington, D.C., New York City, the Pequot Reservation in Connecticut, and the Newberry Library in Chicago, Illinois. Tribal members viewed items significant to them and assessed the ways the tribe could display documents, baskets, bows, arrows, and other cultural items they might acquire and return home. The trips to various libraries by tribal members and their spouses brought about a new awareness of the significance of written documents in tribal history. At the Newberry Library, for example, tribal members found documents and sketches demonstrating the presence of Chemehuevi people working in the Coachella Valley as early as 1900, and later documents showing that some Chemehuevi left the Colorado River to work in the Coachella Valley at least as early as the 1860s and 1870s. This constituted a much longer presence in the Coachella Valley than had been previously known. But more important, the journey to historical repositories and museums in the East encouraged tribal members to support their own historical and cultural programs.[36]

The tribe determined to expand its historical and cultural presentation through a new building project connected with their casino—a space to display museum items, documents, and photographs. The tribe planned, researched, and executed several displays depicting elements of their culture and history. Tribal members asked their designers to create display areas on every floor of their new building, and as the building progressed, the tribe worked closely with curators from the Southwest Museum of Los Angeles to identify material culture they could use in their displays. On the first two floors of the building, the tribe planned fourteen display cases. Some of the displays had elements of material culture borrowed from private collections, while other cases displayed documents and the story of Chemehuevi people from Twenty-Nine Palms based on materials kept in the Twenty-Nine Palms manuscript and archives collection. Jennifer Mike actively worked on the exhibits, and one exhibit depicted her grandmother, Nellie Mike Morongo, and one of Nellie's baskets. On an earlier expedition into Los Angeles to visit the Southwest Museum, Jennifer Mike had photographed many material items, particularly the baskets.

Historian Anthony Madrigal described the basket collection as "superb," and he began assembling ideas about using them in a number of cases found throughout the Spotlight 29 Casino. Unfortunately for the tribe, the week before the exhibit items went into the display cases, the Southwest Museum refused to loan their Chemehuevi items to Chemehuevi people of the Twenty-Nine Palms Tribe—an unprofessional act after a year's worth of close collaboration between the tribe and museum curators. As a result, Jennifer Mike, Anthony Madrigal, Alynn Loupe, and others used photographs of material items to depict elements of tribal culture. They worked closely with the building designers and architects, offering several dramatic exhibits that depict elements of the rich cultural past of the Chemehuevi people as well as contemporary wisdom. Most important, the Business Council of the Twenty-Nine Palms Band viewed the display cases as a continuation of their historical and cultural program radiating out from the reservation and becoming part of their history.[37]

In 1997 the Twenty-Nine Palms Band of Mission Indians shared elements of their history through a short book that introduced Chemehuevi history. Researched and written by scholars Clifford Trafzer, Luke Madrigal, and Anthony Madrigal, *Chemehuevi People of the Coachella Valley* provided the first historical account of Chemehuevi people of Twenty-Nine Palms, based on historical documents and oral histories. The people of the Twenty-Nine Palms Tribe became the first tribe in Southern California to produce their own history. Anthropologist Carobeth Laird had written *The Chemehuevis* in 1976, a cultural anthropological presentation of material provided by her husband, Chemehuevi elder George Laird. That volume offered a historical survey, an introduction to Chemehuevi history, focusing strongly on the Chemehuevi of the Twenty-Nine Palms Tribe. Members of the Business Council wanted an in-depth study of their people and asked historians to begin work. After publication of the first book in 1997, the tribe encouraged the research and writing of a full-length treatment

World acclaimed Chemehuevi basket maker Mary Snyder was the mother of Willie Boy. Chemehuevi elders say that she was a woman of power and had the ability to create the rattlesnake design in her baskets. The Colorado Indian River Tribes Museum holds the most exquisite and extensive Chemehuevi basket collection in the world, including this Rattlesnake basket. Photograph by Wilene Holt-Fisher, Colorado River Indian Tribes Museum, Parker, Arizona.

of the tribe. Efforts to gather more documents, oral histories, and photographs continued for sixteen years, culminating in the present work.

The Twenty-Nine Palms Tribe expanded its interest in preservation in other ways as well. In 2000, Anthony Madrigal of Tribal EPA led efforts to preserve the tribe's history by creating a presentation on the history of the people of

Twenty-Nine Palms. This presentation served as a mnemonic with tribal elders. He conducted several interviews to determine the feasibility and interest in creating a museum program for the tribe. Madrigal wrote a museum and cultural feasibility study for the tribe with the intent of the tribe expanding historical exhibits and cultural demonstrations. In the fall of 2001 the tribe used the document to expand its cultural programs through their Office of Cultural Resources and through the Native American Land Conservancy. The tribe also expanded its work in cultural preservation by supporting Madrigal during his internship at the Smithsonian's National Museum of the American Indian in Washington, D.C. Through his work with the Smithsonian, Madrigal gained valuable knowledge about many aspects of museum work, and he has used these diverse experiences to direct the museum displays in the recent building projects of the Twenty-Nine Palms Tribe.[38]

The Twenty-Nine Palms Tribe supported Madrigal's educational development, just as the tribe has helped many other people with their education through the Theresa A. Mike Scholarship Fund. After losing their daughter in 1997, Dean and Theresa Mike established a scholarship fund in her name. To raise funds to support the scholarship, Theresa created an annual fashion show and dinner. The tribe and many supporters donate their time and money to support the annual event. The scholarship fund originally hosted the annual show and banquet in rented rooms in hotels, but soon the tribe opened its casino stage and seating to thousands of guests. Working initially through the Native American Land Conservancy, the tribe sponsors the Theresa A. Mike Scholarship Fund. Today the scholarship fund is a 501(c)(3) nonprofit corporation. Over the years it has raised more than a million dollars. A scholarship committee, led by Fay McClung, has given thousands of dollars to needy and worthy students to further their education. The fund is available to Indians and non-Indians alike, particularly employees of the Spotlight 29 Casino. Each year, private donors contribute to the fund, and the annual fashion show and dinner brings in more donations that are used exclusively to support the scholarships. The entertainers, ushers, vendors, cooks, and stagehands working the event, drawing hundreds of participants, donate their time. The scholarship is indicative of the tribe's generosity, only one of several charities the tribe donates to each year. The scholarship fund has a special place within the tribe, as it honors a young tribal member taken too early, but it helps hundreds of people receive an education—a process the tribe has always supported. Since the days when the people lived along the Colorado River and in the Mojave Desert, Chemehuevi have supported education of their people and others, first through the oral tradition and later through formal education offered by newcomers. The Twenty-Nine Palms Tribe has continued this tradition through the NALC, exhibit programs, and cultural gatherings, sustaining its ancient focus on education through new venues.

This emphasis on education is seen with the purchase of a valuable collection of material culture depicting elements of past Southern California Indian life.[39] The Twenty-Nine Palms Tribe significantly expanded its cultural program in 2002, when it joined the Native American Land Conservancy and Cabazon Band of Mission Indians to purchase a valuable collection of Southern California Indian artifacts. During the early twentieth century the Cary family raised cattle in several locations in Southern California, including the Santa Rosa Mountains, Anza-Borrego Desert, and Coachella Valley. While herding cattle and camping near the herds, Cary family members started finding material objects left by indigenous peoples near mesquite groves and caves. Over the years sand had buried the objects, so the cowboys dug them out, recorded their finds, and kept stone objects, pottery jars, arrowheads, beads, and other items. In 2001, Al Cary met with Dean and Theresa Mike to ask if they would like to buy the collection. They asked Clifford Trafzer to meet with Cary to determine the worth of the collection. Trafzer met Cary in a recreational vehicle parked near Interstate 10 in Yucaipa, California, where they drank coffee and looked at photographs of the Cary Collection. Trafzer drove to the reservation to urge the tribe to buy the collection, explaining that the one Cahuilla basket was worth the price of Cary's offer.

Al Cary and his family felt the collection should be returned to Native Americans, so he offered it to the first tribe that showed an interest. When Dean Mike presented the idea of the purchase to the tribal council, the tribe decided to buy it. Acting as president of the Native American Land Conservancy, Mike also shared the idea with the conservancy board. Joe Benitez, a member of the Cabazon Band, attended the meeting, and he asked if his tribe could jointly buy the collection. Members of the Native American Land Conservancy board also wanted to help purchase this important collection, so a partnership emerged between the Twenty-Nine Palms Tribe, the Cabazon Tribe, and the Native American Land Conservancy. Trafzer and Madrigal flew to Portland, Oregon, and drove a van to the Oregon coast to the home of Al Cary. They interviewed Cary extensively about every object, video recording the interpretation of every piece. They loaded the collection and drove it to Southern California, to the Cabazon Museum, which had a professional staff on-site. On September 9, 2002, Judy Stapp, director of the Cabazon Cultural Museum, received the material collection. The Cary Collection proved to be far superior than anyone had expected, and some of the objects are on display today at the Cabazon Cultural Museum in Indio, California. Stapp refused to display the objects until a volunteer accessioned them.[40]

In 2003 and 2004, Jeffrey Smith (presently a professor of history at the University of Hawai'i–Hilo) of Yucaipa, California, accessioned the Cary Collection as part of his graduate work in public history at the University of California–Riverside. He assessed, conserved, and photographed each item. Smith then researched every item and its use among Chemehuevi and Cahuilla people. In addition to gathering knowledge from published resources, Smith interviewed several Native Americans about the objects, including Joe Mike Benitez, Dean Mike, and Katherine Saubel. Through his research Smith found the collection contained more than 150 objects, including some rare and unique pieces. The Cary Collection included a few Cahuilla Indian baskets, including one with a rattlesnake design made by a woman from the Torres- Martinez Indian Reservation and sold to Cary's parents by a trader working a post not far from the reservation. The collection also included several large, intact ollas made by Cahuilla and Chemehuevi people. Cary's father found one of these ollas in a cave north of the Cabazon Reservation. Just north of the reservation, rolling sand hills rise up near the base of the Little San Bernardino Mountains. Ancient Lake Cahuilla had created these sand hills.

While grazing cattle near the sand hills just north of Indio, California, Cary's father found a low cave that contained a large olla with the burned image of an antelope head. In the same cave, the elder Cary found two cradleboards made of mesquite wood and woven fibers for a hood to be placed on the baby's head and face to shield the baby from the sun. These cradleboards are the most distinctive items in the collection, and Chemehuevi people made them. During an interpretive session with Cahuilla scholar and elder Katherine Saubel, she emphatically stated that Cahuilla had not made the cradleboards, that Chemehuevi had crafted these distinctive utilitarian pieces. Chemehuevi people had frequently visited Indio and other towns in the Coachella Valley, and they often used the trail that ran from the oasis of Twenty-Nine Palms to Indio. Chemehuevi people had brought the cradleboards and the olla to the area and left them for future use. The Chemehuevi from Twenty-Nine Palms also contributed some of the stone items found in the collection, including arrow straighteners, pipes, and arrowheads. The collection contains many other material items—all of which tell a great deal about the cultures of the Chemehuevi and Cahuilla people. Jeff Smith researched all the material items and wrote his 2006 dissertation on the tribe's collection of "Made Beings."[41] The collection constituted another successful cultural project of the Twenty-Nine Palms Tribe, but the tribe has supported other preservation efforts, including the exhibit "Cahuilla Continuum," sponsored by the Riverside Metropolitan Museum in Riverside, California.

Perhaps the most impressive work of the Twenty-Nine Palms Band of Mission Indians has been to preserve and continue the Salt Songs of the Chemehuevi and other Southern Paiute people. Under the leadership of Matthew Hanks Leivas, Betty Cornelius, Larry Eddy, and Vivienne Jake, the people began a project called "Asi-Huviav Puruakain," or "The Way It Went: The Salt Song." Chemehuevi and Southern Paiute people, who share a common language and culture, formed the Salt Song Project to preserve and continue the songs by passing them on to children. The tribal coalition includes the people at Twenty-Nine Palms, Cedar, Chemehuevi Valley, Kaibab, Koosharem, Moapa, San Juan, Colorado River, Indian Peak, Kanosh, Las Vegas, Pahrump, and Shivwits. The people formed an association to preserve and protect the songs and their meaning, and they have been extremely successful, particularly by singing the songs and creating a masterful CD. The Salt Songs include more than 120 separate songs, telling many stories. The songs are medicine, providing healing for those mourning and directions for the dead so that they may find their way to the next world. The singers used and continue to use the songs at funerals and memorials, retelling the stories and re-creating the ancient paths of the people over a huge geographical area in Arizona, California, Nevada, and Utah. They also sang, and today sing, Salt Songs at social gatherings. The Chemehuevi tradition holds that the songs would travel north, there to be kept until another day, when the songs would return to the Colorado River where they would become strong again. The elders claim that this is indeed happening through the Salt Song Project.[42]

As in the past, men and women join in and sing Salt Songs, sharing their voices in the night air to help the living and the dead make their own journeys. In December 1999, Dean and Theresa Mike hosted a Memorial Ceremony for their daughter, Theresa Andrea Mike, who had died unexpectedly in 1997. They held the ceremony on the Torres-Martinez Reservation and invited Salt Song singers from the Kiabab, Chemehuevi, and Colorado River Indian reservations to sing. Before the ceremony, assistants set up brush arbors and prepared fires for the participants. After sharing an evening meal, the singers began by summoning Spirit people and beginning the first Salt Songs, starting out low and building in force and tempo. A cold, driving wind blew throughout the night and temperatures in the desert dipped below freezing. Still the singers continued as mourners came forward within the brush lodges to pick up a photograph of Theresa A. Mike and dance with it. Numerous people danced back and forth, listening to the singing and sharing tears with those mourning the death of a loved one. At midnight the singers took a break before continuing the songs until about 3:30 A.M., when assistants lit a huge bonfire and the family tossed articles once belonging to Theresa into the fire. Through ritual, the Mike family broke their mourning and sent personal items to the other world. Friends and family greeted the Mike family and grieved with them, sharing a space and time of mourning and relief. Before daylight the songs ended. Singers boarded a van and began their long journey back to their homes, where they waited for their next call to visit a reservation, singing again for the living and the dead.[43]

Chemehuevi songs have become a metaphor for the tribe's recent history. Like the Salt Songs, the tribe has experienced a cultural and political revitalization. Led by Dean Mike, Jennifer Mike, June Mike, Darrell Mike, and other younger members of the tribal council, the Twenty-Nine Palms Tribe has grown in political activities, community donations, educational support, and economic development. Through the Cultural Resources program, the tribe has taken a stand against the government's destruction of cultural resources and human remains by allowing private companies to destroy habitat and cultural features in the Mojave and Colorado Deserts. The federal government, especially the Department of Interior and the Bureau of Land Management, and solar-and wind-generating companies have developed millions of acres through a fast-track process that allows them to destroy desert lands to establish "green" energy projects without fulfilling all the environmental requirements established by federal and state law. The Twenty-Nine Palms Tribe hired Anthony Madrigal, Jr., who has diligently tracked the energy projects and kept the tribal council apprised on the new and rapid development. Like many tribes, the Twenty-Nine Palms Tribe is not opposed to alternative energy, but the leaders have been alarmed at the careless and needless destruction of plants, animals, human remains, and other cultural resources.[44]

In the twentieth century the Chemehuevi living at Twenty-Nine Palms faced great adversity and threats to their existence as a people. They coped with a severe violation of their tribal laws that affected every member of the tribe and all Nüwü people. They faced removal from the oasis and relocation onto the Cabazon Reservation. Most of them moved off the Cabazon Reservation, resettling in Palm Springs, Banning, and other towns where they worked for a living. Through all of this, the families continued their relationships with each

Contemporary Southern Paiute people, including Chemehuevi, keep the ancient Salt Songs alive, using them in ceremony. In addition to singing at funerals and memorials, singers sang Salt Songs at the Oasis of Twenty-Nine Palms and the cemetery of the old Sherman Institute in Riverside, California. This group of Salt Song singers consists of Robert Chavez, Matthew Hanks Leivas, Larry Eddy, Eunice Ohte, Vivienne Jake, and Lalovi Miller. They sang Salt Songs to the mountains near a sacred cave in the Old Woman Mountain Preserve. Photograph by Philip Klasky.

other, marrying others and slowly growing families of their own. Tribal members traveled to the Chemehuevi Valley, the Colorado River Indian Reservation, and visited other Southern Paiute people to share time, food, medicine, ceremony, and song. They never abandoned their identity as Chemehuevi people, and the families continued to work as a tribal entity but one not recognized by the federal government. Most of the people refused to live on the Cabazon Reservation where the government had enrolled them. Instead, they lived as free Nüwü, surviving as carpenters, house cleaners, window washers, cowboys, woodcutters, and farm workers.

During the twentieth century, Chemehuevi people continued their leadership in political matters. Many of them—including Lily Mike, Dorothy Mike, Susie Mike, Jeff Boniface, Avaldo Marcus, and others—joined the Mission Indian Federation. After 1919 and the creation of the Federation, the Chemehuevi

The Theresa A. Mike Scholarship Foundation helped fund consultations with Chemehuevi and Southern Paiute tribal elders who know the Salt Songs and the trail the songs follow. At this consultation on the Moapa Indian Reservation in Utah, elders discuss the route of the Salt Songs and the natural features in their area. The songs poetically describe the landscape that the people have passed down from generation to generation since time immemorial. Photograph by Philip Klasky.

leaders joined many other Southern California Indians to challenge the control of the Office of Indian Affairs over Indian matters. The Chemehuevi and other members of the Mission Indian Federation wanted "home rule," Indian control of all funds and administration of the Indian Office and reservations. The people became most active in the Federation when Congress passed the Wheeler-Howard Act in 1934 and Commissioner of Indian Affairs John Collier reorganized the office. The government asked the tribes to elect to join in the Indian Reorganization Act by voting whether to join in the effort or not. Collier rigged the voting process, however; the government said that Indians who did not vote at all for the act had cast a positive vote through their nonparticipation. Lily Mike voted against the act in 1934, but he was one of the few participants. The Indian Office claimed that the Cabazon Reservation had supported the Indian Reorganization Act. When Lily Mike, Bill Calloway, and other members on the Cabazon Reservation learned this, they asked Adam Castillo, leader of the Mission Indian Federation, to hold a conference on the Cabazon Reservation for Federation members and to support letters to the Commissioner demanding they consider a new vote, which totally defeated the Indian reorganization on the Cabazon Reservation. In a letter to Superintendent John W. Dady of the Mission Indian Agency, several Chemehuevi people from Cabazon, including Lily Mike, Dorothy Mike, Marcus Avaldo, Calavario Quatte, and Jeff Boniface, stated: "We did not vote for the bill at all nor for any spokesman or committee. We do not favor the [Wheeler-Howard] bill."[45] As a result of a new vote, Cabazon did not join in the Indian Reorganization Act and did not reorganize, thwarting Collier's attempt to hoodwink the Chemehuevi and Cahuilla of Cabazon and increase the control of the people by the Indian Bureau.

Despite the fact that Chemehuevi members enrolled on the Cabazon Reservation had participated in the stand against the Wheeler-Howard Act, the Chemehuevi refused to live on the Cabazon Reservation. They lived primarily in Banning and Palm Springs, but they never gave up on their desire to have a place at the Oasis of Mara or Twentynine Palms. On September 6, 1936, Lily Mike returned to the oasis accompanied by Willie Marcus of Palm Springs, Adam Castillo of Soboba, and Purl Willis, a non-Native counselor for the Mission Indian Federation. They were all members of the Mission Indian Federation, and they had traveled to the oasis to inform the owners of the 29 Palms Inn that the Chemehuevi still owned their homeland on the oasis. According to manager Grace G. Brock, an employee of the inn, the Indians demanded the return of the property to the Chemehuevi, the rightful and aboriginal owners of the property. Lily Mike "claimed that the entire section on which the Inn is situated belonged to the Indians." The delegation demanded the return of the entire section. Apparently, after the state sold the land to the Southern Pacific Railroad, the rail company sold it to a Mr. Roberts, who sold it to the owners of the inn. Margaret Kennedy claimed that Purl Willis represented himself as acting on behalf of the secretary of the interior, Harold Ickes, which ignited an investigation by the Office of Indian Affairs and the Federal Bureau of Investigation. The investigations never fully developed or caused trouble for the Twenty-Nine Palms Tribe. However, it serves as an example of Lily Mike's determination to have the oasis returned to the Chemehuevi and initiate a return of the people to their former homeland. In March 2014, Darrell Mike and the current tribal council of the Twenty-Nine Palms Tribe fulfilled their dream and that of their ancestors by returning to the town of Twentynine Palms to open

In 1919 a group of leaders from among the tribes of Southern California, formed the Mission Indian Federation, an intertribal group that stood for tribal sovereignty, self-determination, home rule, and human rights. Members of the Mission Indian Federation, including Lily Mike, Andrea Mike, and Susie Mike, often met in Riverside, California, at the home of counselor Jonathan Tibbet, a man indigenous people called Buffalo Heart. Notice the American flags fluttering between the eucalyptus trees in Tibbet's yard. Photograph by Edward Noble Fairchild. Riverside Metropolitan Museum, Riverside, California.

their new casino, the Tortoise Rock Casino. This small casino, like the Spotlight 29 Casino, promises to take the tribe on new and important paths in the twenty-first century.[46]

In the 1970s members of the Twenty-Nine Palms Tribe continued their tradition of political involvement, tribal sovereignty, and self-determination. Living in Palm Springs, Banning Pass, and other nearby areas, the people met in an informal tribal council to discuss whether to separate from the Cabazon Tribe and receive their own trust land in Coachella, California. After deciding to leave the people of Cabazon, they secured approximately two hundred acres of land

Members of the Twenty-Nine Palms Tribe elected Darrell Mike as chair. He has successfully guided the tribe and led the effort to create the Tortoise Rock Casino on reservation trust lands in the town of Twentynine Palms. The new casino opened its doors in spring 2014. Photograph by the Twenty-Nine Palms Tribe of Mission Indians.

on the southeastern side of the former Cabazon Reservation, and they submitted tribal bylaws to the Bureau of Indian Affairs. In this way they re-created the Twenty-Nine Palms Tribe under a new structure built on their old ways of governance. The action continued the tribe's ethnogenesis as a distinct group within the Nüwü people, specifically the Chemehuevi group. This validated their tribal sovereignty and self-determination to decide for themselves their future course of action as a tribe recognized by the United States. Men and women participated in this endeavor, and the people met in General Council and voted for their Business Council, which handled tribal business on behalf of other members. They survived by exerting their tribal sovereignty and identity as a unique group of Nüwü people. Dorothy Mike Rogers, Jennifer Mike, Susie Mike, June Mike, Darrell Mike Sr., and Dean Mike led the tribe in its new political and economic direction. The children of various tribal members grew into adulthood learning from elder teachers. Parents and grandparents, aunts and uncles served as role models. Since 2000, these children have taken the reins of leadership from their elders, guiding the tribe in innovative and challenging directions, including the management of Spotlight 29 Casino and the new Tortoise Rock Casino located on their reservation lands near the town of Twentynine Palms. The opening of the Turtle Rock Casino offered a new beginning for the tribe as its members returned to their former homeland at the Oasis of Mara on March 31, 2014, to celebrate the opening of their enterprise. Darrell Mike Jr., Angelina Mike, Courtney Andrade Gonzales, Michelle Mike, Dineen Mike, Lloyd Mike, Darrell Mike Miller, Sabrena Mike, Leanna Mike, and Malissa Mike now lead the tribe into the twenty-first century. Like their ancestors before them, they lead with a strong sense of identity and spirit.

The spirit of an ancient culture flows through the veins of the Chemehuevi of Twenty-Nine Palms. Over thousands of years their Nüwü people had drawn on the same spirit to preserve and protect their families, lands, and resources. Ocean Woman had provided for her children by instilling the creative spirit in each person, and they have carried that spirit forward since the beginning of time. The vast region of their traditional homelands remains alive but ever changing. It is an important landscape to the tribe, a gift from the Creator to Nüwüvi people. The spirit place in the land remains alive today, waiting to be used to benefit the people. The spirits of their ancestors have walked with the people of the Twenty-Nine Palms Tribe through adversity and prosperity. Contemporary people stand together in the presence of Spirit just as their ancestors had in the past. Despite differences, they have stood together for the betterment of their people. Members of the Twenty-Nine Palms Tribe have survived as a result of their spiritual songs, their self-determination, and their adherence to tribal sovereignty. They have accepted no government handouts or charity, and they have refused to follow the dictates of foreign rule to live confined on reservations. Like tribal leaders of the past, Chemehuevi leaders of the Twenty-Nine Palms Tribe use song, spirit, and innate intelligence to guide their course. Their future path will draw on their blood memory and Chemehuevi culture to lead them into the centuries ahead.

At one time Chemehuevi people had many songs, both tribal and personal. They believed that song emerged at the time of Creation when Ocean Woman set life into motion by offering her body as the surface of the earth. Coyote, Wild Cat, Bear, Yucca Date, Rat, Joshua Tree, Desert Tortoise, and other plants and animals had songs. The earth and its many places had songs, including caves where the people received instructions. Songs tell stories about the Chemehuevi people and their communities, the animate and inanimate life all around them. Songs helped create the earth and kept it going, and stories changed within the songs as the Chemehuevi changed. Today, the Chemehuevi people and their Southern Paiute relatives have many new songs to sing and share, creating and re-creating a new story based on their rich and colorful past. The songs continue, and with them life continues and grows like the feathering branches of the mesquite trees, reaching out into the desert sunlight and capturing nourishing rays that feed the roots, trunk, branches, and leaves, providing food necessary for life and well-being.

Songs had power and told stories about people, places, and past experiences. They helped create the Nüwü world and keep it in balance. Songs emerged from plants, animals, and places within the Chemehuevi landscape, adding numerous poetic voices and spiritual meaning to life. Songs came from the spirit of being Nüwü, and they spoke of sovereignty and determination. They helped people know who they were and where they were going in this life and the next.

Glossary

Aapanapih. The Chemehuevi name of a chief, meaning White Clay Lightening Flash.

Acjachemen. This is the preferred name for Native Americans associated with California Mission San Juan Capistrano, or the Juaneño Tribe of Mission Indians.

Akawak'heyo:v. A place-name in Mojave Country.

Akuuki. Serrano Indian term for ancestor and the Indian name for Jim Pine.

Alessandro. Serrano cowboy, artist with leather ropes, reins, bridles, hackamore, belts, and so on.

Apache. Athapascan-speaking Indians of eastern Arizona and western New Mexico. Today, many Apache of the Chiracahua Band live at Fort Sill, Oklahoma—descendants of prisoners of war.

Apaily-Kma O'e. Leader of the Chemehuevi people, moved south of Mohave Valley toward Parker, Arizona.

Aratêve. One of the names used in the literature to describe the famed Mojave Indian chief Irataba.

arrastre. A piece of mining equipment used to crush rocks to separate minerals.

Asu-Huviav-Puruakain. "The Way It Went," the Nüwü term for the Salt Song.

Asuket. A Mojave chief who favored peace and led a peace delegation to visit the Chemehuevi.

aya. Chemehuevi term for "desert tortoise."

Avikwame. A sacred mountain to all Yuman-speaking Indians, located in California and Nevada along the Colorado River.

Carriota or Courinote. Jim Mike's Indian name.

Chacar. Chemehuevi war chief and father of Tom Painter, a famous indigenous consultant.

Chemebet. A term used in the literature to describe Chemehuevi people.

Chepeven. Born circa 1792, Chepeven was an elderly man living at the Oasis of Mara in the early twentieth century and known for his hunting ability and generosity.

Chigquata. This is a woman's name, the woman that married Moha, who survived a massive Chemehuevi attack and killing of everyone but Moha.

Chim-e-hue-vas Jim. Chemehuevi warrior and raider.

Chimehuevi Mike. A term found in the literature describing William Mike.

Chi-mi-way-wahs. A term used in the literature to describe Chemehuevi people.

Chooksa homar. A Mojave warrior who provided scholar Alfred Kroeber a detailed Mojave war story.

Comanche. A tribe of Uto-Aztecan speakers related to Shoshone and great warriors of the Southern Plains.

Coyote. This is the English name of the Mother of Matilda Pine.

Cupeño. A Uto-Aztecan tribe related to the Cahuilla people, living near Warner Springs, California.

diggers. A derogatory term used to describe Nüwü, including the Chemehuevi, and later applied to all California Indians.

Diné. Navajo and Apache, both Athapascan-speakers, call themselves Diné.

El Camino del Diablo. The Devil's Highway, an ancient trail that runs on the Arizona side of the Sonoran border.

Gabrieleño. A large tribal group in the Los Angeles Basin and surrounding areas. Today the people prefer Tongva, but they are most closely associated with Mission San Gabriel.

Goffs. A place-name in eastern California Mojave Desert.

gorra blanca · modo de solidéo. A Chemehuevi headdress.

hiyovi. A mourning dove.

Huttamenie. A Quechan Indian chief who made a peace agreement with Major Samuel Peter Heintzelman of Fort Yuma.

Iats. A Chemehuevi term for Mojave.

Irataba. The Mojave chief who fought soldiers at Fort Mojave and negotiated a reservation with President Abraham Lincoln. His efforts resulted in the creation of the Colorado River Indian Reservation on March 3, 1865.

'Isill Héqwas Wáxish. Literally this means "a dried coyote's tail" in the Cahuilla Indian language, and it is the title of a two-volume book by Katherine Siva Saubel on her people.

Itsiyêre. The name of a Mojave war leader.

juncus. A plant used for basket making.

kakara. The Chemehuevi name for Gambel's quail.

Kanosh. A band of Southern Paiute.

Koloma. Coloma, California.

Koosharen. A band of Southern Paiute.

Kumastamho. The son of the Quechan Creator, Kukumat, and Creator in his own right. The spirit of Kumastamho lives on the sacred mountain of Avikwamé.

Luiseño. A Uto-Aztecan-speaking tribe located in Riverside and San Diego Counties.

Maidu. A tribe composed of many bands living in the Sacramento area and the foothills of the Sierra Nevada Mountains. In 1848 the Maidu people helped discover gold at Sutter's Mill.

Malki. The Cahuilla word meaning "dodging" but applied to the reservation now known as the Morongo Indian Reservation.

Mamaytam Maarrenga'yam. This is the Serrano Indian term for the Native American clan from the Oasis of Mara or Twenty-Nine Palms.

Mara or Mar-rah. Serrano word adopted by Chemehuevi people, meaning "little spring, much grass."

Morongo. Originally known as the Malki Reservation, officials of the Mission Indian Agency named the reservation after Serrano leader John Morongo.

Maricopa. A Yuman-speaking tribe of people located near present-day Phoenix, Arizona.

Mike, William. Also known as Chemehuevi Mike, Mike Boniface, and Old Mike. Willie Boy murdred William Mike in 1909.

Moha. This is the name of a Mojave warrior, the only survivor of a fight against Chemehuevi warriors.

Monos. A large tribe of Uto-Aztecan-speaking Indians with bands on the western and eastern side of the Sierra Nevada Mountains.

Moqui. This a term used in the historical literature to describe Hopi Indians.

Mukewiune. The Chemehuevi elder and leader who served as a historical consultant about the nineteenth-century life of Nüwü.

Nacuta. The Cahuilla Indian term for a village in Horse Canyon, California. This was the ancestral home of the Arenas and Madrigal families.

Nez Perce. A tribe in the inland northwest of Idaho, Oregon, and Washington. They call themselves Nim'ipuu.

Nietta. Jim Mike's wife.

Oenyô-hiv'auve. A Chemehuevi leader and warrior during the Chemehuevi-Mojave War.

Pahrimp. This is a term used to describe Pahrump, Nevada, and the Paiute group at the same location.

Pahrump. A place-name in southern Nevada, home of the Pahrump Band of Paiute Indians.

Pah-utahs. A term used in the historical literature for Paiute.

Pahutes. A term used to describe Paiute.

Pakuma. The Serrano name of Chief Santos Manuel.

Pataya. This Yuman term means "ancient" or "old ones" and is used to describe the ancient people of the deserts of California and Arizona.

Patri. Jim Pine's aunt.

Pa-Utche. A term used in the historical literature as Paiute.

Picacho. The term means "peak" and identifies a place on the California side of the Colorado River, located just south of Chemehuevi country.

Pima. A large tribe of people composed of many groups located in south-central Arizona.

Pine, Mathilde or Matilda. The wife of Serrano leader Jim Pine.

Pivan. The name of one of the Chemehuevi people living at Twenty-Nine Palms in the 1890s.

poros. A wooden staff; a spirit or power and medicine staff.

pow wow. A celebration of singing and dancing by Native Americans.

puhwaganti. The Chemehuevi name for a healer or medicine person.

pul. The Cahuilla term for a medicine man.

pul amnawet. The Cahuilla term for the highest level of medicine man.

Purisima de la Concepcíon. A Spanish and Catholic mission located on the California side of the Colorado River at the junction with the Gila River.

Que-o-gan. Chemehuevi chief in 1857.

Quichnailk. Jack Jones Sr., a Mojave leader and interpreter.

samarókwa. A temporary Chemehuevi home made like a domed wickiup.

San Pedro y San Pablo de Bicuñer. A Spanish and Catholic mission located on the California side of the Colorado River north of Purisima de la Concepcion.

Settuma. The name of a Mojave leader and chief.

Surda. The proper name of Maria Mike's mother, mother-in-law of William Mike.

suupaarupi. A winter gathering.

takagani or havagani. A temporary Chemehuevi structure similar to a *ramada*, with vertical poles and a plant-based roof, used for a wake and burned after the wake ceremony.

Tavivo. Wovoka's father.

tcagwara. The Chemehuevi name for a chuckwalla and origin of the English term for this lizard.

Tcate. Irataba's granddaughter.

tcuupikyani. A-framed Chemehuevi home made with poles and arrowweed.

tëhiya. Deer.

Tejón. This is a fort and also the name of a pass in the mountains due north of the Los Angeles Basin.

Tewa. A Tanoan-speaking group of Pueblo Indians.

Ticup, Jim. A Chemehuevi elder who lived at the Oasis of Mara.

Timtimmon. Indian name for the Mike family

tinajas. A Spanish term for rocky indentations that hold water, filling up each time it rains.

tivikyani. One style of Chemehuevi homes made of poles, sticks, and mud.

Tomachi. The Chemehuevi name for Annie Mike, also known as Minnie Mike.

Topock, Arizona. A place-name on the Colorado River near present-day Needles, California.

Tulkapaya. A Yuman term for the Western Yavapai people.

Turat Aiyet. The Mojave word for their homeland.

tutuguuvi. Familiar, spirit helper.

umpahapuhup. Knotted string.

Vanyume. One band of Serrano Indians that inhabited the Mojave Desert of eastern California.

vistidode gamuza. A Chemehuevi shirt made of antelope skin.

Walapai. Hualapai.

Walkara. Ute war chief and raider.

warap. The Chemehuevi term for their great runners.

Washingtonia filifera. The scientific name for the native palm trees at the Oasis of Mara.

Wilepa. This is the proper name for one Chemehuevi female living at Twenty-Nine Palms in the 1890s.

Wovoka. The Ghost Dance prophet, also known as Jack Wilson.

Yartav. This is another term used for Irataba, chief of the Mojave.

Yuhaviatam. A clan of Serrano people that claimed the land and water near present-day Big Bear and Baldwin Lakes.

zapatos. Shoes.

Notes

Introduction

1　In 1998, I attended the memorial ceremony described on the Torres Martinez Indian Reservation in Thermal, California. I followed tribal protocols and did not record the ceremony at the time of the ceremony. I made field notes about the ceremony in my journal, and I later used these notes to recount the ceremony.

2　Native Americans of Southern California and western Arizona often build brush arbors and altars for use in wake and memorial ceremonies. Relatives often place one or more photographs for the deceased on the altars. Southern Paiute protocol allows participants to handle the photographs and dance with the picture within the sacred space under the brush arbor between Salt Song singers and supportive women. People dance "with" the deceased by holding the picture and replace it on the altar after the song. Cahuilla, Luiseño, Serrano, and Kumeyaay do not have this tradition of dancing with the photograph. Among these tribes, it is not proper to take the photo from the altar and dance with it.

3　At mourning and memorial services, an elder speaker explains the rules and proper behavior associated with the ceremony. Larry Eddy served as the spokesman for the Mike family, and he especially warned parents and grandparents to keep control of their children who are not permitted in the sacred space between the dancers in front of the altar.

4　Larry Eddy, Vivienne Jake, Betty Cornelius, and Matthew Hanks Leivas are leaders of the Salt Song Project, which preserves and records the songs. Dean Mike was tribal chair and president of the Native American Land Conservancy when the organization voted to support some activities of the Salt Song Project. The Cultural Conservancy also supports the efforts of the Salt Song Project, and the conservancy has created two documentary films on the Salt Songs, offering authentic information through the voices of Salt Song singers.

5　Oral interview with Matthew Hanks Leivas by Clifford E. Trafzer, Chemehuevi Indian Reservation, Coachella, California, February 17–19, 2013. Oral interview with Larry Eddy by Clifford E. Trafzer, Colorado River Indian Reservation, Parker, Arizona, October 18,

2007. Oral interview with Betty Cornelius by Clifford E. Trafzer, Colorado River Indian Reservation, Parker, Arizona, January 10, 2013.

6   Ibid.

7   Larry Eddy and Betty Cornelius are Chemehuevi elders from the Colorado River Indian Reservation near Parker, Arizona. The reservation is located in Arizona and California. Matthew Hanks Leivas and Iris Burns Leivas were raised on the Colorado River Indian Reservation, but they relocated to the Chemehuevi Indian Reservation in Havasu Lake, California, where they reside today.

8   Trafzer Journal, Field Notes, Winter 1998.

9   Ibid. These are notes from the Yagapi ceremony. For the exact quotation used here, see Philip M. Klasky and Melissa Nelson, "The Salt Song Trail," *News from Native California* (Summer 2005): 10.

10 Ibid.

11 Ibid.; Matthew Hanks Leivas interview, February 17–19, 2013; and see Klasky and Nelson, "Salt Song Trail." Larry Eddy served as the spokesman at this ceremony, and he often shares the same information at each service regarding the origin of the songs and the need to break hearts.

12 Ibid. Singers call the midnight song the "Cake Song" because they take a break after singing the dramatic song during which they eat cake and drink coffee to fortify themselves for singing in the early morning.

13 Ibid.

14 Salt Songs describe the southernmost reaches of Southern Paiute territory, although their landscapes are much broader. Chemehuevi and other Southern Paiute traders traveled into Mexico, Arizona, New Mexico, California, and other points beyond the landscapes normally associated with the people. They do not claim to "own" this vast region, but they used the large landscape and knew many places beyond their villages.

15 Clifford E. Trafzer, *Chemehuevi Indians: Historic Properties of Traditional Lands on the Yuma Proving Ground.* Report to the U.S. Corps of Engineers (Riverside: California Center for Native Nations, 2013), 28–30, 32, 38–41; hereafter cited as Trafzer, *Chemehuevi Indian Report.*

16 Oral interview of anonymous Paiute scholar with Clifford E. Trafzer, October 6, 2012, Spring Mountains, Nevada; hereafter cited as anonymous Paiute scholar interview, October 6, 2012. This scholar wished to remain anonymous.

17 Ibid.

18 Oral interviews with Joe Benitez by Clifford E. Trafzer, Twenty-Nine Palms Reservation, Indio, California, September 10 and 17, 1997. Trafzer, *Chemehuevi Indian Report,* 32–54.

19 Ibid.

20 Oral interviews with Joe Benitez, September 10 and 17, 1997; Trafzer, *Chemehuevi Indian Report,* 44–46; for Mojave testimony about their war with the Chemehuevi, see Alfred Kroeber and C. B. Kroeber, *A Mohave War Reminiscence, 1854–1880* (Berkeley: University of California Press, 1973), 39–47.

21 Oral interview with Dean Mike by Clifford E. Trafzer, Twenty-Nine Palms Indian Reservation, Coachella, California, August 4, 3013.

22 Ibid.

23 Benitez interview, September 10, 17, 1997.

24 Oral interview of Dean Mike by Clifford E. Trafzer, Twenty-Nine Palms Tribe, Coachella, California, September 2–3, 1997.

25 Ibid.

26 In 1999, I learned this information through an informal discussion with tribal chair Dean Mike about Indian gaming on the Twenty-Nine Palms Reservation at Spotlight 29 Casino, Coachella, California.

27 California State Library, "Indian Gaming," online at www.library.ca.gov. This lengthy article presents a history of Indian gaming in California, including the propositions that legalized gaming.

28 Bylaws of the Native American Land Conservancy, copy in possession of the author and on file at Spotlight 29 Casino.

29 Native American Land Conservancy brochure, 2012, in possession of the author.

1. The Chemehuevi Way

1 Richard Stoffle, comp., "The Enugwuhype (Ancestral Numic People): An Ethnogenesis Analysis," unpublished manuscript provided by Stoffle to the author.

2 Trafzer, *Chemehuevi Indian Report*, 8–14, 25–41, 55–62; and Joe Benitez interviews, September 10 and 17, 1997.

3 Stoffle, "Enugwuhype (Ancestral Numic People): An Ethnogenesis Analysis"; and anonymous Southern Paiute scholar to Clifford Trafzer and Matthew Hanks Leivas, Summer 2013.

4 Oral interview with Matthew Hanks Leivas by Clifford E. Trafzer, Palm Desert, California, July 17, 2013.

5 Carobeth Laird, *The Chemehuevis* (Banning, California: Malki Museum Press, 1976). Carobeth Laird uses extensive oral histories with Chemehuevi, particularly George Laird, to present this classic book. Chemehuevi elder George Laird was Carobeth Laird's husband, and he argues that the word "Chemehuevi" is from the Mojave word *tcamuweiva*, meaning "mixed with all." Gertrude Hanks Leivas maintained that the word "Chemehuevi" is a derivative of the word "Mojave," used when they saw Chemehuevi running like roadrunners. The Chemehuevi sometimes wore intricate feathered headpieces and they were known as fast runners; these two elements of Chemehuevi culture may have combined for them to receive this unique name that the people use to this day. George Laird states that the Chemehuevi were called *tuumontcoko,* or black beards, because of their body hair. Throughout this work, the people are referred to as Nüwü, or Chemehuevi. Oral interview with Gertrude Hanks Leivas by Clifford E. Trafzer, Theresa Mike, Matthew Hanks Leivas, Anthony Madrigal, and Bernie Thomas, Chemehuevi Indian Reservation, Havasu Lake, California, March 1999.

6 Richard W. Stoffle and M. Nieves Zedeño, "American Indian World Views: The Concept of Power and Its Connection to People, Places, and Resources," in Richard W. Stoffle, Maria Nieves Zedeño, and David B. Halmo, eds., *American Indians and the Nevada Test Site* (Washington, D.C.: Government Printing Office, 2011), 58–76; and Richard W. Stoffle and M. Nieves Zedeño, "American Indian Worldviews: Power and Cultural Landscapes," in Stoffle, Zedeño, and Halmo, eds., *American Indians and the Nevada Test Site*, 139–52.

7 Telephone interview with Matthew Hanks Leivas by Clifford E. Trafzer, September 12, 2000.

8 Native American Land Conservancy brochure, Coachella, California, Twenty-Nine Palms Tribe Printing.

9 Matthew Hanks Leivas interview, August 4 and 29, 2013; telephone interview with Matthew Hanks Leivas by Clifford E. Trafzer, Chemehuevi Indian Reservation, June 15, 2013; and Betty Cornelius interview, January 10, 2013.

10 The author received this comment from a reviewer of his manuscript on the Palouse Indians of the Northwest for the University of Oklahoma Press in 1985.

11 Oral interviews with Matthew Hanks Leivas and Iris Burns Leivas by Clifford E. Trafzer, Chemehuevi Indian Reservation, Havasu Lake, California, February 17–19, 2013.

12 Clifford E. Trafzer and Richard D. Scheuerman, eds., *Mourning Dove's Stories.* Publications in American Indian Studies (San Diego: San Diego State University Press, 1991), vi, 2.

13 Laird, *The Chemehuevis,* 148–49; and Carobeth Laird, *Mirror and Pattern: George Laird's World of Chemehuevi Mythology* (Banning, California: Malki Museum Press, 1984), 32.

14 Laird, *Mirror and Pattern,* 32. Chemehuevi also called Ocean Woman, Ocean Old Woman. She is one of the many Naminiwigaipi, or people who are gone, spirit people, holy people, immortal ones.

15 Ibid.

16 Ibid.; Laird, *The Chemehuevis,* 148–49.

17 Laird, *The Chemehuevis,* 149.

18 Ibid.

19 Ibid.

20 Ibid., 150–51.

21 Oral interview with Larry Eddy by Clifford E. Trafzer, Colorado River Reservation, Parker, Arizona, October 18, 2007. I wish to thank Mr. Eddy for sharing deep and personal information about his tribal culture and history.

22 Ibid.

23 Stoffle, Zedeño, and, eds., *American Indians and the Nevada Test Site,* 73.

24 Contemporary Chemehuevi and their Southern Paiute neighbors continue to revere Charleston Peak and many other sites in the Mojave Desert and beyond. The people consider these sites sacred, still tied to their spiritual beliefs through story and song. Although their reservations are not located on most of the sites, the people have a special relationship with their places and the characters associated with particular sites. The people still tell stories about these places, and they sing songs about many of them. In 1999, Chemehuevi cultural preservationist Matthew Hanks Leivas and other Southern Paiute people began the Salt Song Project, an intertribal effort to take young people to places mentioned in the songs and teach the young people the words and songs as well as the cultural context of the Salt Songs. The Native American Land Conservancy and the Theresa A. Mike Scholarship Foundation supports the Salt Song Project. The project preserves the songs by teaching the children and protects sacred sites mentioned in the songs.

25 John P. Harrington, "The Chemehuevi: Their Name, Character, and Habitat," papers of John P. Harrington, Smithsonian Institution, Microfilm Collection, Rivera Library, University of California–Riverside, Reel 147, Part 3, p. 4; hereafter cited as Harrington Papers.

26 Matthew Hanks Leivas interview, June 15, 2013.

27 Ibid.

28 Alfred Kroeber, "A Report of the Aboriginal Territory and Occupancy of the Mohave Tribe," in *Indian Claims Commission Findings on the Mohave* (New York: Garland Press, 1974), 45, 70–71, 75; Henry F. Dobyns, Paul Ezell, and Greta Ezell, "Death of a Society," *Ethnohistory* 10 (Spring 1963): 125–37; oral interview with Michael Tsosie by Clifford Trafzer, Colorado River Reservation, Parker, Arizona, April 21–22, 2010; Clifford E. Trafzer, *Mojave of the Colorado River Indian Reservation: Historic Property Inventory Traditional Cultural Properties on the Yuma Proving Ground.* Report to the United States Corps of Engineers

(Riverside: California Center for Native Nations, 2011), 124–41; and Trafzer, *Chemehuevi Indian Report.*

29 Ibid.; and Betty Cornelius interview, January 10, 2013.

30 Trafzer, *Chemehuevi Indian Report*, 28–30.

31 Ibid.

32 Alfred Kroeber, *Handbook of the Indians of California* (Berkeley: University of California Press, 1953), 595.

33 Oral interview with Matthew Hanks Leivas by Clifford E. Trafzer, Twenty-Nine Palms Reservation, Coachella, California, July 23, 2013.

34 Harrington, "The Chemehuevis," Harrington Papers, 3, 21, 23; and Ronald Dean Miller and Peggy Jean Miller, *The Chemehuevi Indians of Southern California* (Banning, California: Malki Museum Press, 1967), 9. During an informal conversation with anthropologist Lowell Bean about the ability of the Southern Paiute to travel great distances, Bean commented that during the early nineteenth century, more Paiute people lived in Los Angeles than any other Native American group, thereby attesting to the traveling proclivity of Paiute people.

35 Oral interview with Dean Mike by Clifford E. Trafzer, Luke Madrigal, and Anthony Madrigal, Twenty-Nine Palms Reservation, Coachella, California, September 3, 1997. Also see Joe Benitez interviews, September 10 and 17, 1997.

36 Generally Chemehuevi transferred ownership of their hereditary Deer and Mountain Sheep Songs from father to son. However, the owner of a song could give the song to a daughter, sister-in-law, brother, brother-in-law, or close friend, especially if the owner had no children with whom to share it. In the late nineteenth and early twentieth centuries, the Chemehuevi population declined because of high death rates, low birth rates, and movement away from the Mojave Desert to border towns and reservations along the Colorado River, in southern Nevada, and California. As a result of language loss and diaspora, many songs passed out of use or were shared with anyone who might perpetuate them. Other songs, particularly personal songs for hunting and gathering, disappeared.

37 Laird, *The Chemehuevis*, 9.

38 Gertrude Hanks Leivas interview, March 1999; and Joe Benitez interviews, September 10 and 17, 1997.

39 Clifford E. Trafzer, Luke Madrigal, and Anthony Madrigal, *Chemehuevi People of the Coachella Valley* (Coachella, California: Chemehuevi Press of the Twenty-Nine Palms Tribe, 1997), 14.

40 Martha C. Knack, *Boundaries Between: The Southern Paiutes, 1775–1995* (Lincoln: University of Nebraska Press, 2001), 13, 15–20, 25–26; and Stoffle, Zedeño, and Halmo, eds., *American Indians and the Nevada Test Site*, 72–75, 102–3, 106–7, 111–12. Both of these books are community based and contain excellent information on Southern Paiute people.

41 Richard C. Jenkins, "A Study of Aboriginal Land Use: Southern Paiute Subsistence in the Eastern Mojave Desert," master's thesis, Department of Anthropology, University of California–Riverside, 1982, pp. 28–30.

42 Ibid., 14–16.

43 Ibid., 16–18.

44 Ibid., 20.

45 Ibid., 18–22.

46 Ibid., 22.

47 Ibid., 24–26. Oral interview of anonymous Paiute scholar, October 6, 2012. I recorded the interview in my field notes.

48 Laird, *The Chemehuevis*, 7–8; and Pearl Eddy as quoted in the Matthew Hanks Leivas interview, September 5, 2000.

49 The narrative describes a desert and mountain range hunted by the Chemehuevi. Since the 1990s, no ownership songs have come to light among the people. From the landscape and actions of animal, song makers created cryptic verse in phrases, much like a poem, and sang about the region and the hunting there. This description provides an example of graphic possibilities Chemehuevi would have used in song.

50 Ibid., 15.

51 Ibid., 14.

52 Ibid, 25.

53 In 1999, Matthew Hanks Leivas, Vivienne Jake, and Betty Cornelius led a small group of Chemehuevi to unite in a Salt Song Project to preserve remaining Salt Songs, to teach young people to sing the songs, and to travel to the sites sung about in the songs. Soon the Native American Land Conservancy began to sponsor the project. Larry Eddy made this statement about Salt Songs at the memorial wake for Theresa A. Mike on the Torres-Martinez Indian Reservation, Thermal, California. Also see Philip Klasky and Melissa K. Nelson, "The Salt Song Trail," *News from Native California* (Summer 2005): 10–12.

54 Many contemporary Chemehuevi know Bird Songs, and they explain that they learned them from Mojave, Quechan, Hualapai, Cahuilla, and other groups. According to Native American scholar Paul Apodaca of Chapman University, Bird Songs originated with Cahuilla, not Chemehuevi or other Native Americans. However, Nüwü and many other tribes learned the Bird Songs and shared them widely, adopting them through the process of indigenization. This learning of Bird Songs and other fascinating songs that tell of places and travels during the early years of Creation demonstrates cultural adaptation by the Chemehuevi. Apodaca is the foremost scholar researching Bird Songs today. See Paul Apodaca, "Tradition, Myth, and Performance of Cahuilla Bird Songs," PhD dissertation, University of California–Los Angeles, 1999.

55 Trafzer, Madrigal, and Madrigal, *Chemehuevi People*, 33–34.

56 Elliott Coues, ed., *On the Trail of a Spanish Pioneer: The Diary and Itinerary of Francisco Garces* (New York: Francis P. Harper, 1900), 213–25.

57 Laird, *The Chemehuevis*, 26–27, 42, 47, 95.

58 Twenty-Nine Palms tribal chair Dean Mike and Theresa Mike hosted the *yagapi* ceremony, and I had the honor of attending and participating in the singing, dancing, and burning. The ceremony was very moving, a sacred event hosted by the parents of Theresa Andrea Mike, and I extend my sincere appreciation to the Mike family for their invitation to enter this element of their lives so that I might understand further the significance of the sacred within the lives of Chemehuevi people.

59 Joe Benitez interviews, September 10 and 17, 1997.

60 Laird, *The Chemehuevis*, 48.

61 Joe Benitez interviews, September 10 and 17, 1997.

62 Laird, *The Chemehuevis*, 48.

63 Ibid.

64 Ibid.

65 Harrington, "The Chemehuevi," Harrington Papers, 3, 9–10, 21, 23.

66 Carobeth Laird, "Chemehuevi Religious Beliefs and Practices," *Journal of California Anthropology* I (Spring 1974): 19–25; Laird, *The Chemehuevis*, 148–52; Carobeth Laird, "Chemehuevi Religious Beliefs and Practices," *AVAS Newsletter* (March 1982), in Gerald A. Smith Collection, Smiley Library, Redlands, California; Carobeth Laird, "Chemehuevi

Shamanism, Sorcery, and Charms," *Journal of California and Great Basing Anthropology* 2 (1980): 80–87; and R. A. Musser-Lopez, "Yaa vya's Poro: The Singular Power Object of a Chemehuevi Shaman," *Journal of California and Great Basin Anthropology* 5 (1983): 260–64.

67 On December 29, 2002, at 5:30 A.M., Cahuilla elder Katherine Saubel and I drove to the airport. On the way we drove down Malki Road on the Morongo Indian Reservation near Banning, California. At that time she shared this story. She often told stories when we traveled to meetings of the Native American Heritage Commission from Banning, California, to Sacramento, California.

68 Florence McClintock to W. B. Wells, April 18, 1931, Box 6, Mission Indian Agency, National Archives, Pacific Southwest Region, Record Group 75, Perris, California.

69 Larry Eddy interview, October 18, 2007.

70 In 2013, Serrano and Cahuilla scholar and elder Ernest Siva shared a medicine story about a man who abused a medicine bundle by opening it to show non-Indians the contents. As a result of this transgression, the man became ill and died. Within many Native American communities, tribal elders know of numerous examples of people who violated traditional laws and suffered disease and death as a result. Oral interview of anonymous Chemehuevi elders with Clifford E. Trafzer, August 2013. The elders asked not to be identified as they shared information about Eddy's relative.

71 Larry Eddy interview, October 18, 2007.

72 Ibid.

73 Ibid.

74 Ibid. The power was that of the bat.

75 Ibid.; and Laird, *The Chemehuevis*, 31–39.

76 Laird, *The Chemehuevis*, 31–33.

77 Anonymous Chemehuevi elders, August 2013.

78 Clifford E. Trafzer, "Tuberculosis Death and Survival among Southern California Indians, 1922–1944," *Canadian Bulletin of Medical History* 18 (2001): 85–107; and Clifford E. Trafzer, "Medical Circles Defeating Tuberculosis in Southern California," *Canadian Bulletin of Medical History* 23 (2006): 477–98.

79 I attended the meeting at the Presbyterian Church in Redlands, California, with Theresa Mike, Joe Mike Benitez, and representatives of the Presbyterian Synod of Southern California and Hawai'i. The non-Indian representative from the Upland Church wanted to triple the price for the land in comparison to all other owners. One representative of the church explained: "You can talk all you want about how the land has spirit and that it is a cultural place. The land has no meaning to us; you may do with the land whatever you want; what we want is the money." Native people attending the meeting looked at each other, wondering if they should leave. The crass statement nearly ended the meeting, but we remained seated in the hope of resolving our differences. In September 2000, representatives of the Native American Land Conservancy participated in a conference call with two representatives of the Synod, including a representative of the Native American committee of the church. We talked about the land and its role in the church's professed interest in reconciliation with Native Hawai'ians and American Indians. Ultimately the Synod sold their interest in the Old Woman Mountains to the Native American Land Conservancy for the same amount, one hundred dollars an acre, as the other owners. The sale of the land in the Old Woman Mountains concluded, in large part because of the support of the Twenty-Nine Palms Tribe and the U.S. Fish and Wildlife Service, a federal agency that has supported the programs of the conservancy.

80 Kurt Russo, *In the Land of Three Peaks: The Old Woman Mountain Preserve* (Coachella, California: Native American Land Conservancy, 2005).

81 In July 2013, Richard Stoffle, compiler, provided me an informative manuscript assembled by Stoffle on behalf of numerous Southern Paiute people, "The Enugwuhype (Ancestral Numic People): An Ethnogenesis Analysis." The quotations are found on page 1 of this document.

82 Ibid.

83 Ibid.

84 Laird, *The Chemehuevis*, 104; *kani* in the Chemehuevi language literally means "bird nest."

85 Ibid., 105.

86 Gertrude Hanks Leivas interview, March 1999.

87 Laird, *The Chemehuevis*, 105.

88 Oral interview of Joe Mike Benitez by Clifford E. Trafzer, Morongo Reservation, Banning, California, September 29, 2000. Isabel Truesdell Kelly, *Southern Paiute Ethnography* (New York: Garland Publishing, 1976), 59. Within Kelly's book, Richard F. Van Valkenburg published "Chemehuevi Notes 1974," 225–53. Scholars may find the "Chemehuevi Notes 1974" at the Museum of Northern Arizona in Flagstaff. Laird does not mention sweat bath in her work on the Chemehuevi. Many consider Catherine Fowler one of the leading scholars of Paiute people, and she has spent her life studying the people and sharing information with Native American scholars.

89 For the most comprehensive study of non-Native views toward Native Americans, see James Rawls, *Indians of California: The Changing Image* (Norman: University of Oklahoma Press, 1984), 49–59, 97–99, 155, 172, 187, 190–99. Historians Edward Castillo and George Philips have also stated in classroom and scholarly presentations that there is a strong connection between the two pejorative terms.

90 Laird, *The Chemehuevis*, 5, 23, 104–16, 152–55; and Kelly, *Southern Paiute Ethnography*, 152–80.

91 Geoffrey Smith, "Made Beings: Cahuilla and Chemehuevi Material Culture As Seen through the Cary Collection," PhD dissertation, University of California–Riverside, 2006.

92 Harrington, "The Chemehuevi," Harrington Papers, 9–10.

93 Robert F. Heizer and M. A. Whipple, *The California Indians: A Source Book* (Berkeley: University of California Press, 1971), 16, 322.

94 Laird, *The Chemehuevis*, 13.

95 Joseph Christmas Ives, "Report Upon the Colorado River of the West," *Report of the Secretary of War, 1861,* in *Senate Executive Document*, 36th Congress, 1st Session, p. 55; hereafter cited as Ives Report.

96 In 1999–2000 the Twenty-Nine Palms Tribe borrowed a feathered headdress from the Los Angeles County Museum and created a special exhibit for the honored museum piece. In a ceremony a group of Chemehuevi and other Native Americans transferred the headdress from the container into its new home within a walnut case built specifically for the headdress. With eagle feathers, white sage, prayers, and songs, the people of Twenty-Nine Palms ceremonially placed the headdress into the case, where it remains today, on the second floor of Spotlight 29 Casino near other exhibits depicting the history and culture of the tribe.

97 Miller and Miller, *Chemehuevi Indians of Southern California,* 8.

98 Smith, "Made Beings," 52–76.

99 Laird, *The Chemehuevis*, 5.

100 Joe Benitez interviews, September 10 and 17, 1997.

101 Katherine Siva Sauvel and Eric Elliott, *'Isill Héqwas Wáxish: A Dried Coyote's Tail,* vol. 1 (Banning, California: Malki Museum Press, 2004), 140, 149, 201–2, 291, 296, 528, 653.

102 Anyone interested in detailing the use of Native Americans living in the Mojave and Colorado Deserts must consult the entire classic work, Lowell J. Bean and Katherine Siva Saubel, *Temalpakh: Cahuilla Indian Knowledge and Usage of Plants* (Banning, California: Malki Museum Press, 1972).

103 Ibid., 97. Chester King and Dennis Casebier, *Background to Historic and Prehistoric Resources of the East Mojave Desert Region* (Riverside, California: U.S. Department of Interior, Bureau of Land Management, 1981), 58.

104 Bean and Saubel, *Temalpakh*, 95, 150–53, 67–68; and King and Casebier, *East Mojave Desert*, 58.

105 Bean and Saubel, *Temalpakh*, 18, 20, 31–36. Oral interview with Pauline Murillo by Clifford E. Trafzer, San Manuel Reservation, Highland, California, March 2000. Jenkins, "Study of Aboriginal Land Use," 72–73.

106 Jenkins, "Study of Aboriginal Land Use," 73; Bean and Saubel, *Temalpakh*, 17, 20, 107–17; and King and Casebier, *East Mojave Desert*, 55, 57.

107 King and Casebier, *East Mojave Desert*, 54; Bean and Saubel, *Temalpakh*, 81. In the 1960s and 1970s, Mike Mendival, Lee Emerson, and Henry DeCorse explained the use of tule roots by Native people living along the Colorado River and shared some of the root with me.

108 Jenkins, "Study of Aboriginal Land Use," 72.

109 King and Casebier, *East Mojave Desert*, 66.

110 Don D. Fowler and Catherine S. Fowler, eds., "Anthropology of the Numa: John Wesley Powell's Manuscripts on the Numic Peoples of Western North America, 1868–1880," in *Contributions to Anthropology,* vol. 14 (Washington, D.C.: Smithsonian Institution Press, 1971), 47; and Julian H. Steward, "Basin-Plateau Aboriginal Sociopolitical Groups," in *Bureau of American Ethnology Bulletin,* vol. 120 (Washington, D.C.: Government Printing Office, 1938), 184.

111 King and Casebier, *East Mojave Desert*, 63.

112 Fowler and Fowler, "Anthropology of the Numa," 48; and Heinrich Bauduin Möllhausen, *Diary of a Journey from the Mississippi to the Coasts of the Pacific,* vol. 2 (New York: Johnson Reprint Company, 1969), from the original published in 1858, 287.

113 King and Casebier, *East Mojave Desert*, 64–65. Note that this crooked staff was not the sacred *poro* used by medicine people. For a discussion of the difference, see Musser-Lopez, "Yaa vya's Poro," 260–64.

114 W. J. Hoffman, "Miscellaneous Ethnographic Observations on Indians Inhabiting Nevada, California, and Arizona," in *Tenth Annual Report of the United States Geological and Geographical Survey of the Territories—Being a Report of Progress of the Exploration for the Year 1876* (Washington, D.C.: Government Printing Office, 1878), 465–66.

115 Fowler and Fowler, "Anthropology of the Numa," 48.

116 Oral interview with Matthew Hanks Leivas by Clifford E. Trafzer, Palm Desert, California, August 24, 2013.

117 Gertrude Hanks Leivas interview, March 1999.

118 Bean and Saubel, *Temalpakh*, 29, 76, 136–39, 206.

119 King and Casebier, *East Mojave Desert*, 54–60.

120 Ibid.

121 Edward Palmer, "Plants Used by the Indians of the United States," *American Naturalist*

12 (1878): 601–2; and Matthew Hanks Leivas interview, August 24, 2013.

122 Ibid.

123 Möhausen, *Diary of a Journey*, 287.

124 Grant Foreman, ed., *A Pathfinder in the Southwest: The Itinerary of Lt. A. W. Whipple during His Explorations for a Railway Route from Fort Smith to Los Angeles in the Years 1853 and 1854* (Norman: University of Oklahoma Press, 1941), 250.

125 Armstrong, in *Annual Report of the Commissioner of Indian Affairs, 1857*, 234.

126 Powell, in *Annual Report of the Commissioner of Indian Affairs, 1870*, 203.

127 Frederick V. Colville, "The Panamint Indians of California," *American Anthropologist* 5 (1892): 352.

128 King and Casebier, *East Mojave Desert*, 62.

129 On August 24, 2013, Matthew Hanks Leivas sang Salt Songs, a talent he shares often at public meetings. As a singer, he sings most often at funerals and memorial services throughout California, the Great Basin, and the Southwest.

130 The original song "Chemehuevi," by Matthew Hanks Leivas, is located at the Leivas residence, Chemehuevi Indian Reservation. Leivas gave a copy to me to use in historical and cultural publications.

131 Since 1997, some Chemehuevi and their Southern Paiute relatives have shared elements of their history, culture, religion, and beliefs with me, and throughout this intellectual journey, the people have sung songs, an important method of transferring knowledge. As a result, this book is entitled *A Chemehuevi Song*. There are many songs, not one, and this attempt at representation provides only one perspective of Nüwü. There are many Chemehuevi songs, and I hope that this one leads other scholars and the Chemehuevi people themselves to share other songs, so that the broader world may come to know Nüwü peoples, their relatives, and their neighbors.

132 This book is an ethnohistorical work based on many sources, including archaeological works. However, the work has not claim to archaeology. In the past, archaeologists have offered the best work on the Oasis at Twentynine Palms and the entire landscape known today as Joshua Tree National Park. Archaeologists Elizabeth and William Campbell, Jan Sabala, Joan Schneider, G. Dicken Everson, Martyn Tagg, Michael Lerch, JoAnne Leonard, Jan Keswick, Rosie Pepito, and Claude Warren have conducted the major works of the area and must be consulted. A sample of their works include Joan S. Schneider and G. Dicken Everson, "Archaeological Investigations at the Oasis of Mara," National Park Service Document, Twentynine Palms, California, 2003; Martyn D. Tagg, *Excavations at the Oasis of Mara* (Washington, D.C.: National Park Service, 1983); Michael K. Lerch, *Cultural Resources Mitigation . . . Twentynine Palms* (Yucca Valley, California: Warner Engineering, 1982); JoAnne C. Leonard and Michael Lerch, *An Archaeological Evaluation of the Shuffler Property (Oasis of Mara)* (Redlands, California: San Bernardino County Museum Association, 1980).

2. Invading and Defaming Chemehuevi

1 Catherine S. Fowler, "Reconstructing Southern Paiute–Chemehuevi Trails in the Mojave Desert of Southern Nevada and California: Ethnographic Perspectives from the 1930s," in James Snead, Clark Erickson, and J. Andrew Darling, eds., *Landscapes of Movement* (Philadelphia: University of Pennsylvania Museum of Archaeology and Anthropology, 2009), 84, 91.

2   Ibid.

3   Ibid.

4   Clifford E. Trafzer, *Yuma: Frontier Crossing of the Far Southwest* (Wichita, Kansas: Western Heritage Press, 1981), 8–21.

5   Laird, *The Chemehuevis*, 7–9.

6   Robert C. Euler, *The Paiute People* (Phoenix: Indian Tribal Series, 1972), 2.

7   Herbert Eugene Bolton, *Coronado: Knight of Pueblo and Plains* (Albuquerque: University of New Mexico Press, 1950), 23–50.

8   Ibid., 115–32, 133–41.

9   Ibid., 153–78. Scholars are uncertain of the exact location of these two hills. I believe these two prominent hills are known today as Prison Hill in Yuma, Arizona, and Fort Yuma Hill in California on the Fort Yuma Indian Reservation.

10 Ibid.; and Trafzer, *Yuma*, 8–21.

11 Hubert Howe Bancroft, *History of Arizona and New Mexico* (San Francisco: The History Company, 1889), 9.

12 Ibid., 110–51, 346–48.

13 For information regarding the Native responses to the Spanish invasion of California, readers are urged to read the works of Edward D. Castillo, a noted scholar and Cahuilla man. See Edward D. Castillo, "The Impact of Euro-American Exploration and Settlement," in Robert F. Heizer, ed., *Handbook of North American Indians: California*, vol. 8 (Washington, D.C.: Smithsonian Institution Press, 1978), 99–104. Also see Hubert Howe Bancroft, *History of California*, vol. 1 (San Francisco: The History Company, 1886), 126–63.

14 For concepts of resettlement and invasion, see Francis Jennings, *The Invasion of America: Indians, Colonialism, and the Cant of Conquest* (Chapel Hill: University of North Carolina Press, 1975).

15 Oral interview with anonymous Chemehuevi man by Clifford E. Trafzer, Riverside, California.

16 James J. Rawls, *Indians of California: The Changing Image* (Norman: University of Oklahoma Press, 1986), 13; and Castillo, "Impact of Euro-American Exploration and Settlement," 100.

17 Euler, *Paiute People*, 11–12.

18 Ibid., 17–18; and Coues, ed., *On the Trail of a Spanish Pioneer*, 219.

19 Trafzer, *Yuma*, 15.

20 Matthew Hanks Leivas interview, August 29, 2013.

21 Trafzer, *Yuma*, 15–17; and Bancroft, *History of California*, 257–97.

22 Trafzer, *Yuma*, 15–17.

23 Ibid.; Couse, *On the Trail of a Spanish Pioneer*, 213.

24 Couse, *On the Trail of a Spanish Pioneer*, 219–20.

25 Ibid., 225.

26 Ibid., 220–21.

27 Ibid., 221.

28 Ibid.

29 Ibid., 224–25.

30 As mentioned in chapter 1, the report of Joseph Christmas Ives is extremely important in presenting a firsthand account regarding the interaction of the people with early American explorers. See the Ives Report.

31 During the 1970s, I informally interviewed both Henry DeCorse and Lee Emerson, members of the Quechan Fort Yuma Tribe. In addition, I interviewed Lee Emerson formally at

his home on the Fort Yuma Indian Reservation, in Winterhaven, California, and published the interview in *Quechan Voices*, cited below. Both men shared many accounts informally, including information on Chemehuevi. Both men had the utmost respect for the great hunting and running ability of Chemehuevi that lived in small groups in the desert and along the Colorado River. For more formal interviews and additional information on Quechan landscape, see Clifford E. Trafzer, ed., *Quechan Voices* (Riverside: California Center for Native Nations, University of California–Riverside, 2012).

32 Trafzer, *Yuma*, 15–21.
33 Ibid.
34 Ibid., 15–18.
35 King and Casebier, *Eastern Mojave Desert*, 284.
36 Euler, *Paiute People*, 20.
37 Robert C. Euler, *Southern Paiute Ethnography* (Salt Lake City: Anthropological Papers, University of Utah Press, 1966), 38.
38 Ibid., 39.
39 Brendan C. Lindsay, *Murder State: California's Native American Genocide, 1846–1873* (Lincoln: University of Nebraska Press, 2012), 70–108.
40 Ibid.
41 Euler, *Southern Paiute Ethnohistory*, 40.
42 Ibid.
43 Ibid., 41.
44 Charles L. Camp, "The Chronicle of George C. Yount," *California Historical Society Quarterly* 2 (1923): 38–39.
45 Ibid.
46 Lynn R. Bailey, *Indian Slave Trade in the Southwest* (Los Angeles: Westernlore Press, 1966), 140. For a masterful, short, and clear examination of "civilized" versus "uncivilized," see Thomas C. Patterson, *Inventing Western Civilization* (New York: Monthly Review Press, 1997).
47 Thomas J. Farnham, *Farnham's Travels in the Great Western Prairies, the Anahuac and Rocky Mountains and in the Oregon Territory* (1843; reprint Carlisle, Massachusetts: Applewood Books, 2007), 248–49. In recent years, publishers Houghton Mifflin and McGraw Hill have worked to correct this portrayal of California's Indian people in their textbooks.
48 Ibid.
49 Pierre DeSmet, *Voyages aux Montag Rocheuses* (Paris: Lille, 1845), 32–33.
50 Ibid.
51 Ibid.
52 Clinton E. Brooks and Frank D. Reeves, eds., "James A. Bennett: A Dragoon in New Mexico, 1850–1856," *New Mexico Historical Review* 22 (1947): 51–97, 69.
53 Matthew Hanks Leivas interview, August 29, 2013.
54 Ibid.
55 As quoted in G. H. Heap, *Central Route to the Pacific* (Philadelphia: Lippincott, Grambo & Company, 1854), 99–100.
56 Garland Hurt, "Message of the President of the United States, Communication . . . Information in Relation to the Massacres in Utah Territory," in *Senate Executive Document* 42, 36th Congress, 1st Session, 1860.
57 Gertrude Hanks Leivas interview, March 1999.
58 George Harwood Phillips, *Vineyards and Vaqueros: Indian Labor and Economic Expansion of Southern California, 1771–1887* (Norman: Arthur H. Clark, 2010), 202.

59 Joe Benitez interviews, September 10 and 17, 2013; and Matthew Hanks Leivas interview, August 19, 2013.

60 Oral interview with Joe Benitez by Clifford E. Trafzer, Twenty-Nine Palms Reservation, Coachella, California, September 6, 2000. For details on the Indian slave trade, see Bailey, *Indian Slave Trade in the Southwest.*

61 Orville C. Pratt, "Diary of Orville C. Pratt," in LeRoy R. Hafen and Ann W. Hafen, *Journals of Forty-Niners* (Cleveland, Ohio: Arthur H. Clark Company, 1954), 341–59; and Euler, *Southern Paiute Ethnohistory*, 50.

62 Euler, *Southern Paiute Ethnohistory*, 49–50.

63 Trafzer, *Yuma*, 31.

64 Ibid, 31–34.

65 Euler, *Southern Paiute Ethnohistory*, 55–60.

66 Andrew Jensen, "History of the Las Vegas Mission," unpublished manuscript, Reno, Nevada State Historical Society, 1926, as quoted in Euler, *Southern Paiute Ethnohistory*, 67.

67 Pratt, "Diary of Orville C. Pratt," 341–49.

68 Euler, *Southern Paiute Ethnohistory*, 52; also see the public exhibit of the Gold Rush in Southern California by Paul Smith in the city of Twentynine Palms, California.

69 Thomas W. Sweeney, *Journal of Lt. Thomas W. Sweeney, 1849–1853*, edited by Arthur Woodward (Los Angeles: Westernlore Press, 1956), 55–61, 111, 249.

70 Euler, *Southern Paiute Ethnohistory*, 71; and L. Sitgreaves, "Report on an Expedition down the Zuni and Colorado Rivers," in *Senate Executive Document* 59, 32nd Congress, 2nd Session (Washington, D.C.: Beverly Tucker, 1854).

71 Amiel Weeks Whipple, "Reports of Exploration and Surveys to Ascertain the Most Practicable and Economical Route for a Railroad from the Mississippi River to the Pacific Ocean," in *Senate Executive Document* 78, 33rd Congress, 2nd Session, 1856 (Washington, D.C.: Beverly Tucker, 1856).

72 Ibid., 17–18, 41.

73 Ibid., 121.

74 Möhausen, *Diary of a Journey from the Mississippi to the Coast of the Pacific*, vol. 2, 295.

75 Ibid.

76 Euler, *Southern Paiute Ethnohistory*, 73.

77 Samuel Peter Heintzelman, "Report of Captain S. P. Heintzelman to Major Townsend from Fort Yuma, July 15, 1853," in *House Executive Document* 76, 34th Congress, 3rd Session, 1857 (Washington, D.C.: Government Printing Office, 1857), 34, 44, 53.

78 Robert F. Heizer and Alan F. Almquist, *The Other Californians* (Berkeley: University of California Press, 1971), 23–64.

79 Trafzer, *Yuma*, 85–88; Lewis Burt Lesley, ed., *Uncle Sam's Camels* (Cambridge, Massachusetts: Harvard University Press, 1929; reprint, Glorieta, New Mexico: Rio Grande Press, 1970), 112–15; and for the best study of the Camel Corps, see Odie B. Faulk, *The U.S. Camel Corps* (New York: Oxford University Press, 1976).

80 Ives Report, 54–55.

81 Ibid.

82 Ibid., 55.

83 James Sandos and Larry Burgess, *The Hunt for Willie Boy: Indian-Hating and Popular Culture* (Norman: University of Oklahoma Press, 1994), 97.

84 Dean Mike interview, September 3, 1997; and Joe Benitez interviews, September 10 and 17, 1997.

85 Ives Report, 56.

86 Ibid.
87 Ibid.
88 Ibid.
89 Ibid.
90 Ibid., 72.
91 Ibid., 59.
92 Ibid, 73.
93 Ibid.
94 Ibid., 57.
95 Ibid.
96 Ibid., 72.
97 Ibid., 80.

3. War, Resistance, and Survival

1   Clifford E. Trafzer, *As Long As the Grass Shall Grow and Rivers Flow: A History of Native Americans* (Fort Worth, Texas: Harcourt, 2000), 192–93.
2   Ibid., 196–99, 343–44.
3   Ibid, 196–99; and Clifford E. Trafzer and Joel R. Hyer, eds., *Exterminate Them! Written Accounts of the Murder, Rape, and Enslavement of Native Americans during the California Gold Rush* (East Lansing: Michigan State University Press, 1999), 15–25.
4   Ibid., xiii.
5   Trafzer and Hyer, *Exterminate Them!.*, 28–30.
6   Trafzer, *Yuma*, 74–76.
7   Ibid., 52–63.
8   Euler, *Southern Paiute Ethnohistory*, 74.
9   Amiel Weeks Whipple, "General Description of Route Traversed from Rio del Norte to Port of San Pedro," chapter 4, in *Reports of Explorations and Surveys, to Ascertain the Most Practicable and Economical Route for a Railroad from the Mississippi River to the Pacific Ocean, 1853–54*, volume 3 (Washington, D.C.: Beverly Tucker Printer, 1856), 17. Hereafter cited as Whipple's Report.
10 Ibid., 17–18.
11 Ibid., 18–19.
12 Joe Benitez interviews, September 10 and 17, 1997.
13 Oral interview with Matthew Hanks Leivas by Clifford E. Trafzer, Twenty-Nine Palms Reservation, September 12, 2000.
14 A. S. Burton to S. Cooper, August 11, 1860, National Archives, Record Group 94, Letters Received, Adjutant General's Office, 233-B, as quoted in Euler, *Southern Paiute Ethnohistory*, 75.
15 Euler, *Southern Paiute Ethnohistory*, 74.
16 Matthew Hanks Leivas interview, September 12, 2000.
17 For the best study of the corps, see Faulk, *U.S. Camel Corps*.
18 Robert Utley, *Frontiersmen in Blue: The United States Army and the Indian, 1848–1865* (New York: Macmillan, 1967), 164.
19 This quotation is from George Devereux, "Mohave Chieftainship in Action: A Narrative of the First Contacts of the Mohave Indians with the United States," *Plateau* 23 (January 1951): 38. Also see Hoffman's "Report from Fort Mohave, January 16, 1859," in *Report of the Secretary of War, 1859* (Washington, D.C.: Government Printing Office, 1860).

20 Hoffman's "Report from Fort Mohave," 164.

21 Ibid.

22 From *Report of the Secretary of War, 1859*, 387–413.

23 Census of Los Angeles, California, 1840, as provided by Professor Lowell John Bean to Clifford Trafzer, March 2000.

24 George H. Phillips, *Chiefs and Challengers: Indian Resistance and Cooperation in Southern California* (Berkeley: University of California Press, 1975), 165–72. See the updated version published in 2014 by the University of Oklahoma Press.

25 "Important from the South: The Indian Rising—The Attack on Warner's Rancho, Departure of Volunteers," *Daily Alta California*, December 3, 1851; "The Southern Indian War," *Daily Alta California*, December 4, 1851; "Letter from San Diego," *Daily Alta California*, December 10, 1851; and "Letter From the South—The Indian War," *Daily Alta California*, December 12, 1851; and "Trial of Antonio Garra, the Hostile Indian Chief," *San Diego Herald*, January 17, 1852.

26 Phillips, *Chiefs and Challengers*, 164.

27 David Earl provided this insight in a paper presented at Chaffey College during the California Indian Conference.

28 Trafzer, *Yuma*, 82–96. The best overview of the steamboats on the Colorado River through Chemehuevi country is Richard Lingenfelter, *Steamboats on the Colorado* (Tucson: University of Arizona Press, 1976).

29 The chaos in Southern California is addressed in Trafzer and Hyer, eds., *Exterminate Them!*, 81–112; and Trafzer, Madrigal, and Madrigal, *Chemehuevi People*, 52–67.

30 Trafzer, Madrigal, and Madrigal, *Chemehuevi People*, 59; and A. L. Kroeber ad C. B. Kroeber, *A Mohave War Reminiscence, 1854–1880* (Berkeley: University of California Press, 1973), 83.

31 Richard F. Van Valkenburgh, "Chemehuevi Notes," in Isabel T. Kelly, ed., *Southern Paiute Ethnography* (New York: Garland Publishing, 1976), 227, 230–31.

32 Ibid.

33 Ibid.

34 Ibid.

35 Ibid.

36 Ibid.

37 Ibid.

38 Ibid., 231–32.

39 Ibid. For another Chemehuevi version, see ibid., 234–35.

40 Ibid., 232, 234–35.

41 Ibid., 232.

42 Ibid., 235.

43 Ibid.

44 Ibid., 232.

45 Ibid., 233.

46 Ibid., 232.

47 The Chemehuevi people have a history of being tricksters. For eight years I worked with Chemehuevi from the Colorado River and the Twenty-Nine Palms Band, and every person is skilled with words intended to tease, joke, and provide good humor among the people. It is easy to imagine that they teased the Mojave about a dangerous situation, even though the danger impacted the lives of Chemehuevi as much as Mojave.

48 Matthew Hanks Leivas interview, September 12, 2000; and Joe Benitez interviews, September 10 and 17, 1997.

49 Kroeber and Kroeber, *Mohave War Reminiscence*, vii, 5.
50 Ibid., 39.
51 Van Valkenburgh, "Chemehuevi Notes," 2. On the same page, Van Valkenburgh explains that the Mojave say that this was when they brought the Chemehuevi to Cottonwood Island, but other evidence suggests that the Chemehuevi were already living north, south, and west of the Mojave.
52 Kroeber and Kroeber, *Mohave War Reminiscence*, 39–40.
53 Ibid.
54 Ibid.
55 Ibid., 39–42.
56 Van Valkenburgh, "Chemehuevi Notes," 233, and for another version and information on the knotted strings, see ibid., 239–40.
57 Ibid., 233.
58 Ibid.
59 Ibid.
60 Dean Mike interviews, September 3 and October 24, 1997; and Joe Benitez interviews, September 10 and 17, 1997.
61 Kroeber and Kroeber, *Mohave War Reminiscence*, 39–42.
62 Ibid., 39–43.
63 Ibid., 43.
64 Ibid.
65 Captain W. R. Johnson manuscript as cited in Euler, *Southern Paiute Ethnography*, 77–78.
66 Ibid., 78.
67 Ibid.
68 *Arizona Citizen*, September 28, 1872.
69 Oral interview with Chief Pancoyer, Chemehuevi, by Agent William Stanley, in the Coachella Valley in William Stanley to George W. Dent, Records of the Arizona Superintendent of Indian Affairs, National Archives, Microfilm 734, Reel 2.
70 G. W. Ingalls to Commissioner of Indian Affairs A. Walker, November 1, 1872, in *House Executive Document 66*, 42nd Congress, 3rd Session, 1872; and "Report of Special Agent John G. Ames, in Regards to the Conditions of the Mission Indians of California, October 28, 1873," in "Western Americana: Frontier History of the Trans-Mississippi West," Microfilm Collection 139, Reel 9, Beinecke Library, Yale University, New Haven, Connecticut.
71 Colonel O. B. Wilcox, "Chemehuevi Near Ehrenberg," in *Annual Report of the War Department, 1880*, as quoted in Euler, *Southern Paiute Ethnography*, 79.
72 George Roth, "The Calloway Affair of 1880: Chemehuevi Adaptation and Chemehuevi-Mohave Relations," *Journal of California Anthropology* 4 (1977): 275–76.
73 Ibid.
74 As in *Annual Report of the Commissioner of Indian Affairs, 1880*.
75 Letter of Lieutenant C. Worthington, April 23, 1880, Fort Mojave, Arizona Historical Society, as quoted in Roth, "Calloway Affair," 277.
76 Kroeber and Kroeber, *Mohave War Reminiscence*, 91; and Roth, "Calloway Affair," 277.
77 Dean Mike interview, September 3, 1997.
78 Ibid.
79 Trafzer, *As Long As the Grass Shall Grow and Rivers Flow*, 318–19.
80 Ibid.
81 John Wesley Powell, *Fourteenth Annual Report of the Bureau of Ethnology to the Secretary of the Smithsonian Institution, 1892–93* (Washington, D. C.: Government Printing Office, 1896), 814.

82   Dean Mike interviews, September 3 and October 24, 1997.
83   Ibid.; and Joe Benitez interviews, September 10 and 17, 1997.

4. Chemehuevi at Twenty-Nine Palms

1   Maud Carrico Russell, "The Yesterdays of Twenty-Nine Palms," unpublished manuscript, Old Schoolhouse, Twenty-Nine Palms Historical Society (TNPHS), Twentynine Palms, California. Hereafter cited as Russell Manuscript.
2   Dorothy Ramon and Eric Elliott, *Wayta' Yawa': Always Believe* (Banning, California: Malki Museum Press, 2000), 200, 439. Ramon reported that her father lived at Twenty-Nine Palms, but he was Muhatna'yam, a different clan than most Serrano at the oasis. At one time the oasis attracted Indian people from many backgrounds, including Chemehuevi.
3   Dean Mike interviews, September 3 and October 24, 1997; and Joe Benitez interviews, September 10 and 17, 1997.
4   Trafzer, Madrigal, and Madrigal, *Chemehuevi People*, 18–22.
5   Ramon and Elliot, *Wayta' Yawa'*, 592.
6   Joe Benitez interviews, September 7 and 10, 1997.
7   Lowell J. Bean and Lisa J. Bourgeault, *The Cahuilla* (New York: Chelsea House Publishers, 1989), 83, 89.
8   Joe Benitez interviews, September 10 and 17, 1997.
9   Ibid.; and Ramon and Elliott, *Wayta' Yawa'*, 701.
10   Ramon and Elliott, *Wayta' Yawa'*, 472.
11   Ibid.
12   Ibid., 282.
13   Joe Benitez interviews, September 10 and 17, 1997; and Dean Mike interview, September 3, 1997.
14   Russell Manuscript.
15   Joe Benitez interviews, September 10 and 17, 1997.
16   A copy of Washington's report is found in the Russell Manuscript; and John D. Adams to Maud Russell, September 23, 1943, TNPHS.
17   A copy of Green's report is found in the Russell Manuscript.
18   Ibid.; and Adams to Russell, September 23, 1943, TNPHS.
19   See both surveys in the Russell Manuscript.
20   Oral interview with Ben de Crevecoeur by Maud Russell, n.d., in the Russell Manuscript.
21   Oral interview with Pauline Murillo by Clifford E. Trafzer, San Manuel Reservation, May 15, 200. Ramon and Elliot, *Wayta' Yawa'*, 280–81.
22   Notes of Paul Smith, Twentynine Palms Inn; hereafter cited as Smith Notes.
23   Green Report, in the Russell Manuscript.
24   Ibid.
25   Joe Benitez interviews, September 10 and 17, 1997. Benitez believes the name Boniface originated from non-Indians in Banning, California. When the Mike families worked in the Banning area for cash, they allowed their children to attend the Saint Boniface Indian School in Banning. Priests, nuns, and others started calling the children Boniface children and the name caught on with non-Indians. One family of Mikes, Jeff Boniface, kept the name, which his family on the Soboba Reservation still uses.
26   Oral interview with Paul and Jane Smith by Clifford E. Trafzer, Twentynine Palms, California, June 1999.
27   Ibid.

28 Ibid.; Russell Manuscript; and Smith Notes.

29 Smith Notes.

30 Charles D. Poston to William P. Dole, September 30, 1864, in *Annual Report of the Commissioner of Indian Affairs, 1864.*

31 The Southwest Museum and the museum on the Colorado River Indian Reservation contain excellent examples of basketry. Dr. Gerald Smith collected Serrano baskets, and some are found in the San Bernardino County Museum. Pauline Murillo, an elder from the San Manuel Reservation, has a wonderful collection of her grandmother's baskets, those of Jesusa Manuel. However, Jesusa was Cahuilla from the Los Coyotes Reservation, although the Serrano may have influenced her designs and techniques.

32 Smith Notes; and Russell Manuscript.

33 Ibid.

34 In 2000, Paul Smith created an important exhibit depicting the impact of the Gold Rush and gold discoveries in Southern California. Smith Notes.

35 According to Harvey Johnson, the foremost scholar studying the history of the lower Colorado River, Heintzelman's notes indicate that the major invested time and money prospecting for gold, hoping to supplement his military income with a gold strike. Oral interview with Harvey Johnson by Clifford Trafzer, Yuma, Arizona, June 1973. See the Johnson Collection, Yuma County Historical Society, Yuma, Arizona.

36 Laird, *The Chemehuevis*, 83–85.

37 For information about miners and their relationship with other Southern Paiute, see Knack, *Boundaries Between*, 4–6.

38 Russell Manuscript.

39 Ibid.

40 Ibid.

41 Ibid.

42 Clara True to Maud Russell, May 3, 1942, Russell Collection, TNPHS; and James A. Sandos and Larry E. Burgess, *The Hunt for Willie Boy: Indian Hating and Popular Culture* (Norman: University of Oklahoma Press, 1994), 109.

43 Russell Manuscript.

44 Ibid.

45 "Report of Superintendent Charles D. Poston, Arizona Superintendency," in *Annual Report of the Commissioner of Indian Affairs, 1863.*

46 From *Handbook of American Indians North of Mexico*, Bulletin 30, Office of Indian Affairs, Department of Interior, 1912.

47 Census of the Twenty-Nine Palms Band, 1890, Mission Indian Agency, National Archives, Record Group 75, Microfilm 595, Roll 257. Hereafter cited as Census of the Twenty-Nine Palms Band, 1890.

48 Joe Benitez interviews, September 10 and 17, 1997; and Dean Mike interview, September 3, 1997.

49 Smith Notes.

50 Russell Manuscript; and Census of the Twenty-Nine Palms Band, 1892, Mission Indian Agency, National Archives, Microfilm 595, Roll 257.

51 Census of the Twenty-Nine Palms Band, 1894, Mission Indian Agency, National Archives, Microfilm 595, Roll 258.

52 Ibid.

53 Ramon and Elliott, *Wayta' Yawa'*, 696.

54 Smith Notes.

55 Ibid.
56 Ibid.
57 Smith Notes.
58 Ibid.
59 Censuses of 1910, Typescript, Twenty-Nine Palms Band of Mission Indians Library, Coachella, California. Jean Farnam and Helen Haworth, Genealogy of Mike Family, Jennifer Mike's Personal Collection; hereafter cited as Mike Genealogy. Also see Smith Notes.
60 Mike Genealogy; and Smith Notes.
61 Ibid.; and Ramon and Elliot, *Wayta' Yawa'*, 281–82.
62 Censuses of the Twenty-Nine Palms Band, 1895 and 1896, Microfilm 595, Roll 258.
63 True to Russell, May 3, 1942, Russell Collection, TNPHS.
64 Census of 1897, Microfilm 595, Roll 258.
65 Ibid.
66 Russell Manuscript; and Smith Notes.
67 Maud Carrico Russell, "Old Indian Burial Grounds," *Desert Spotlight*, pp. 5, 16, vertical files, Twentynine Palms Library, Twentynine Palms, California.
68 True to Russell, May 3, 1942, Russell Collection, TNPHS.
69 Russell, "Old Indian Burial Grounds," 5.
70 Joe Benitez interviews, September 10 and 17, 1997; and Dean Mike interview, September 3, 1997.
71 Russell, "Old Indian Burial Grounds," 5, 16.
72 *Desert Trails*, September 6, 1967, vertical files, Twenty-Nine Palms Library.
73 In 1997, Trafzer, Madrigal, and Madrigal published *Chemehuevi People of the Coachella Valley*. At that time the authors did not believe that the smallpox epidemic reached Twenty-Nine Palms, but today it is clear the disease reached the oasis, although we have few details of the exact effect of the disease on or other Indians living within the greater Mojave Desert.
74 Wayne Biddle, *A Field Guide to Germs* (New York: Doubleday, 1995), 127.
75 Russell Manuscript. For a classic study of tuberculosis, see Rene and Jean Dubois, *The White Plague: Tuberculosis, Man, and Society* (New Brunswick, New Jersey: Rutgers University Press, 1992).
76 Ibid.
77 Ibid.
78 Maud Carrico Russell, "Early Days at Twenty-Nine Palms," *Desert Spotlight*, vertical files, Twentynine Palms Library, Twentynine Palms, California.
79 Trafzer, Madrigal, and Madrigal, *Chemehuevi People of the Coachella Valley*, 69–76.
80 Ibid.
81 Lowell J. Bean, ed., *California Indian Shamanism* (Menlo Park, California: Ballena Press, 1992), 7–32.
82 Russell, "Old Indian Burial Grounds," 5, 16.
83 Ibid.
84 De Crevecoeur had earned a reputation as a storyteller and a man known to create stories illustrating that Indians were "save," uncivilized, barbarians, reflecting his own negative views of Indians.
85 Telephone interviews with Katherine Saubel and Pauline Murillo by Clifford E. Trafzer, May 8, 2001.
86 Russell, "Old Indian Burial Grounds," 16.
87 Russell Manuscript; and Smith Notes.

88 Tribal sovereignty and Native law originated from traditional oral narratives and songs of the people, not from the United States. The tribes asserted their sovereignty throughout their histories, including the early twentieth century. The decision of tribal elders at Twenty-Nine Palms not to move from their homes illustrates the assertion of tribal sovereignty.

89 Marriage laws among them required people to examine familial relationships to ensure that cousins, even remote cousins, did not marry. The marriage laws of the Chemehuevi played a significant role in the death of William Mike.

90 Sandos and Burgess, *Hunt for Willie Boy*, 106.

91 Scholar Martha Knack provides an excellent discussion and analysis of the importance of family and marriage laws in her book *Boundaries Between*, 21–23, 27–29, 204–6.

92 Exhibit at the Gilman Ranch, Riverside County Park, Banning, California; and Russell Manuscript.

93 Ibid.

94 Joe Benitez interviews, September 10 and 17, 1997.

95 True to Russell, May 3, 1942, Russell Collection, TNPHS.

96 Ibid.

97 Sandos and Burgess, *Hunt for Willie Boy*, 23–24.

5. Unvanished Americans

1 Maud Russell, "Indian Reservations at Twenty-Nine Palms," and Clara True to Commissioner of Indian Affairs, October 28, 1943, both in Russell Collection, Twenty-Nine Palms Historical Society, Twentynine Palms, California; hereafter cited as Russell Collection.

2 Trafzer and Hyer, *Exterminate Them!*

3 "An Act for Relief of the Mission Indians in the State of California," in *Statutes at Large of United States of America*, 26 (Washington, D.C.: Government Printing Office, 1891), 712–14; hereafter cited as "An Act for the Relief."

4 Larry Burgess, "Commission to the Mission Indians, 1891," manuscript, A. K. Smiley Library, Redlands, California; hereafter cited as Burgess Manuscript. The author used the original manuscript and a published version of the Burgess Manuscript; see Larry Burgess, "Commission to the Mission Indians, 1891," *San Bernardino County Museum Quarterly* 35 (1988): 31.

5 Ibid.; and "An Act for the Relief."

6 Constance Goddard DuBois, *The Condition of the Mission Indians of Southern California* (Philadelphia: Office of Indian Rights Association, 1901), 5.

7 Ibid., 6.

8 Telephone interview with Larry Burgess by Clifford E. Trafzer, September 18, 2001, and with Valerie Mathes by Clifford E. Trafzer, September 30, 2001.

9 Burgess Manuscript.

10 See oral interview by John Harrington with Pakuuma, Harrington Papers; and Clifford E. Trafzer, *The People of San Manuel* (Highland, California: San Manuel Band of Mission Indians, 2002), 16–19.

11 Albert K. Smiley, "Account of a Trip through Southern California Spring 1891 as Chairman of Mission Indian Commission," Smiley Collection, Smiley Library, Redlands, California.

12 Valerie Sherer Mathes, *Helen Hunt Jackson and Her Indian Reform Legacy* (Austin: University of Texas Press, 1990), 114. Professor Mathes generously provided more information to me through a telephone interview, September 29, 2001.

13 According to the Twenty-Nine Palms tribal census of 1897, "Sumehweva Mike" was fifty-four years old and married to Marcelmu, age fifty. The couple had five children, but the family is not that of Jim Mike or William Mike, the two known leaders of the tribe at the time. Although Painter may have spoken to this man, it is more than likely that Chemehuevi Mike is either Jim or William.

14 "Smiley Commission Report, December, 1891," Smiley Library, Redlands, California; hereafter cited as Smiley Report. Also, Burgess, "Commission to the Mission Indians, 1891," 31.

15 Smiley Commission Report, December 1991.

16 The Smiley Commission acted in good faith as pointed out by noted scholars Larry Burgess and Florence Shipek in *Pushed into the Rocks: Southern California Indian Land Tenure, 1769–1986* (Lincoln: University of Nebraska Press, 1988). Also see Burgess Manuscript, Burgess, "Commission to the Mission Indians, 1891, and oral history notes by Maud Russell with Nellie Morongo, circa 1940, Twenty-Nine Palms Historical Society, Twentynine Palms, California.

17 Descriptions of the village are made from my personal observations after an extensive survey of the land led by Paul and Jane Smith, Twentynine Palms Inn.

18 Larry Burgess interview, September 18, 2001. The quotation is from the oral history, but also see Burgess, "Commission to the Mission Indians 1891."

19 Trafzer, *Yuma*, 112–21.

20 Oral interview by Gerald Smith with unidentified elder, n.d., Smith Collection, Smiley Library, Redlands, California.

21 H. M. Critchfield to Maud Russell, December 2, 1943, Russell Collection, Twentynine Palms Historical Society.

22 Ibid.

23 J. M. Stewart to J. R. Sterling, January 25, 1937, Russell Collection, Twentynine Palms Historical Society.

24 Oral interview with Paul Smith by Clifford E. Trafzer, Twentynine Palms Inn, March 3, 2000.

25 Ted R. Carpenter and A. R. Schultz to Maud Russell, October 14, 1943, Russell Collection, Twentynine Palms Historical Society.

26 See the map of the oasis area in the Twenty-Nine Palms Archives, Coachella, California. Also see Executive Order of President Grover Cleveland, November 11, 1895, in the tribal archives.

27 William T. Sullivan to Commissioner of Indian Affairs, December 5, 1910, NAPSWR, RG 75, Mission Agency.

28 Smith Interview.

29 Mike Genealogy.

30 Gilman Ranch is a Riverside County Park that contains exhibits about William Mike's death. See Burgess and Sandos, *Hunt for Willie Boy*.

6. Willie, William, and Carlotta

1 In 1994, authors James Sandos and Larry Burgess published a remarkable book that carefully incorporated Chemehuevi voices about the events surrounding the killing of William Mike by Willie Boy and the death of Carlota. See Sandos and Burgess, *Hunt for Willie Boy*.

2 Ramon and Elliott, *Wayta' Yawa'*, 696.

3 Joe Benitez interviews, September 10 and 17, 1997.

4 Today Riverside County, California, operates the Gilman Ranch as a historical site. The trees where William Mike and his family camped still stand beside the small creek running through the property.

5 This information is taken from a display at the Gilman Ranch in Banning, California.

6 Oral interview with Alberta Van Fleet by James Sandos and Larry E. Burgess, January 5 and February 15, 1991, in Sandos and Burgess, *Hunt for Willie Boy*, 105–6.

7 Oral interview with Joe Benitez by James A. Sandos and Larry E. Burgess, August 12, 1989, in Sandos and Burgess, *Hunt for Willie Boy*, 105–6; Joe Benitez interview, interviews also took place on February 10, 1990, and March 23, 1991.

8 Alberta Van Fleet interview in Sandos and Burgess, *Hunt for Willie Boy*, 106.

9 Trafzer, *As Long As the Grass Shall Grow*, 319; and Gregory E. Smoak, *Ghost Dances and Identity: Prophetic Religion and American Indian Ethnogenesis in the Nineteenth Century.* (Berkeley: University of California Press, 2006), 165–75.

10 For information on Wovoka and the Ghost Dance, see Michael Hittman, *Wovoka and the Ghost Dance* (Yerington, Nevada: Yerington Paiute Tribe, 1990); James Mooney, *The Ghost-Dance Religion and Wounded Knee* (New York: Dover Publications, Reprint, 1973); A. H. Gayton, "The Ghost Dance of 1870 in South-Central California," *University of California Publications in American Archaeology and Ethnology* 28 (1930–31): 57–82; and L. G. Moses, "The Father Tells Me So! Wovoka: The Ghost Dance Prophet," *American Indian Quarterly* 9 (1985): 335–51.

11 Clara True to the Commissioner of Indian Affairs, October 20, 1909, "The Willie Boy Case and Attendant Circumstances," Office of Indian Affairs, file number 79987–09, published by Harry Lawton in *Journal of California Anthropology* 5 (Summer 1978): 115–23; hereafter cited as True Report. In an oral interview by James Sandos and Larry Burgess with Mary Lou Brown, February 15, 1991, in Sandos and Burgess, *Hunt for Willie Boy*, 113, the Chemehuevi elder stated that Willie was young, wanted a wife, "but there were no young women nearby." She suggests that he wanted a wife, not that he *had* a wife.

12 Joe Benitez interview, March 1, 2001, Twenty-Nine Palms Reservation. In addition, during a 2012 gathering in the Spring Mountains, a Southern Paiute scholar who wished to be unidentified provided me detailed information about the marriage laws and their significance.

13 Sandos and Burgess, *Hunt for Willie Boy*, 29. Conflicting reports suggest that Willie Boy served twenty, forty, or ninety days in jail in either 1905 or 1906. The fact that he served time is confirmed and his mug shot has been preserved.

14 Joe Benitez interviews, September 10 and 17, 1997.

15 Peter Nabokov, *Indian Running: Native American History and Tradition* (Santa Fe: Ancient City Press, 1981), 70.

16 Joe Benitez interviews, September 10 and 17, 1997; Alberta Van Fleet interviews, January 5 and February 15, 1991, in Sandos and Burgess, *Hunt for Willie Boy*; Mary Lou Brown interview, February 15, 1991, in Sandos and Burgess, *Hunt for Willie Boy*, 113; and Joe Benitez interviews, August 12, 1989, February 10, 1990, and March 23, 1991.

17 Mary Lou Brown interview, February 15, 1991, in Sandos and Burgess, *Hunt for Willie Boy*, 113.

18 Ibid.

19 Ibid.

20 Joe Benitez interviews, September 10 and 17, 1997; and oral interview with park ranger by Clifford E. Trafzer, Gilman Ranch, Riverside County Park, Banning, California, June 2000.

21 Mary Lou Brown interview, February 15, 1991, in Sandos and Burgess, *Hunt for Willie Boy*, 113.

22 Ibid.

23 Sandos and Burgess, *Hunt for Willie Boy*, 74–82.

24 Mary Lou Brown interview, February 15, 1991, in Sandos and Burgess, *Hunt for Willie Boy*, 113.

25 This citation emerges from an unpublished manuscript of Maud Carrico Russell found in her collection at the Twentynine Palms Historical Society Library, Old Schoolhouse Museum, Twentynine Palms, California. Within the body of a short manuscript Russell wrote, she inserted an excerpt from Clara True, the former Indian agent at the Malki Agency, Banning, California. True provided Russell a brief report, quoted in this chapter as the True Report. Neither True nor Russell provides a title or a date, although True and Russell likely wrote the document after 1946 when Russell was publisher of the *Desert Spotlight*, a newsletter publication; and *Redlands Daily Review*, September 30 and October 5, 1909.

26 Ibid.

27 Ethel Gilman to sister, n.d., Gilman Ranch, Riverside County Park, Banning, California. Portrero is located on the Morongo Indian Reservation east of Banning, and the Mike family placed a headstone at the cemetery site during the first decade of the twenty-first century, offering a ceremony that included Salt Songs.

28 According to Chemehuevi elder Larry Eddy, Chino was part Chemehuevi. Eddy knew his lineage and said Chino was of mixed-blood Chemehuevi heritage. Cahuilla elder Katherine Saubel claimed that Chino, a longtime friend of her family, was Cahuilla. When I asked her if she knew the lineages of his mother and father, she could not rule out a Chemehuevi relationship of one or more of Chino's parents or grandparents.

29 The newspapers and past scholarship has identified Hyde as Yaqui, but Cahuilla elder Katherine Saubel corrected me, saying that Hyde was Kumeyaay or Diegueño from San Diego County. She personally knew his family.

30 If the trackers had really gotten close enough to Willie Boy and Carlota, they would have shot at Willie, or Willie at them. Logic dictates that the lawmen exaggerated their proximity to the couple just as they did other aspects of the chase.

31 This ridiculous story is found in James L. Carling, "On the Trail of Willie Boy," *Desert Magazine* (November 1946), 6.

32 Ibid.; Willard S. Wood, "Bad Indian in the Morongos," *Westways* 27 (April 1935): 10–11, 34; and Tom Hughes, *History of Banning and San Gorgonio Pass* (Banning, California: Banning Record Print, 1939), 173–74. For the finest analysis of these sources, see Sandos and Burgess, *Hunt for Willie Boy*, 38–41, 75.

33 Wood, "Bad Indian in the Morongos," 10–11.

34 Sandos and Burgess, *Hunt for Willie Boy*, 120–21.

35 Today Highway 62 runs north from Interstate 10 through a pass that separates the San Bernardino and Little San Bernardino Mountains. Willie Boy and Carlota used a route near Highway 62, traveling through two steep and rugged passes, the Morongo and Yucca Valleys, which take travelers from the Coachella Valley, through the mountain passes and inland valleys into the higher reaches of the western Mojave Desert. The couple passed along Mission Creek, where the government had established an Indian reservation. They traveled through the Morongo Valley into The Pipes, an arid and rustic landscape at the base of the San Bernardino Mountains filled with huge boulders often seen in television and film presentations about the American West.

36 Mary Lou Brown interview, February 1, 1991, in Sandos and Burgess, *Hunt for Willie Boy*, 113.
37 Sandos and Burgess, *Hunt for Willie Boy*, 25, 120.
38 Matthew Hanks Leivas interview, June 23, 2013. The Chemehuevi consultants interviewed by Sandos and Burgess offer this interpretation in *The Hunt for Willie Boy*.
39 Ibid., 120.
40 Ibid., 25, 120.
41 Most often, the Chemehuevi sing Salt Songs at funerals. They sing from dusk to dawn, the songs take the singers and listeners on an expansive journey through western Arizona, southern Nevada, and eastern California—the land of the Chemehuevi people. Songs are central to Chemehuevi culture, and the people continue to sing Salt Songs and others. Like all Chemehuevi of his time, Willie Boy knew several songs and likely spent his time near the place where Carlota died, singing and praying out of respect for her.
42 Wanted Poster, 1909, "Arrest for Double Murder," Special Collections, Rivera Library, University of California–Riverside.
43 Mary Lou Brown interview, February 15, 1991, in Sandos and Burgess, *Hunt for Willie Boy*, 113.
44 True Report.
45 Ibid.
46 Sandos and Burgess, *Hunt for Willie Boy*, 80–82.
47 True Report.
48 Genealogical chart of Chemehuevi elder Jennifer Mike, granddaughter of Nellie Morongo and Billy Mike.
49 The area surrounding Ruby Mountain contains little fuel that could be used to burn a body. Cremation of any body requires a great deal of fuel and little can be found in the rocky landscape of Ruby Mountain.
50 Ann Japenga, an investigative reporter, conducted the interview with Gray. Find her significant report, "A Legend Undone," *Palms Springs Life* (August 2008): 1. During a recent tour of the Autry Museum in Los Angeles, I studied the graphic photographs of the Dalton Gang. Whenever possible, lawmen took photographs of slain criminals, particularly famous outlaws. All photographs examined offered close-ups. The posse took photographs at Ruby Mountain, but all of them were distant shots. The posse took no close-up photographs of Willie Boy, the most logical explanation being that they had no body to photograph.
51 Paul Trachtman, *The Gunfighters* (Alexandria, Virginia: Time-Life Books, 1974), 224–31. Remarkably, the posse chasing Willie Boy never took a close-up photograph of the outlaw, arguably because they never found him. Willie Boy would have fled Ruby Mountain, leaving the posse an empty nest.
52 Sandos and Burgess, *Hunt for Willie Boy*, 123.
53 Lawton, *Willie Boy,* 194.
54 Oral interview with Katherine Saubel by Clifford E. Trafzer, Sacramento, California, June 15, 2001.
55 Lucullus Virgil McWhorter, *Yellow Wolf: His Own Story* (Caldwell, Idaho: Caxton Press, 1940), 291.
56 Mary Lou Brown interview, February 15, 1991, in Sandos and Burgess, *Hunt for Willie Boy*, 113; Joe Benitez interviews, September 10 and 17, 1997; and Dean Mike interviews, September 3 and October 24, 1997.

57 Joe Benitez interviews, September 10 and 17, 1997; and Dean Mike interview, September 3, 1997.

58 Ibid.

59 Oral interview with Katherine Saubel by Clifford E. Trafzer, Southwest Airlines Flight, Sacramento to Ontario, California, and Morongo Indian Reservation, September 15, 2000.

60 Ibid.

61 Ibid.

62 McWhorter, *Yellow Wolf,* 291.

63 Alberta Van Fleet interviews, January 5 and February 15, 1991, in Sandos and Burgess, *Hunt for Willie Boy,* 100.

64 Mary Lou Brown interview, February 15, 1991, in Sandos and Burgess, *Hunt for Willie Boy,* 107.

65 Oral interview with Larry Burgess by Clifford E. Trafzer, Redlands, California, August 29, 2013.

66 Sandos and Burgess, *Hunt for Willie Boy,* 425.

67 Ibid., 123.

68 Carlota's family and friends sang Salt Songs for her shortly after the posse returned her body. In July 2005 the Mike family held a ceremony to commemorate their dead buried at the Morongo Reservation cemetery, and they placed new headstones on the graves of all of their loved ones. During the ceremony they remembered all their relatives, particularly William Mike and his daughter, Carlota.

69 Katherine Saubel interview, September 15, 2000.

70 Russell, "Old Indian Burial Ground," 1.

71 Ibid.

72 Genealogical chart of Chemehuevi elder Jennifer Mike, granddaughter of Nellie Morongo and Billy Mike; and Mission Indian Census, 1896.

73 Interview with Jane and Paul Smith by Clifford E. Trafzer, Twentynine Palms Inn, Twentynine Palms, California, May 7, 2001.

74 Russell, "Old Indian Burial Ground," 1.

75 True Report.

76 Joe Benitez interview, June 5, 2001.

77 Ibid.

78 E-mail communication, Joe Benitez to Clifford E. Trafzer, June 5, 2001.

79 Oral history of anonymous Paiute scholar, October 6, 2012.

80 Telephone interview with Matthew Hanks Leivas by Clifford E. Trafzer, May 16, 2001.

81 Mary Lou Brown interview, February 15, 1991, in Sandos and Burgess, *Hunt for Willie Boy,* 107.

82 Oral interview with Alfreda Mitre by Clifford E. Trafzer, Las Vegas Paiute Indian Reservation, July 10–11, 2006.

83 Ramon and Elliott, *Wayta' Yawa',* 696.

84 Maud Carrico Russell, "Pioneer Days," *Desert Spotlight,* vertical files, Twentynine Palms City Library, Twentynine Palms, California.

85 Joe Benitez interview, June 13, 2001.

86 Clifford E. Trafzer, "Tell Them Willie Boy Is Here," in LeAnne Howe, Harvey Markowitz, and Denise K. Cummings, eds., *Seeing Red: Hollywood's Pixeled Skins* (East Lansing: Michigan State University Press, 2013), 154.

87 Ibid., 155.

88 Census of the Twenty-Nine Palms Tribe, microfilm 595, multiple rolls.

89 Russell, "Early Days at Twenty-Nine Palms."

90 Tillie Lopez, Juanito Alimo, Miguel Williams, Pablo Kintano, Julian Augustine, and Bill Colloway to John Dady, March 10, 1935, "Hearings before the Subcommittee on General Bills of the Committee on Indian Affairs, House of Representatives, H.R. 7781," February 11, 1935, in *Indian Conditions and Affairs* (Washington, D.C.: Government Printing Office, 1935); and J. H. Hanson to Director of the Federal Bureau of Investigation, December 16, 1936, L.A. File 70–184, Papers of the Federal Bureau of Investigation, declassified and obtained through the Freedom of Information Act. Robert Przeklasa provided the document to the author.

7. Cultural Preservation, Ethnogenesis, and Revitalization

1   The Chemehuevi elder who commented about his mother felt deprived of learning more about his culture, although he understood the parent's concerns.

2   "The Enugwuhype (Ancestral Numi People): An Ethnogenesis." Unpublished manuscript provided by Richard W. Stoffle to Clifford Trafzer.

3   Joe Benitez interview, September 14, 2001.

4   Details taken from 1890–1920, Twenty-Nine Palms Tribal Census, NAPSWR, RG 75. The Office of Indian Affairs did not make a tribal census for the Mission Indian Agent every year; rather, agents took the censuses irregularly from 1890 to 1920.

5   Oral interview with Dean Mike by Clifford E. Trafzer, Twenty-Nine Palms Indian Reservation, August 8, 2013.

6   Joe Benitez interviews, September 10 and 17, 1997.

7   Jennifer Mike interview, March 3, 2000.

8   Dean Mike interviews, September 2 and October 24, 1997.

9   Joe Benitez interviews, September 10 and 17, 1997.

10 Matthew Hanks Leivas interviews, September 27, 2001, and August 29, 2013; and "Enugwuhype (Ancestral Numic People): An Ethnogenesis."

11 Theresa Mike interview, August 31, 2005.

12 I have attended the Tobacco Ceremony several times, and hosted a blessing ceremony in 2012 on the campus of the University of California–Riverside.

13 Programs for Cultural Night, 1997–99, Twenty-Nine Palms Band Archives, Coachella, California.

14 Ibid.

15 Oral interview with Theresa Mike by Clifford E. Trafzer, November 15, 1997, Twenty-Nine Palms reservation.

16 Dean Mike, "Comments Offered at Cultural Night," November, 1997, Twenty-Nine Palms Band Archives, Coachella, California.

17 Oral interview with Dean Mike by Clifford E. Trafzer, Twenty-Nine Palms Indian Reservation, August 4, 2013.

18 Ibid.

19 Bylaws of the Native American Land Conservancy, Twenty-Nine Palms Band Archives, Coachella, California.

20 Minutes of meetings, Native American Land Conservancy, September–December, 1998, Twenty-Nine Palms Band Archives, Coachella, California.

21 Ibid.

22 Ibid.

23 Ibid., January–March 1999.

24 I attended these meetings and recorded the proceedings in my journal. This discussion is derived from my field notes.

25 Oral interview with Theresa Mike by Clifford E. Trafzer, Twenty-Nine Palms Reservation, March 1, 2001.

26 Ibid.

27 Grant Proposals, Native American Land Conservancy, Twenty-Nine Palms Band Archives, Coachella, California.

28 Theresa Mike interview, March 1, 2001.

29 Kurt Russo, *In the Land of Three Peaks: The Old Woman Mountain Preserve* (Coachella, California: Native American Land Conservancy, 2005), 19–28.

30 E-mail communication from Kurt Russo to Clifford E. Trafzer, August 29, 2005.

31 Oral interview with Kurt Russo by Clifford E. Trafzer, Cabazon and Twenty-Nine Palms Reservations, Indio and Coachella, California, May 7, 2006.

32 Ibid.; Theresa Mike interview, March 1, 2001; and Kurt Russo, *Visitor's Guide: Old Woman Mountains* (Coachella, California: Native American Land Conservancy, 2005).

33 All of these oral histories are archived in the tribe's files located in the Tribal EPA offices, Coachella, California.

34 Jennifer Mike interview, March 2, 2000.

35 See the tribal archives consisting of several boxes of documents, Twenty-Nine Palms Band Archives, Coachella, California.

36 Letters of agreement, Twenty-Nine Palms and Chemehuevi Valley tribes, Twenty-Nine Palms Band Archives, Coachella, California.

37 Notes of material items found at Southwest Museum, Twenty-Nine Palms Band Archives, Coachella, California.

38 Anthony Madrigal, "Field Report," University of California–Riverside. The report is a museum study containing oral histories with elders.

39 Telephone interview with Theresa Mike by Clifford E. Trafzer, August 31, 2005.

40 I used my field notes to reconstruct this narrative. The Cary Collection remains in the Cabazon Museum today.

41 Jeff Smith, Accession Notes, Cary Collection, Cabazon Cultural Museum, Indio, California; and Journal Entry, Clifford E. Trafzer, September 9, 2002.

42 Matthew Hanks Leivas interview, September 27, 2001.

43 Ibid.

44 Anthony Madrigal Sr., Jeffrey Smith, and Anthony Madrigal Jr. have all led the Cultural Resources programs of the Twenty-Nine Palms Tribe, in the past under the supervision of the Tribal EPA program. The program has developed into a sophisticated part of tribal government.

45 "Petition Against the Wheeler-Howard bill," within Tillie Lopez, Juanito Alimo, Miguel Williams, William Levy, Pablo Kintano, Ulian Augustine, and Bill Colloway to John W. Dady, March 10, 1935, *Indian Conditions and Affairs*, H.R. 7781, February 11, 1935 (Washington, D.C.: Government Printing Office, 1935); and *Palm Springs Band of Mission Indians*, H.R. 7450 (Washington, D.C.: Government Printing Office, 1938).

46 Robert Przeklasa of the University of California–Riverside provided these documents he had received on CD from the FBI through the Freedom of Information Act. Przeklasa shared these documents and a brief narrative explanation to the author and the leaders of the Twenty-Nine Palms Tribe. Testimony of Margaret Kennedy, December 1, 1936, "J. Edgar Hoover FBI Internal Memorandum," and J. H. Hanson to Director of the Federal

Bureau of Investigation, December 16, 1936, "J. Edgar Hoover FBI Internal Memorandum," declassified through the Freedom of Information Act, Records of the Federal Bureau of Investigation, Washington, D.C.

Bibliography

Archival Collections

American Indian Claims Commission Papers. National Archives. College Park, Maryland.

Brendan Lindsay Collection. California Center for Native Nations. University of California–Riverside.

Bureau of Land Management Collection. Yuma District. Yuma, Arizona.

Cabazon Tribal Museum. Cabazon Indian Reservation. Indio, California.

Cary Collection. Cabazon Cultural Museum. Indio, California.

Colorado River Indian Tribes Library and Museum. Parker, Arizona.

Costo Library. University of California–Riverside.

Federal Bureau of Investigation Papers. "J. Edgar Hoover FBI Internal Memorandum." Declassified through the Freedom of Information Act, Records of the Federal Bureau of Investigation, Washington, D.C.

Gerald Smith Collection. Smiley Library. Redlands, California.

Gilman Ranch. Riverside County Park. Banning, California.

Harvey Johnson Collection. Arizona Historical Society. Yuma, Arizona.

John P. Harrington. National Anthropological Archives. Smithsonian Institution. Washington, D.C. Microfilm copy at Rivera Library. University of California–Riverside.

Johnson Collection. Arizona Historical Society. Yuma, Arizona.

Matthew Hanks Leivas Family Collection. Havasu Lake, California.

Maud Russell Collection. Twenty-Nine Palms Historical Society (TNPHS). Twentynine Palms, California.

Office of Indian Affairs. Records of the Mission Agency. Record Group 75. National Archives. Pacific Southwest Region. Riverside, California.

Paul Smith Collection. Twentynine Palms Inn. Twentynine Palms, California.

President Grover Cleveland. "The United States of America To All To Whom These Presents Shall Come." Executive Order, November 11, 1895. Copy in the Tribal Library, Twenty-Nine Palms Tribe. Coachella, California.

Records of the Bureau of Indian Affairs. Record Group 75. National Archives and Records Administration. Pacific Southwest Region. Riverside, California.

Records of the Indian Claims Commission. National Archives and Records Administration. Suitland, Maryland. .

Records of the State Department. National Archives and Records Center. Pacific Southwest Region. Riverside, California.

Records of the War Department. National Archives and Records Center. Pacific Southwest Region. Riverside, California.

Saint Boniface Indian School Collection. Microfilm Copies, California Center for Native Nations. University of California–Riverside.

Sherman Indian School Museum. Archives and Photographic Collection. Riverside, California.

Special Collections and University Archives. University of California–Riverside.

Twentynine Palms Branch Library. Twentynine Palms, California.

Twentynine Palms Historical Society. Old Schoolhouse. Twentynine Palms, California.

Twenty-Nine Palms Indian Tribe Archives. Coachella, California.

Twenty-Nine Palms Band of Mission Indians files. Bureau of Indian Affairs. Southern California Agency. Riverside, California.

Yuma County Library Newspaper Collection. Yuma, Arizona.

Yuma Proving Ground. Cultural Resources Collections. United States Army. Yuma, Arizona.

Oral Histories

Anderson, Kenneth. Interview by Clifford E. Trafzer. Las Vegas Paiute Indian Reservation. Las Vegas, Nevada. July 10–11, 2006.

Anonymous Paiute Scholar. Interview by Clifford E. Trafzer. Spring Mountains, Nevada. October 6, 2012.

Bean, Lowell John. Interview by Clifford E. Trafzer. Telephone interview. March 1, 2012.

Benitez, Joe. E-mail communication with Clifford E. Trafzer. June 5, 2001.

———. Interview by Clifford E. Trafzer. Cabazon Indian Reservation. Indio, California. September 29, 2000, and November 30, 2001.

———. Interview by Clifford E. Trafzer. Twenty-Nine Palms Indian Reservation. Coachella, California. September 10 and 17, 1997.

———. Interview by Clifford E. Trafzer. Cabazon Indian Reservation. Indio, California. September 14, 2001.

———. Interview by James Sandos and Larry E. Burgess. Colorado River Indian Reservation. Parker, Arizona. August 12, 1989. Interview appears in James Sandos and Larry Burgess, *The Hunt for Willie Boy: Indian-Hating and Popular Culture*. Norman: University of Oklahoma Press, 1994.

Brown, Mary Lou. Interview by James Sandos and Larry E. Burgess. February 1 and 15, 1991. Colorado River Indian Reservation, Parker, Arizona. Interview appears in James Sandos and Larry Burgess, *The Hunt for Willie Boy: Indian-Hating and Popular Culture*. Norman: University of Oklahoma Press, 1994.

Burgess, Larry. Interview by Clifford E. Trafzer. Redlands, California. August 29, 2013.

———. Telephone interview by Clifford E. Trafzer. September 18, 2001.

Chief Pancoyer, Chemehuevi. Oral interview by Agent J. L. Stanley, in the Coachella Valley in Stanley to Dent. Records of the Arizona Superintendent of Indian Affairs. National Archives. Microfilm 734, Reel 2. Washington, D.C.

Cornelius, Betty. Interview by Clifford E. Trafzer. Colorado River Indian Reservation. Parker, Arizona. January 10, 2013.

Davis, Jason. Interview by Clifford E. Trafzer. University of California–Riverside. Riverside, California. February 2013.

DeCorse, Henry. Informal interviews by Clifford E. Trafzer. Century House Museum. Arizona Historical Society. Yuma, Arizona. 1974–1977.

De Crevecoeur, Ben. Interview by Maud Carrico Russell. Russell Manuscript. This statement is part of the unpublished manuscript "The Yesterdays of Twenty-Nine Palms." Twentynine Palms, California.

Earl, David. Paper delivered at California Indian Conference. Chaffey College. Rancho Cucamonga, California. October 15, 2000.

Eddy, Larry. Interview by Clifford E. Trafzer. California State University–San Bernardino, San Bernardino, California. September 28, 2001.

———. Interview by Clifford E. Trafzer. Colorado River Indian Reservation. Parker, Arizona. October 18, 2007.

Emerson, Lee. Interview by Clifford E. Trafzer and Mary Lou Wilkie. Fort Yuma Indian Reservation. Winterhaven, California. 1974.

———. Interview by Shirley Kerson. Fort Yuma Indian Reservation. Yuma, California. 1977.

Johnson, Harvey. Interview by Clifford E. Trafzer. Yuma, Arizona. June 1973.

Leivas, Ace Hanks, and Matthew Hanks Leivas. Interview by Clifford E. Trafzer. Riverside, California. August 29, 2013.

Leivas, Gertrude Hanks. Interview by Clifford E. Trafzer, Theresa Mike, Matthew Hanks Leivas, Anthony Madrigal, and Bernie Thomas. Chemehuevi Indian Reservation. Havasu Lake, California. March 1999.

Leivas, Iris, and Matthew Hanks Leivas. Interview by Clifford E. Trafzer. Chemehuevi Indian Reservation. Havasu Lake, California. February 17–19, 2013.

Leivas, Jake, Vivienne, and Matthew Hanks. Public Presentation of Salt Songs. Twentynine Palms, California. March 1999.

Leivas, Matthew Hanks. Interview by Clifford E. Trafzer. Chemehuevi Indian Reservation. Havasu Lake, California. September 5, 2000; April 8, 2002; December 5, 2005; November 27, 2011; and October 5, 2012.

———. Interview by Clifford E. Trafzer. "Hawai'iyo, East of the Chemehuevi Indian Reservation, 2010," as found in Clifford E. Trafzer, *Keeping the Songs Alive*. DVD. 2010.

———. Interview by Clifford E. Trafzer. Palm Desert, California. August 4, 2013.

———. Interview by Clifford E. Trafzer. Twenty-Nine Palms Reservation. Coachella, California. September 12, 2000; and July 23, 2013.

———. Interview by Clifford E. Trafzer. San Bernardino, California. September 27, 2001.

———. Telephone interview by Clifford E. Trafzer. October 15, 1997; May 16, 2001; and June 15, 2013.

Mahone, Keith. Interview by Clifford E. Trafzer. Twenty-Nine Palms Indian Reservation. Coachella, California. November 1997.

Mathes, Valerie. Telephone interview by Clifford E. Trafzer. September 29–30, 2001.

Mike, Dean. Interview by Clifford E. Trafzer. Twenty-Nine Palms Indian Reservation. Coachella, California. September 2–3, 1997; October 24, 1997; September 10, 2001; August 4, 2013; and August 8, 2013.

Mike, Jennifer. Interview by Anthony Madrigal. Twenty-Nine Palms Reservation. Coachella, California. March 2–3, 2000.

Mike, Jennifer Estama. Interview by Clifford E. Trafzer. Twenty-Nine Palms Reservation. Coachella, California. January 28, 2002.

Mike, Theresa. Interview by Clifford E. Trafzer. Twenty-Nine Palms Reservation. Coachella, California. November 15, 1997; and March 1, 2001.

———. Telephone interview by Clifford E. Trafzer. August 31, 2005.

Mitre, Alfreda. Interview by Clifford E. Trafzer. Las Vegas Paiute Indian Reservation. Las Vegas, Nevada. July 10–11, 2006.

Morongo, Nellie. Oral history notes by Maud Carrico Russell. Twentynine Palms Historical Society. Old Schoolhouse. Twentynine Palms, California. Circa 1940.

Murillo, Pauline Ormego. Interview by Clifford E. Trafzer. San Manuel Indian Reservation. Highland, California. March 2000 and May 15, 2001.

———. Telephone interview by Clifford E. Trafzer. May 8, 2001.

Pakuuma. Interview by John Harrington. Harrington Papers. Interview took place in 1915 at Big Bear, California, and the microfilm is found in the Rivera Library, University of California–Riverside.

Park ranger. Interview by Clifford E. Trafzer. Gilman Ranch. Riverside County Park. Banning, California. June 2000.

Russell, Maud Carrico. "The Yesterdays of Twenty-Nine Palms." Unpublished manuscript (prepared during the 1940s). Old Schoolhouse. Twenty-Nine Palms Historical Society. Twentynine Palms, California.

Russo, Kurt. E-mail communication with Clifford E. Trafzer. August 29, 2005.

———. Interview by Clifford E. Trafzer. Cabazon and Twenty-Nine Palms Reservation. Cabazon, California, and Coachella, California. May 7, 2006.

Saubel, Katherine. Interview by Clifford E. Trafzer. Southwest Airlines Flight (Sacramento to Ontario, California) and Morongo Indian Reservation. Banning, California. September 15, 2000.

———. Telephone interview by Clifford E. Trafzer. May 8, 2001.

Smith, Paul. Interview with Clifford E. Trafzer. Twentynine Palms Inn. Twentynine Palms, California. March 3, 2000.

Smith, Paul, and Jane Smith. Interview by Clifford E. Trafzer. Twentynine Palms, California. June 1999 and May 7, 2001.

Unidentified elder. Interview by Gerald Smith. Smith Collection. Smiley Library. Redlands, California. Circa 1955.

Van Fleet, Alberta. Interview by James Sandos and Larry E. Burgess. January 5 and February 15, 1991. Colorado River Indian Reservation. Parker, Arizona. In James Sandos and Larry Burgess, *The Hunt for Willie Boy: Indian-Hating and Popular Culture*. Norman: University of Oklahoma Press, 1994.

Vaughn, Ted. Interviews with Clifford E. Trafzer. Yavapai-Prescott Indian Reservation. Prescott, Arizona. November 6, 2008, and January 8, 2009.

Books, Reports, Articles, and Multimedia

Adams, John D. Letter, September 23, 1943. In Maud Carrico Russell, "The Yesterdays of Twenty-Nine Palms." Unpublished manuscript. Old Schoolhouse. Twenty-Nine Palms Historical Society. Twentynine Palms, California. Circa 1948.

"Annual Wildflower Plant List." Yuma Proving Ground. Yuma, Arizona. 2001.

Bailey, Lynn R. *Indian Slave Trade in the Southwest*. Los Angeles: Westernlore Press, 1966.

Bancroft, Hubert H. *History of Arizona and New Mexico*. San Francisco: The History Company, 1889.

———. *History of California*. 7 volumes. San Francisco: The History Company, 1886.

———. *History of Nevada, Colorado, and Wyoming*. San Francisco: The History Company, 1890.

Bean, Lowell J., and Katherine Siva Saubel. *Temalpakh: Cahuilla Indian Knowledge and Usage of Plants*. Banning, California: Malki Museum Press, 1972.

Bean, Lowell J., and Lisa J. Bourgeault. *The Cahuilla*. New York: Chelsea House Publishers, 1989.

Bean, Lowell J., ed. *California Indian Shamanism*. Menlo Park, California: Ballena Press, 1992.

Bee, Robert L. *Crosscurrents along the Colorado: The Impact of Government Policy on the Quechan Indians*. Tucson: University of Arizona Press, 1981.

Biddle, Wayne. *A Field Guide to Germs*. New York: Doubleday, 1995.

"Bird List." Yuma Proving Ground. Yuma, Arizona. 2001.

Bolton, Herbert Eugene. *Coronado: Knight of Pueblos and Plains*. Albuquerque: University of New Mexico Press, 1949.

Brand, Donald. *Aboriginal Trade Routes of Sea Shells in the Southwest*. Cheney, Washington: Yearbook of the Association of Pacific Coast Geographers. Volume 4, 1938.

Brooks, Clinton E., and Frank D. Reeves, eds. "James A. Bennett: A Dragoon in New Mexico, 1850–1856." *New Mexico Historical Review* 22 (1947): 51–97.

Brown, Alan K., trans. and ed. *With Anza to California, 1775–1776: The Journal of Pedro Font, O.F.M.* Norman, Oklahoma: Arthur H. Clark Company, 2011.

Browne, J. Ross. "A Tour through Arizona." In Richard Hinton, ed., *The Handbook to Arizona*, pp. 172–73. New York: Payot, 1878.

Burgess, Larry. "Commission to the Mission Indians, 1891." Manuscript. A. K. Smiley Library. Redlands, California.

———. "Commission to the Mission Indians, 1891." *San Bernardino County Museum Association* 35 (Spring 1988): 1–46.

California Center for Native Nations. "Keeping the Songs Alive: Southern California Indians." DVD. University of California–Riverside, 2011. Producer Clifford E. Trafzer. Digitat Studios. Riverside, California.

Camp, Charles L. "The Chronicle of George C. Yount." *California Historical Society Quarterly* 2 (1923): 3–66.

Carling, James L. "On the Trail of Willie Boy." *Desert Magazine* (November 1946): 6–11.

Carrico, Richard. *Strangers in a Stolen Land: Indians of San Diego from Prehistory to the New Deal*. Newcastle, California: Sierra Oaks Publishing, 1987. Reprint, San Diego: Sunbelt Publishers, 2008.

Castillo, Edward D. "The Impact of Euro-American Exploration and Settlement." In Robert F. Heizer, ed., *Handbook of North American Indians: California*, vol. 8, pp. 99–127. Washington, D.C.: Smithsonian Institution Press, 1978.

Censuses of 1910. Typescript. Twenty-Nine Palms Band of Mission Indians Library. Coachella, California.

Census of Los Angeles, California. 1840. Information provided by Lowell Bean to Clifford Trafzer. Telephone interview, March 1, 2012.

Census of the Twenty-Nine Palms Band. 1890. Mission Indian Agency. National Archives. Record Group 75. Microfilm 595. Roll 257.

———. 1892. Mission Indian Agency. National Archives. Record Group 75, Microfilm 595. Roll 257.

———. 1894–1897. Mission Indian Agency. National Archives. Record Group 75, Microfilm 595. Roll 258.

Colorado River Indian Reservation. Congressional Act. March 3, 1865.

Colville, Frederick V. "The Panamint Indians of California." *American Anthropologist* 5 (1892): 351–56.

Culp, Georgia Laird. "The Chemehuevis." *Desert* (March 1975): 18–21, 38.

Cultural Conservancy. "The Salt Song Trail." Produced by Melissa Nelson and Philip Klasky and Ester Figueroa. San Francisco, California. 2005.

———. "The Salt Song Trail: A Living Documentary." Produced by Melissa Nelson, Phillip Klasky,

Nicola Wagenberg, Cara McCoy, and Bridget Sandate. San Francisco, California. 2007.

Davis, Sarah Ann. *The Mohave of the Colorado: The Story of the Mojave Indians of the Colorado River and Their Meetings with the Explorers of the Southwest*. El Centro, California: Pages of History, 1960.

Dent, George W. "Report of the Superintendent of Indian Affairs to the Commissioner of Indian Affairs." In *Annual Report of the Commissioner of Indian Affairs*. Washington, D.C.: Government Printing Office, 1868.

DeSmet, Pierre. *Voyages aux Montag Rocheuses*. Paris: Lille, 1845.

Devereux, George. "Mohave Chieftainship in Action: A Narrative of the First Contacts of the Mohave Indians with the United States." *Plateau* 23 (January 1951): 33–48.

Dobyns, Henry, Paul Ezell, and Greta Ezell. "Death of a Society." *Ethnohistory* 10 (Spring 1963): 105–61.

DuBois, Constance Goddard. *The Condition of the Mission Indians of Southern California*. Philadelphia: Office of Indian Rights Association, 1901.

Dubois, Rene, and Jean Dubois. *The White Plague: Tuberculosis, Man, and Society*. New Brunswick, New Jersey: Rutgers University Press, 1992.

Euler, Robert C. *The Paiute People*. Phoenix: Indian Tribal Series, 1972.

———. *Southern Paiute Ethnography*. Salt Lake City: Anthropological Papers, University of Utah Press, 1966.

Farnam, Jean, and Helen Haworth. Genealogy of Mike Family. Jennifer Mike's Personal Collection. Coachella, California.

Farnham, Thomas J. *Farnham's Travels in the Great Western Prairies, the Anahuac and Rocky Mountains and in the Oregon Territory*. New York: Wiley & Putnam, 1843. Reprint, Carlisle, Massachusetts: Applewood Books, 2007.

Faulk, Odie B. *Land of Many Frontiers: A History of the American Southwest*. New York: Oxford University Press, 1968.

———. *The U.S. Camel Corps*. New York: Oxford University Press, 1976.

Fowler, Catherine S. "Reconstructing Southern Paiute-Chemehuevi Trails in the Mojave Desert of Southern Nevada and California: Ethnographic Perspectives from the 1930s." In James Snead, Clark Erickson, and J. Andrew Darling, eds., *Landscapes of Movement: Trails, Paths, and Roads in Anthropological Perspective,* pp. 84–105. Philadelphia: University of Pennsylvania Museum of Archaeology and Anthropology, 2009.

Fowler, Don D., and Catherine S. Fowler, eds. "Anthropology of the Numa: John Wesley Powell's Manuscripts on the Numic Peoples of Western North America, 1868–1880." *Contributions to Anthropology*. Volume 14, pp. 1–142. Washington, D.C.: Smithsonian Institution Press, 1971.

Foreman, Grant, ed. *A Pathfinder in the Southwest: The Itinerary of Lt. A. W. Whipple during His Explorations for a Railway Route from Fort Smith to Los Angeles in the Years 1853 and 1854*. Norman: University of Oklahoma Press, 1941.

Garcés, Francisco. *On the Trail of a Spanish Pioneer: The Diary and Itinerary of Francisco Garces*. Edited by Elliott Coues. New York: Francis P. Harper, 1900.

Gayton, A. H. "The Ghost Dance of 1870 in South-Central California." *University of California Publications in American Archaeology and Ethnology* 28 (1930–31): 57–82.

Green, A. P. "Report." In Maud Carrico Russell, "The Yesterdays of Twenty-Nine Palms." Unpublished manuscript. Old Schoolhouse. Twenty-Nine Palms Historical Society. Twentynine Palms, California. Circa 1946.

Griswold del Castillo, Richard. *The Treaty of Guadalupe Hidalgo: A Legacy of Conflict*. Norman: University of Oklahoma Press, 1992.

Hanks, Richard A. *This War Is for a Whole Life: The Culture of Resistance among Southern California Indians, 1850–1966*. Banning, California: Dorothy Ramon Learning Center, 2012.

Heap, G. H. *Central Route to the Pacific*. Philadelphia: Lippincott, Grambo & Company, 1854.

Heintzelman, Samuel Peter. "Report of Captain S. P. Heintzelman to Major Townsend from Fort Yuma, July 15, 1853." In *House Executive Document* 76, 34th Congress, 3rd Session, Washington, D.C.: Government Printing Office, 1857.

Heizer, Robert F., and Alan F. Almquist. *The Other Californians*. Berkeley: University of California Press, 1971.

Heizer, Robert F., and M. A. Whipple. *The California Indians: A Source Book*. Berkeley: University of California Press, 1971.

Heizer, Robert F., ed. *Handbook of North American Indians: California*. Washington, D.C.: Smithsonian Institution Press, 1978.

Hittman, Michael. *Wovoka and the Ghost Dance*. Yerington, Nevada: Yerington Paiute Tribe, 1990.

Hodge, Frederick W. *Handbook of American Indians North of Mexico*. Bulletin 30. Office of Indian Affairs. Department of Interior. 1912.

Hoffman, W. J. "Miscellaneous Ethnographic Observations on Indians Inhabiting Nevada, California, and Arizona." In *Tenth Annual Report of the United States Geological and Geographical Survey of the Territories—Being a Report of Progress of the Exploration for the Year 1876*. Washington, D.C.: Government Printing Office, 1878.

———. "Report from Fort Mohave, January 16, 1859." In *Report of the Secretary of War, 1859*. Washington, D.C.: Government Printing Office, 1860.

Hughes, Tom. *History of Banning and San Gorgonio Pass*. Banning, California: Banning Record Print, 1939.

Hurt, Garland. "Message of the President of the United States, Communication . . . Information in Relation to the Massacres in Utah Territory." In *Senate Executive Document* 42, 36th Congress, 1st Session, 1860. Washington, D.C.: Government Printing Office. 1860.

Indian Conditions and Affairs. House Report 7781. Government Printing Office. Washington, D. C. 1935.

"Indian Gaming." Chapter 4 in *Gambling in California*, by Roger Dunstan. California Research Bureau. California State Library. Online at www.library.ca.gov/crb/97/03/Chapt4.html.

Ingalls, G. W., to Commissioner of Indian Affairs A. Walker. November 1, 1872. In *House Executive Document 66*, 42nd Congress, 3rd Session. Washington, D.C.: Government Printing Office. 1872.

Ives, Joseph Christmas. "Report upon the Colorado River of the West." *Report of the Secretary of War, 1861*. In *Senate Executive Document*, 36th Congress, 1st Session. Washington, D.C.: Beverly Tucker, 1861.

Japenga, Ann. "A Legend Undone." *Palm Springs Life* (August 2008): 1.

Jenkins, Richard C. "A Study of Aboriginal Land Use: Southern Paiute Subsistence in the Eastern Mojave Desert." Master's thesis, University of California–Riverside, 1982.

Jennings, Francis. *The Invasion of America: Indians, Colonialism, and the Cant of Conquest*. Chapel Hill: University of North Carolina Press, 1975.

Jensen, Andrew. "History of the Las Vegas Mission." Unpublished manuscript. Nevada State Historical Society. Reno. 1926.

Johnson, Captain W. R. "Manuscript." In Robert C. Euler, *Southern Paiute Ethnography*. Salt Lake City: Anthropological Papers, University of Utah Press, 1966.

Kelly, Isabel. "Southern Paiute Ethnography." Glen Canyon Series 21. In *University of Utah Anthropological Papers 69*. Salt Lake City: University of Utah, 1964.

————. *Southern Paiute Ethnohistory*. New York: Garland Publishing, 1976.

King, Chester, and Dennis Casebier. *Background to Historic and Prehistoric Resources of the East Mojave Desert Region*. Riverside, California: U.S. Department of Interior, Bureau of Land Management, 1981.

Knack, Martha C. *Boundaries Between: The Southern Paiutes, 1775–1995*. Lincoln: University of Nebraska Press, 2001.

Kroeber, Alfred. *Handbook of the Indians of California*. Berkeley: University of California Press, 1953.

————, and C. B. Kroeber. *A Mohave War Reminiscence, 1854–1880*. Berkeley: University of California Press, 1973.

Kroeber, Clifton B. "The Mohave as Nationalist, 1859–1874." *Proceedings of the American Philosophical Society* 109 (May 1965): 1–20.

Laird, Carobeth. "Chemehuevi Religious Beliefs and Practices." *AVAS Newsletter* (March 1982). In Gerald A. Smith Collection. Smiley Library. Redlands, California.

————. "Chemehuevi Religious Beliefs and Practices." *Journal of California Anthropology* 1 (Spring 1974): 19–25.

————. *The Chemehuevis*. Banning, California: Malki Museum Press, 1976.

————. "Chemehuevi Shamanism, Sorcery, and Charms." *Journal of California and Great Basin Anthropology* 2 (1980): 80–87.

————. *Mirror and Pattern: George Laird's World of Chemehuevi Mythology*. Banning, California: Malki Museum Press, 1984.

Lawton, Harry. *Willie Boy: A Western Manhunt*. Balboa Island, California: Paisano Press, 1960.

Leivas, Matthew Hanks. "Chemehuevi: Nuwu Who-vee-up." Unpublished song by Matthew Leivas. Personal collection of Clifford Trafzer.

Leivas, Matthew Hanks, and Kurt Russo. "Ways of Knowing Landscapes: Representations of Sacred Landscapes." Unpublished manuscript. In possession of Matthew Hanks Leivas.

Leonard, JoAnne C., and Michael Lerch. *An Archaeological Evaluation of the Shuffler Property (Oasis of Mara)*. Redlands, California: San Bernardino County Museum Association, 1980.

Lerch, Michael K. *Cultural Resources Mitigation . . . Twentynine Palms*. Yucca Valley, California: Warner Engineering, 1982.

Lesley, Lewis Burt, ed. *Uncle Sam's Camels: The Journal of May Humphreys Stacey, Supplemented by the Report of Edward Fitzgerald Beale (1857–1858)*. Cambridge: Harvard University Press, 1929.

Lindsay, Brendan C. *Murder State: California's Native American Genocide, 1846–1873*. Lincoln: University of Nebraska Press, 2012.

Lingenfelter, Richard. *Steamboats on the Colorado*. Tucson: University of Arizona Press, 1976.

Madrigal, Anthony. "Field Report." University of California–Riverside.

"Mammal List." Yuma Proving Ground. Yuma, Arizona. 2001.

Martineau, LaVan. *Southern Paiutes: Legends, Lore, Language, and Lineage*. Las Vegas: K. C. Publications, 1992.

Mathes, Valerie Sherer. *Helen Hunt Jackson and Her Indian Reform Legacy*. Austin: University of Texas Press, 1990.

McGuire, Randall H., and Michael B. Schiffer. *Hohokam and Patayan: Prehistory of Southwestern Arizona*. New York: Academic Press, 1982.

McWhorter, Lucullus Virgil. *Yellow Wolf: His Own Story*. Caldwell, Idaho: Caxton Printers, 1940. Reprinted in 1995.

Mike, Dean. "Comments Offered at Cultural Night." November 1997. Coachella, California. Twenty-Nine Palms Indian Reservation.

Miller, Ronald Dean, and Peggy Jean Miller. *The Chemehuevi Indians of Southern California.* Banning, California: Malki Museum Press, 1967.

Möllhausen, Heinrich Bauduin. *Diary of a Journey from the Mississippi to the Coasts of the Pacific.* Volume 2. New York: Johnson Reprint Company, 1969. From the original published in 1858.

Mooney, James. *The Ghost-Dance Religion and Wounded Knee.* Reprint, New York: Dover Publications, 1973.

Moses, L. G. "The Father Tells Me So! Wovoka: The Ghost Dance Prophet." *American Indian Quarterly* 9 (1985): 335–51.

Musser-Lopez, R. A. "Yaa vya's Poro: The Singular Power Object of a Chemehuevi Shaman." *Journal of California and Great Basin Anthropology* 5 (1983): 260–64.

Nabokov, Peter. *Indian Running: Native American History and Tradition.* Santa Fe, New Mexico: Ancient City Press, 1981.

Native American Land Conservancy. Brochure. Twenty-Nine Palms Tribe Printing. Coachella, California.

Ogden, Peter S. *Traits of American Indian Life and Character.* San Francisco: Gabhorn Press, 1933.

Palmer, Edward. "Plants Used by the Indians of the United States." *American Naturalist* 12 (1878): 1–23.

Palm Springs Band of Mission Indians. H.R. 7450. (Washington, D.C.: Government Printing Office, 1938).

Patent. 240 Acres to the Twenty-Nine Palms Band of Mission Indians. April 21, 1976. Bureau of Indian Affairs, Southern California Agency. Riverside, California. Copy in Tribal Library, Twenty-Nine Palms Band of Mission Indians. Coachella, California.

"Perennial Plant List." U.S. Army Command, Yuma Proving Ground. Yuma, Arizona. 2001.

Phillips, George H. *Chiefs and Challengers: Indian Resistance and Cooperation in Southern California.* Berkeley: University of California Press, 1975. Second Edition, 2014, University of Oklahoma Press.

Vineyards and Vaqueros: Indian Labor and the Economic Expansion of Southern California, 1771–1877. Norman, Oklahoma: Arthur H. Clark Company, 2010.

Poston, Charles D., to William P. Dole. Letter. September 30, 1864. In *Annual Report of the Commissioner of Indian Affairs,* 1864. Microfilm M1314. Record Group 75. National Archives, Washington, D.C.

———. "Report of Superintendent Charles D. Poston, Arizona Superintendency." In *Annual Report of the Commissioner of Indian Affairs,* 1863. Microfilm M1314. Record Group 75. National Archives, Washington, D.C.

Powell, John Wesley. *Fourteenth Annual Report of the Bureau of Ethnology to the Secretary of the Smithsonian Institution, 1892–93.* Washington, D.C.: Government Printing Office, 1896.

Pratt, Orville C. "Diary of Orville C. Pratt." In LeRoy R. Hafen and Ann W. Hafen, *Old Spanish Trail,* pp. 341–58. Cleveland, Ohio: Arthur H. Clark Company, 1954.

Public Law 94–271. 94th Congress. H. R. 1465. April 21, 1976. "An Act to Provide for the Division of Assets between the Twenty-Nine Palms Band and the Cabazon Band of Mission Indians, California." Copy in Tribal Library, Twenty-Nine Palms Band of Mission Indians. Coachella, California.

Ramon, Dorothy, and Eric Elliot. *Wayta' Yawa': Always Believe.* Banning, California: Malki Museum Press, 2000.

Rawls, James J. *Indians of California: The Changing Image.* Norman: University of Oklahoma Press, 1986.

Reader's Report of Clifford Trafzer and Richard D. Scheuerman, "Renegade Tribe: The Palouse Indians and the Invasion of the Inland Northwest." University of Oklahoma Press. 1985.

"Report of the Mission Indian Commissioners, December 7, 1891." Copy in the Tribal Library, Twenty-Nine Palms Band of Mission Indians. Coachella, California.

"Report of Special Agent John G. Ames, In Regards to the Conditions of the Mission Indians of California, October 28, 1873." Western Americana: Frontier History of the Trans-Mississippi West. Microfilm Collection 139, Reel 9. Beinecke Library, Yale University.

"Reptile and Amphibian List." Yuma Proving Ground. Yuma, Arizona. 2001.

Roth, George. "The Calloway Affair of 1880: Chemehuevi Adaptation and Chemehuevi-Mohave Relations." *Journal of California Anthropology* 4 (1977): 273–86.

Russell, Maud Carrico. "Early Days at Twenty-Nine Palms." *Desert Spotlight*. February 1948. Vertical files. Twentynine Palms Branch Library. Twentynine Palms, California.

———. "Indian Reservations at Twenty-Nine Palms." Russell Collection. Twenty-Nine Palms Historical Society. Twentynine Palms, California. Circa 1940s.

———. "Old Indian Burial Grounds." *Desert Spotlight*. Vertical files. Twentynine Palms Branch Library. Twentynine Palms, California. Circa 1948.

———. "Pioneer Days." *Desert Spotlight*. Vertical files. Circa 1940s. Twentynine Palms Branch Library. Twentynine Palms, California.

———. "The Yesterdays of Twenty-Nine Palms." Unpublished manuscript. Old Schoolhouse. Twenty-Nine Palms Historical Society (TNPHS). Twentynine Palms, California. Circa 1940s.

Russo, Kurt. *In the Land of Three Peaks: The Old Woman Mountain Preserve*. Coachella, California: Native American Land Conservancy, 2005.

———. *Visitor's Guide: Old Woman Mountains*. Coachella, California: Native American Land Conservancy, 2005.

Sandos, James, and Larry Burgess. *The Hunt for Willie Boy: Indian-Hating and Popular Culture*. Norman: University of Oklahoma Press, 1994.

Saubel, Katherine Siva, and Eric Elliott. *'Isill Héqwas Wáxish*. Volumes 1 and 2. Banning, California: Malki Museum Press, 2004.

Schneider, Joan S., and G. Dicken Everson. "Archaeological Investigations at the Oasis of Mara." National Park Service document. Twentynine Palms, California. 2003.

Scott, Lalla. *Karnee: A Paiute Narrative*. Reno: University of Nevada Press, 1966.

Seymour, Gregory, and Hoski Schaafsma. *Archaeological Inventory and Historic Context of the Colorado-Gila Trail*. Yuma, Arizona: Zia Engineering, 2012.

Shipek, Florence. *Pushed into the Rocks: Southern California Indian Land Tenure, 1769–1986*. Lincoln: University of Nebraska Press, 1988.

Singletary, Otis. *The Mexican War*. Chicago: University of Chicago Press, 1960.

Sitgreaves, L. "Report on an Expedition down the Zuni and Colorado Rivers." *Senate Executive Document* 59. 32nd Congress, 2nd Session, 1853. Washington, D.C.: Beverly Tucker, 1854.

Smiley, Albert K. "Account of a Trip through Southern California Spring 1891 as Chairman of Mission Indian Commission." Smiley Collection. Smiley Library. Redlands, California.

———. "Smiley Commission Report, December, 1891." Smiley Library. Redlands, California.

Smith, Jeffrey Allen. "Made Beings: Cahuilla and Chemehuevi Material Culture as Seen through the Cary Collection." PhD dissertation. University of California–Riverside. 2006.

Smith, Justin H. *The War with Mexico*. 2 volumes. New York: MacMillan, 1919.

Smith, Paul. Notes. Twenty-Nine Palms Inn. Twentynine Palms, California.

Smoak, Gregory E. *Ghost Dances and Identity: Prophetic Religion and American Indian Ethnogenesis in the Nineteenth Century.* Berkeley: University of California Press, 2006.

Steward, Julian H. "Basin-Plateau Aboriginal Sociopolitical Groups." *Bureau of American Ethnology Bulletin* 120 (1938): 1–20.

Stewart, Kenneth M. "The Mohave Indians in Hispanic Times." *Kiva* 32 (Fall 1966): 1–20.

Stoffle, Richard W., compiler. "The Enugwuhype (Ancestral Numic People): An Ethnogenesis Analysis."

Stoffle, Richard W., Maria Nieves Zedeño, and David B. Halmo, eds. *American Indians and the Nevada Test Site.* Washington, D.C.: Government Printing Office, 2001.

Stoffle, Richard W., Richard Arnold, and Kathleen Van Vlack. "Facing the Unimaginable: Hopi and Southern Paiutes Respond to Massive Risk Events." May 14, 2013. Unpublished manuscript.

"Summary Testimony by Richard Arnold in Response, Hidden Hills Generating System." February 4, 2013. Provided by Matthew Hanks Leivas.

Sweeny, Thomas W. Journal of Lt. Thomas W. Sweeny. Edited by Arthur Woodward. Los Angeles: Westernlore Press, 1956.

Tagg, Martyn D. *Excavations at the Oasis of Mara.* Washington, D.C.: National Park Service, 1983.

Testimony of Margaret Kennedy. December 1, 1936, "J. Edgar Hoover FBI Internal Memorandum," and J. H. Hanson to director of the Federal Bureau of Investigation J. Edgar Hoover, December 16, 1936. Declassified through the Freedom of Information Act, Records of the Federal Bureau of Investigation, Washington, D.C.

Thwaites, Reuben Gold, ed. "Patties Personal Narrative, 1824–1830." In *Early Western Travels, 1748–1846.* Volume 8, pp. 23–369. Cleveland, Ohio: Arthur H. Clark Co., 1905.

Trachtman, Paul. *The Gunfighters.* Alexandria, Virginia: Time-Life Books, 1974.

Trafzer, Clifford E. *As Long as the Grass Shall Grow and Rivers Flow: A History of Native Americans.* Fort Worth, Texas: Harcourt, 2000.

———. "Chemehuevi Indian Creation." In Ruth Nolan, ed., *No Place for a Puritan: The Literature of California's Deserts,* pp. 197–201. Berkeley, California: Heyday Books, 2009.

———. *Chemehuevi Indians: Historic Properties of Traditional Lands on the Yuma Proving Ground.* Riverside: University of California–Riverside, California Center for Native Nations, 2013.

———. *Historic Property Inventory, Traditional Cultural Properties: Yavapai-Prescott Cultural Ethnography of Lands on the Yuma Proving Ground.* Riverside: University of California–Riverside, California Center for Native Nations, 2010.

———. "Invisible Enemies: Ranching, Farming, and Quechan Indian Deaths at the Fort Yuma Agency, California, 1915–1925." *American Indian Culture and Research Journal* 21 (1997): 83–117.

———. "Medical Circles Defeating Tuberculosis in Southern California." *Canadian Bulletin of Medical History* 23 (2006): 477–98.

———. *Mojave of the Colorado River Indian Reservation: Historic Property Inventory Traditional Cultural Properties: Mojave of the Colorado River Indian Reservation Cultural Ethnography of the Lands on the Yuma Proving Ground.* Riverside: University of California–Riverside, California Center for Native Nations, 2011.

———. *The People of San Manuel.* Highland, California: San Manuel Band of Mission Indians, 2002.

———. *Quechan Indian Historic Properties of Traditional Lands on the Yuma Proving Ground.* Riverside: University of California–Riverside, California Center for Native Nations, 2012.

———. "Tuberculosis Death and Survival among Southern California Indians, 1922–1944." *Canadian Bulletin of Medical History* 18 (2000): 85–107.

———. *Yuma: Frontier Crossing of the Far Southwest*. Wichita, Kansas: Western Heritage Press, 1980.

———, ed. *Quechan Voices: Lee Emerson and Patrick Miguel*. Riverside: University of California–Riverside, California Center for Native Nations, 2012.

Trafzer, Clifford E., and Joel R. Hyer, eds. *Exterminate Them! Written Accounts of the Murder, Rape, and Enslavement of Native Americans during the California Gold Rush*. East Lansing: Michigan State University Press, 1999.

Trafzer, Clifford E., and Richard D. Scheuerman, eds. *Mourning Dove Stories*. Publications in American Indian Studies. San Diego: San Diego State University Press, 1991.

Trafzer, Clifford E., Luke Madrigal, and Anthony Madrigal. *Chemehuevi People of the Coachella Valley*. Coachella, California: Chemehuevi Press of the Twenty-Nine Palms Tribe, 1997.

Trafzer Journal. Field Notes. 2001–7. In possession of the author.

True, Clara. "The Willie Boy Case and Attendant Circumstances." Office of Indian Affairs, file number 79987–09. Originally published by Harry Lawton in *Journal of California Anthropology* 5 (Summer 1978): 115–23.

Utley, Robert. *Frontiersmen in Blue: The United States Army and the Indian, 1848–1865*. New York: Macmillan, 1967.

Van Valkenburgh, Richard F. "Chemehuevi Notes." In Isabel T. Kelly, *Southern Paiute Ethnography*, pp. 225–53. New York: Garland Publishing, 1976.

Washington, Henry. "Report." In Maud Carrico Russell, "The Yesterdays of Twenty-Nine Palms." Unpublished manuscript. Old Schoolhouse. Twenty-Nine Palms Historical Society (TNPHS). Twentynine Palms, California.

Whipple, Amiel W. *A Pathfinder in the Southwest: The Itinerary of Lt. A. W. Whipple during His Explorations for a Railway Route from Fort Smith to Los Angeles in the Years 1853 and 1854*. Edited by Grant Foreman. Norman: University of Oklahoma Press, 1941.

———. "Reports of Exploration and Surveys to Ascertain the Most Practicable and Economical Route for a Railroad from the Mississippi River to the Pacific Ocean." Volume 3. In *Senate Executive Document* 78. 33rd Congress, 2nd Session. Washington, D.C.: Beverly Tucker, 1856.

Wilcox, Colonel O. B. "Chemehuevi Near Ehrenberg." *Annual Report of the War Department, 1880*. In Robert C. Euler, ed., *Southern Paiute Ethnography*. Salt Lake City: Anthropological Papers, University of Utah Press, 1966.

Wood, Willard S. "Bad Indian in the Morongos." *Westways* (April 1935): 10–11, 34.

Worthington, Lieutenant C. Letter, April 23, 1880. Fort Mojave. Arizona Historical Society. In George Roth, "The Calloway Affair of 1880: Chemehuevi Adaptation and Chemehuevi-Mohave Relations." *Journal of California Anthropology* 4 (1977): 286.

Index